D1625726

278

R10-75

# THE
# S★VIET
# WAR MACHINE

## An encyclopedia of Russian military equipment and strategy

# THE SOVIET WAR MACHINE

## An encyclopedia of Russian military equipment and strategy

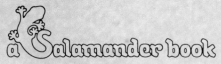

a Salamander book

Published by

**HAMLYN**

London · New York · Sydney · Toronto

# A Salamander Book

*This edition published 1976 by*
The Hamlyn Publishing Group Limited
London · New York · Sydney · Toronto
Astronaut House, Feltham
Middlesex, England

ISBN 0 600 38228 1

© Salamander Books Ltd 1976
52 James Street
London W1
United Kingdom

All rights reserved. Except for use in a
review, no part of this book may be
reproduced, stored in a retrieval system, or
transmitted, in any form or by any means,
electronic, mechanical, photocopying,
recording or otherwise, without the prior
permission of Salamander Books Ltd.

All correspondence concerning the content
of this volume should be addressed to
Salamander Books Limited. Trade enquiries
should be addressed to the publisher.

# Credits

**Consultant:** Air Vice-Marshal S.W.B. Menaul

**Editor:** Ray Bonds

**Design Director:** Chris Steer

**Designer:** Barry Savage

Colour drawings of armoured fighting vehicles, missiles and small arms: John W. Wood
and Gordon Davies.

Line drawings of aircraft: © Pilot Press Ltd.

Line drawings of armoured fighting vehicles, missiles and small arms: © US Army Europe,
Seventh Army; and Miles Walker.

Line drawings of warships: © Siegfried Breyer.

Maps prepared by Richard Natkiel

**Filmset by** SX Composing, Leigh-on-Sea, Essex, England; and Adtype Ltd, 29 Clerkenwell
Road, London EC1, England

**Colour reproduction by** Metric Reproductions Ltd, Chelmsford, Essex, England; and
Paramount Litho Company, 4 Robert Way, Wickford, Essex, England

PRINTED BY BEN JOHNSON AND CO. LTD. YORK ENGLAND.

# Acknowledgements

There has never before been a book on the Soviet military forces with so many amazing colour illustrations as there are in THE SOVIET WAR MACHINE. Many of the colour photographs have been processed as "stills" from recent Soviet colour documentary film. We thank Educational and TV Films Ltd., London, for allowing us to obtain colour transparencies from the films. When processing still transparencies from duplicated 35mm film the quality of reproduction of the resultant picture is unavoidably degraded; nevertheless, these revealing photographs have helped to make the book unique.

In addition to our expert team of authors, we are extremely grateful to Air Vice-Marshal Menaul, for introducing us to many of them and are indebted to the Royal United Services Institute for Defence Studies, London, for its help and guidance in obtaining material for publication.

Bill Gunston, who contributed the itemised technical descriptions of Soviet aircraft, warships and army weapons, assisted greatly in the compilation of the book, for which we owe him our gratitude. The table at the beginning of the chapter "Soviet Aircraft" was compiled by Charles Gilson, Defence Editor, *Flight International* magazine.

We also thank Macdonald and Jane's for permitting us to use the information in tables published in Captain J. E. Moore's excellent book, "The Soviet Navy Today", in the compilation of our table on page 127, which has been updated by Captain Moore.

Our special thanks also go to the publishers of *Air Force* magazine for permitting us to use as a basis their map of major Warsaw Pact and NATO airfields in Europe.

# Contents

# Foreword

Operation Barbarossa, Hitler's plan to conquer the Soviet Union in June 1941, was based on the swift massacre of the Red Army. Though the Russian casualties in men and equipment were grievous, the final outcome was victory for the Soviet Union. This victory was not gained by numbers alone. In many cases, most notably the T-34 tank, the Soviet weapons were the best in the world. Throughout what the Soviets call The Great Patriotic War they were also supplied with arms and equipment by their Allies. This may have surprised Stalin and his fellow-members of the Politburo, because according to the teaching of Marx and Lenin the Capitalists forever seek to destroy the Communist world.

The massive Allied help demonstrated the falsity of this teaching. So too did the years after 1945 when the Communist world could indeed have been destroyed by American nuclear weapons, but was not. Instead the Allies watched sadly as their former comrades in arms pulled down the Iron Curtain and embarked on The Cold War. At that time the advanced Capitalist nations called themselves "The Free World", and though this is no longer fashionable its accuracy continues to be a devastating indictment of the Soviet way of life. It serves no useful purpose for anyone in the Free World to proclaim that the Capitalists have no wish to harm the Communist world. The readers of this book know this to be true, but it still cuts no ice with the Soviet government, any more than do the facts of history related above. From the Kremlin pours a ceaseless barrage of propaganda concerning the wicked intentions of the Capitalists. These intentions were spelt out by Marx and Lenin, so there is nothing more to be said. It is this rigid dogma which has both spurred and made possible today's Soviet War Machine.

This build-up of armed forces would be a phenomenon of great academic interest were it not directed so powerfully against us. As it is, it is disquieting and even terrifying. That there are millions of Russians under arms is not news. What is disquieting is that the vast forces of the Soviet Union are no longer simple peasants with simple weapons. They are skilled and dedicated troops deploying equipment that is beating the Free World across the board. In quantity, beyond question. In quality, increasingly often.

Today, and for years past, the Soviet Union has so many people planning, designing, developing

and producing armaments that the potentially more powerful Western nations can no longer compete. Increasingly, the newest weapons in the Western countries are attempts to answer Soviet weapons of the previous generation. This is a new situation, but the trend is accentuating it year by year.

An even more fearsome menace is presented by what the Soviet Union calls "weapons of mass destruction". We do not know much about their chemical and biological weapons, beyond the announced fact that these are regarded by Soviet commanders as routine options to be used whenever the circumstances are correct. But we do know quite a lot about the Strategic Rocket Forces, the élite and most exalted of all Soviet services. Ordinary people are not familiar with "throw weights" and "megatons", but if they study these forces they will inescapably conclude that with their planned overkill the Russians could destroy the whole animal life on this planet, and probably ten or twenty times over.

There are many who refuse to believe such claims about the phenomenal and ever-increasing strength of the Soviet War Machine. Let them read this book.

# The Roots of Discord

**P. H. Vigor**

The Soviet Union did not arise out of nothing in November 1917, a state newborn, devoid of roots with the past. On the contrary, it was an old state, a state which had been called Russia; and although as a result of the Revolution it admittedly became possessed of a new ideology, nevertheless it continued to be possessed of the old, old problems that had plagued the Russia of the tsars. For instance, it was too big a country to be administered easily and efficiently, and the Bolsheviks found the

running of it as big a problem as the Romanov emperors had done. It was a country where the good farming land formed only a comparatively small proportion of the total surface area, and the Bolsheviks found it as difficult to feed the towns of Soviet Russia as Nicholas II had found it difficult to feed those of Imperial Russia. More specifically related to our present purpose, Soviet Russia, like Imperial Russia, was bordered by a number of other countries which were sometimes friendly and sometimes hostile, but which could never be wholly ignored. In the military sense, therefore, just because she was Russia, and situated on the same spot on the globe where Russia had always been situated, the USSR, like Imperial Russia, was confronted by the need to possess armed forces that could guard those lengthy borders.

Nor was the purpose of the Soviet forces invariably defensive, any more than the purpose of those of the tsars had been. The one, like the other, resorted to the offensive on occasions, in order either to extend their existing dominions (Georgia in 1921, eastern Poland and Finland in 1939, Latvia, Lithuania and Estonia in 1940) or to chastise what their government considered to be intolerable provocation (China in 1929).

We therefore see that the Soviet Union needed, and so created, armies, navies and air forces for the same sort of reasons that other countries (what the average reader might mentally label 'ordinary' countries) needed and created theirs. On top of this, however, there was a further reason, derived from the Soviet Union's political and economic ideology, which increased the pressure on her Bolshevik rulers to create their military forces of a particular and unusual type, and to create them, moreover, on a very large scale indeed. Consequently, it is impossible to proceed any further with this discussion without examining, at least in outline, the nature of Soviet ideology; for this provides an essential clue to the type of armed forces that materialised.

The ideology in question is Marxism–Leninism. This comprises those parts of Marx's theories which Lenin thought to be useful to him, coupled with his own views on politics and economics and, in particular, with his invention of a new type of political

Lenin and a group of Red Guards during the October Revolution. The Guards were the precursors of the Red Army, their job being to seize power for the Bolsheviks

party (which is usually called a 'communist' party), whose function was to plan the seizure of power, to cling on to that power after its successful seizure and to make use of its grip on the various levers of government to force the population to evolve in particular directions towards a specific goal called 'communism'.

The ultimate goal of Marxism–Leninism, therefore, is the achievement of communism, a goal which the USSR, on its own admission, has not yet managed to reach. At the present moment, the USSR is a 'Union of Soviet *Socialist* Republics'; and it has advanced along the Leninist evolutionary chain only so far as the half-way house of socialism. Leninist-style socialism, unlike communism, permits the use of money; it also permits tremendous differentials in wages, as Soviet practice demonstrates. Thus in the Soviet Union today there are a great many people with a low standard of living and a great many others with one which, by comparison, must be rated extremely high. On the other hand, Leninist-style socialism concurs with communism in forbidding private enterprise, in the sense of the private ownership of factories, farms and so on; and with the exception of the peasant's private plot, that is exactly the position in practice in the USSR today.

Moreover, Marxism–Leninism envisages this change-over from capitalism to communism as taking place eventually over the whole world. In other words, it will not just be Russia, together with the rest of what we often refer to as the 'Communist bloc' that will experience this transformation, but the United States, Great Britain, West Germany, France, Japan and all the capitalist countries as well. It is true that no actual date was set by either Marx or Lenin for the accomplishment of this worldwide transformation; but it is also true that they were sure that it would eventually happen.

Successive rulers in the communist countries have continued to share this belief. Khrushchev proclaimed it in the course of a number of his speeches, such as those he made at the 22nd Party Congress; Brezhnev and his colleagues have continued to proclaim it in the days since Khrushchev's overthrow. Thus, in the most recent party congress yet to have taken place, Brezhnev declared not merely that 'the total triumph of Socialism all over the world is inevitable', but also that it was the bounden duty of the Soviet Communist Party to speed up this process.

But as well as the actual date of this transformation being, even now, a matter of considerable uncertainty, a further degree of uncertainty hangs over the question concerning the means to be employed for bringing it about. A careful reading of Marx, Engels and Lenin, and indeed of such figures as Stalin, Khrushchev and Brezhnev, allows the reader to deduce from their works two answers, each of which, in its purest form, flatly contradicts the other. One answer says, or can be interpreted as saying, that time alone will be sufficient for its accomplishment; the other says that force will have to be used. The degree of force and the kind of force that will be necessary are, once again, enveloped in obscurity; but that a use of force of some kind is not only desirable but essential under certain circumstances has been asserted only quite recently by the newspaper *Pravda* in its issue of 6 August 1975.

Leaving aside the degree of force to be applied, the kind of force is relevant to our present purposes; for although some com-

*Right:* **Armed force as an ingredient for the holding of power. A modest but efficient guard outside the Bolshevik HQ in Petrograd in 1917**

*Below:* **Armed force as an ingredient for the seizure of power. A pro-Bolshevik automobile and machine gun detachment, patrolling the streets of Moscow during the uprising**

munist governments have indeed gained
power by little more than an extension of
civil violence (Kerala in India in 1957, for
instance), others, including the Soviet Union
itself, have required the application of a kind
of force which must at least be called para-
military throughout (Red Guards from the
factories armed with rifles and machine-
guns). Sometimes this has resulted in a
purely professional military operation undertaken not by para-military, but by regular
military units (the activities of the Petrograd
Garrison and the Baltic Fleet in 1917 are an
obvious example of this). Further down the
scale come instances where the installation of
a communist government in a country has
been effected virtually single-handed by that
country's regular armed forces. At the time
of writing, it is not yet certain whether the
1975 revolution in Portugal is going to result
in the coming to power of a communist
government in that country; but if it is, it is
both a recent and also a clear example of the
use of force of this kind.

Finally, there are the instances where
communist governments have been installed
in countries as a result of invasion from
without. In such cases, the Soviet Army has
marched across their frontiers and forcibly
'bolshevised' them. (The armies of Communist China did the same thing in the case
of Tibet, although a purist may object that
the use of the word 'bolshevised' is in-
appropriate here.) Attempts are frequently
made by the Soviet Communist Party to
conceal from us this fact, generally by
spouting the old quotation from Engels to
the effect that one cannot thrust communism on people with a bayonet. Despite
this quotation, the fact remains that on a
number of occasions the Soviet armed
forces have done precisely that.

This was done only when the circumstances were right, of course. And in this
connection it is pertinent to remark that
Soviet theory considers that circumstances
are wrong for the undertaking of a military
expedition unless its success can be virtually
taken for granted. And, historically speaking,
there have been none too many occasions
when an expedition undertaken by the
Soviet armed forces was well-nigh bound to
be successful: the Red Army and the Red
Navy were weak both in respect of numbers
and of quality of equipment until well into
the late 1930s, and for a number of years
after the end of World War II they had little
hope of attacking successfully any but a
primitive and poorly armed opponent, as a
result of their tremendous losses in men and
material which they incurred on the
Eastern Front.

Nevertheless, despite these qualifications,
circumstances have been sufficiently favourable at various moments in the history of the
Soviet armed forces for them to be employed
on more than one occasion for the invasion
of another country and its forcible 'bol-
shevisation'. Some of these occasions have
already been mentioned above – Georgia in
1921, Latvia, Lithuania and Estonia in 1940
– but to these we must add the enforced
'communisation' of the countries of Eastern
Europe at the end of World War II. Admittedly the entry of the Red Army into
these latter countries was dictated by the
need to pursue the forces of Nazi Germany;
but once installed in them, it proceeded to

make use of its presence to see that the governments brought to power in them should be communist in all but name. Of course it is virtually certain that if the peoples of those countries had had the chance of expressing their wishes, and expressing them freely and without constraint, they would not have wanted exactly that form of society that prevailed in them prior to the war. It is also certain, however, that the kind of society they wanted was not the sort they were forced to acquire as a result of the presence in their countries of the Soviet Army. In other words, in the case of the 'satellite' countries the Soviet armed forces produced, and were intended to produce, a 'communisation' of their societies and governments that can only be described as 'enforced'.

But the ideology of Marxism–Leninism has served not merely to equip the Soviet armed forces with a particular kind of offensive, in the sense that it has given them a motive to attack some other country which they might otherwise have left in peace; it has served also to equip them with a particular kind of defensive.

By this is meant that just as Marxism–Leninism indicated targets which might conceivably be suitable for military invasion but which Russian nationalism, if left to itself, would have rejected as unsuitable (Lenin's plan for the Red Army to march into Hungary in 1919 is a case in point), so it also created for Russia a number of enemies who, in the absence of any such ideological conflict, would probably never have been her enemies at all. The prime example undoubtedly is the United States of America.

The younger generation may be reasonably expected to imagine that the United States and the USSR have always been natural enemies; but a brief look at the history of these two countries will show that this view is wrong, or rather, to be accurate, that it is true only of the Russia of the Soviet period. It is not true of the Russia before the revolution.

Furthermore, it was no part of the classic Marxist tradition that the United States was to be regarded as particularly damnable by every good revolutionary. On the contrary, Marx and Engels themselves were, generally speaking, favourably inclined to the USA, holding that country to be a great deal more democratic and more progressive than the Britain, France, Germany, Austria, Italy, Spain and Russia of their time. Lenin before World War I was also of the same opinion, and it was not until the American intervention in the Civil War of 1918–1920 that he altered his view of that country. But since that intervention was itself ideologically motivated, in the sense that its avowed purpose was to get rid of the communists from Russia; and since the American government's subsequent refusal to have diplomatic relations with the Soviet Union (a refusal with which it persisted until 1933)

A propaganda poster of a parade in Red Square. The value of these parades, as far as the Kremlin is concerned, has always been to give foreigners an exaggerated idea of Soviet military might

15

was also ideologically motivated, it is reasonable to say that it was the very existence of a communist government as such in control of Russia that led to the enmity between the latter and America which seems so natural today.

But although America is the most notable, it is not the only example of enmity between Russia and another country being mostly ideologically inspired. France must be counted another such, and so must Holland and Belgium. Admittedly France invaded Russia in the course of the Napoleonic wars, and repeated the experiment (although on a smaller scale) in the course of the Crimean War; but in the long sweep of the history of Franco–Russian relations these two incidents distinguish themselves as being very much of an exception. Relations between France and Russia were usually good, the huge distances separating the two countries being largely responsible for this. In addition, French civilization was traditionally very much admired by the educated classes of Russia; and the Russian aristocracy generally spoke French as fluently as they did Russian.

In the cases of Holland and Belgium, again it was the great distances which separated them from Russia that must be accounted chiefly responsible for their relations being so friendly. This situation held good so long as Imperial Russia continued in existence; it is only since the communists took power and threatened (or at any rate, seemed to threaten) the integrity of the whole of Western Europe that the Dutch and the Belgians joined an alliance that was aimed at resisting, militarily if necessary, the ambitions of the USSR.

Britain provides an example, however, of an old enmity having been merged and assimilated into a new one. For very many years, Britain was an opponent of Russia, fearing an advance eastwards by tsarist forces for the purpose of invading India. She was also afraid of the imbalance in Europe that would be created if Russia were to gain direct access to the Mediterranean Sea. That Britain now finds herself in the North Atlantic Treaty Organisation (NATO), with the object of blocking further Soviet advance in central, southern and western Europe, is merely to say that today she fears the invasion of her own homeland rather than that of any former colonial possessions, but that the traditional British suspicion of Russian intentions, and hence the traditional antagonism towards Russian policies, continues unchecked.

The case of Japan is similar. Japanese policies came into conflict with those of Imperial Russia almost from the moment when Commodore Perry with his squadron of American warships in 1854 made the Japanese abandon their isolation and take their place in the world. The Russo–Japanese War of 1904–1905 was the first explosion between them; but the Japanese invasion of eastern Siberia during the Russian Civil War, the clashes in Mongolia between Soviet and Japanese forces in 1938 and 1939, and the Soviet attack on the Japanese army in Manchuria in 1945 are merely further examples of such explosions, which embrace both the tsarist and the communist periods. Nor, so long as the ownership of the Kuril Islands and the southern half of Sakhalin Island continues to be allotted as it is at

ВПЕРЕД!
ПОБЕДА БЛИЗКА!

*Above left:* **The famous Soviet aeronautical engineer A. N. Tupolev with one of his earliest designs, the ANT-1 'sport plane' of 1923**

*Above:* **A Soviet propaganda placard from World War II. The caption reads, 'Forward! Victory is near'**

*Right:* **A typical example of the work of Soviet artists during WWII. This canvas depicts a Soviet tank unit resting in a pine forest during a lull in the fighting**

*Left:* **Part of a propaganda poster of 1938 designed to foster in the Soviet people a spirit of readiness to fight in defence of their country. A caption with it read, 'If war breaks out tomorrow'**

present, can one truthfully say that Soviet–Japanese antagonism can possibly be regarded as dead.

We may sum up, therefore, by saying that the Soviet Union's need to possess armed forces, and the policies that will guide her use of them, derive both from her traditional past and from her ideological present. Some of her most implacable enemies of the tsarist period (Poland, for instance, or Sweden) have been eliminated, either by outright absorption into the Russian bailiwick, as has been the case with Poland, or else by neutralisation; but then the neigh-

bours of the absorbed countries have become *de facto* neighbours of the Soviet Union, with all the suspicions and antagonisms which proximity so often brings. Other traditional enemies have remained her opponents to this day (Turkey and Britain); while Japan, though her case is somewhat unique, can hardly be described as friendly.

By contrast there are still other countries which, judged by that selfsame standard, must also be reckoned the opponents of the Soviet Union, but whose opposition originally derived from strong ideological differences. Of these the United States is the

prime example, as has already been mentioned above.

Finally, there is China. Here is a country which, during the nineteenth century, was preyed on by tsarist Russia, just as she was preyed on by the Western European countries and by America and Japan. The predatory policies of Alexander III and Nicholas II naturally engendered hostility between China and Russia; but it was to be expected that, when the tsars were evicted and a confessedly anti-colonialist government took power in the Soviet Union, the causes of that hostility, essentially colonialist

in their origin, should speedily be extinguished. This did not happen.

Nor did it happen later, which was even more remarkable, when China herself became subject to a communist government, and both the USSR and China were therefore ideologically akin. So far from that hostility being extinguished, it has, if anything, grown. Thus the Soviet Union now keeps a strong army of over 50 divisions, together with supporting arms, along the Chinese border. Here is an old enemy, which is now also a new enemy, but whose enmity is based partly on traditional grievances and partly on ideological differences, despite the fact that, in this particular instance, the differences are between two rival interpretations of one and the same ideology. For, nominally at least, the USSR and China are both Marxist–Leninist societies, and hence nominally ideologically identical.

The Soviet armed forces must therefore be designed and trained and equipped and organised and deployed to cope with these different antagonisms. They must also be able to suppress revolt within the 'satellite' countries and the USSR herself. Leaving aside the 'satellites', though, and concentrating on the Soviet Union's external enemies or potential enemies, it is clear that these forces must be able to implement, with regard to each single one of them, both an offensive and a defensive policy. If the Kremlin decides that the task of the Soviet armed forces is to confine themselves to preserving intact the present frontiers of Russia (i.e. to implementing a purely defensive policy), then the Russian generals and admirals must be able to achieve this. It should perhaps be added that Soviet military science insists on basing its whole strategy upon the concept of the counter-

offensive even in the case of a defensive war – in other words, that an invading army is to be counter-attacked so soon as this is possible, and pushed back into its own territory, where the rest of the war is to be fought.

If, on the other hand, the Kremlin decides on launching an offensive war on one or other of its neighbours, or on all of them, then this too the generals and admirals must be able to accomplish. As a third possibility, they may be required to defend one section of their frontiers, and attack in another.

The motive for this attack or this defence will, as has been seen, be partly due to the traditional sorts of causes that have sparked off warfare for centuries between one country and another (the desire to grab more territory or to prevent the loss of one's own territory, the wish to chastise an insult, the urge to gain access to markets or raw materials or to extend one's sphere of

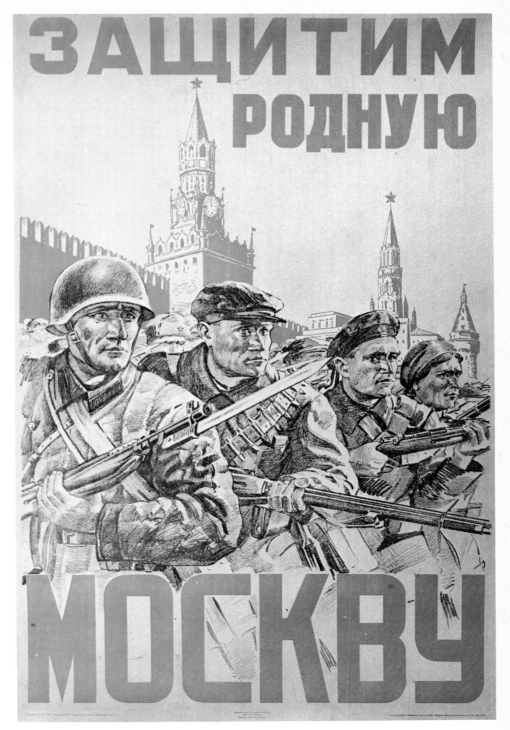

ЗАЩИТИМ РОДНУЮ МОСКВУ

*Above left:* **The modern Soviet Army holding a defensive position against Communist Chinese forces on the 'Kamennaya' Ridge in the Semipalatinsk region in 1969**

*Above:* **A wartime poster from the early stages of the German invasion. Loosely translated, the caption reads, 'Let us defend our native Moscow'**

*Left:* **A house in Leningrad shattered by German shell fire. The placard is headed, 'Death to the Killers of Children'**

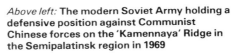

influence, and other factors). The USSR, like her tsarist predecessor, has on several occasions initiated wars of this sort, and has moreover suffered them at the hands of others. But another motive for attack or defence will be mainly ideological; and, once again, examples of each are to be met with in Soviet history.

Today, however, it is not very likely that either motive of itself would be sufficient to spark off actual hostilities. The USSR, even now, is bitterly opposed to our Western form of society, and asserts this almost hourly. But this kind of spiritual antagonism is hardly enough, in an age where both sides bristle with nuclear weapons, to spark off another war. The same sort of thing may be said about the Russians' relations with China. In each case, it is only if the traditional (i.e. material) interest is strong, and coincides firmly with the ideological interest, so that both these interests point decisively in the same direction, that actual war is likely to break out; and this is true whether the putative aggressor is to be assumed to be the West or Communist China or the USSR herself.

# The History of the Soviet Armed Forces

P. H. Vigor

According to Soviet sources, the Red Army was born on what, according to the modern calendar, was 28 January 1918. Recruitment was originally intended to be voluntary; and the voluntary basis was successful enough to have attracted more than 100,000 recruits by the end of March 1918. This number was insufficient, however, and on 22 April 1918 the Bolsheviks were obliged to issue a decree making service in the Red Army compulsory.

The purpose of having a specifically 'Red' Army, instead of continuing with the old Imperial Russian Army, was to provide the Bolshevik government with an armed force which could be relied upon to use its weapons to keep that government in office. Lenin's view of the way a revolution would develop caused him to expect the dispossessed propertied classes to attempt to stage a 'come-back' (or 'counter-revolution' as Marxist terminology would call it). Consequently, unless the army at the communists' disposal was in strong political sympathy with the aims of the Revolution, there was grave danger that it might not fight enthusiastically enough to prevent the come-back succeeding. In Lenin's opinion, therefore, it was essential that those who served in the Red Army should only be drawn from such sections of the old Russian society as might be expected to be revolutionary sympathisers; and it was for this reason that, right from the very beginning, the Red Army refused to accept in its ranks recruits drawn from those sections of the old Russian society which the communists considered 'reactionary'. Not that the old aristocracy or the old middle classes were prevented from making any contribution whatever to the military capacity of the communists: on the contrary, they too were conscripted. They were not, however, al-

lowed to serve in any of the 'teeth' arms or technical services, but instead were recruited into so-called 'auxiliary units', generally labour battalions.

It is true that the exigencies of the Civil War compelled the Bolsheviks to admit into the ranks of their officer corps a considerable number of ex-tsarist officers, despite their 'bourgeois' background; but this was done only under the pressure of a most compelling necessity. Furthermore, the device was discontinued as soon as circumstances permitted; and throughout the period of their service with the Red Army, the so-called 'military specialists' worked under the vigilant supervision of a body of men termed 'military commissars', whose job it was to see that the suspect 'military specialists' did not betray their employers.

There was thus implanted in the Soviet armed forces, right from the very beginning of their existence, the basic principle that in a communist state political reliability is of the first importance, to which all else, in-

The famous 'Tachanka' (a machine gun mounted in a horse-drawn cart) widely used by the Red Army in its early days

cluding professional ability, must be subordinated. Marx, Engels and Lenin, and all the other revolutionary leaders, had studied with care the part that was played by Napoleon in the history of the French Revolution; and they were all determined that no *Brumaire* coup (such as that which elevated Bonaparte to the office of 1st Consul in November 1799) should frustrate their own revolution. The armed forces of the USSR were then, and are now, the only body in the country that is physically capable of destroying the communist government; and the communist government was aware of it then, and is equally aware of it now. The institution of the political commissars, the authority vested in the Main Political Directorate of the Armed Forces and the political requirements demanded of Soviet officers are all symptoms of the profound influence which the ghost of Napoleon Bonaparte exerts, and has always exerted, on those in power in the Kremlin.

The needs of the Civil War (1918–1920) caused a rapid rise in the numbers of the Red Army. If in March 1918 its strength was only a little over 100,000, this had risen to over 306,000 by May of that same year, to over 1,000,000 by February 1919 and to over 3,000,000 by January 1920. At its peak in the Civil War years, the official strength of the Red Army was 5,498,000 (1 October 1920).

It must not be supposed that these enormous numbers were deployed *en masse*, like some titanic hammer, on a particular sector of the front. Nor were they ever deployed simultaneously over all the fronts together:

official strengths were one thing, and reality another. Moreover, the nominal strength of the Red Army was much reduced by desertion. Furthermore, as Soviet generals testify, the nature of the Civil War was such that large numbers of so-called soldiers had to be employed by the communist leaders on very unsoldierly duties. When whole areas the size of Britain had been devastated by the continual fighting, the supply problem was appalling; thus soldiers were used to catch fish, to repair windmills, to provide firewood for railway engines, and even to operate match factories.

The Civil War was also an important milestone in the history of the Soviet armed forces from the point of view of strategy and tactics. So much emotion has entered into the study of this period, both on the side of the Reds and on that of the Whites, that it is important, when attempting an assessment of it, to try to be objective. And so far as the military aspects of this struggle are concerned, the objective facts are that although the numbers of the men involved in the war were vast, they were not nearly so vast as the territories over which they fought. Consequently, it was physically impossible for a static front to be formed, of the kind which was formed across Western Europe between 1914 and 1918. The Civil War in Russia therefore inculcated in its participants a belief in the virtues of the offensive as opposed to the defensive, and of speed and manoeuvrability in the execution of it, which has remained to this day the hallmark of Soviet tactics.

The Civil War ended in a Red victory in

December 1920; but in many ways the victory was Pyrrhic. The industry, the commerce, the agriculture of Soviet Russia were on the verge of collapse, and the armed forces had to be demobilised speedily in order to provide the manpower necessary for their reconstruction. Trotsky, the chief military architect of the Bolshevik victory, was in some disagreement with his colleagues as to how this should best be accomplished, but he too was emphatic that it had to be done. Consequently, whereas in 1920 the strength of the Soviet armed forces was over 5,000,000, by 1923 it had fallen to 610,000 and by 1924 had reached its nadir of 562,000. When it is remembered that this figure includes not only the army and navy but also the frontier guards, it will be apparent to what a degree of military impotence the Soviet Union had fallen.

But the Soviet leaders' Marxism constrained them to believe that the capitalist nations were always on the watch for an opportunity to make use of their military strength to invade Russia and put an end to communism. From which it followed that the above-mentioned military impotence could not be tolerated for a moment longer than was necessary, and that, so soon as the Soviet economy began to recover, the battle effectiveness of the Soviet armed forces should begin to recover too. The worsening of the international situation at the end of the 1920s and in the early 1930s gave added impetus to this train of thought, which was soon translated into action. Thus whereas, as has been said, the Soviet armed forces in 1924 numbered only 562,000, they had risen

*Far left:* **A Red Army artillery unit during the Civil War period**

*Above:* **Red Army artillery during the Civil War.**

*Left:* **Red Army infantry on the march. Their rifles are the old Tsarist 'Nagent'**

to a figure of 617,000 in 1928, of 885,000 in 1933 and of 1,513,000 by 1938.

This increase in strength of the Soviet armed forces took place simultaneously with an equally impressive increase in Soviet industrial production. The years 1928–1932 were the period of the first of the 5-year plans upon the results of which depended the degree to which Soviet rearmament was possible. According to the published figures, this was considerable. Thus the total number of aircraft in service in 1928 is given as 1,394; by 1932 this had risen to 3,285; and by 1935 it had increased still further to 6,672. The figures for guns of a calibre of 76-mm or greater were 6,645 in 1928, 10,684 in 1932 and 13,837 in 1935. For tanks the corresponding figures were 92, 1,401 and 10,180 respectively.

The increased technological capability of

the Red Army was backed by a military doctrine of corresponding efficacy. From its earliest days, it had been •blessed with strategists and tacticians whose views of war were, if anything, in advance of their time. No doubt they had been assisted in their professional development by their contacts with the highly efficient German army officers which had been developed as a result of the Treaty of Rapallo (1922); but the fact remained that, as early as the middle 1920s, there were propounded in Soviet official circles views which were at least as advanced as any in Western Europe. The successes of the various 5-year plans allowed the Soviet leaders to put flesh on them. As a result, the USSR in 1932 produced the world's first mechanised corps, which included in its establishment more than 500 tanks. By 1936 the Soviet Union had a total of four mechanised corps, six independent

mechanised brigades and six independent tank regiments. This approach to the use of armour contrasts strongly with that of some Western countries, whose conversion to the idea of using armour *en masse* was a very great deal more dilatory.

Soviet progress in this direction was brought to a halt, however, by Stalin's wrong evaluation of the Soviet experience of using tanks during the Spanish Civil War (1936–1939). As a result, the mechanised corps were disbanded, and their component tanks returned to their original task of fighting in penny packets in support of the infantry. It was not until after the German invasion of Russia in 1941 that this decision was reversed.

Despite all this, however, the efficacy of the Red Army was clearly demonstrated when Soviet forces clashed with Japanese forces in Mongolia. The first clash, the

Battle of Lake Khasan (July 1938), was a comparatively small-scale affair. But in the following year, in the Battle of Khalkin Gol, over 60 battalions of Soviet and Japanese infantry were embroiled in the fighting, together with appropriate supporting arms, including 600 tanks. The result was an undoubted victory for the USSR. It is an ironic comment on Stalin's Russia that the man who won the victory for the Soviet Union, Marshal Blyukher, was arrested and shot by the *NKVD* only a very short time after he had done so.

And, of course, the purge of the officer corps in 1937–1938 had a great effect on the battleworthiness of the Soviet armed forces. Its most famous victim was Marshal Tukhachevsky; but, according to Robert Conquest's *The Great Terror*, the Soviet Union lost, in addition, two more of the five marshals, 14 of the 16 army commanders,

*Top left:* **The motorised version of the 'Tachanka' (pictured earlier) taking part in a parade in Red Square**

*Left:* **A Soviet tank of the 1930s taking part in a parade in Red Square. The design clearly foreshadows the famous T-34, the battle-winning Red Army tank of World War II**

*Above:* **Mobile anti-aircraft guns of the 1940 period parading through Red Square**

all eight of the full admirals, 60 of the 67 corps commanders, 136 of the 199 divisional commanders, 221 of the 397 brigade commanders and all 11 of the Vice-Commissars for Defence, together with 75 of the 80 members of the Supreme Military Soviet.

In all, according to Conquest, approximately 35,000 officers of all ranks were shot or imprisoned.

It can, of course, be argued (and has been argued) that the removal from office of many of these was of direct benefit to the Soviet armed forces, in that a considerable number of the victims were elderly men, 'dead wood', whose savage pruning did much to rejuvenate the Red Army. On the other hand, it can hardly be denied that the command and control of the Red Army during the early stages of the Russo–Finnish War of 1939–1940 left much to be desired; and that, although the rank-and-file fought sturdily and in the best traditions of the Russian army, the generalship and the logistics were extremely defective. Other causes for the initial Russian disasters include the unusual severity of the weather during that winter, the lack of proper skiing equipment among the Soviet forces and the great heroism and military ability displayed by the Finns.

Nevertheless, despite its initial setbacks, the Red Army did ultimately win the war, which came to an end in March 1940. As things turned out, this gave the Soviet leaders a breathing space of approximately 15 months in which to prepare for their forthcoming struggle with Germany. Events, however, proved that this was not really long enough. The numbers of planes, tanks and other equipment available to the Soviet armed forces looked very formidable on paper; but much of the stuff was obsolescent, and incapable of meeting their Nazi counter-parts on anything like equal terms. That admirable tank, the T-34, had admittedly come off the drawing-board and gone into production by the time of Hitler's invasion in 1941, but the numbers actually available were extremely small. A similar comment applies to Soviet aircraft.

The part played by the Soviet armed forces in helping to win World War II is so well known that, in an outline history, there seems not much point in doing more than sketch in its salient features. An important cause of Hitler's failure in Russia was his underestimation of the size of the forces necessary to allow him to achieve victory. Including the troops of his allies, he had less than 190 divisions available for the pur-pose; and these proved far too few. If just his occupation policies had been less bar-barous, his troops might have sufficed; but the treatment meted out to Russian civilians in the areas occupied by Hitler's armies was so cruel as to drive into armed opposition the bulk of the inhabitants of those regions. Consequently, the holding down of the occupied territories was an important military task for the Nazi generals, and troops which might otherwise have been used for fighting against the Red Army were pinned down in garrison duties in the rear.

The milestones of the war on the Eastern Front were the appalling losses of the Soviet armed forces in the first few weeks of the war there, due to the strategic and tactical surprise which the Nazi generals were able to achieve (itself due largely to Stalin's lunatic policies); the success of the Red Army in preventing the fall of Moscow in the winter of 1941; the defence of Lenin-grad; the heroic resistance of the Russian soldiers to the German attacks on Stalingrad in the autumn of 1942, and their subsequent going over to that offensive which resulted in the encirclement and total destruction of Paulus' 6th Army in February 1943; the Battle of Kursk in the same year, which has been authoritatively described as the real turning-point of the war on the Eastern Front; the Red Army's offensive in the summer of 1944, which drove the Nazis back across Central Europe to the borders of Germany itself; and finally, in 1945, the Soviet invasion of Germany, culminating in the capture of Berlin. Nor, when speaking of the Soviet armed forces' contribution to the winning of World War II, should we forget their campaign in the Far East against the Japanese Kwantung Army in the summer of 1945 (militarily irrelevant though that campaign may have been so far as the attain-ment of victory over Imperial Japan was concerned).

But although World War II had been won, the cost to the Russians had been appalling. The destruction of towns and villages in European Russia had been horrific; and the toll in Soviet lives, accord-ing to Molotov, was of the order of

*Right:* **Yak-9 fighters in action against the Germans towards the end of World War II. These machines were among the best of Soviet wartime designs**

*Below:* **T-34 tanks entering Poznan in Poland in 1945. The vehicle in the foreground is one of thousands of Jeeps supplied to the USSR by the Americans**

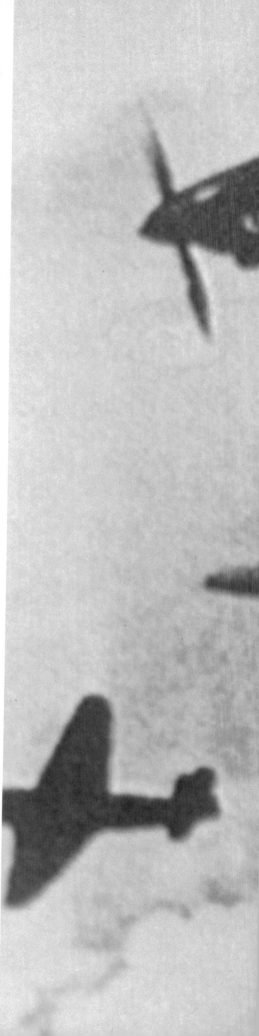

20,000,000. Recent demographic studies suggest that this figure may be even higher. Fortunately for the Soviet Union, however, there was no enemy left on this earth who wanted to go to war with her. Although there were undoubtedly voices to be heard in the West, declaring that a preventive war on Russia was highly desirable, the major Western powers, so far from preparing for it, began to demobilise their armies and navies as soon as Germany and Japan had been decisively beaten.

The history of the Soviet armed forces since 1945 is therefore one of very little fighting, but at the same time one of continual modernisation, of continual pondering over the lessons of the 'Great Patriotic War', and of an unremitting determination to prevent a repetition of a capitalist invasion of the 'Socialist Motherland'. This determination has found its practical expression in the size of the forces kept under arms by the Kremlin since the end of World War II and in the number and quality of the weapons with which these forces have been equipped. In addition, the period 1945–1953 saw the Soviet armed forces being used by Stalin to support his expansionist foreign policy; as a result of their help, a considerable area of Europe fell under the sway of the USSR for the first time.

The end of World War II saw the first use of atomic weapons, which subsequently evolved into nuclear ones. The Soviet attitude towards these weapons was strongly influenced by the fact that the West possessed them, a circumstance which made the Kremlin devote great energy to producing Soviet versions of them as soon as it could. The first Soviet atomic device was tested in 1949, and the first Soviet nuclear device in 1953. At the same time, as Soviet industry recovered from the ravages of World War II, a good deal of the output of its more sophisticated branches was directed towards the production of modern equipment for the use of the Soviet armed forces. Ever newer tanks, ever more formidable artillery, ever more effective aircraft poured out of the Soviet factories; while in the means of delivering a missile on to a very far distant target the Russian technicians succeeded in outstripping the West. The year 1957 was a milestone in the history of the Soviet armed forces, for in that year the USSR successfully tested a missile which, launched from Soviet territory, was capable of hitting the territory of the United States. In that year, therefore, the total immunity to destruction by Soviet weapons which the USA had enjoyed since the dawn of time, was brought to an end, and the world's strategic balance significantly altered. It was this policy which allowed Khrushchev to seek to adopt a policy of relying almost exclusively upon nuclear weapons for the defence of the Soviet Union, and thereby make it possible to effect drastic reductions in the conventional forces. That this policy was unpopular with the Soviet military goes without saying; and after the fall of Khrushchev in 1964 the conventional forces of the USSR were restored to their traditional importance.

The postwar years were also those of the growth of the Soviet Navy, which moved ever farther away from those coastal waters which had been its customary playground, and went out on to the high seas after the fashion of the British and American navies, and began to sail the oceans of the world. Prior to World War II, it had consisted of little more than large numbers of small ships and small, short-range submarines designed for coastal defence. In 1970, however, the great naval manoeuvres, code-named 'Okean', proved to even the most sceptical Western observer that the Soviet Navy had made great progress since the end of World War II. Since that date, the steady growth in the numbers of nuclear submarines, the building of the series of helicopter/VTOL carriers, and the impressive total of modern surface vessels of every conceivable kind available to Soviet admirals are further evidence of the Soviet Navy's ever increasing power. How it will use that power has not yet been satisfactorily assessed by Western observers; but many of the latter, who once assumed that the motive behind the growth of the Soviet Navy was essentially defensive, are now beginning to have second thoughts on the matter.

As for the air forces, the Soviet leaders traditionally refused to regard them as a separate service. Before World War II, therefore, their function was to co-operate either with the army or else with the navy; and their machines were designed for the purpose of fulfilling those functions and nothing else. Consequently, the planes allotted to the army were designed for reconnaissance and ground support, and heavy bombers simply were not made in significant quantities. Similarly, those intended for the navy naturally had to conform to the navy's strategic and tactical doctrines of the time. Since these were concerned exclusively with the prevention of an enemy seaborne landing on Soviet territory, and since the Soviet economy of the 1920s and 1930s would not allow of the construction of a modern fleet, the aim of the Soviet admirals was to have very large numbers of light forces which could engage the enemy like a cloud of mosquitoes, but (like mosquitoes) only near their base. The aircraft allotted to the support of the Soviet Navy had therefore also only a very short range, which proved a serious handicap in World War II, as Admiral Gorshkov has testified.

Today, however, the picture looks very different. Although, once again, the Soviet Air Force as such can hardly be said to exist, the aircraft available to the Russian leaders form an impressive 'mix'. Apart from those allotted to the support of the ground forces and of the navy, there are first-class machines to be found in the ranks of Air Defence Command (*PVO Strany*) and Air Transport Command. Nor is the long-range bomber now omitted from the inventory of Soviet aircraft. The Long-Range Air Force now has a total of over 800 long-range and medium-range machines. Unlike the air forces of the West, the Soviet capability in long-range strategic aircraft is not weakening but growing.

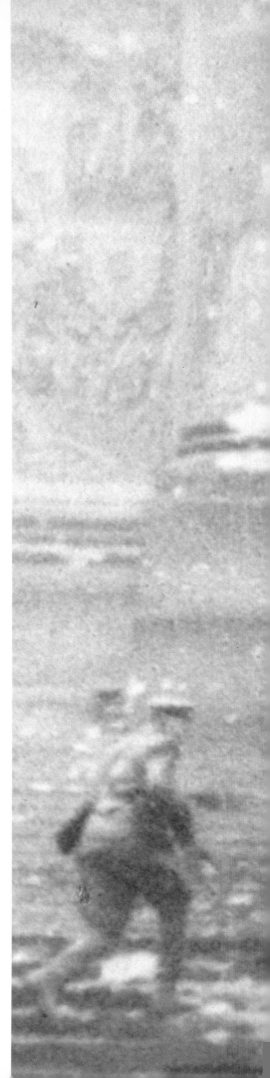

The storming of the Reichstag (the parliament building) in Berlin by units of the Red Army in 1945. The race to the Nazi capital cost the Russians 200,000 casualties

# Military/Political Infrastructure

**Christopher Donnelly**

It is the role of the Communist Party of the Soviet Union (CPSU) to guide and direct Soviet society along the road to communism. In fulfilment of this (its historic mission, as it believes), the Communist Party feels that it is obliged to exert its control over every aspect of human behaviour.

Every branch of that organism which is Soviet society is subject to the direction and supervision of the CPSU, and the armed forces are no exception. Indeed, because they constitute the party's main instrument for controlling Soviet society as a whole, yet are at the same time the only organisation within that society which could ever succeed in overthrowing the dictatorship of the party, the armed forces are singled out for especially thorough control and supervision by the party.

The brain of an army can usually be found in its General Staff, and the Soviet Army (or Red Army, as it was entitled until World War II) is no exception. However, the CPSU can justifiably claim to be the Soviet Army's central nervous system and animating spirit. Moreover, it is precisely because the CPSU fulfils this same function in the whole of Soviet society that we can talk of a Soviet 'war machine'.

By inserting party members into every social institution at all levels, and by ensuring that professional promotion relies on party approval, the CPSU contrives to achieve, however enforced, a unity of aim and purpose in Soviet society which is rarely to be found in a Western country.

Because Marxist ideology insists that the hostile capitalist West will seek to destroy the Soviet state and end the rule of the Communist Party (and the history of the USSR over the past 50 years tends to reinforce this belief in the minds of Soviet citizens), it is hardly surprising that the party has made use of its position of power during this time to prepare the Soviet economy and the Soviet people for war. While it is difficult to reach a precise figure, many Western specialists would agree that a good third of all public expenditure and

Party leader Brezhnev looks on as Marshal Grechko takes the salute at a military parade. Brezhev served as a political officer under Grechko during WWII

31

# Military and Political Infrastructure of the Soviet Union

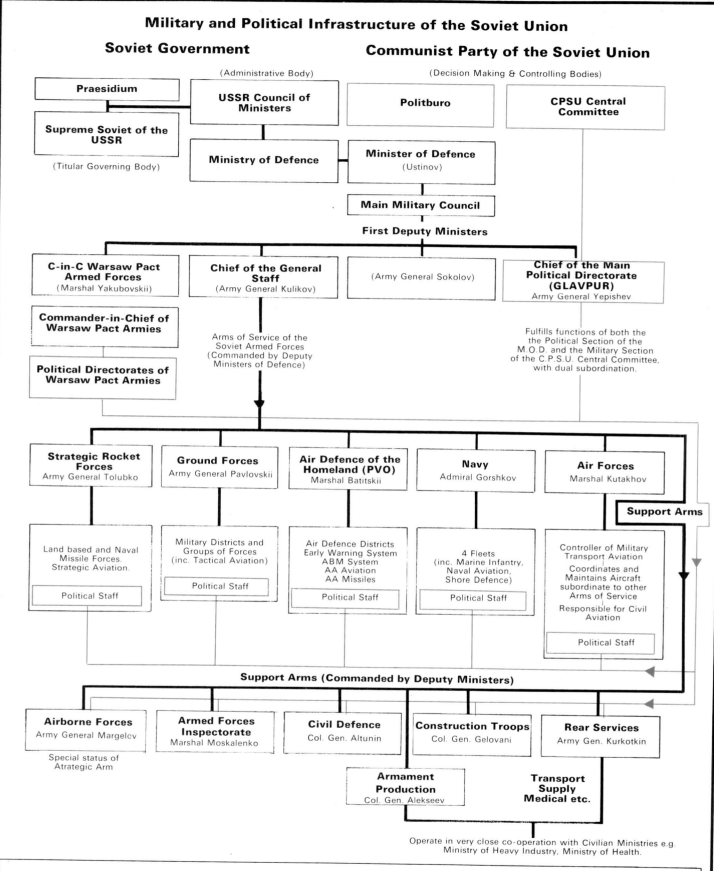

## Soviet Government

(Administrative Body)

**Praesidium**

**Supreme Soviet of the USSR**

(Titular Governing Body)

**USSR Council of Ministers**

**Ministry of Defence**

## Communist Party of the Soviet Union

(Decision Making & Controlling Bodies)

**Politburo**

**CPSU Central Committee**

**Minister of Defence**
(Ustinov)

**Main Military Council**

**First Deputy Ministers**

**C-in-C Warsaw Pact Armed Forces**
(Marshal Yakubovskii)

**Commander-in-Chief of Warsaw Pact Armies**

**Political Directorates of Warsaw Pact Armies**

**Chief of the General Staff**
(Army General Kulikov)

Arms of Service of the Soviet Armed Forces (Commanded by Deputy Ministers of Defence)

(Army General Sokolov)

**Chief of the Main Political Directorate (GLAVPUR)**
Army General Yepishev

Fulfills functions of both the the Political Section of the M.O.D. and the Military Section of the C.P.S.U. Central Committee, with dual subordination.

**Strategic Rocket Forces**
Army General Tolubko

Land based and Naval Missile Forces. Strategic Aviation.

Political Staff

**Ground Forces**
Army General Pavlovskii

Military Districts and Groups of Forces (inc. Tactical Aviation)

Political Staff

**Air Defence of the Homeland (PVO)**
Marshal Batitskii

Air Defence Districts Early Warning System ABM System AA Aviation AA Missiles

Political Staff

**Navy**
Admiral Gorshkov

4 Fleets (inc. Marine Infantry, Naval Aviation, Shore Defence)

Political Staff

**Air Forces**
Marshal Kutakhov

**Support Arms**

Controller of Military Transport Aviation

Coordinates and Maintains Aircraft subordinate to other Arms of Service

Responsible for Civil Aviation

Political Staff

**Support Arms (Commanded by Deputy Ministers)**

**Airborne Forces**
Army General Margelov

Special status of Atrategic Arm

**Armed Forces Inspectorate**
Marshal Moskalenko

**Civil Defence**
Col. Gen. Altunin

**Construction Troops**
Col. Gen. Gelovani

**Rear Services**
Army Gen. Kurkotkin

**Armament Production**
Col. Gen. Alekseev

**Transport Supply Medical etc.**

Operate in very close co-operation with Civilian Ministries e.g. Ministry of Heavy Industry, Ministry of Health.

---

Chaired by the Minister of Defence, the Military Council directs the work of the USSR Ministry of Defence. Members of the Military Council include all First Deputy and Deputy Ministers of Defence and most senior officers of all Arms of Service, such as Commanders of Military Districts or Fleets; senior political officers and members of the Central Committee, and senior civilians from relevant positions, e.g. those responsible for industrial production. A Military Council meeting called by the Minister of Defence may involve only the First Deputy Ministers plus a few other members,

e.g. heads of organisations involved in matters on the agenda of the meeting.
A senior commander, such as the Chief of an Arm of Service, directs his organisation through his own Military Council composed of his deputy commanders and senior subordinates. At all levels, the Military Council includes at least one member of the Political Administration, who is directly subordinate to his superior in the GLAVPUR organisation, as well as to the senior military commander.

*Above:* **When fresh conscripts arrive at a Soviet unit, the troops parade to greet them and "show them the ropes"**

resources in the Soviet Union is earmarked for arms. What is more, the characteristics of the Soviet system mean that it is far easier to divert effort into defence projects than it would be in a Western society.

The secret lies in total centralisation allied with close control and supervision. The Soviet economy is a planned economy. That is to say that the production of every item down to, for instance, every cup and saucer or every rifle bullet, is done according to a master plan produced by *Gosplan* – the State Planning Ministry – in Moscow. A revised plan is produced every five years or so to take account of changes in requirements and conditions. The market influences of supply and demand which control capitalist economy are not allowed to operate, and state control of the mass media and all means of public expression make it very difficult for individuals to make their complaints heard. The net result is that public opinion has little or no effect on the plan.

The function of the various economic ministries of the Soviet government is to see to the implementation of that part of the plan which concerns them, and to advise the planners as to what could be expected to be achieved. Decisions concerning the economic developments of the country are made by the ruling bodies of the Communist Party, particularly by the *Politburo*, headed at the moment by Brezhnev. In the same way, the other ministries, such as the Ministry of Education, the Ministry of Health and the Ministry of Defence, to name but a few, simply exist to put into practice the decisions of the party leaders, and advise them in their own special field when requested to do

so. The Minister of Defence, for example, was co-opted into the *Politburo* in 1973 because at that time the Party chiefs felt the need of specialised and competent advice when entering into such important negotiations as the SALT (Strategic Arms Limitation Talks) and MBFR (Mutual Balanced Force Reductions) discussions. When the party no longer feels the need for such close collaboration with the military, no doubt the Minister of Defence will lose his seat on the party's ruling body.

Should, then, the party decide that it needs a larger army and more tanks, it will simply instruct *Gosplan* to allot a larger slice of the economic cake to tank production in the next plan, building new factories or converting existing ones to cope with the increased demand.

This, then, is the first practical step to the creation of a single-minded war machine. It has an important and useful spin-off in that, with such centralised direction on such a large scale, standardisation of military equipment is far easier than in capitalist economies where each firm involved in defence industries is likely to produce equipment to its own specifications.

At the present time, as indeed since the economy was first effectively industrialised in the 1930s, the party allots a very high priority to the defence industry. Factories engaged in defence work are assured better supplies of raw materials plus higher wages and bonuses than are factories working for the civilian economy.

The second step towards establishing a functioning war machine is the psychological preparation of the population. The state makes good use of its total control of the educational system and the information networks to keep the spirit of war alive in the population. This takes two forms: firstly, the propaganda line in schools and in the mass media emphasises the military threat which capitalist nations and blocs pose to the

Soviet Union, and glorifies the feats of the Soviet Army, widely publicising exercises, holding public parades and celebrating anniversaries of glorious victories; secondly, the civilian economy is run in military fashion with periodic 'storming' of the economic targets, and decorating 'Heroes of Labour' for victories achieved in the struggle to build socialism. Indeed, in its whole atmosphere the Soviet Union strikes the casual visitor as a nation at war, and the patriotic posters with their calls to work harder and the general scarcity of consumer goods tend to accentuate this feeling. The above must not be construed as meaning that the Soviet people want a war. They most definitely do not. However, they are kept aware that they might have to fight a war if capitalism, that most evil of social systems, attempts to destroy socialism; and they are told that by whatever means that war would be fought, the Soviet Union would be bound to win.

The third step to the creation of an effective war machine is to ensure the total integration of civilians and the military within society. The idea of a 'nation in arms' is dear to the Marxist's heart; and although the Soviet system may fall some way short of that ideal, it does nevertheless go a good way towards it. All young men are required to do two or three years national service, and though in fact two-fifths are exempted, these are expected to complete a part-time course of training to give them a reserve capability in the event of mobilisation. When the pre-service training system is working properly, all young men will do basic military training before they reach the age of 18, regardless of whether or not they are to be conscripted.

There have also existed in the Soviet Union, almost since the days of the revolution, sports organisations under party control which provide excellent facilities for any youth or girl wishing to take up such para-military sports as shooting, gliding, parachuting or skiing. Physical training is widely encouraged by the party's youth organisations; and all school children, as part of their normal school curriculum, do a physical training exam and receive a certificate declaring them to be 'Ready for Labour and Defence'. There is a widespread and flourishing civil defence organisation which works in close co-operation with hospitals, local authorities and local military units, and which holds rallies, lectures and demonstrations to involve the public in such communist feasts as 'Soviet Army Day'. All hospitals are supposed to practise dealing with the mass casualties produced by a nuclear, biological or chemical war.

On the other side of the coin, integration is effected by the posting of military personnel into civilian appointments. It is usual for factories engaged in defence work to have serving officers filling administrative or technical posts on their staff. The senior military commander in any city or district is automatically appointed to a seat on the local government body at that level, e.g. the commandant of a garrison located in a town would have a seat on the town council; the commander in chief of a military district would be appointed as a Deputy to the Supreme Soviet of the republic in which the district was situated, and also probably to

33

the Supreme Soviet of the USSR.

It must also be borne in mind that the army in Russia traditionally fulfilled the function of bringing the members of the different races of the empire into close contact with each other, subjecting them to a single unifying discipline and programme of education. The Soviet Army continues to fulfil this useful function, and thus contributes greatly to increasing the cohesion of the Soviet Union.

But it is Communist Party direction and its control of Soviet society (and particularly of the armed forces) which provides that essential motivation which makes the Soviet war machine what it is. The first and most obvious means of control available to the party is that which is available to any government up to a point – the party, by controlling the economy, controls the purse which pays the men and provides the equipment and the expensive exercises. The Soviet military press is daily filled with acclamations about how concerned the party is for the well-being of the armed forces, and how the armed forces owe their all to the party. Such a level of control is, however, far from sufficient. There are three further means of control – firstly there is the *KGB*. The Committee for State Security, as its title means, is the latest name for the paramilitary security and intelligence organisation which is in fact the Communist Party's own private army; some of its earlier titles were the *Cheka*, the *OGPU* and the *NKVD*. It is the senior of all Soviet police organisations and has a special branch which deals with the security and reliability of the armed forces. *KGB* agents and informers are to be found at all levels and in all branches of the Soviet armed forces.

Important though it is, the *KGB* is interested mainly in seeing that the normal means of political direction in the armed forces are functioning properly. These normal means are, firstly, the Communist Party organisation which exists at all levels within the armed forces, as it does within any branch of Soviet society and, secondly, the Main Political Directorate of the Soviet Army and Navy (its Russian title is abbreviated to *GLAVPUR*). This latter is a large, separate and extremely influential corps in the armed forces, and is responsible for the political reliability of those forces at all times.

The Communist Party organisation in the armed forces exists primarily to ensure that the personnel, particularly the regular cadre of officers, ensigns and extended service NCOs, identify their own interests with those of the party. A great deal of pressure is exerted, most of all on the officers, to encourage them to become members of the party or, if under 25 years of age, members of the Young Communist League (*Komsomol*). In fact, of junior officers, probably about two-thirds are Communist Party or active *Komsomol* members; for senior captains and majors, the figure is about three out of every four; while membership of the party is more or less obligatory for senior officers, or any post of especial responsibility.

Party or *Komsomol* meetings are held regularly at company level or equivalent; but rarely, if ever, will the company commander be the senior party member. On

principle, political and military control is separated at all levels except the very highest, in order to provide an extra means of control. The senior party official, the secretary, is responsible for party affairs to his immediate party boss at battalion level and not to the company commander, and so on up the entire organisation.

The responsibility for the functioning of any unit, including the political education of the men, their discipline, morale and spiritual well-being belongs entirely to the unit commander himself. In the ground forces, for example, for the normal unit, i.e. a regiment of three or four battalions, this will be a lieutenant-colonel or colonel. To assist him in running the unit, the commander has on his staff several deputies, each with a special area of responsibility, e.g. the Deputy Regimental Commander for Rear Services, who normally hold the rank of major. One of these deputies will invariably be the Deputy Commander for Political Affairs, or '*Zampolit*'. His job, as a member of the Political Directorate, is to remove the burden of political education from the shoulders of the unit commander and organise, co-ordinate or run all unit political activities.

The *Zampolit*'s task is to assist the commander to maintain discipline and morale and thus keep the men fighting and obeying orders. The political activities are in fact merely the means by which this is done, ensuring at the same time, of course, that loyalties are strictly in favour of the party. To help him in his duties, the *Zampolit* has several assistants in each battalion and company of the regiment: these may be officers or ensigns. He can also call on the Communist Party organisation in the unit to assist him in his programme; indeed, he will normally work in close co-ordination with the party at all times.

The latest party regulations insist that each soldier in the armed forces is to receive the following political instruction as a basic minimum: two two-hour classes in Marxist–Leninist theory per week; one hour per week of Marxist interpretation of current events, either as two 30-minute classes or as one 10-minute talk six days out of seven; and special talks in the field lasting up to three hours during major exercises. There are also to be permanent propaganda displays in all barracks, clubhouses and messes, troops are to participate in rallies and parades on communist 'feast-days' and the weekly or fortnightly unit news bulletin is to carry political instruction.

In addition to sharing the burden of organising the above, all officers must attend at least 50 hours of political instruction per year. This normally takes the form of attendance at a week-long course on a specific theme (such as how best to engender a true hatred of imperialism in the men under one's command), plus attendance at rallies or classes in current affairs.

It must be remembered that, in addition,

*Left:* **An officer of the GLAVPUR (Political Directorate) delivers a propaganda lecture on the battlefield, indoctrination being one of his regular duties**

35

most officers will be involved in sparetime work for the Communist Party or *Komsomol,* or studying for promotion or staff academy entrance exams, of which political studies are an obligatory part.

The only cultural organisations and activities countenanced in the USSR are those sponsored or approved by the party. This means that activities which in the armed forces of a Western state would be considered amusement or recreational activities will inevitably bear a communist message if performed in the Soviet armed forces. Popular Soviet examples are: 'brains trusts', when the men may quiz a panel of experts; the contents of libraries, and library displays; unit film shows, concerts or amateur dramatics; and, of course, all programmes on the services radio stations.

The job of the political deputy of a unit is not merely to co-ordinate and supervise all this activity – a mammoth task in itself – but he must also do the jobs that the education officer and padre do in a British unit. He must organise and supervise all education classes, arranging, for example, Russian classes for non-Russian speakers. (In the belief that military units comprised principally of one nationality, e.g. Ukrainians or Armenians, pose a threat of nationalist dissent to party rule, the Soviet leaders take great care nowadays to split up all national groups right down to section level, despite the linguistic problem this presents to those given the task of training conscripts, 20 per

cent of whom may have only the faintest grasp of Russian.) Soldiers are encouraged to take all their welfare problems to the political deputy when the unit commander is busy; and should the Soviet high command have any urgent message for the troops, the political deputy is made responsible for conveying it. As an example of this last point, one might quote the campaigns organised to prevent wastage of bread in those years when the Soviet grain harvest has been abnormally low.

This enforced political involvement is in direct contrast with most Western armies, which forbid political involvement on the part of their officers and men; and it constitutes what is certainly the most striking difference between the armed forces of a communist-style state and those of a Western country.

The following brief description of the purely military side of the personnel structure of the Soviet armed forces is designed to show the career structure and conditions for the Soviet military; but the reader is warned to remember at all times that, in the Soviet view, the military and political spheres are totally indivisible.

The personnel structure of the army is based on a large corps of regular volunteer officers, assisted by a somewhat lesser number of regular NCOs, who together make up approximately one-third of the army's manpower. The other two-thirds are conscripts, inducted for two or three years.

*Above:* **Taking the military oath. This is always carried out with great ceremony to impress on the soldier the burden of his duty — and the penalties for failure**

*Above right:* **Officer cadets of an air force technical academy receive instruction in one of the many aspects of highly-developed Soviet aeronautics**

*Right:* **A standard tactic of Soviet penetration forces is to capture a sentry from a logistics unit and gain entry to supply dumps by impersonating him**

From earliest infancy, the young Soviet citizen learns to accept that he must do national service, and he learns to respect and honour the armed forces as the means of defending 'Socialism' and the 'Soviet Homeland' from the capitalists who would love to destroy them.

His first actual contact with military service will probably be at school or at work where, between the ages of 15 and 18, he is expected to complete 100–140 hours of basic military training to prepare him for military service. Military departments exist in all schools and industrial or agricultural establishments having over 10 young men in the 15–18 age group; and for perhaps two hours per week the young man must learn shoot-

ing, drill and minor tactics at the hands of serving or retired officers posted to the school or factory for that purpose.

The system, introduced in 1968, does have drawbacks, including 'consumer resistance' and lack of funds. However it was estimated that, by the end of 1974 approximately, two-thirds of boys in the relevant age group had received a significant amount of basic military training. In addition, there exists an organisation called *DOSAAF* which provides at very little cost excellent facilities in many urban areas for those in their mid and late 'teens who wish to learn and practise sports which have a military application, such as shooting, gliding, parachuting and skiing.

At the age of 18, the young man will be ordered to report for conscription. Though universal military service is the law, exemption or deferment can be obtained for the usual health or family reasons, and also if the young man is going to study at a university or other higher educational establishment. If this deferment takes them beyond the age of 23, they are unlikely to be conscripted, but will pass onto the reserve. Those attending university are expected to spend one afternoon per week (for at least two of the five years of their course) doing basic military studies, and training as future reserve officers. Those conscripted will do two years service in the Army or three years in the Navy, Air Force or Internal Security Forces (*KGB* or *MOOP*).

Induction takes place in spring and autumn every year, and is always accompanied by a large-scale public relations campaign, parades and an impressive induction ceremony in each major town. After a brief kitting-out period in their local barracks, the conscripts will be sorted and despatched to their units for training and service. A serious attempt is made to fit the young man into the service in which he can be of most use. The Air Forces, Navy and Strategic Rocket Forces will get those best qualified technically, and the Airborne Forces and Marine Infantry take only volunteers who are above average in physical fitness. As far as the Army is concerned, those whose educational, military training or *DOSAAF* records mark them as above average material are sent direct to training regiments to be trained as junior NCOs. After a six-month course, they are sent out to units to do their national service as junior sergeants.

Because of the limited training time and constant rapid turnover of personnel, particularly in the Army, the conscript is subjected to an intensive and stereotyped training cycle which will teach him to do two basic jobs; for example a tank driver should be capable not only of driving but also performing necessary servicing jobs on his tank.

*Above left:* **Sailors of the Baltic Fleet undergoing political indoctrination**

*Above:* **A member of the military branch of the KGB in parade dress**

*Left:* **The late Marshal A. A. Grechko addresses a military parade. Until his death in April 1976, Grechko was Minister of Defence of the USSR. His successor, Dmitrii F. Ustinov, a civilian, was given the rank of Army General on his appointment: previously he had been in charge of military defence industries. Shortly afterwards, in May 1976, Party leader Brezhnev assumed the rank of Marshal of the Soviet Union. This probably indicates a strengthening of Party control over the armed forces and a curtailment of the independence of the military as a group**

Conditions of service for the conscript are rigorous by modern Western standards. He gets little or no leave (naval ratings are rarely allowed the run of a foreign port except under the supervision of a petty officer) and only four or five roubles (about £2) per month pocket money. Moreover, the standard of food and accommodation is very low, especially in remote areas.

However, for those who, in their second year of service, volunteer and are accepted for extended service as regular NCOs, life improves enormously. The regular NCO gets a wage equivalent to his civilian position, 40 days leave per year and various fringe benefits such as subsidised shops and accommodation. Despite this, his status has never approached that of a responsible NCO in the British army, and the duties he is employed on are much less demanding of initiative and ability. Consequently, in an attempt to create a class of 'warrant officers',

i.e. NCOs capable of holding responsible command positions, the Soviet authorities in 1972 revived the ranks of ensign and midshipman, with enhanced status, privilege and conditions of service, and the offer of the possibility of an eventual commission for those considered suitable. It was hoped that more well qualified soldiers and sailors would be tempted to sign on in these new ranks, which run parallel to the extended service ranks of sergeant, senior sergeant and petty officer, or that extended service NCOs would be tempted to increase their technical qualifications to achieve the higher standard demanded of the new 'warrant officers'. It is also hoped that the ensign and midshipman will eventually do many of the tedious tasks that are at present done by junior officers in the Soviet armed forces.

Despite Soviet insistence that there is no 'class' distinction between officers and men in the armed forces (indeed if one uses 'class' in its Marxist meaning this may be true), nevertheless there is nowadays a noticeable difference between the backgrounds of the average officer and soldier. An officer's education can start as early as 13 at a special Suvorov (Army) or Nakhimov (Naval) college where, in the rank of cadet, a boy receives a traditional military education in an elite boarding school environment. It is demonstrably easier for a serving or retired officer or senior party official to get his son into such a school than it is for someone who does not have such a background.

At the age of 18–19 the potential officer begins a three- to six-year course at any one of 150 all-arms or special-to-arm academies,

from which he will emerge as a junior lieutenant holding an accepted educational qualification relevant to the number of years spent under training. Officer candidates come from Suvorov and Nakhimov colleges, straight from school or university, or in rare cases, having completed one year of national service. Their social and educational background is usually a fair degree higher than that of the conscript and regular NCO. The courses at the military and naval academies are thorough and extensive, concerned with both the theory and the practice of war.

The young army officer, as platoon and later company commander, is wholly responsible for the day-to-day training of his conscript soldiers. He is allowed much less initiative in arranging training schedules than is his Western counterpart; and the tight timing of the training cycle permits the young Soviet officer few, if any, of the more pleasurable 'adventure training' activities that his NATO equivalent might expect to enjoy. Not until he has completed the three-year staff course at the Frunze Military Academy or a technical staff academy, does the officer, as a major commanding a battalion, achieve any real ability to practise initiative, and even then it is more limited than it would be in the case of a NATO officer.

However, lack of opportunity for displaying initiative at lower levels is not such a fault in Soviet eyes. The army depends for its effectiveness on strict and efficient command and control from higher command levels. Not until he attains command of a

regiment or even a division will a Soviet officer be expected or allowed to display tactical initiative in the Western sense. The battalion commander is expected to carry out his orders and play his part in the grand plan according to the book. Any sudden burst of initiative or independent action on his part might simply ruin the overall plan. In general terms, initiative and spontaneity are not regarded as virtues anywhere in Soviet society, and in this respect the army is no exception.

Conditions of service for officers are very good, and raise their standard of living well above the Soviet average. They are well paid, and receive substantial privileges in terms of subsidised accommodation, special education for their children in many cases, special subsidised shops for food and consumer goods, and 40 days leave per year. However, the tedium of a young officer's early career, plus the general rise in the standard of living of the civilian population, has meant a drop in the quality and quantity of volunteers for officers' service in recent years. The recent increases in pay and privileges afforded officers, and the attempt to relieve them of tedious administrative work at lower levels, plus a steadily increasing public relations and advertising campaign for the military academies, is evidence of the concern that this causes the Soviet high command.

While his career structure is very similar, a naval officer is less subject to the pressures of the training cycle and more able to exercise his initiative than his army colleagues. The uncertainties of life and war at sea do anyway tend to require a more flexible ap-

*Far left:* T-54/55 tank unit seen near a housing estate in the suburbs of Prague, Czechoslovakia, on September 15, 1968

*Above:* At the XXV CPSU Congress in the Kremlin in February 1976. Brezhnev reviewed Soviet military, economic and political performance of the previous half-decade

*Left:* Senior officers on a course at the General Staff Academy. Soviet officers spend longer on training courses than their counterparts in many NATO armies

proach to command and control than is usually necessary on land. It is perhaps for this reason that the problems of young officer recruitment and service are less acute in the navy.

Generals and admirals attend a course of up to two years at the General Staff Academy (to equip them for command of large formations), academies, research establishments, or senior appointments in the Ministry of Defence. On completion of 25 years service an officer gets a very generous pension, and those who have achieved a senior rank also retain a great many of their privileges. The statutory retirement ages are often ignored; and many of the very senior army commanders, even today, are in their late 60s.

# Current Objectives and Political Strategy

**Brigadier Shelford Bidwell**

We have already seen in an earlier chapter how the whole dynamic of Soviet behaviour is governed by its peculiar, all-embracing Marxist view of the world. To those unfamiliar with it, Soviet foreign policy, the deployment of its military power and its occasional use of this military power may seem illogical or inconsistent. In fact it is wholly consistent, and both its distant goals and all Soviet manoeuvres, the pursuit of *détente*, the staging of the European Security Conference, the SALT talks, intervention in the Arab–Israeli quarrel, supplying arms to non-Marxist insurgents and the activities of the new Soviet Navy, are all based on the most careful and painstaking analysis made with reference to Marxist principles. (If things go wong, as they did, for instance, in Greece in 1948 and the confrontation with the US over Cuba, it is out of the question for the principles to be found wanting: the analysis or the analysts must be at fault.)

War, in the Marxist view, is basically an evil thing, but it is one of the inevitable consequences of capitalism in its last and most virulent phase of 'imperialism'. It might be wondered what 'empires' now exist, but the Marxist interpretation of the present state of affairs is that the former colonial empires and the third, undeveloped world are still exploited by the capitalist bloc of countries as surely as if they were still under direct rule. To oversimplify, they have shaken off imperial rule, and next they must shake off native bourgeois capitalist rule finally to join the progressive socialist 'camp'. In South-East Asia, South America and Africa, therefore, we see 'wars of liberation'

attempted or in progress. The liberation movements may not be of the correct Marxist hue, but none the less they favour the onward march of revolution to its correct, socialist conclusion.

In the phase of imperialist-capitalism, the capitalist states will either fight each other, suppress wars of liberation by force or, and this is the biggest threat of all, attempt to arrest the progress of history by attacking the socialist camp. Strategically speaking, this socialist camp is a firm base and a fortress of which the satellite states of Central and Eastern Europe form the outer defences and the Soviet Union the citadel. It is useless to argue that the West has neither the intention nor the necessary military power to do any such thing. The dogma derives from the central part of

Aggressive reconnaissance and electronic intelligence gathering is not solely the task of small ad hoc ships, as shown here by a Kotlin class destroyer probing a British oil rig in the North Sea

Marxist philosophy, and may not be questioned. (Marxists see confirmation of theory in the wars of intervention of 1919 and the German invasion in World War II. It does not explain very satisfactorily why the United States did not make its bid to destroy socialism when it possessed nuclear weapons and the Soviet Union did not.)

The Soviet attitude to war is therefore very clear. As war is inevitable, the Soviet Union must be prepared to win it. Further, and somewhat perplexingly, part of the Marxist theory is that although the cyclic evolution of society through capitalism and socialism to communism is inevitable, it may at the same time be helped by force on every level and every occasion. ('Force is the midwife of revolution.') Accordingly warfare or military force must be used as an instrument of policy when it is safe and profitable to do so.

Soviet strategy therefore has three major goals. The first is to make the Soviet Union, or rather the Soviet bloc as represented by the Warsaw Treaty Organisation (WTO), or Warsaw Pact, impregnable against attack from every quarter. The second is to reduce the power and influence of the United States and the Western alliance (NATO is seen by the Russians as the predicted ganging-up by the desperate capitalist states in preparation for an assault on socialism. The third is the support of 'wars of liberation' everywhere.

There is one very important conditioning factor which must be emphasised here. According to Marxist theory success in war must inevitably go to the side which is economically the stronger. At present Soviet analysts consider that economically the Western bloc is undoubtedly the stronger, and therefore as long as that situation prevails the Soviet leaders will at all costs avoid a global war. They are ready to test Western, or more particularly United States, resolution, as they did over Berlin (1948) and Cuba (1962), and more recently over the Arab–Israeli war, and they will push into any soft spot, but they will never take a risk. They will back down as readily as they will bluster: 'face' means nothing. War and peace are a continuum in Soviet strategy, and objectives are always to be pursued by the most effective and economical means.

The first of these objectives, the security of the Soviet homeland, rests on two pillars.

Marxist theory was formulated before the invention of nuclear weapons, but even Marxists can see that neither socialism nor any other world order can by historic inevitability survive a nuclear holocaust. Therefore one of the two pillars is the creation of a powerful strategic nuclear force capable of surviving a first strike and retaliating in kind.

The essential point to grasp is that the Soviet aim is to establish a strategic missile force superior in quality and numbers to the American one so as to make a pre-emptive strike against the Soviet Union too dangerous to contemplate. A secondary objective is to provide a strong bargaining base from which to launch diplomatic offensives such as the SALT talks, whose real aim is to

*Right:* In October 1973 few Israeli aircraft could evade deadly SA-6 Gainful missiles, fired from triple launchers on vehicles such as these, which also carry the guidance radars

*Far right:* The annual May Day Parade of armed might through Moscow's Red Square is attended not only by Soviet leaders but by guests from many countries

*Below:* Shore leave in a foreign port for the crew of a Kashin class ship. Soviet crews have to obey rigid rules during such visits

*Above:* **This Soviet warhead test underscores the fact that the West can no longer use a dominant nuclear capability to make up a deficiency in conventional armaments**

*Left:* **The swift victory of the MPLA in Angola was a textbook example of Soviet political domination and arms supply. These MPLA recruits in Luanda in November 1975 have RPG-7 rocket launchers**

weaken the relative position of the United States. As we have seen, from the first introduction of nuclear weapons Soviet propagandists have skilfully used native left-wing opinion in the Western countries to discredit the Western possession of nuclear weapons, while ignoring or condoning the existence of the Soviet Strategic Rocket Forces and the massive nuclear testing carried out by the Soviet Union.

Whereas the West follows a strategy of small, but efficient, purely defensive forces backed by a graduated nuclear deterrent, there are indications that the Soviet leaders believe that the balance of nuclear terror is such that a purely 'conventional' war is possible and that they are preparing for it.

Soviet conventional strategy is based on the principle of mass, as contrasted with Western 'classical' ideas in which success in war depends on the practical application of certain guide-lines (known in the British army as the 'principles of war') and on the art of generalship. Soviet military experts do

not dismiss such considerations as surprise and flexibility, but regard them as subsidiary and tactical. They firmly believe in the preponderance of numbers over any amount of tactical skill and subtlety in manoeuvre. In World War II they ground the Germans, down, bringing a manpower superiority of 4:1 to bear in the battle zone and from 160–240 pieces of artillery per mile of front. (A perfect example of Russian methods was seen on the Arab side in the war of October 1973.)

Although Soviet military technology is very good, the Russians forego the extreme sophistication of Western designers, which results in great cost per item, in favour of more numerous, less elaborate, cheaper but nevertheless robust and serviceable equipments. This difference is purely relative and, in the missile field for instance, Soviet weapon systems are fully up to the role for which they have been designed.

The deployment of Soviet forces facing NATO in north-west Europe illustrates this basic principle of the preponderance of numerical superiority in determining the outcome of any armed clash, on whatever scale. According to the best overt appreciation (*The Military Balance 1975–1976*, published by the International Institute for Strategic Studies) the Warsaw Pact maintains 68 divisions to guard against attack by 27 NATO divisions, which in terms of tanks is 19,000 against 5,000, supported by 5,000 strike aircraft against 2,000, plus a powerful force of short-range nuclear missiles and nuclear heavy artillery. It might be wondered what this vast force is really for.

The probable answers to this are three, or threefold, for they are interlinked. Firstly, it is Soviet doctrine that if policy is to be implemented by war, then it is essential that the war be won conclusively, and this can only be ensured by overwhelming superiority in numbers and resources. Secondly, Soviet military theory in a way endorses a passive, 'virtuous' defence – virtuous in the sense that aggression must be first clearly seen or 'identified' before it is responded to. To forego the initiative in war is a rash, self-imposed handicap. The correct strategy is an offensive-defensive to carry the war to the aggressor's territory and defeat his armed forces completely there, and not in one's own homeland. (The Russians had enough of this in the war against Germany.) In any case it is not impossible with the present ratio of forces for the Warsaw Pact to overrun the central sector before tactical nuclear weapons are brought into play, or at least before they begin to bite. (Their own tactical nuclear force may be designed as a deterrent so as to ensure a purely conventional clash that will be entirely in the favour of the Warsaw Pact.) Thirdly, although current indications are that the Soviet leaders will at all costs avoid a global, all-out struggle unless the integrity of the Soviet homeland is threatened, this immensely powerful force geared for offensive action remains poised to take advantage of any serious deterioration in the resolution or defensive capability of the Western alliance. This might take the form of an American withdrawal or the rise of neutralist, leftist governments in Europe.

There is also a fourth possible use for so large and threatening a force, although so far the Western nations have not fallen into the trap: rather the reverse. Any attempt to match Soviet power in terms of numbers can only have a distorting effect on Western economy and on Western standards of living, which would hasten the revolutionary process or, alternatively, force the West to seek strategic safety in qualitative rather than quantitative terms, which according to Soviet doctrine is a false solution. In the Soviet view they win either way.

With a major military clash with the imperialist camp ruled out for the time being, the Soviet strategic goals are pursued by political means, but before examining these the role of the Soviet Navy should be briefly mentioned. The Soviet homeland, unlike the West, is not dependent for its existence on vital imports carried by sea. The Soviet Navy must therefore be, in war-fighting terms, an offensive weapon. The Soviet leaders, however, have grasped by the British and American examples that in peace, or rather in periods of confrontation, an ocean-going navy is a powerful political instrument. It is a visible symbol of military power and furthermore it gives a largely landlocked power access to all the areas of strategic interest to it. The Soviet Navy's most striking success so far, according to Admiral Zumwalt, US Chief of Naval Operations during the period of the 1973 Arab-Israeli war, was in backing the demand to the United States to order the Israelis to withdraw from their successful foray on the west bank of the Suez Canal.

What then are the specific Soviet political goals? Soviet trade and diplomacy are indeed active everywhere – in this the Soviet Union is no different from any other power – but priority is given to areas of instability where local conditions favour the rise of radical or revolutionary governments, and above all where there is actual conflict. (These areas are the targets for infiltration and subversion, as are the strongholds of the West. This is a most important subject but one too lengthy and complex to be discussed in a short chapter.) The significant areas are Latin America, South-East Asia, the Middle East and the northern and southern flanks (or 'tiers' as they would be called in Warsaw Pact terminology) of NATO – in ascending order of importance.

Latin America is a fruitful area for intervention: politically unstable, poor, resentful of 'Yankee' economic domination and with a tradition of revolutions, coups and military regimes. Strategically speaking, it is also the United States' 'backyard': an area where the US can be injured with an economical outlay of Soviet effort. The same is likely to be said of Portugal, although it is permissible to guess that there the Marxist analysts will blame the local Communist Party for attempting too much too soon. The workers were not in fact fully educated and (following the original Russian model) the peasants were reactionary in clinging to the private ownership of land. The gain to the Soviet bloc of a neutralist Portugal, let alone a communist Portugal with Soviet naval bases on the Atlantic coast, is so great that the Soviet leaders will certainly proceed slowly and with great caution in that area, to avoid precipitating a right-wing reaction.

In South-East Asia, of course, the Soviet Union has won a great political victory. It has not been lost on the leaders of the third-world nations in that area that it was Soviet weapons carried in Soviet ships guarded (although indeed remotely and indirectly) by the Soviet Navy that ensured the fall of the Saigon regime. The future objectives are the toppling of the regimes in Thailand, the Philippines, Malaya, Singapore and Burma. With the exception of Singapore there is in all these left-wing insurgency which, if given Soviet advice and weapons, may eventually prove too much for the existing regimes to snuff out – all the more so in the aftermath of US disengagement. The only real competition left is with the left – i.e., with the intervention by the Chinese People's Republic.

Of great importance, but only in the long term, is the balance of power in southern Africa, for in the event of global war Soviet naval squadrons with bases on the coast could threaten—indeed disrupt—the vital sea-routes along which the bulk of the oil supplies of the West are carried round the Cape of Good Hope. The 'capture' of African states by Moscow-orientated Marxist parties furthers this strategy, and the Soviet Union will not hesitate to intervene, as it has done in Angola, provided it can do so without risk of a major conflagration and using indirect or proxy methods.

The greatest single obstacle to this aspect of Soviet strategy is the existence of a strong, developed, industrial, anti-Marxist state lying in a key position to protect the sea-routes connecting the South Atlantic with the Indian Ocean: the Republic of

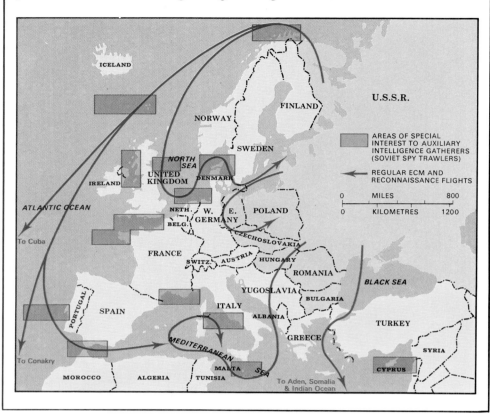

**Soviet ECM and reconnaissance aircraft routes over Europe, and regular patrol areas of Soviet intelligence-gathering "trawlers"**

## SOVIET ARMS AND INFLUENCE IN ANGOLA

There is scarcely a country in the world where the Soviet Union does not pursue some military, economic or political interest; and as, to a Soviet Marxist politician, economics and military affairs are merely different tools to achieve the same end, it is perhaps unwise to concentrate merely on military involvement as a measure of Soviet power or influence abroad. However, we give below a list of countries where representatives of the Soviet military are involved, as opposed to countries with whom arms deals have been concluded without direct involvement of Soviet personnel: Afghanistan, Algeria, Angola, Cuba, Egypt, Guinea, Indo China, Iraq, Libya, Somalia, Syria, Uganda, Yemen.

In their February 1976 issue, the *International Defence Review* quoted one source as having reported that the totals in weapons, vehicles and equipment supplied to MPLA forces in Angola included:

*Infantry weapons and equipment:* 10,000 AK-47 rifles; 10,000 AKM rifles; 10,000 SKS rifes; 2,000 Tokarev pistols; 80,000 hand grenades; 40,000 anti-tank and anti-personnel mines; 290 belt-fed heavy machine-guns; an unknown number of AT-3 *Sagger* anti-tank missiles; an unknown number of SA-7 SAMs; 1,100 RPG-2 anti-tank rocket launchers; 1,700 B-10 82 mm recoilless anti-tank guns; 1,000 82 mm mortars; 240 tactical communications sets;
*Artillery:* over 100 truck-mounted BM-21 40-tube 122 mm artillery rocket systems; 12,000 rounds for single-tube 122 mm rocket launchers; an unspecified number of old 76 mm ZIS-3 anti-tank cannon; 25 "heavy calibre" anti-aircraft guns; 300 AA guns "on armoured vehicles" (presumably either the ZSU-57-2 or ZSU-23-4);
*Combat vehicles:* at least 30 T-54 battle tanks; about 80 older T-34 battle tanks; 68 PT-76 amphibious light tanks; 92 BTR-50 amphibious tracked APCs; 74 BTR-60PA amphibious wheeled APCs; 20 BRDM armoured cars with heavy machine-guns; 32 old BRT-40 light armoured vehicles; 877 unspecified reconnaissance vehicles;
*Logistics vehicles:* 384 GAZ-51 trucks; 55 1 ¼ ton trucks; 80 ¼ ton trucks; 160 heavy trailers; 30 medium trailers; 40 generators;
*Aircraft:* 12 MiG-21 fighter-bombers; 3 MiG-15 fighter-bombers (a GCI net is reported to have been set up recently in MPLA territory by Russian "advisers");
*Ships:* 5 modified Soviet landing craft; 3 unspecified other ships (one from East Germany, 2 from Cuba); 5 smaller vessels bought with Soviet funds from the defunct Angola Shipping Co, SOTRAL.

Apparently all this equipment had been airlifted to Luanda and Henrique de Carvalho by Soviet Air Force Antonov An-12 and An-22 transport aircraft.

*Above:* In the Middle East, Soviet-supplied armour such as this T-10M heavy tank has out-gunned all opposition. Its effect however, has often been nullified through crew mishandling

*Right:* In many parts of the world, the Royal Navy's absence is underlined by the Soviet Navy's new presence. Here, a missile-armed Kildin draws the crowds at Lagos, Nigeria

South Africa. The immediate aim there is to use every propaganda effort to sever all diplomatic and defence associations between South Africa and the NATO countries, a strategy unhappily facilitated by the South African government's domestic policies. So far this Soviet policy has been highly successful.

More immediate, and far more important, is the war by proxy situation in the Middle East, in which the Soviet Union has invested far too heavily to tolerate a complete and utter defeat of the Arabs. Soviet policy has been well thought out, the key factor in the appreciation being the dependence of the European members of NATO on Arab oil, a fact which can be used as a direct weapon and also an indirect one to lever apart the Europeans, who are very prone to act in their own selfish interests and also to give way to anti-Americanism, and the United States. So far the plan has been twice wrecked only by the extraordinary military ability and valour of the Israelis, but some indication of the tenacity of the Soviet Union in this area is that the enormous losses suffered by the Arabs (the Syrians alone lost 1,200 main battle tanks) have all been made good. Nevertheless, an outright victory by the Arabs resulting in the liquidation of the state of Israel as a Jewish entity would not be entirely welcome. The Arabs can be very adroit and difficult in negotiations, and are by no means likely to accept the position of a Soviet cat's-paw. They in their turn see the Russian connexion as a means of overcoming a bitterly hated enemy. Once this is achieved they would certainly follow quite an independent course, perceiving as they do that the West has far more to offer the undeveloped world. Soviet policy in the Middle East is therefore aimed not at positive outcomes, but the promotion of instability which can be exploited to embarrass the United States and weaken the West.

None of the objectives so far discussed is absolutely vital to Soviet security although they may be essential to the promotion of the revolutionary struggle; but whether they progress quickly or slowly, or even fail, they are part of the historical process which must take its predestined course. What is vital is the head and front of the imperialist plot against the socialist camp – NATO. NATO has manifold problems,

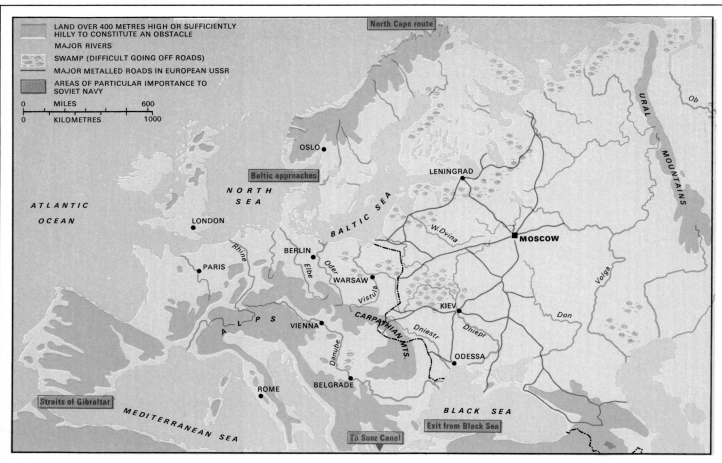

LAND OVER 400 METRES HIGH OR SUFFICIENTLY HILLY TO CONSTITUTE AN OBSTACLE
MAJOR RIVERS
SWAMP (DIFFICULT GOING OFF ROADS)
MAJOR METALLED ROADS IN EUROPEAN USSR
AREAS OF PARTICULAR IMPORTANCE TO SOVIET NAVY

MILES          600
KILOMETRES          1000

## European geographic features of strategic importance to USSR

When seen from Moscow, the strategic geography of the USSR is not at all attractive from the point of view of defence. Almost the whole of the European USSR is an enormous plain which stretches unbroken from the Ural mountains to the English Channel, and from the Black Sea to the Arctic Ocean. The major natural obstacles to any invader are the very size of the country, its lack of all-weather roads, and the frequent large rivers and areas of marshland. To the south and east of Moscow, the plain stretches to the Pamirs and Tien Shan mountains, where the border with China runs. The only strategic land link with the Soviet Far East is the Trans Siberian railway, whose tortuous route runs south of Lake Baikal and along the Chinese boarder for some 1,500 miles. The urgency with which the Soviet authorities are at present constructing a second railway several hundred miles further north is proof of the importance they attach to reducing this strategic vulnerability.

## Major road network in European USSR

Although the USSR has an extensive road network, less than 8% is metalled, the remainder being graded or simply compacted earth. There are no metalled roads linking European Russia with Asiatic USSR, and there are large tracts of country with no all-weather roads between towns at all, especially east of the Urals. There are only 6 through all-weather roads linking the Soviet industrial regions with Eastern Europe. These are: along the Baltic coast, from Moscow via Minsk to Warsaw; from Kiev into Poland, Czechoslovakia and Hungary; and from Odessa via Kishinev into Romania. These roads are in the main 20-24ft wide concrete or tarmacadam. Travel off these roads in Spring and Autumn, or during a wet summer, is often extremely difficult; a good example of this are the Pripet marshes in Belorussia, which cover an area the size of Wales astride the Moscow-Warsaw road.

Ninety five per cent of Soviet freight goes by rail or river, and long distance passenger travel is almost entirely by rail or air. Military re-supply to Soviet forces in Europe relies on rail transport, with a rapidly increasing percentage of personnel movement by civil or military air transport. The completion of the "Druzhba" oil pipeline from West Siberia to East Germany has reduced the need for strategic transport of fuel by rail. Because of the poorly developed road system, most Soviet cilivian goods vehicles are in effect "cross-country" vehicles and are therefore eminently suited to military use in the event of mobilisation.

but its centre is fairly solid. The vulnerable areas are the 'flanks.' The balance of forces is even more favourable to the Russians in the north, and Norway and Denmark are cautious and conciliatory if not neutralistic. A great Soviet gain would be a neutral Scandinavia and an Iceland free of any NATO commitment. The northern gateway to the Atlantic (which Britain fought so hard to keep shut in World War II) would then be open in time of war. That is one important target; vulnerable, but with no real immediate signs of movement.

The situation on the south-eastern flank is far more promising. There the Cyprus situation has embroiled the Greeks and Turks, led to Greek withdrawal from the military side of NATO and a quarrel between the Turks and the US over the misuse of arms supplied for NATO defence. There is also a quarrel brewing up over the ownership of the Aegean continental shelf and the oil to be found there. All this is grist to the Soviet mill. The problem is how to exploit it. The Turks are naturally hostile to Russians; the Greeks now have a parliamentary government much more to the taste of the West Europeans than the rule of the colonels and are seeking admission to the European Economic Community (EEC), the other organisation anathema to the Russians. It is a situation difficult to analyse along Marxist lines, as economic factors and the class struggle are not dominant factors; or factors at all, some would say. Nevertheless, given patience and a turn to the left in Greece, the situation has great possibilities.

Of one thing we can be sure: of all Soviet objectives the weakening and disruption of NATO under the cover of *détente* and mutual force reductions has absolute priority and wherever a crack opens, a lever of intrigue and subversion will be introduced.

In the October 1973 Middle East war, total Arab losses of Soviet fighters and tanks equalled the front-line strengths of the combined nations of Western Europe

# Air Defence of the Homeland

**Air Vice-Marshal S. W. B. Menaul**

The Russians have been obsessed with the defence and security of their homeland since Napoleonic times – and with good reason. It is hardly surprising therefore that those who direct the affairs of the Soviet Union today are sparing no effort to provide their people with the most effective defence possible, both passive and active, against air attack by aircraft or missiles. The forces assigned to the task of defending the Soviet homeland and their Eastern European empire are known as the troops of the National Air Defence Command (*PVO Strany*). This force ranks third in order of precedence after the Strategic Rocket Forces and the Ground Forces, and became an independent arm of the Soviet armed forces in 1954, with its own commander-in-chief responsible through the Services of the Armed Forces (Deputy Ministers of Defence) to the Ministry of Defence in Moscow.

At the end of World War II the Russians lacked a comprehensive air defence organisation. They had no effective radar early warning or tracking system and only a rudimentary fighter control organisation operating along their western front. The rapid development of United States Strategic Air Command (SAC), armed with atomic and thermo-nuclear weapons, and the British Bomber Command's nuclear V-bomber force posed a threat to the Soviet Union in the 1950s that its government could not ignore. It would have been possible even as late as 1957 to penetrate into Soviet territory with manned aircraft almost anywhere along the 1,300-mile frontier from Murmansk to Odessa and attack industrial targets deep inside the Soviet Union in the knowledge that there would be only light opposition – despite the advanced technology in air defence which fell into Soviet hands in Germany in 1945 and which should have been put to better use in the decade that followed.

In 1955 the most effective interceptor aircraft deployed by the Soviet Air Force was the MiG-15. Although produced in large numbers, the type was beginning to be replaced by the more advanced MiG-17 and MiG-19. But none of these simple aircraft were all-weather fighters, and they posed only a modest threat to SAC and Bomber Command. The interceptor fighter force was, however, being augmented by the first of the surface-to-air missile systems, the SA-1, which posed a formidable threat to all types of aircraft as the destruction of a Lockheed U-2 reconnaissance aircraft over central Russia demonstrated in 1960. Between 1956 and 1960 American U-2 reconnaissance aircraft had roamed at will over the entire Soviet Union from bases in Norway, Turkey, Germany and Japan, but on 1 May 1960 Gary Powers in a U-2 was shot down at 65,000 feet by a surface-to-air missile (SAM). By the late 1950s the entire system of air defence including aircraft, radars, surface-to-air missiles and anti-aircraft guns had developed into a cohesive organisation centrally directed from Moscow through a single command structure. The aircraft element was provided by the Soviet Air Force and administered by it, but came under the operational control of the Commander-in-Chief of the Air Defence Command. The organisation for the air defence of the Soviet homeland and Warsaw Pact countries could be said to have been completed in 1966 by the addition of the first anti-ballistic missile (ABM) defences, the 'Galosh' system, deployed around Moscow. SALT-1 and subsequent agreements, however, have limited the deployment of ABM systems by both the 'superpowers' and imposed certain limitations on the future deployment of radars. But research and development into ABM systems continues, and there is the possibility that the Soviets

Salvo launch of SA-1 Guild surface-to-air missiles. This weapon, operated from fixed sites, is similar to the transportable and more widely deployed SA-2 Guideline.

may have developed an existing anti-aircraft missile system to give it a limited anti-ballistic missile capability.

The Warsaw Pact nations are of course included in the current *PVO Strany* organisation, and collectively they provide a formidable additional forward air defence system against manned aircraft attempting to penetrate to targets deep in the Soviet Union. But the advent of long-range, stand-off missiles launched from aircraft would largely nullify the air defence interceptor capability currently deployed. The ABM system around Moscow would give some, but by no means total, protection to the citizens of the Soviet capital against strategic nuclear missile attack, and a degree of area protection beyond the limits of the city of Moscow itself, but cruise missiles, if fully developed by the United States, will further complicate the Soviet defence problem.

The manpower strength of the national Air Defence Command is over 500,000 Soviet troops, to which must be added about 100,000 Warsaw Pact forces. Western observers might well ask if such an elaborate air defence system is necessary, since the manned aircraft threat posed by the West is less than 1,000 aircraft, of which only about 500 are categorised as strategic nuclear bombers. But the Soviets have a vast air space to protect against attack from almost any direction, and their 3,500 interceptor aircraft and 11,000 surface-to-air missile launchers must be deployed over a wide area. Soviet concepts of air defence, although similar to those in the West, must take account of attacks from high and low altitude and by nearly every type of weapon in the strategic inventory and some in the tactical forces of the West as well. The missile is currently the predominant strategic nuclear threat to the Soviet Union, both from the West and in due course from China, and active defence against strategic missile attack, in view of the ABM Treaty, is little more than symbolic. Civil defence, however, is a very important and highly organised aspect of the defence of the Soviet homeland. It is integrated into the active air defence structure and comes directly under the Ministry of Defence. It operates under its own commander (currently Marshal Altunin) and training is compulsory for all Soviet citizens. There are elaborate plans for the evacuation of urban areas and resiting of important industrial complexes in the event of war. No other country in the world has such a complete civil defence organisation fully integrated with early warning and air defence, and there is no sign that the Soviet authorities are reducing the emphasis placed on the importance of civil defence despite *détente*, the ABM Treaty and other agreements achieved in SALT discussions.

## PVO Strany organisation

*PVO Strany*, which became independent in 1954, is one of the five major elements of the Soviet armed forces. These are, in order of precedence: the Strategic Rocket Forces, the Ground Forces, the National Air Defence Command (*PVO Strany*), the Air Forces and the Naval Forces. The Commander-in-Chief of the National Air Defence Command is Marshal of the Soviet

Union P. V. Batitskii. He operates directly under the Ministry of Defence in Moscow and controls his command through subsidiary headquarters, which in turn control the main elements of his command. These are:

(a) Radar Troops (*Radiotekhnicheskie Voiska*)
(b) Anti-Aircraft Artillery Troops (*Zenitnaya Artilleriya*)
(c) Anti-Aircraft Missile Troops (*Zenitno-Raketmye Voiska*)
(d) Fighter Aviation of the Air Force (*Istrebitel'naya Aviatsiya*)

As its name implies, *PVO Strany* is concerned primarily with the air defence of the Soviet homeland, but since aircraft of similar types operate to provide air defence for ground forces (*PVO Voisk*) in the Frontal Aviation forces, they work in close co-operation with the *PVO Strany* but are under the operational control of the C-in-C Ground Forces. They too could be employed in the air defence of the Soviet homeland if required, and inter-operability is a recognised procedure. Naval air defence interceptors are part of the *PVO*'s Air Defence Fighter Command (*IA-PVO*). There is an additional element of *PVO* not much heard of in the West. It is known as *Protivokozmicheskaya Oborona* (*PKO*) and is charged with the defence of the homeland against space weapons, nuclear or conventional, and with monitoring the activities of intelligence and reconnaissance space vehicles. With the conclusion in 1965 of the space agreement which prohibited the use of vehicles with bombs in space, the *PKO* is currently maintained at a low profile, although it has certainly not been abandoned. It all sounds inordinately complicated to Western minds, but in a fully centralised, rigidly controlled system where every policy decision emanates from one central organisation in Moscow, it appears to work efficiently. It is debatable if it would function smoothly in war, however.

The operational direction and control of the Air Defence Command, exercised from Moscow through the commander-in-chief, extends to 16 air defence districts, of which six are in the Warsaw Pact countries and the remainder in the Soviet Union. Early warning and interceptor control organisations within each district are linked to a central controlling authority and to Soviet air defence units. There is a similar chain of command to air defence units of the Warsaw Pact countries.

**Radar Troops**

Radar early warning and control systems cover the entire Soviet land mass and include the Warsaw Pact countries. More than 5,000 surveillance radars are currently deployed and are increasing in number and complexity as the Soviets strive to maintain effective early warning and interception systems against attack from both East and

*Above, left:* **The Barlock ground-controlled interception (GCI) radar, known in Russia as the P-50, is used to guide fighters such as the MiG-21 and later types to their targets.**

*Left:* **The widely deployed SA-2 Guideline surface-to-air missile can be transported on a trailer towed by a truck. It is transferred to a rotating launcher for firing.**

West and in the face of increased jamming capabilities by potential enemies. This is a never-ending process in the battle of measure, counter-measure and counter-counter-measure. The radar troops' task is to provide early warning of approaching enemy aircraft or missiles, identify and track them, and direct missiles or aircraft to intercept and destroy them.

Coming late into the field of advanced technology in radar, early warning, control and interception, the Soviet Union has made strenuous efforts to catch up with the West and in one respect at least has succeeded. In airborne early warning and control the Soviet Union moved ahead of the West with the deployment in 1973 of airborne early warning and control systems (AWACS) using the Tu-126 'Moss' aircraft. The techniques employed are similar in concept to the US system, which deploys the Boeing E-3A, but the radar and control equipments are almost certainly inferior to US equipments. There is as yet no airborne early warning and control system deployed in NATO although discussions on procurement of AWAC aircraft are proceeding.

Early warning and acquisition of incoming enemy targets in the Warsaw Pact area are provided by 'Tall King' radars with associated range-, azimuth- and height-finding radars feeding into a command and control centre in the area where the decision to intercept by surface-to-air missiles or interceptor aircraft is taken. In the case of missiles, data are transmitted to a 'Fan-song' radar at an SA-2 missile site which combines target-tracking and missile-guidance in the same unit, or 'Low Blow' in the case of SA-3s and 'Long Track' for SA-4s and SA-6s, both of which have 'Pat Hand' radars for direction and launch control. Although lagging behind the United States and the West in electronic techniques, the Soviets are increasingly deploying the more modern phased array radars to replace the older manually-controlled equipments. The anti-ballistic missile system deployed around Moscow has modern radars, the three major components of which are a long-range early warning radar ('Hen House') believed to be capable of locating targets at ranges of 3,000 miles, a second radar ('Dog House') capable of identifying and discriminating between war-heads and decoys at ranges of 1,500 miles, the information filtered and assessed being fed to the third element, the 'Try Add' radars, for launch control of the 'Galosh' ABM missiles of which there are 64 launchers in a ring around Moscow.

## AA Artillery Troops

Although the Soviet Union earned something of a reputation for its proficiency in all aspects of artillery before and during World War II, it did not produce efficient anti-aircraft defences either during that war or immediately after it. The threat of atomic attack by strategic bombers did, however, galvanise Soviet planners into action in the 1950s and the advent of surface-to-air missiles as defence against high-flying air-craft rapidly replaced anti-aircraft artillery in the late 1950s and early 1960s. The destruction of a United States U-2 aircraft by a Soviet surface-to-air missile in May 1960 compelled those concerned with the operation of strategic bomber forces in the West

to reassess the chances of survival of high-flying aircraft penetrating the new Soviet air defence system, which was rapidly developing into a missile and interceptor air-craft organisation with a high degree of effectiveness against such high-flying aircraft.

Eventually, strategic bomber forces in the West were compelled to adopt low-level tactics, which in turn demanded changes in the air defence weapons systems of the Soviet Union. The counter to low-flying air-craft in the form of missiles and guns has now been deployed and was shown to be effective in the Yom Kippur War of 1973. In the Vietnam war, US tactics and the use of electronic counter-measures (ECM) did much to nullify the effectiveness of SAM systems and enabled US Boeing B-52 bombers to operate with acceptable losses at high level. But such relative immunity would be unlikely over the Soviet Union or Eastern Europe, and changes in tactics from high- to low-level must be expected as the measure/counter-measure war in the ether develops.

Modern Soviet anti-aircraft guns range from 14.5 mm to 130 mm in calibre. The most effective weapons against low-flying aircraft in the Yom Kippur War were the ZSU-23-4 23-mm four-barrelled system and the ZSU-57-2 57-mm twin-barrel systems, with their accompanying radars code-named 'Gun Dish' and 'Fire Can'. Of the larger calibre anti-aircraft gun systems, the 130-mm gun served by 'Flap Wheel' radar was prominent in the Vietnam war. The smaller calibre guns, mounted in pairs or fours on self-propelled vehicles, are

*Above:* **The SA-4 Ganef surface-to-air missile is transported by and launched from a tracked vehicle. The weapon is launched by four rockets and thereafter propelled by a ramjet.**

*Right:* **An SA-2 belches smoke and flame as its liquid-propellant boost motor ignites. Propulsion is later taken over by a solid-propellant sustainer.**

now widely deployed not only for the air defence of the homeland, but as part of the mobile air defence capability of ground troops.

## AA Missile Troops

The first surface-to-air missile (SAM) defences were deployed around Moscow in 1956 and the first missile, the SA-1, although obsolete, is still deployed today. But the mainstay of the surface-to-air system is the SA-2 'Guideline' widely deployed throughout the Soviet Union as part of the extensive defence system estimated at more than 11,000 missiles on 1,650 sites. It is also widely deployed in satellite countries, the Middle East, the Far East and some African countries. The SA-2 has a slant range (the distance between two points of different altitude) of 25 miles and is effective at altitudes of 2,000–80,000 feet. It has a conventional war-head of about 300 lbs of high explosive. There are six launchers surrounding a central fire-control unit. Guidance is automatic radio-command with radar target-tracking. The SA-3 'Goa' is a low-

altitude missile with a slant range of 15 miles and is twin-mounted on a tracked chassis. It too is widely used inside and outside the Soviet Union. It complements the SA-2 and is radio-command guided with radar terminal homing. It has a conventional HE war-head. The SA-5 'Gammon', the most advanced Soviet missile, is deployed in the Moscow–Leningrad complex for long range, high-altitude interception and has a possible anti-ballistic missile capability. It has a slant range approaching 100 miles, an effective ceiling of 95,000 feet and an intercept speed of Mach 5. Its guidance system is radar-homing. The SA-4 'Ganef', twin-mounted on tracked carriers, and the SA-6 'Gainful', triple-mounted on tracked carriers, have ramjet propulsion, and are designed to counter battlefield air threats at medium- and low-level and to protect rear areas of the military districts providing support to the forward forces in Soviet military districts and in the Warsaw Pact countries. Between them, these two radio-command guided missiles also provide the major elements of SAM support to advancing troops on the battlefield and were noticeably successful against Israeli aircraft in the Yom Kippur War. But like all radio/radar-directed systems they are vulnerable to jamming, and an ECM counter based on examination of a captured system has already been developed in the United States. Although primarily for use on the battlefield, the man-portable SA-7 'Strela' shoulder-fired missile, which has passive infra-red homing for guidance, has been produced in enormous quantities and is widely used for defence against low-flying aircraft. It has a maximum range of about two miles and can engage targets between 150 and 4,000 feet.

Under the terms of the ABM Treaty of 1972, modified in 1973, the two superpowers are permitted to deploy only one ABM system each. The system is limited to 100 launchers and 100 missiles, which may be deployed either around the national capital or around an inter-continental ballistic missile (ICBM) complex. The Soviet ABM system was already deployed around Moscow when the ABM Treaty was agreed and it remains the only system so far deployed by the Soviet Union. A further 36 launchers and 'Try Add' engagement radars are in process of construction to bring the 'Galosh' system up to the maximum of 100 launchers and missiles with associated radars permitted under the ABM Treaty. The SA-5 'Gammon' may have an ABM capability, and research and development into new ABM systems continues. At least one new missile has been tested in recent months.

**Fighter Aviation**
The defences against manned aircraft in the Soviet Union have made enormous progress in recent years from the original Tallinn line system deployed along the western boundary of the Soviet Union in the late 1950s and early 1960s. Today the air defence system has been improved in quality and quantity of the radars and interceptors deployed along the entire western border from Murmansk in the north to the Turkish frontier, and in depth, with particular emphasis on the Leningrad/Moscow area and Baku. More than 3,500 interceptor fighters are deployed

*Above, left:* **A Tupolev Tu-28P Fiddler interceptor carrying AA-5 Ash air-to-air missiles. A total of four rounds — two radar guided and two with infra-red warheads — can be fitted.**

*Above:* **An SA-2 Guideline surface-to-air missile about to leave its rotating launcher, which can be operated by remote control or manually positioned by the firing crew.**

*Left:* **The MiG-21 Fishbed fighter can be fitted with two under-fuselage rocket packs to reduce its take-off run. Other types such as the Su-7 carry similar packs.**

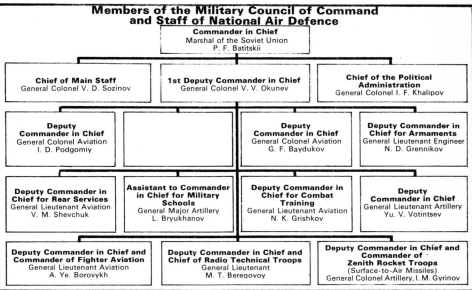

### Members of the Military Council of Command and Staff of National Air Defence

| | | |
|---|---|---|
| | **Commander in Chief**<br>Marshal of the Soviet Union<br>P. F. Batitskii | |
| **Chief of Main Staff**<br>General Colonel V. D. Sozinov | **1st Deputy Commander in Chief**<br>General Colonel V. V. Okunev | **Chief of the Political Administration**<br>General Colonel I. F. Khalipov |
| **Deputy Commander in Chief**<br>General Colonel Aviation<br>I. D. Podgomiy | **Deputy Commander in Chief**<br>General Colonel Aviation<br>G. F. Baydukov | **Deputy Commander in Chief for Armaments**<br>General Lieutenant Engineer<br>N. D. Grennikov |
| **Deputy Commander in Chief for Rear Services**<br>General Lieutenant Aviation<br>V. M. Shevchuk | **Assistant to Commander in Chief for Military Schools**<br>General Major Artillery<br>L. Bryukhanov | **Deputy Commander in Chief for Combat Training**<br>General Lieutenant Aviation<br>N. K. Grishkov | **Deputy Commander in Chief**<br>General Lieutenant Artillery<br>Yu. V. Votintsev |
| **Deputy Commander in Chief and Commander of Fighter Aviation**<br>General Lieutenant Aviation<br>A. Ye. Borovykh | **Deputy Commander in Chief and Chief of Radio Technical Troops**<br>General Lieutenant<br>M. T. Beregovoy | **Deputy Commander in Chief and Commander of Zenith Rocket Troops**<br>(Surface-to-Air Missiles)<br>General Colonel Artillery, I. M. Gyrinov |

in the *IA-PVO*, many of which have all-weather capability. They consist in the main of MiG-21 'Fishbed', Su-9 'Fishpot', Su-11 'Fishpot-C' and Su-15 'Flagon', supplemented by increasing numbers of the newest and latest MiG-25 'Foxbat'. The Yak-28P 'Firebar' and Tu-28 'Fiddler' are also deployed in strength. Fighter Aviation is currently commanded by General-Lieutenant A. Borovykh who is responsible to the C-in-C of the *PVO*, Marshal Batitskii.

To this force must be added aircraft of the Warsaw Pact countries, particularly those of the Polish, Czech and East German air forces, which together have over 1,000 interceptors, mostly MiG-21s. Nearly all are armed with air-to-air missiles ('Alkali', 'Anab', 'Ash', 'Atoll' and 'Awl'), either radar or infra-red homing, or a combination of both. The aircraft are also fitted with guns of various calibres and rockets.

### The weapons
The MiG-21 'Fishbed', of which there are something like 20 different versions, is the most widely deployed fighter interceptor in the world. In keeping with Soviet aviation practice, each succeeding version of an aircraft already deployed operationally has some improvement incorporated to enhance its performance: sometimes increased engine power, modifications to the airframe or the introduction of new weapons systems or avionics. The MiG-21F 'Fishbed-C' is a straightforward, clear-weather, single-seat fighter armed with one 30-mm NR-30 cannon and two 'Atoll' air-to-air missiles (AAMs) or 57-mm rockets. It is still in service.

The MiG-21PF 'Fishbed-D' was the first of a new series with search/track radar to improve all-weather capability. It has an uprated engine with afterburner and rocket-assisted take-off. A further development, the MiG-21PFM 'Fishbed-F', was soon

superseded by the MiG-21PFMA 'Fishbed-J' which is a multi-role aircraft with four underwing pylons and a GSh 23-mm twin-barrel gun. It also carries four radar-homing 'Atoll' air-to-air missiles. Other versions are the 'Fishbed-K' and 'L' which have modifications to the airframe of the basic 'MF' type. Performance characteristics are similar and a typical war load for all versions would be one twin-barrel 23-mm GSh gun with 200 rounds of ammunition and, on the underwing pylons, two K-13A 'Atoll' (infra-red homing) and two 'Advanced Atoll' (radar-homing) air-to-air missiles or two pods of 16 57-mm rockets or two drop-tanks. Alternative loads would be rockets or bombs on the pylons instead of air-to-air missiles.

The MiG-25 'Foxbat' of 1965 was a new aircraft in the Soviet inventory instead of a modified version of an original design. It is of very advanced design incorporating new features not previously seen in Soviet aircraft. It is a twin-engined aircraft equipped for operations in the interceptor and reconnaissance roles, and both versions are fitted with two Tumansky 24,250-lb static thrust engines with afterburners. The MiG-25 has a maximum speed of Mach 3.2 at height and has a service ceiling of 80,000 feet. Although the interceptor version, equipped with advanced avionics and radar intercept equipment and new air-to-air missiles, is now deployed in the air defence role in the Soviet Union, it could also be deployed in Frontal Aviation in support of ground forces. It has a 'look-down, shoot-down' capability and can operate in close co-operation with the

airborne early warning and control (AWACS) 'Moss' aircraft against low-flying enemy aircraft. The reconnaissance version, fitted with cameras, radar and infra-red equipment, is already operational and operated over the Mediterranean during and after the Yom Kippur War.

The Sukhoi family of interceptors makes a substantial contribution to the *PVO Strany*'s interceptor force of nearly 3,500 aircraft. The Su-9 'Fishpot' is the longest serving variant, having entered operational service in 1959. It is a single-engined, single-seat fighter carrying four 'Alkali' air-to-air missiles under the the wings but usually no cannon. The Su-11 'Fishpot-C' is an improved version of the Su-9 with a more powerful engine, the Lyulka AL-7F turbojet of 22,000 lbs thrust with afterburner. It has a maximum speed of Mach 1.8 at 36,000 feet and carries two 'Anab' air-to-air missiles, one radar-homing and one infra-red. Yet another Sukhoi variation is the Su-15 'Flagon', a twin-jet all-weather interceptor of improved design and considerably increased performance. The single-seat operational versions 'Flagon-D' and 'E' have a maximum speed of Mach 2.5 at 40,000 feet. They carry two 'Anab' missiles, one radar-homing and one infra-red, under the wings. There are also two pylons under the fuselage which could carry additional missiles or fuel tanks.

The Tupolev Tu-28P 'Fiddler' is a long-range interceptor deployed mainly in the north of the Soviet Union and is armed with four air-to-air 'Ash' missiles. It is a twin-jet,

two-seater aircraft with a maximum speed of Mach 1.75. Not many of them are in service.

The Yakovlev Yak-28P 'Firebar' is a two-seater transonic all-weather twin-jet interceptor with a maximum speed of Mach 1.1 at 35,000 feet and a service ceiling of 55,000 feet. It is armed with two air-to-air 'Anab' missiles on pylons under the outer wings.

Up to 1970 Soviet air defence with manned aircraft, guns and surface-to-air missiles and associated radars followed patterns already well established in the West, particularly in the United States. Research and development to improve the performance of ground-based radars in range and discrimination was a continuous process in most advanced industrialised countries, and one of the major problems facing technologists was to find effective means of acquiring and tracking aircraft at low level over land and sea. The answer appeared to lie in deploying airborne radar for search and tracking and for the direction of controlled interception, either by manned fighters or missiles.

The Tu-126 'Moss' was the first Soviet system to be deployed operationally and is still the only Soviet airborne warning and control system. About 12 aircraft are currently operational and have been in service since 1970. The object of any AWACS aircraft is to provide detection and tracking of approaching enemy aircraft at any altitude over land or sea, but particularly at low level where detection, acquisition and tracking by

*Far left:* **A development of the Tu-114 airliner. the Tu-126 Moss airborne early warning and control aircraft carries powerful radar and computers. Western Europe does not even have such aircraft on order.**

*Above:* **Capable of speeds up to Mach 3, the MiG-25 Foxbat A interceptor can carry four of the largest air-to-air missiles in the world. A reconnaissance version can map the earth's surface with cameras and radar from more than 75,000 feet.**

*Left:* **An Su-9 Fishpot all-weather fighter launches one of its four underwing AA-1 Alkali missiles. The type carried no fixed guns, but current combat aircraft show a return to the use of built-in armament.**

ground-based radars is difficult, and often impossible, because of interference by radar returns from ground objects (clutter). Having detected enemy aircraft the AWACS must have a communications system with which to alert, control and direct fighters or missiles to intercept the enemy either from land bases or from on board ship. Detection and subsequent tracking is achieved by means of a large, rotating scanner operating a surveillance radar, information from which is fed to radar receivers, electronic processing equipment and display consoles in the fuselage of the aircraft, which also houses computers and a data-link system to transmit information to intercept systems which can use the information either for direct interception or as further directed by the AWACS aircraft. Not enough is known

of the individual equipments in the 'Moss' system to establish how efficient they are, but it is known that these aircraft were deployed operationally in the Indo-Pakistan War of 1971, apparently with considerable success.

The Tu-126 'Moss' aircraft carries a crew of 12. It is powered by four NK-12MV turboprop engines and has a range of 7,700 miles at a cruise speed of 380–485 mph. The endurance at cruising speed for a 1,250-mile radius is six hours, which with flight refuelling can be extended to 17 hours. AWACS aircraft can be deployed in air defence systems such as the *PVO Strany* or in the battlefield area in the role of surveillance, control of friendly aircraft and the direction of interceptors or missiles, or they can equally well be deployed in maritime operations in similar roles. They are highly mobile and flexible systems, but like any other aircraft the Tu-126 is vulner-

able to interception by aircraft, missiles or AA guns, which to some extent limits its deployment even where ECM and other forms of protection are provided. But the risk of destruction is not as high as might be supposed, and the value of the AWACS will almost certainly outweigh the risks of destruction in time of war. The airborne radar itself can, of course, be jammed, but measures to overcome this deficiency can also be taken, even to the extent of locating and destroying the offending jammer.

The Soviet air defence of the homeland, the *PVO Strany*, now embraces all known modern methods of air defence and follows doctrines similar to those adopted in the West, although the strategy for implementing these doctrines often differs. Despite the limited threat from manned aircraft the Soviets show no sign of down-grading the size or efficiency of their air defence system. Among the advantages which could be

claimed for the *PVO Strany* over Western systems are total standardisation of doctrine, organisation and equipment, common logistic supply, and inter-operability between units deployed in widely differing areas. All these come under one central controlling authority, and yet by its very nature such a monolithic system could, and sometimes does, create problems of inflexibility in deployment and decision-making. In war, major decisions would be made by the central staffs, with little initiative permitted to the commanders on the spot.

In air warfare conditions change more rapidly than in any other environment, and rigidity in command and control could produce fatal weaknesses in defence, however good the weapons and equipment might be. But it must be said that despite advances which Soviet technology has made in the last decade, their weapons systems (including aircraft, avionics and missiles) are still

*Above, left:* **The ZSU-23-4SP Shilka carries four radar-directed 23-mm cannon on an armoured vehicle. The Shilka had considerable success during the October 1967 Middle East war.**

**A heavy anti-aircraft gun on a fixed site in the USSR. A large number of these weapons are still maintained and permanently manned by the PVO.**

*Left:* **A Russian surface-to-air missile intercepts its target. Many such weapons are fitted with proximity fuses which detonate the warhead even if a direct hit is not made.**

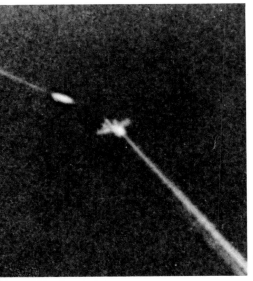

inferior to those available to the West. As described in another section, the Soviets have had ample opportunity to test their equipment under operational conditions in Vietnam and in the 1973 Middle East war. They found many deficiencies in their aircraft and weapons, and have no doubt renewed their efforts in research and development to improve the quality of their equipment.

It is vital that the West should maintain research and development in the field of aeronautics, avionics and weapons systems at a high level, to ensure that the present lead which they undoubtedly enjoy is not surrendered to the Soviet Union. The air-launched ballistic missile, the supersonic bomber with stand-off missiles, new guidance systems to reduce inaccuracies in delivery, penetration aids and total all-weather capability must be the goal in future developments of air power as part of the strategic threat of retaliation against the Soviet Union implicit in the West's strategy of deterrence, defence and *détente* in that order.

A Sukhoi Su-7B Fitter A close support fighter releasing unguided air-to-surface rockets from its two underwing pods. A 30mm cannon is carried in each wing root.

# The Soviet Air Forces

Air Vice-Marshal S. W. B. Menaul

The Russians are rightly included among the pioneers of aviation, but their claim to have preceded the Wright brothers in the achievement of powered flight is treated with a certain amount of scepticism by most Western nations. Even if it is conceded that Alexander Mozhaisky may have designed and built an aircraft powered by a steam engine in 1884, the claim that he also flew it taxes the imagination too far. There were, however, many pioneer aircraft designers in Russia at the turn of the century, and the name of Igor Sikorsky is too well known in aviation history to question the authenticity of Soviet claims that he was designing and building aircraft of various types as early as 1908. He has the further distinction of having designed, built and tested the first multi-engined aircraft in the world, the *Russian Knight* of May 1913.

During World War I the Russo–Baltic Wagon Works produced at least 80 great four-engined bombers of the Ilya Mouro-metz type, based on the *Russian Knight,* and these equipped the world's first strategic bomber force, the EVK or Squadron of Flying Ships. Many hundreds of other Russian aircraft, built by many factories led by the Anatra, Shchetinin, Lebed' and Mosca groups, played a significant part in the mighty campaigns on the Eastern Front in 1914–17. As today, tsarist airpower was deployed by the Imperial Navy as well as by the army air force.

But in 1917 the Revolution interrupted Soviet developments in aeronautical engineering as indeed it interrupted and retarded progress in many other fields of engineering activity. In the aftermath of the Revolution many Russian aviation engineers were to disappear for ever, while others escaped to Europe or America. Sikorsky settled in the United States, where today his name is synonymous with the design and production of helicopters. From 1917, for a period of about 10 years, Soviet aviation was virtually at a standstill while the industrialised nations of Europe and the United States were advancing the science of aeronautics for civil and military application. There was neither the will on the part of the new rulers of the Soviet Union nor the brain power and engineering skills on the part of the designers to develop aviation on a par with the West; and to some extent the gap is still evident even today, though great progress has been made by the Soviets in the last 20 years.

One name which has become a household word, not only in the Soviet Union but in aviation circles throughout the world, is that of Andrei Tupolev, who as a young man trained as an engineer and then decided to make a career in aviation, which he believed held the key to the future development of the vast land mass of the Soviet Union. He was a founder, together with Professor Zhukovski, of the Central Aero-Dynamics and Hydro-Dynamics Research Institute (*TsAGI*) in Moscow in 1918. In 1922 Tupolev designed his ANT-1, pictured on page 16. But such was the scarcity of aeronautical engineering talent in the early

1920s that the Soviet Union not only imported foreign aircraft and engines, but foreign engineers and mechanics, especially from France and Germany. Nevertheless, throughout the 1920s Soviet engineers produced a variety of aircraft, most of which relied on engines of foreign origin either directly imported or made under licence – chiefly British, French and German.

Among the more enlightened and progressive of the new generation of Soviet designers was Sergei Ilyushin, who as a youth had served as a mechanic in the Russian air force in World War I. After graduating from the Air Academy he went to the *TsAGI*, where he was much influenced by Tupolev. His first design was unambitious – a glider – but in subsequent designs he established a reputation for thoroughness and simplicity which exists to this day. He was one of a number of dedicated individualists involved in the new science of aeronautics whose enthusiasm was not shared by officialdom, so that at the end of the communists' much vaunted first 5-year plan, introduced in 1928, Soviet aviation

*Above:* The turbo-prop-powered Tu-95 Bear D seeks out targets for the missiles of other aircraft, surface ships or submarines. It can also issue its own guidance commands.

*Left:* A close-up of the twin 23mm cannon tail 'stinger' of a Tu-16 Badger showing the gun-directing radar at the base of the rudder. This sub-type carries seven of these 23mm weapons.

Above: A diving MiG-21 PFM firing two K-13A infra-red homing missiles from outboard wing pylons. The MiG-21 has been in service since 1959.

Left: A Tu-16 Badger B bomber launches an AS-1 Kennel turbojet-powered air-to-surface anti-ship missile.

had made only modest progress. Most of the home-produced aircraft were light, single-engined types used mainly for communications purposes and as fighters.

Tupolev's contribution during this period was the ANT-6, a four-engined aircraft suitable for use as a bomber or transport, but unfortunately Soviet engine designers could not produce sufficiently powerful and reliable engines to meet the specifications of Tupolev's design. The ANT-6 entered service as a bomber in 1932 and subsequently as a transport aircraft for use with the rapidly expanding Soviet parachute force, for which the Russians were to become famous just before World War II.

The second 5-year plan coincided with Hitler's rise to power in Germany in the early 1930s, and since the Soviet Union had depended to a large extent on German technology and manpower in the development of her aviation industry, she now had to seek assistance elsewhere. By 1939, with help from the United States, the Soviet Union was producing about 4,500 aircraft a year, of which something less than 2,000

were fighters, about 1,000 bombers (of which about 200 were four-engined) and the rest transport and training types of various designs. The quality of Soviet aviation products, however, did not compare favourably with those being manufactured in Britain, the United States or Germany, and Soviet doctrine for the employment of air power in the event of war was different from that currently being advocated in the West.

While air strategists in the West, led by Douhet, Mitchell and Trenchard, were advocating independent air operations based on the concept of strategic bombing, the Soviets decided on a policy of subordinating air power to the role of army support, and to a lesser extent support of naval operations. They drew lessons from the Spanish Civil War which were not accepted by the USA, Britain, France or Germany. The four-engined bombers designed by Tupolev were not, therefore, destined to provide a strategic bomber force comparable with the US 8th Air Force or RAF Bomber Command. Had they done so, the course of World War II so far as the Russo–German front was concerned might have taken a different turn. Soviet emphasis in World War II was almost entirely on interception and tactical air support for the armies. The best Russian aircraft at the beginning of World War II were the Lavochkin LaGG-1 and 3 single-engined monoplane fighters and the Petlyakov Pe-2 light bomber, both of which were produced in large numbers.

Among the outstanding designers of World War II who has since achieved a lasting reputation was Artem Mikoyan who, with Mikhail Gurevich, was to produce a long and distinguished line of MiG fighters. The first design, the MiG-1, produced in 1940, was a single-engined fighter whose performance on test was disappointing. It was quickly superseded by a modified version, the MiG-3, which had a more powerful engine. This was followed by the MiG-5, a radial-engined progressive development of the MiG-3. The type saw limited service in 1943, but further work on the variant was halted in favour of the generally superior Lavochkin La-5 mentioned later.

Before World War II few Soviet aircraft had the performance of contemporary US, British or German aircraft, except for the outstanding Polikarpov I-16 fighter. But the traumatic experiences in the early days of the German assault on the Soviet Union in 1941 acted as a stimulus to the design and production of higher-performance aircraft and encouraged new designers. During the 1930s the name of Aleksandir Yakovlev began to be heard with increasing frequency among Soviet designers. He served his apprenticeship under Tupolev, designed a long and successful series of Yak single-engined fighters, and eventually became a chief designer in the Soviet Union.

By 1941 Soviet factories were producing approximately 1,000 aircraft a month, an

*Above:* The Tu-22 Blinder B bomber can carry a single AS-4 Kitchen air-to-surface missile partially recessed in the belly. The bomb-bay doors indicate the shape of the weapon.

*Above right:* A pair of MiG-25 Foxbat A interceptors each carrying four underwing AA-6 Acrid air-to-air missiles. Those with white noses are infra-red homing, the others being radar-guided.

*Right:* The variable-geometry MiG-23 fighter is now in widespread service in the Middle East. It can carry missiles, bombs and rockets in addition to its built-in cannon.

increasing percentage of them Ilyushin Il-2 *Shturmovik* ground-attack machines. This was an excellent type, and was destined to play a very considerable part in Russia's final defeat of Nazi Germany. Other designs in major production were the LaGG, MiG and Yak single-engined fighters, and the Petlyakov Pe-2, Tupolev SB-2 and Ilyushin Il-4 twin-engined bombers. As the German invasion of the Soviet Union in 1941 gathered momentum it became apparent that the Soviet Air Force was no match for the German *Luftwaffe*. More than 5,000 Soviet aircraft were destroyed in the first few months of the war. The only Soviet aircraft that appeared to contribute anything

to the support of the ground forces in those desperate days was the Il-2, which was specially suited to attacks against tanks. Of wood and metal construction with considerable armour plating, it survived heavy ground-to-air defences, but was vulnerable to air attack from the rear. A two-seat version was therefore introduced with a rear gunner operating a 12.7-mm machine-gun.

The almost total rout of the Soviet armies and the rapid advance of the German land forces compelled the Soviet authorities to move their aircraft factories eastwards to the Urals and beyond for safety, an operation conducted under great difficulty and one which was bound to interrupt the production of aircraft urgently needed for air defence and support of the ground forces. The first production aircraft from the new factories was the Lavochkin La-5, whose sturdy wooden construction was well suited to the available materials and skills. Its performance kept up with German progress, and right to the end of the war Lavochkin fighters were able to take on German fighters at the low to medium altitudes favoured by the Russians with every chance of success.

By the time the tide turned in the Russians' favour in 1943, with considerable help from the United States and Britain, the Russians were producing about 3,000 aircraft a month, the majority of them designed for interception and close army support. But in 1942 it had been decided to establish a long-range force, whose main role was to be supply dropping to partisans behind the enemy lines. The force was equipped with Petlyakov Pe-8 four engined aircraft, which had been designed for long-range bombing missions, though few were used in this role.

When eventually the Russians entered Berlin, their armies were supported by over 20,000 aircraft and production was running at over 40,000 machines a year. They did not, however, possess an effective long-range bomber force except for the Pe-8s and a few North American B-25 Mitchells which were given to the Soviet Air Force in late 1943. They had no jet interceptor aircraft and no radar early warning or controlled interception system. It was not until after the German surrender that the Russian political and military leaders, including Stalin, were able to witness at first hand the effects of the British and US strategic bomber offensive, which impressed them deeply and from which they learned the right lessons, even if they were slow to act on them.

The destruction of Hiroshima and Nagasaki by strategic air power and the atomic bomb also contributed to the Soviet decision to revise its concepts for the use of air power in war. A great mass of German high-technology equipment and documents captured by the Russian armies was transported back to the Soviet Union, together with a considerable number of scientists, engineers and technicians, enabling the Russians from 1945 onwards to develop modern concepts of air power. This included the development of an elaborate air defence system and strategic bomber forces, which in the early 1950s were to be the only means of delivery of their atomic and thermo-nuclear weapons, the first of which was tested in 1949, much to the surprise of the West. But one aspect of air power which

the Soviets had neglected in World War II was strategic bombing. Although they had a large bomber force at the beginning of the war, they had very few four-engined bomber aircraft and no modern blind bombing equipment equivalent to the British H2S or United States H2X radar aids to navigation and bombing. So the Soviets had to embark on the creation of a bomber force entirely from their own resources. They were fortunate in acquiring three American Boeing B-29s that had force-landed in Soviet territory late in World War II. These they copied under the direction of Tupolev and produced in quantity as the Tu-4, NATO code-named 'Bull'. By 1954 more than 1,400 of them had been produced as the forerunners of the Myasishchev Mya-4 'Bison', Tupolev Tu-16 'Badger' and Tupolev Tu-95 'Bear' strategic turbojet and turboprop bomber and reconnaissance aircraft that form the principal elements of the long-range air force today.

Although captured German engines included the German Junkers Jumo 004 and BMW 003 turbojets, the real boost to Soviet jet engine design came with the transfer of British Rolls-Royce Nene and Derwent centrifugal flow turbojet engines provided by a benevolent British Labour Government in 1946. The Soviet version of the Nene engine, the RD-45, produced 5,000 lb thrust which, when installed in the MiG-15, enabled this aircraft to achieve speeds of 660 miles per hour. Eventually more than 15,000 MiG-15s were produced and found their way into many air forces throughout the world, being particularly conspicuous in the Chinese and North Korean air forces during the Korean War.

## The Soviet Air Force (*Voenno-Vozdushnye Sily, V-VS*)

The modern Soviet Air Force is one of five major elements of the Soviet armed forces and ranks fourth in the Soviet order of precedence. It is commanded by Marshal of Aviation P. S. Kutakhov, and has over 400,000 men and 12,000 combat aircraft. The Soviet Air Force consists of three major commands and a further two which, although part of the Soviet Air Force for administrative, research and supply purposes, do not come under the operational command and control of the air force commander-in-chief. The three primary arms are Frontal Aviation (*Frontovaya Aviatsiya*), Long-Range Aviation (*Dal'naya Aviatsiya*) and Air Transport (*Voenno-Transportnaya Aviatsiya*). The two other elements are Fighter Aviation/Air Defence Command (*Istrebitel'naya Aviatsiya*) which forms part of the National Air Defence Command (*Protivo-Vozdushnaya Oborona Strany* or *PVO Strany*) and Naval Aviation (*Aviatsiya Voenno-Morskogo Flota*) which provides air support for Soviet naval operations. The Commander-in-Chief of the Soviet Air Force exercises administrative control over the first three elements, all of which have a certain amount of operational independence in peacetime, but operational control of the Air Defence Fighter Command units (*IA-*

*Left:* In addition to its basic bomber role, the Tu-95 Bear is used for reconnaissance, the dropping of air-to-surface missiles and to provide target information to other forces.

*PVO*) is vested in the Commander-in-Chief, Air Defence Command, while Naval Aviation is under the operational command and control of the Commander-in-Chief, Naval Forces. Both these forces use common facilities with the Soviet Air Force e.g. airfields.

## Frontal Aviation

With a strength of more than 5,000 aircraft, of which 4,000 are deployed in support of Warsaw Pact forces opposing NATO in the European theatre, Frontal Aviation, the Russian version of the West's tactical air forces, is by far the largest element of the Soviet Air Forces. The primary role of this command is the air support of the Ground Forces, for which it is equipped with fighters to provide counter air operations (to gain and maintain local air superiority); ground-attack aircraft for close air support of ground troops; strike aircraft for interdiction missions; photographic- and radar-reconnaissance aircraft; tactical transports

*Right:* The MiG-19PM Farmer D all-weather fighter can carry four AA-1 Alkali air-to-air missiles under its inboard wing leading edges. No guns are carried by this variant.

*Below:* Excess fuel vaporises as a Myasishchev M-4 Bison C breaks contact after refuelling. Some Bisons have themselves been converted to the tanker role.

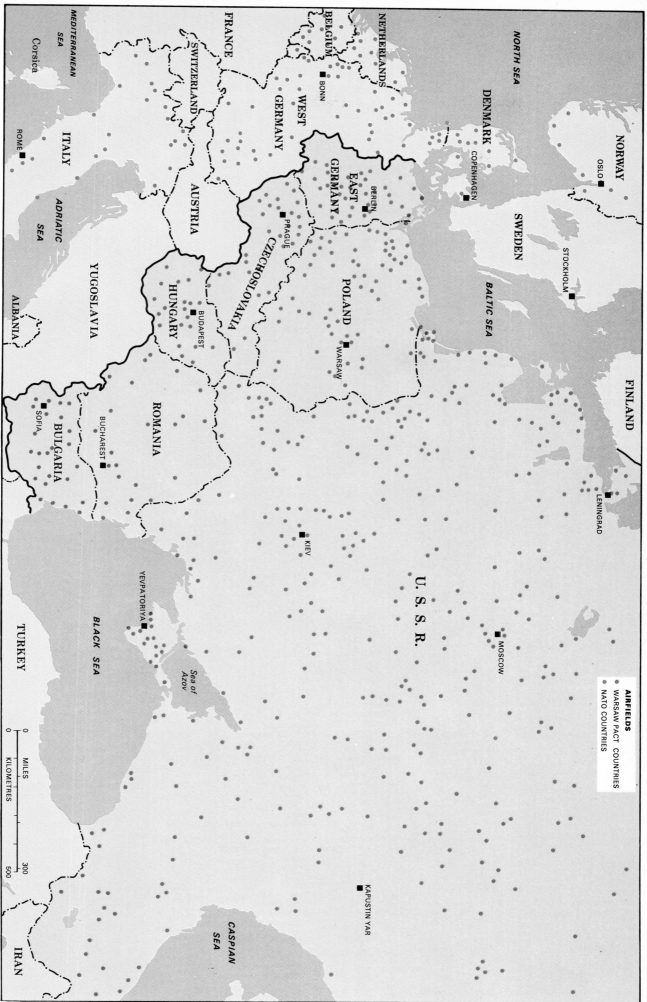

Shown on this map (which has been adapted from one which appeared in **Air Force Magazine** March 1976, © Air Force Association) are the approximate locations of airfields with at least one runway 4,000 feet or more in length, and highway landing strips that can accommodate military aircraft. Fields in the USSR

and other Warsaw Pact countries are marked in red; those of the NATO countries in blue. Airfields in France are not shown since their availability in time of crisis is uncertain. Austria, Sweden and Switzerland, neutral countries, have been excluded, as has Yugoslavia, which is not a member of the Warsaw Pact. Military, civilian, and

joint-use fields are shown. It is likely that all civilian fields in the western part of the Pact area and many of those in the USSR have at least minimum provisions for military use. In addition to the airfields shown, there are many sod strips in the Pact countries from which military jets operate frequently.

**AIRFIELDS**
- ● WARSAW PACT COUNTRIES
- ● NATO COUNTRIES

NORTH SEA

NORWAY
OSLO

SWEDEN
STOCKHOLM

DENMARK
COPENHAGEN

BALTIC SEA

FINLAND

LENINGRAD

NETHERLANDS

BELGIUM

BONN

WEST GERMANY

EAST GERMANY
BERLIN

FRANCE

SWITZERLAND

AUSTRIA

CZECHOSLOVAKIA
PRAGUE

POLAND
WARSAW

U. S. S. R.

MOSCOW

HUNGARY
BUDAPEST

ROMANIA

YUGOSLAVIA

ITALY

ROME

CORSICA

MEDITERRANEAN SEA

ADRIATIC SEA

ALBANIA

BULGARIA
SOFIA

BUCHAREST

KIEV

YEVPATORIYA

Sea of Azov

BLACK SEA

TURKEY

KAPUSTIN YAR

CASPIAN SEA

IRAN

MILES
0
300

KILOMETRES
0
500

and helicopters to provide air mobility for the Ground Forces; armed helicopters for employment in the anti-tank role; and electronic counter-measures (ECM) aircraft for operations in the battle zone. The size of the Frontal Aviation forces, together with their equipment and the command structure under which they operate, are indicative of the importance which the Soviet High Command attaches to close co-operation between air and ground forces in the land battle, and emphasises the Soviet doctrinal principle of 'all arms co-ordination' as the key to success in modern warfare.

Frontal Aviation is organised in 16 Tactical Air Armies, more than half of which are deployed in the western USSR and Warsaw Pact countries. Each military district in the European Soviet Union has its own Frontal Aviation Army. In addition, there are four 'groups of forces' in the Warsaw Pact area, pride of place being

awarded to the 16th Frontal Aviation Army supporting the elite Group of Soviet Forces in (East) Germany (GSFG). Each military district has its own commander and under him the air and land forces of that district form 'groups of forces', the most important being the European groups designated Northern, Central, Southern and GSFG. Overall command and control is exercised by the General Staff, and in war *STAVKA* (the Supreme High Command) would control the battle or the redeployment of forces through the commander-in-chief according to the requirements of a particular front at any given time. Air armies or elements of them could be redeployed from one group to another as required.

An air army consists of three corps, each of three divisions, sub-divided into three regiments, each of which is composed of three squadrons. In round figures this adds up to 81 squadrons when an air army is at

full strength. From the MiG-15s and 17s of the Korean War (some of which are still in service) the modern air army has been expanded and re-equipped with MiG-21 'Fishbed', Sukhoi Su-7 'Fitter', Yakovlev Yak-28 'Brewer', and more recently with the MiG-23 'Flogger', Sukhoi Su-19 'Fencer' and Sukhoi Su-17 'Fitter-C'. There are also a few Ilyushin Il-28 'Beagle' and some Yak-28 and Antonov An-12 'Cub' electronic warfare aircraft. The MiG-17 'Fresco', of which there are about 700, is employed mainly in close air support missions but has been almost entirely replaced by the MiG-23 'Flogger'. But the reluctance of the Soviet Union to withdraw weapons systems from operational service is seen in the extremely long life of the MiG-17 in the same way as tanks, armoured personnel carriers (APCs) and guns are retained long after they have ceased to be capable of fulfilling their primary role. The

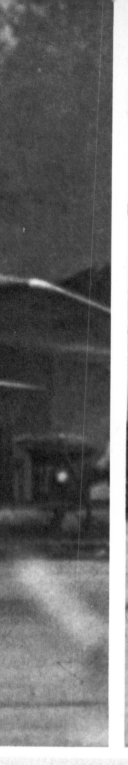

*Above, left:* The MiG-23B Flogger D ground-attack aircraft carries no radar, unlike the fighter version. It is armed with a multi-barrel Gatling gun as well as bombs and rockets.

*Above:* Tu-28P Fiddler all weather interceptors on the flightline about to be loaded with AA-5 Ash air-to-air missiles, which can use infra-red or semi-active radar seeker warheads.

*Left:* The Sukhoi Su-17 Fitter C fighter is a variable-geometry development of the Su-7. Poland and Czechoslovakia have been supplied with the very similar Su-20 export variant.

Soviet emphasis on numbers obviously influences this attitude to obsolete equipment, and the high attrition rates in the Yom Kippur War of October 1973 tend to confirm the Soviet view that however unsophisticated aircraft may be, there comes a time when numbers matter.

The MiG-21 variants ('J', 'K' and 'L') are employed in the interceptor air superiority role in combat zones, with counter air and battlefield interdiction as secondary roles. Although these aircraft are supersonic, they have a strictly limited performance in speed, range and manoeuvrability. They normally carry a twin 23-mm cannon pack and four air-to-air 'Atoll' infra-red or radar missiles. They can also carry four 240-mm rockets or two 1,102-lb bombs.

The Su-19 'Fencer' is one of three new, advanced aircraft lately introduced into Frontal Aviation squadrons of the Soviet

Air Force. It is a variable-geometry, two-seater aircraft designed specifically as a fighter-bomber and bears a striking resemblance to the US General Dynamics F-111, but is smaller and lighter. Its warload is 10,000 lb and includes nuclear weapons and air-to-surface missiles. Few details of performance are available but it probably has a radius of action of about 280 miles and its primary role is likely to be interdiction into Western Europe, probably at low level. Maximum speed is about Mach 2.3 at 36,000 feet.

The Su-17 'Fitter-C' is a variable-geometry version of the well established ground-attack aircraft, the Su-7 'Fitter', the major design improvements being a large portion of each wing (about 13 feet) pivoted to improve take-off and landing and range performance over the Su-7. The Su-17 retains the same fuselage and the same arrangements for armament, i.e. wing-root guns and under-fuselage pylons for bombs or rockets. It has improved avionics equipment for navigation and attack. Maximum speed is about Mach 1.6 at 36,000 feet. Export models are designated Su-20.

The Su-7 ground-attack aircraft has been in operational service for nearly two decades and has seen active operations in the Middle East wars and in the 1971 Indo/Pakistan war. It is a single-engined, single-seat aircraft with a maximum speed of Mach 1.6 at high level. It carries two 30-mm cannon in the wing roots and has underwing attachments for bombs or rockets up to a total

weight of about 5,500 lb. It can also carry two air-to-air missiles. Its primary role is close air support.

The MiG-23 'Flogger' variable-geometry Mach-2 aircraft is the most advanced of the new additions to the Soviet Air Force Frontal Aviation. It is clearly a high-performance aircraft comparable with the best deployed in the Western alliance. It has been introduced in increasing numbers into Soviet units in Eastern Europe, especially East Germany. There are several versions employed in the roles of air superiority in the combat zone, and of battlefield and rear area interdiction. The single-seat fighter version can be armed with four 'Atoll' air-to-air missiles in addition to a twin 23-mm cannon pack, while the two-seat fighter-bomber version can carry four 1,102-lb bombs, or four 57-mm rocket packs (each with 16 rockets), a twin 23-mm cannon pack and four 'Atoll' missiles. The two-seat version is also capable of tactical nuclear strikes. It probably does not have advanced avionics comparable with the latest equipment installed in such aircraft as the US General Dynamics F-16 or European Panavia Multi-Role Combat Aircraft (MRCA), nor is there any sign as yet that the Soviets have a range of precision guided munitions to equal the US laser, infra-red and electro-optical weapons. But, unlike the Western aircraft, it is already in large-scale service.

The Yak-28 is used in the reconnaissance role, and the 'E' version has recently been

identified in the ECM role. There is also evidence that additional reconnaissance is provided to units in the Warsaw Pact countries and particularly to the 16th Frontal Aviation Army stationed in the German Democratic Republic, by the Mach-3 high-flying MiG-25 'Foxbat' operating from airfields in Poland.

**Long-Range Aviation**

The Long-Range Aviation force consists of three air components, two deployed in European Russia and one in the East. It is commanded by Colonel-General V. V. Reshetnikov and is a subordinate command of the Soviet Air Force, although it has a fair measure of operational independence. The strength in aircraft has remained comparatively constant in recent years and until the introduction of the new Tupolev 'Backfire' supersonic variable-geometry strategic bomber, the older 'Bears' and 'Badgers', with a few 'Bisons', formed the major strategic bombing capability for a decade and are still in service. For medium-range targets the 'Badgers' are augmented by the supersonic Tupolev Tu-22 'Blinder'.

The total strength of the force today is about 900 combat aircraft, made up of 100 Tu-95 'Bears', 450 Tu-16 'Badgers', 180 Tu-22 'Blinders' and about 80 of the new supersonic 'Backfires' in two versions. Approximately 85 Mya-4 'Bison' aircraft operate in the tanker role and occasionally 'Bears' are employed for in-flight refuelling simply by transferring fuel from one bomber to another. The tankers serve both the long-range bomber aircraft and the reconnaissance force of Naval Aviation, of which there are about 100 Tu-95 'Bear-B' reconnaissance and ECM aircraft, augmented by variants of the Mya-4 and Tu-16.

The principal role of the 'Bear' and other heavy aircraft which make up the force of 130 long-range nuclear strike aircraft is nuclear (or conventional) weapon delivery by free-fall bombs and air-to-surface missiles (AS-3 'Kangaroo' and AS-2 'Kipper'). The Tu-22 'Blinder' carries the more modern AS-4 'Kitchen' missile, which has a range of 465 miles. Priority targets for attack would be nuclear delivery systems in the United States and Europe, and industrial complexes, transportation and supply depots.

The latest addition to the Soviet long-range fleet is the Tupolev Tu-122, code-named 'Backfire', about 80 of which are already deployed in operational squadrons. The 'Backfire' epitomises Soviet deter-

mination to maintain the triad of strategic nuclear delivery systems, i.e., silo-based missiles, submarine-launched missiles and manned aircraft – a system which the United States has maintained since the late 1950s. The addition of the Rockwell B-1 to the Strategic Air Command's B-52 force indicates US determination to maintain manned aircraft in the strategic role as part of its deterrent forces for many years to come, and it was only to be expected that the Russians would pursue a similar policy. Unlike the Soviet bomber the B-1 is still many years from service, and could even be cancelled.

The 'Backfire' is a twin-engined, variable-geometry, supersonic aircraft powered by two NK-144 turbofan engines with afterburners. It carries a crew of three and includes many new aerodynamic design features and advanced equipment. It has a modern doppler radar and inertial navigation system, terrain-following radar, a computer and radar warning devices. It is equipped with a tail-mounted 37-mm cannon and has a normal war load of 15 1,102-lb conventional bombs or 17,637 lb of nuclear weapons. It can also carry two AS-6 air-to-ground missiles on underwing pylons. The missiles are believed to have a range of about 500 miles. They are inertially guided with radar terminal homing. The 'Backfire' has a combat radius of action of 3,570 miles in a high-level profile and 1,550 miles in a low-level role Variations in flight profile – high–low–high – may be adopted for combat missions between the upper and lower range limits, but with in-flight refuelling the combat radius in all modes can be considerably extended. The maximum speed at high level is Mach 2 + , and at sea level Mach 0.9.

*Left:* A pair of Sukhoi Su-7 Fitter A fighters on a ground attack mission using unguided rockets. Two external fuel tanks are mounted under the belly to give extra range at low altitudes.

*Below:* A flight of four MiG-25 Foxbat A interceptors armed with AA-6 Acrid missiles which are normally fired in salvoes of two about one second apart. These 20 foot weapons are the largest air-to-air missiles in the world.

Cruising speed at optimum altitude is Mach 0.82.

The design of the 'Backfire' and its performance characteristics give rise to some controversy on the precise operational role in which the aircraft might be operated in war. It can certainly be used in either the strategic or tactical interdiction roles in Europe. It could also be used in maritime operations against shipping in the Atlantic from Soviet land bases. At subsonic speeds at optimum altitude and allowing for the 500-mile range of the AS-6 air-to-surface missile (ASM), the maximum radius of action would be 4,070 miles, which just reaches Greenland. With a single in-flight refuelling the radius of action can be extended to 5,280 miles, which brings targets throughout the United States within striking distance from bases in northern Russia and Siberia.

The effectiveness of the 'Backfire' in the strategic nuclear role against targets in the United States will therefore depend on the in-flight refuelling capacity which the Soviets decide to provide. They already operate in-flight refuelling with all their strategic aircraft, but it is likely that a special development of the Ilyushin Il-76 'Candid' transport aircraft will be produced as a specialised tanker.

The 'Backfire' is a smaller and lighter aircraft than the US Rockwell B-1, but it is in every respect a modern, efficient, high-technology bomber aircraft capable of being deployed in either the conventional or nuclear role against land or sea targets.

The long-range air units are deployed throughout the Soviet Union, with many staging bases in the Arctic region and the Leningrad Military District from which they carry out their roles of armed reconnaissance over the Atlantic in peacetime, and from which they would operate in the reconnaissance and attack roles against targets in the United States and Europe and in support of maritime operations in war.

But the majority of the Soviet long-range aircraft ('Bears', 'Badgers' and 'Bisons') are getting old and would be highly vulnerable to modern interceptor aircraft and surface-to-air missiles despite the ECM capability with which they are now equipped. It is questionable, therefore, in view of the enormous build-up of Soviet inter-continental missiles, both silo-based and submarine-launched, whether any of these subsonic ECM/tankers would be employed in strategic nuclear attack deep into the United States or even over Western Europe. They would almost certainly be confined to peripheral targets and to attacks at sea. Certainly the reduction in the United States Continental Air Defence System (CONAD), particularly in manned interceptors, gives the impression that the United States does not consider Soviet long-range nuclear bombers as a serious threat. All the strategic Nike-Hercules surface-to-air missiles deployed in the United States are being phased out except for two areas, one in Alaska and the other in Florida, and interceptor aircraft are to be further reduced to less than 150 – nearly 5,000 fewer than in the Warsaw Pact forces!

## Military Air Transport

The Military Air Transport force is commanded by Lieutenant-General G. N. Pakilev. It has always been an important element in Soviet aviation since Tupolev, in 1918, first propounded his theory that aviation held the key to the development of the Soviet land mass. In more recent years Military Air Transport has played an important role in extending Soviet influence

*Right:* **Condensation trails stream from the jetpipes of a Tu-95 Bear bomber carrying an AS-2 Kipper turbojet-powered air-to-surface missile slung beneath its belly.**

*Below:* **An Su-7 Fitter A streams is braking parachute is to reduce its landing run. Low-pressure tyres are fitted to allow operations from dispersed airfields with soft or uneven surfaces.**

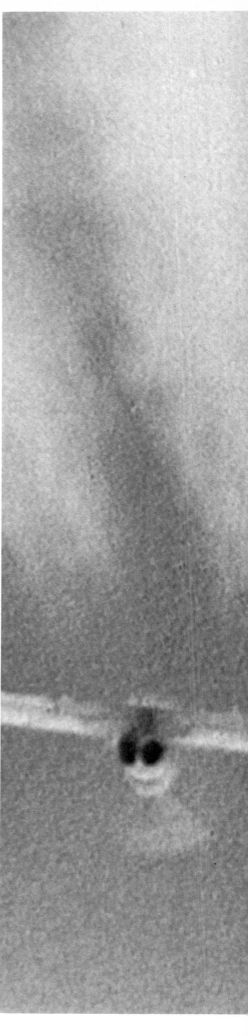

beyond national frontiers. In the Yom Kippur War, the Soviet Union gave an impressive demonstration of the importance of Military Air Transport not only in re-supplying Egypt and Syria with much needed replacement weapons of war, but also in its ability to mobilise large airborne forces for deployment by air outside Soviet frontiers. It is possible that if conditions in this Middle East war had deteriorated to the disadvantage of the Arabs, to the extent that Cairo would have been threatened by Israeli armoured columns, the threat of Soviet intervention to save Egypt would have been very real. But the threat met with a prompt response from the United States, which culminated in a general alert of US forces. Fortunately, wiser counsels prevailed and a

*Right:* **The Su-7 has a 30mm cannon in each wing root for ground-attack missions, the guns being complemented by rockets fired from underwing pods.**

*Below:* **An AS-3 Kangaroo air-to-surface missile drops away after release from a Tu-95 Bear. Other versions of the Bear can guide surface-launched weapons or seek out enemy ships. Nearly all are serving in the electronic reconnaissance and missile-director role.**

*Far right:* **A squadron of MiG-21 Fishbeds prepares to scramble for a night mission. The latest versions of the fighter have a rear-view mirror mounted on top of the canopy.**

cease-fire was agreed with the approval of both the superpowers.

In addition to purely military transport aircraft there is of course a very large reserve backing provided by the Civil Air Fleet (*Aeroflot*) which is by far the largest civil air organisation in the world. It is directed by P. B. Bugayev, who holds the rank of Marshal of Aviation in the Soviet Air Force. The Air Transport forces at present consist of about 1,600 aircraft made up of 600 An-24 light transports; 900 An-12 and Il-18 medium transports; and about 100 An-22 heavy-lift aircraft. The superb Il-76 heavy turbofan-engined freighter is coming into large-scale use, replacing the An-12. There are also some smaller tactical transport/communications aircraft and a very large complement of some 2,000 helicopters varying in size from the small communications and troop-carrying Mil Mi-2, through the medium Mi-4, Mi-6, Mi-8 and Mi-10, to the enormous Mi-12, the largest heavy-lift helicopter in service anywhere in the world. The Soviets are acutely conscious of the strategic and tactical advantages which air mobility can confer on ground forces, and they have also recognised the utility of the helicopter in many other roles including anti-tank, casualty evacuation and re-supply.

Recently there has been a considerable increase in helicopter production and deployment to equip new helicopter assault forces currently being deployed on both western and eastern fronts. The Mi-4 helicopter is used primarily for troop-transport in assault attacks while the Mi-6, also suitable for troop-transport, has been adapted for the carriage of light 57-mm self-propelled guns and their crews, which provide anti-aircraft support to troops deployed in flank manoeuvres. The Mi-8 is the primary vehicle for assault troops and also carries rockets to supply supporting fire to disembarking troops. The Mi-24 'Hind' is the latest addition to the Soviet 'heliborne' forces. It is armed with one 12.7-mm machine-gun mounted in the nose, four anti-tank missiles, and four rocket-pods mounted under stub wings. The Mi-12 is probably designed to lift heavy equipment such as tanks and missiles, but few have so far been observed in operational units.

## Naval Aviation

Soviet Naval Aviation, though under the operational control of the navy and commanded by Colonel-General Mironenko, comes under the Soviet Air Force for supply of aircraft and other administrative functions. It often uses air force bases and command facilities, and the aircraft flown by Naval Aviation are similar to those operated by other arms of the air force but with modifications to meet the particular requirements of a maritime role. Naval Aviation supports the four Soviet fleets – the Northern, Baltic, Black Sea and Far Eastern Fleets. The aircraft front-line strength is currently about 1,200. This includes 50 Tu-95 'Bear' aircraft for long-range reconnaissance, 400 Tu-16 'Badger' bombers, about 50 Tu-22 'Blinder' supersonic medium bombers and a small number of Il-28 torpedo-bombers. The 'Badger' bombers carry AS-5 'Kelt' or AS-2 'Kipper' long-range air-to-surface missiles and are also capable of carrying free-fall bombs, both conventional and

*Above left:* **The Mil Mi-10 Harke flying crane can carry loads of up to 15 tons on its wheeled platform. Cargo can also be carried beneath the helicopter, as well as freight or passengers in the cabin.**

*Above:* **The crew of a Tu-16 Badger D parade in front of their maritime reconnaissance aircraft. Other versions of the Tu-16 can carry air-to-surface missiles and unguided weapons.**

*Left:* **Kamov Ka-25 Hormone anti-submarine helicopters operate from many of the Soviet Navy's larger warships. They carry 'dunking' sonar to detect submarines.**

*Right:* **The shipborne ASW version of the twin-turboshaft Ka-25 is equipped with a chin-mounted radar and carries torpedoes and depth charges. It can also mark the position of a submarine for attack by accompanying ships of the fleet.**

nuclear. The Tu-22 'Blinders', of which there are four versions, are employed mainly on medium-range strike/reconnaissance missions and carry the more effective AS-4 'Kitchen' air-to-surface missile. There are also approximately 50 Il-38 'May' anti-submarine warfare and reconnaissance aircraft.

The navy has its own force of approximately 250 helicopters, mostly Mi-4 'Hound' and Ka-25 'Hormone' anti-submarine warfare aircraft. The first of the new carriers, the *Kiev*, will be equipped with helicopters and V/STOL aircraft (probably the Yak-36 'Freehand' or a development of it) and should join the Black Sea Fleet in 1976. Two anti-submarine helicopter cruisers (the *Moskva*

and the *Leningrad*) carry their own force of helicopters. In war the main role of Naval Aviation will be the attack of enemy naval forces, particularly the US carrier task forces in the Atlantic and Mediterranean.

**Equipment and technology**
The Soviet Union took every opportunity to test its military equipment in the Vietnamese War and in the Yom Kippur War of October 1973. All kinds of modern arms were supplied to the North Vietnamese together with Soviet advisers, who helped to operate them and to train the North Vietnamese to operate some of the more

sophisticated equipments. But so far as the air was concerned, the major emphasis in Vietnam was on air defence of North Vietnam against formidable US and South Vietnamese air attack. The North Vietnam air force was small, poorly trained and not very efficient. It had no bombing or strike capability against the South Vietnam forces and only rarely did North Vietnam aircraft venture across the demilitarised zone into South Vietnam air space, and then only in the closing stages of the war, when the North Vietnamese communist ground forces swept rapidly south through South Vietnam to occupy Saigon and force the surrender of

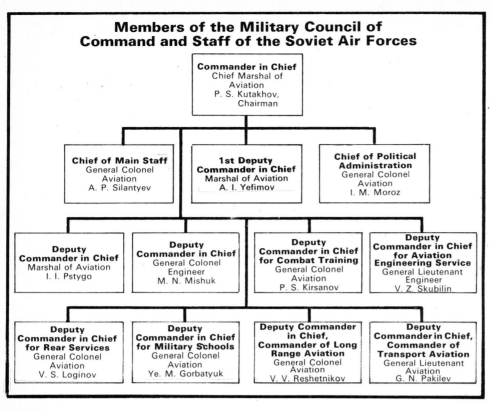

## Members of the Military Council of Command and Staff of the Soviet Air Forces

**Commander in Chief**
Chief Marshal of Aviation
P. S. Kutakhov, Chairman

**Chief of Main Staff**
General Colonel Aviation
A. P. Silantyev

**1st Deputy Commander in Chief**
Marshal of Aviation
A. I. Yefimov

**Chief of Political Administration**
General Colonel Aviation
I. M. Moroz

**Deputy Commander in Chief**
Marshal of Aviation
I. I. Pstygo

**Deputy Commander in Chief**
General Colonel Engineer
M. N. Mishuk

**Deputy Commander in Chief for Combat Training**
General Colonel Aviation
P. S. Kirsanov

**Deputy Commander in Chief for Aviation Engineering Service**
General Lieutenant Engineer
V. Z. Skubilin

**Deputy Commander in Chief for Rear Services**
General Colonel Aviation
V. S. Loginov

**Deputy Commander in Chief for Military Schools**
General Colonel Aviation
Ye. M. Gorbatyuk

**Deputy Commander in Chief, Commander of Long Range Aviation**
General Colonel Aviation
V. V. Reshetnikov

**Deputy Commander in Chief, Commander of Transport Aviation**
General Lieutenant Aviation
G. N. Pakilev

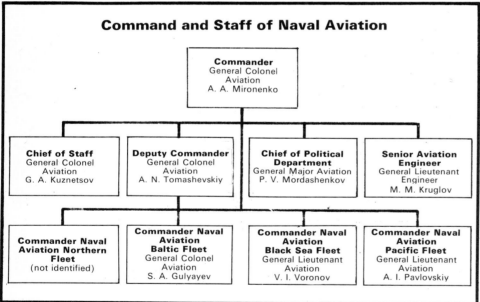

## Command and Staff of Naval Aviation

**Commander**
General Colonel Aviation
A. A. Mironenko

**Chief of Staff**
General Colonel Aviation
G. A. Kuznetsov

**Deputy Commander**
General Colonel Aviation
A. N. Tomashevskiy

**Chief of Political Department**
General Major Aviation
P. V. Mordashenkov

**Senior Aviation Engineer**
General Lieutenant Engineer
M. M. Kruglov

**Commander Naval Aviation Northern Fleet**
(not identified)

**Commander Naval Aviation Baltic Fleet**
General Colonel Aviation
S. A. Gulyayev

**Commander Naval Aviation Black Sea Fleet**
General Lieutenant Aviation
V. I. Voronov

**Commander Naval Aviation Pacific Fleet**
General Lieutenant Aviation
A. I. Pavlovskiy

the South Vietnam government. The air defence of Hanoi, Haiphong and industrial areas of the north against the massive air assault by United States strategic and tactical bombers required a vast arsenal of over 6,000 anti-aircraft guns of all calibres and 200 surface-to-air missiles, mostly SA-2 'Guidelines'. Despite the proliferation of defences, however, US strategic air attacks against targets in the North were conducted with relatively small losses except in 1972, during the resumed bomber onslaught against the North, when US bombers met the heaviest concentration of missile and gun air defences ever encountered. In the period between 18 and 30 December 1972 the United States lost 15 B-52s, which represented a loss rate of just over 2 per cent. This was certainly tolerable, and could have been sustained for much longer if the war had not ended in early 1973. Counter-measures, both evasive action and ECM,

did much to keep the losses down and to nullify the effectiveness of the Soviet SA-2 missiles, and escorting US fighters were able to deal effectively with the small number of MiG interceptors which the North Vietnamese deployed against the US bomber forces. But the Vietnam War, despite the intensity of operations and the losses sustained by US strategic and tactical air units, particularly in helicopters, provided relatively few lessons that would be applicable to a war in central Europe, but it did provide the Soviet Union with the opportunity to use its defensive equipment in a sophisticated air environment.

The Yom Kippur War of October 1973 provided a much more realistic scenario from which to assess the effectiveness of Soviet and US air weapons systems, both offensive and defensive. Most of the Arab air forces were supplied with Soviet aircraft and equipment, while the majority of

Israeli squadrons had US or French aircraft. The Egyptians had a massive SAM defence system deployed along the Suez Canal, under cover of which the Egyptian army made its initial assault across the canal into Sinai. The Israelis had no similar SAM defence system, although they did have anti-aircraft guns and some missiles. The war lasted only 18 days, however, and although attrition rates in sophisticated and expensive weapons systems were high, the cease-fire prevented an accurate assessment of how the air weapons systems deployed by both sides would have influenced the course of the war had it not ended abruptly because of the intervention of the super-powers. What is clear is that after the initial Egyptian offensive across the canal, during which the SAM defences provided a very effective umbrella and took a heavy toll of Israeli aircraft, the Egyptian army lost the initiative to the Israelis and thereafter

| Soviet Naval Aviation | | | |
|---|---|---|---|
| several | Tu-16 | Badger-A | bomber-trainer |
| 290 | Tu-16 | Badger-C/G | bomber (ASM) |
| 50 | Tu-22 | Blinder-A | bomber |
| few | | Backfire | bomber (ASM) |
| 20 | Il-28 | Beagle | attack-trainer |
| 50 | Tu-16 | Badger-D | reconnaissance |
| 50 | Tu-95 | Bear-D | reconnaissance |
| few | An-12 | Cub-C | reconnaissance (ECM) |
| 75 | Be-12 | Mail | maritime patrol/ASW |
| 55 | Il-38 | May | maritime patrol/ASW |
| few | Tu-95 | Bear-F | maritime patrol |
| several | Tu-16 | Badger | ECM |
| 75+ | Tu-16 | Badger | tankers |
| 160 { | Ka-25 | Hormone-A | helicopter-reconnaissance |
| | Ka-25 | Hormone-B | helicopter-ASW |
| 50 | Mi-4 | Hound | helicopter-ASW |
| few | Mi-8 | Hip | helicopter-minesweeper |

Approximately 300 transport, training, and utility aircraft also are operated by Soviet Naval Aviation.

Missile-armed MiG-25 Foxbats roll down the runway during a dusk take-off. The taxi lights are retracted in flight to protect them from the heat generated by the airframe at speeds of Mach 3.

fought defensive actions against qualitatively superior Israeli forces employing better tactics and imbued with the offensive spirit. Israeli aircraft on the whole were shown to be superior to the MiG-21s and Su-7s, but the Egyptian SAM systems proved highly successful in the opening phases of the war though were later shown to be susceptible to ECM and anti-radiation suppression weapons. The Israelis had no answer to the SAM-6 and their ECM system against the SAM-3s and 4s was limited. The capture of Soviet equipment has, however, provided the United States with all the information it required to develop electronic counter-measures against most of the currently deployed Soviet SAM systems.

Despite prodigious efforts in research and development, and the acquisition of advanced technology from the West by various means, it is generally conceded that the standard of Soviet arms and equipment in all three elements – land, sea and air – is generally inferior to that of the West, although in certain categories of technology the Soviets may have a slight lead. But the Soviets are indulging in research and development projects that far exceed the efforts of the United States and Western Europe, and despite the disadvantages of lower efficiency in a totally state-controlled system the Soviets are prepared to seek parity with the West in modern weapons technology whatever the cost; moreover, what they lack in quality they make up for abundantly in numbers.

# Soviet Aircraft

**Bill Gunston**

## Soviet Military Aircraft Since World War II

| Manufacturer Designation Nato code name | Role | First flight | Entry into service | Total production number | Current production status |
|---|---|---|---|---|---|
| **Antonov** | | | | | |
| An-2 Colt | Observation/parachute training | 1947 | c. 1949/50 | 5,000-plus by 1960 | Civil versions in production to at least 1968 |
| An-8 Camp | Tactical transport | 1955 | Not known | 100 | Out of production, replaced by AN-12 |
| An-12 Cub | Freighter/transport/ECM | 1957/58 | c.1959 | 900-plus | Out of production, c.600 still in service |
| An-14 Clod | Light general-purpose | 15 March, 1958 | 1965–66 | 300-plus | Not known |
| An-22 Cock | Strategic freighter/transport | 27 February, 1965 | 1967 | c.100 | Believed out of production during 1974 |
| An-26 Curl | Tactical transport | Probably 1967 | Probably 1968 | Not known | In production |
| **Beriev** | | | | | |
| Be-6 Madge | Maritime reconnaissance | 1945 | 1949 | Not known | Out of production |
| Be-12 Mail | Maritime reconnaissance | pre-1961 | c.1964 | c.100 | Out of production, c.80 still in service |
| **Ilyushin** | | | | | |
| Il-12 Coach | Transport | 1946 | 1947 (civil version) | c.500 | Out of production |
| Il-14 Crate | Transport | 1950 | 1954 | 700-plus by 1958 | Out of production |
| Il-28 Beagle/ Mascot | Medium bomber | August 8, 1948 | Probably 1951 | Not known, c.1,000 exported | Out of production |
| Il-38 May | Anti-sumbarine warfare/ maritime patrol | Probably 1967/68 | 1970 | 65–70 | Small number being built for export |
| Il-76 Candid | Freighter/transport | March 1971 | 1974 | Not known | In production. Possible tanker version in development |
| **Kamov** | | | | | |
| Ka-15 Hen | Naval observation/anti-submarine helicopter | Probably 1953 | c.1955/56 | Not known | Out of production |
| Ka-18 Hog | Utility helicopter | 1957 | c.1958/59 | Not known | Out of production |
| Ka-25 Hormone | Anti-submarine/multi-purpose | pre-1961 | c.1962/63 | Not known | Not known |
| **Mikoyan** | | | | | |
| MiG-9 Fargo | Fighter | 24 April, 1946 | 1947 | c.550 | Out of production in July 1948 |
| MiG-15 Fagot/ Midget | Fighter/trainer | 2 July, 1947 | 1948 | Not known, several thousands | Out of production |
| MiG-17 Fresco | Fighter-bomber | Probably 1949 | Probably 1951/52 | c.9,000 | Out of production in 1957 |
| MiG-19 Farmer | Fighter-bomber | September 1953 | 1955 | Not known | Out of production |
| MiG-21 Fishbed Mongol | Fighter and ground attack/trainer | 1955 | 1959 | Not known, 1,500-plus in USSR | Four-five a week |
| MiG-23 Flogger | Fighter and strike/attack | Probably 1966 | 1971 | Some hundreds so far | At least 20 per month, probable eventual requirement c.5,000 |
| MiG-25 Foxbat | Interception/reconnaissance | Probably 1963/64 | 1971 | c.250 so far | Two-three per month |
| **Mil** | | | | | |
| Mi-1 Hare | Communications helicopter | Probably 1948 | 1949/50 | Not known | Out of production |
| Mi-4 Hound | Utility helicopter, close support, anti-submarine | 1952 | 1952/53 | Several thousand | Out of production |
| Mi-6 Hook | Freighter/transport helicopter | 1957 | Probably 1958/59 | c.550 | Not known, but was c. eight per month in 1970 |
| Mi-8 Hip | Transport helicopter | 1961 | 1964 | c.1,150 | In production |
| Mi-10 Harke | Crane helicopter | 1960 | Probably 1961/62 | Not known | Probably still in limited production |
| Mi-12 Homer | Heavy general-purpose | 1968 | 1973 | Not known | In production |
| Mi-24 Hind | Assault helicopter | Probably 1971/72 | 1974 | Not known | In production |
| **Myasishchev** | | | | | |
| Mya-4 Bison | Strategic bomber/maritime reconnaissance | Probably 1953 | Prpbably 1956 | Not known | Out of production, c.100 still in service |
| **Sukhoi** | | | | | |
| Su-7 Fitter/Moujik | Tactical fighter-bomber/trainer | pre-1956 | c.1958 | Not known | Probably out of production, c.500 still in service |
| Su-9 Fishpot-B | All-weather fighter | pre-1956 | 1959 | Not known | Out of production |
| Su-11 Fishpot-C/ Maiden | All-weather fighter/trainer | pre-1967 | pre-1969 | Not known | Out of production |
| Su-15 Flagon | All-weather interceptor | pre-1967 | c.1967 | Not known, 1971 production rate put at 15/month | In production, low rate |
| Su-17/20 Fitter-C | Tactical fighter-bomber | pre-1967 | 1971/72 | Not known | In production |
| Su-19 Fencer | Strike/attack | Probably 1970 | 1974 | More than 100 so far | In prpduction |
| **Tupolev** | | | | | |
| Tu-14 Bosun | Bomber | 24 October, 1947 | 1951 | Not known | Out of production |
| Tu-16 Badger | Bomber/tanker/maritime/strike/ECM | pre-1954 | 1954/55 | c.2,000 | Out of production, c.900 still in service |
| Tu-20/95 Bear | Bomber/maritime reconnaissance | 1954 | 1957 | c.300 | Out of production, c.100 still in service |
| Tu-22 Blinder | Bomber/maritime reconnaissance | pre-1961 | c.1962/63 | c.275 | Possibly still in very limited production |
| Tu-26 Backfire | Strategic bomber | 1969 | 1974 | c.65 so far | About five per month |
| Tu-28 Fiddler | All-weather interceptor | pre-1961 | 1962/63 | Not known | Out of production, c.150 still in service |
| Tu-126 Moss | Early warning and control | Possibly 1963 | Probably 1967/68 | c.30 | Possibly still in production |
| **Yakovlev** | | | | | |
| Yak-11 Moose | Trainer | 1946 | 1947 | 3,859 | Out of production in 1956 |
| Yak-12 Creek | Liaison | Probably 1946 | c.1948 | Not known | Out of production |
| Yak-15 | Fighter | 24 April, 1946 | 1947 | c.400 | Out of production in March 1948 |
| Yak-17 Feather Magnet | Fighter/trainer | 1947 | 1948 | c.700 | Out of production |
| Yak-18 Max | Trainer | 1946 | 1947 | 6,760 | Out of production |
| Yak-23 Flora | Fighter | 1947 | 1948/49 | Not known | Out of production |
| Yak-24 Horse | Transport helicopter | 1952/53 | 1956 | c.100 | Out of production |
| Yak-25 Flashlight | All-weather interceptor/ reconnaissance | 1952 | 1955 | Not known | Out of production |
| Yak-26 Mandrake | High-altitude reconnaissance | Not known | 1963 | Not known | Out of production |
| Yak-27 Flashlight-C/ Mangrove | All-weather interceptor/tactical reconnaissance | pre-1956 | Not known | Relatively small numbers | Out of production |
| Yak-28 Brewer/Fire- bar/Maestro | Light bomber, reconnaissance and ECM/all-weather fighter/trainer | pre-1961 | Probably 1962 | Not known | Out of production |

(1) In service = with Soviet Forces or in USSR, i.e. no export customers included.
(2) Pre-1961, e.g., usually means this was date of first public showing.
(3) Production numbers may include civil versions.

# Antonov An-12

**An-12**
**Type:** Paratroop, passenger and freight transport.
**Engines:** four 4,000 ehp Ivchenko AI-20K single-shaft turboprops.
**Dimensions:** span 124 ft 8 in (38 m); length 121 ft 4½ in (37 m); height 32 ft 3 in (9·83 m).
**Weights:** empty 61,730 lb (28,000 kg); loaded 121,475 lb (55,100 kg).
**Performance:** maximum speed 482 mph (777 km/h); maximum cruising speed 416 mph (670 km/h); maximum rate of climb 1,970 ft (600 m)/min; service ceiling 33,500 ft (10,200 m); range with full payload 2,236 miles (3600 km).
**Armament:** powered tail turret with two 23 mm NR-23 cannon.
**History:** first flight (civil An-10) 1957; (An-12) believed 1958.

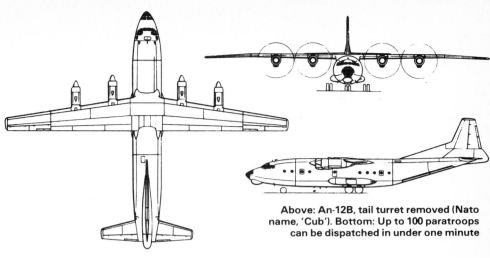

**Above: An-12B, tail turret removed (Nato name, 'Cub'). Bottom: Up to 100 paratroops can be dispatched in under one minute**

With the big An-2 biplane Oleg K. Antonov, previously noted mainly for his smaller glider designs, established himself as pre-eminent supplier of utility transport and freight aircraft in the Soviet Union. In 1958 he flew a large twin-turboprop which owed something to German designs of World War II and the C-130. From this evolved the An-10 airliner and the An-12, which since 1960 has been a standard transport with many air forces. Fully pressurised, the An-12 has an exceptionally high performance yet can operate from unpaved surfaces. At least one was fitted with large skis with shallow V planing surfaces equipped with heating (to prevent sticking to ice or snow) and brakes. Nearly all have the tail turret, and under the transparent nose is a weather and mapping radar, which in most Soviet Air Force An-12s has been changed to a more powerful and larger design. The rear ramp door is made in left and right halves which can be folded upwards inside the fuselage, either for loading heavy freight with the aid of a built-in gantry or for the dispatch of 100 paratroops in less than one minute. Huge numbers of these capable logistic transports have taken part in manoeuvres of Warsaw Pact forces, and others have been supplied to the air forces of India, Egypt, Indonesia, Poland, Iraq, Algeria and Bangladesh, and to many other operators. The total number built almost certainly exceeds 1,000.

# Beriev Be-12 (M-12)

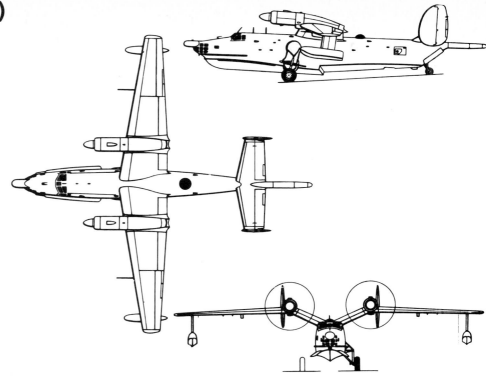

### Be-12 (M-12) Tchaika

**Type:** ocean reconnaissance and utility amphibian.
**Engines:** two 4,190 ehp Ivchenko AI-20D single-shaft turboprops.
**Dimensions:** span 97 ft 6 in (29·7 m); length overall 99 ft 0 in (30·2 m); height on land 22 ft 11½ in (7 m).
**Weights:** empty approximately 48,000 lb (21,772 kg); maximum approximately 66,140 lb (30,000 kg).
**Performance:** maximum speed about 380 mph (612 km/h); cruising speed 199 mph (320 km/h); service ceiling 38,000 ft (11,582 m); range with full equipment 2,485 miles (4000 km).
**Armament:** at least 6,600 lb (3000 kg) sonobuoys and AS bombs in internal weapon bay; one to three external hard points for stores under each outer wing.
**History:** first flight 1960 or earlier; combat service probably about 1962; set many world records in 1964, 1968, 1972 and 1973.

The bureau of Georgi M. Beriev, at Taganrog on the Azov Sea, is the centre for Soviet marine aircraft. The Be-6, powered by two 2,300 hp ASh-73TK radial engines and in the class of the Martin PBM or P5M, served as the standard long-range ocean patrol flying boat from 1949 until about 1967. In 1961 Beriev flew a remarkable large flying boat, the Be-10, powered by two Lyulka AL-7PB turbojets, but though this set world records it never entered major operational service. Instead a more pedestrian turboprop aircraft, first seen at the 1961 Moscow Aviation Day at the same time as the swept-wing Be-10, has fast become the Soviet Union's standard large marine aircraft. The Be-12 Tchaika (Seagull) is an amphibian, with retractable tailwheel-type landing gear. Its twin fins are unusual on modern aircraft, and the gull wing, which puts the engines high above the spray, gives an air of gracefulness. The Be-12 is extremely versatile. The search and mapping radar projects far ahead of the glazed nose, and a MAD (magnetic anomaly detector) extends 15 ft behind the tail. Much of the hull is filled with equipment and there is a weapon and sonobuoy bay aft of the wing with watertight doors in the bottom aft of the step. Be-12s, known as M-12s in service with the Soviet naval air fleets, have set many class records for speed, height and load-carrying. They are based all around the Soviet shores and in Egypt and, possibly, other countries.

# Ilyushin Il-28

**Il-28, 28R, 28T and 28U**

**Type:** three-seat bomber and ground attack; (28R) reconnaissance; (28T) torpedo carrier; (28U) dual trainer.

**Engines:** two 5,952 lb (2700 kg) thrust Klimov VK-1 single-shaft centrifugal turbojets.

**Dimensions:** span (without tip tanks) 70 ft 4¼ in (21·45 m); length 57 ft 10¾ in (17·65 m); height 22 ft (6·7 m).

**Weights:** empty 28,417 lb (12,890 kg); maximum loaded 46,297 lb (21,000 kg).

**Performance:** maximum speed 559 mph (900 km/h); initial climb 2,953 ft (900 m)/min; service ceiling 40,355 ft (12,300 m); range with bomb load 684 miles (1100 km).

**Armament:** (Il-28, typical) two 23 mm NR-23 cannon fixed in nose and two NR-23 in powered tail turret; internal bomb capacity of 2,205 lb (1000 kg), with option of carrying double this load or external load (such as two 400 mm light torpedoes).

**History:** first flight (prototype) 8 August 1948; (production Il-28) early 1950; service delivery 1950; final delivery (USSR) about 1960, (China) after 1968.

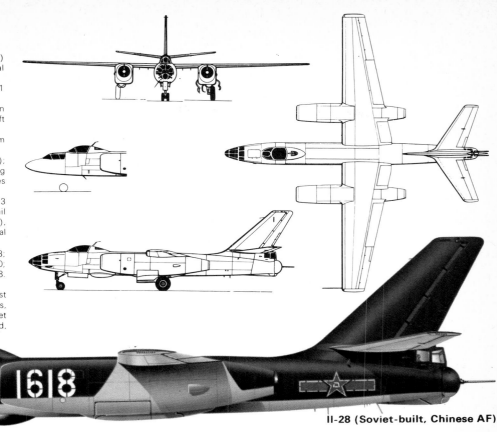

After World War II the popular media in the West published a succession of indistinct photographs, drawings and other pictures purporting to show Soviet jet aircraft. Apart from the MiG-9 and Yak-15 (and,

II-28 (Soviet-built, Chinese AF)

after 1951, MiG-15) all were fictitious and by chance none happened to bear much resemblance to aircraft that actually existed. Thus, whereas the 1950 *Jane's* published a drawing and "details" of an Ilyushin four-jet bomber, it knew nothing of the extremely important Il-28 programme then coming to the production stage. Roughly in the class of the Canberra, the Il-28 prototype flew on two RD-10 (Jumo 004 development) turbojets, but the much superior British Nene was

quickly substituted and, in VK-1 form, remained standard in the 10,000 or more subsequent examples. Unusual features are the sharply swept tail surfaces, the single-wheel main gears retracting in bulges under the jetpipes, the fixed nose cannon and the rear turret manned by the radio operator. Known to NATO as "Beagle", it equipped all the Warsaw Pact light bomber units in 1955–70 and was also adopted by the AV-MF as the Il-28T torpedo bomber (that service

having originally chosen the rival Tu-14T). The Il-28U dual trainer has distinctive stepped cockpits, and the 28R reconnaissance versions (many probably converted bombers) carry a wide range of electronics and sensors. No longer a front-line type in the Soviet Union, the Il-28 remains in service with some 15 air forces outside Europe, the most important being that of China where some hundreds were built under a licence granted before 1960.

*Below:* **Il-28T torpedo-bomber while serving with AV-MF.**

# Ilyushin Il-38

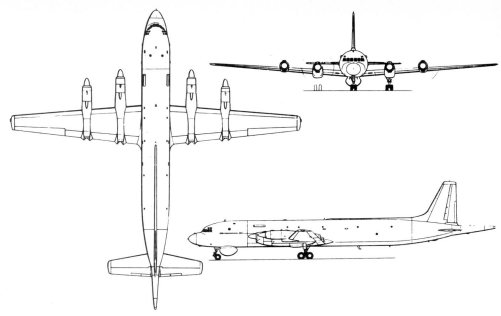

## Il-38

**Type:** maritime patrol and anti-submarine.
**Engines:** four Ivchenko AI-20 single-shaft turbo-props, probably rated at about 5,000 shp each.
**Dimensions:** span 122 ft 8½ in (37·4 m); length 129 ft 10 in (39·6 m); height about 35 ft (10·7 m).
**Weights:** empty, approximately 90,000 lb (40,820 kg); maximum loaded, approximately 180,000 lb (81,650 kg).
**Performance:** maximum speed, about 450 mph (724 km/h); maximum cruising speed, about 400 mph (644 km/h); range with typical mission load, about 4,500 miles (7240 km); endurance, about 15 hr.
**Armament:** internal weapon bay ahead of and behind wing accommodating full range of anti-submarine torpedoes, bombs, mines and other stores; possibly external racks for stores such as guided missiles between weapon-bay doors under wing and beneath outer wings.
**History:** first flight (Il-18 transport) July 1957; first disclosure of Il-38, 1974, by which time it was well established in operational service.

Following the example of the US Navy and Lockheed with the Electra/P-3 Orion transformation, the Soviet Naval Air Arm (AV-MF) used the Il-18 transport as the basis for the considerably changed Il-38, known to NATO by the code-name of "May". Compared with the transport it has a wing moved forward and a considerably longer rear fuselage, showing the gross shift in centre of gravity resulting from the changed role. Whereas in the transport the payload is distributed evenly ahead of and behind the wing, the rear fuselage of the Il-38 contains only sensors, sono-buoy launchers of several kinds and a galley, with the main tactical compartment just behind and above the wing, with a probable tactical crew of eight. Most of the heavy stores and consoles are ahead of the wing, together with the search radar. The only added item at the rear is the MAD (magnetic anomaly detector) stinger, not a heavy item. So far little is known of the Il-38 and photographs show few of the items one would expect to see. There is no weapon bay below the wing and pressurised fuselage, as in the Nimrod and P-3, no major sensor outlets and aerials and no apparent external stores pylons. On the other hand the Il-38 is undeniably a major new operational type, used not only by the Soviet AV-MF but also by the Egyptian Air Force and probably other countries.

# Ilyushin Il-76

## Il-76

**Type:** heavy freight transport.
**Engines:** four 26,455 lb (12,000 kg) thrust Soloviev D-30KP two-shaft turbofans.
**Dimensions:** span 165 ft 8 in (50·5 m); length 152 ft 10½ in (46·59 m); height 48 ft 5 in (14·76 m).
**Weights:** empty, about 159,000 lb (72,000 kg); maximum loaded 346,125 lb (157,000 kg).
**Performance:** maximum speed, about 560 mph (900 km/h); maximum cruising speed 528 mph (850 km/h); normal long-range cruising height 42,650 ft (13,000 m); range with maximum payload of 88,185 lb (40,000 kg) 3,100 miles (5000 km).
**Armament:** normally none.
**History:** first flight 25 March 1971; production deliveries 1973.

First seen in the West at the 1971 Paris Salon, the Il-76 created a most favourable impression. Though superficially seeming to be another Ilyushin copy of a Lockheed design, in this case the C-141 StarLifter, in fact the resemblance is coincidental. The design was prepared to meet a basic need in the Soviet Union for a really capable freighter which, while carrying large indivisible loads, with a high cruising speed and intercontinental range, could operate from relatively poor airstrips. The result is a very useful aircraft which, though initially being used by Aeroflot in the 1971–5 and 1976–80 plans for opening up Siberia, the far north and far east of the Soviet Union, is obviously a first-class strategic and tactical transport for military use. It has very powerful engines, all fitted with reversers, a high-lift wing for good STOL performance and a high-flotation landing gear with 20 wheels. The nose is typical of modern Soviet aircraft for "outback" operation, and closely resembles that of the An-22. The big fuselage, usefully larger in cross-section than that of the C-141, is fully pressurised and incorporates a powerful auxiliary power unit and freight handling systems. There seems no reason why the rear clamshell doors should not be opened in flight to permit heavy dropping. The Il-76 has the NATO code name of "Candid"

**Above and below: Ilyushin Il 76 (Nato name, 'Candid') which can fulfil both military and civil roles**

# Kamov Ka-25

**Ka-25 (several versions, designations unknown)**
**Type:** ship-based ASW, search/rescue and utility helicopter.
**Engines:** two 900 hp Glushenkov GTD-3 free-turbine turboshaft.
**Dimensions:** main rotor diameter (both) 51 ft 8 in (15·75 m); fuselage length, about 34 ft (10·36 m); height 17 ft 8 in (5·4 m).
**Weights:** empty, about 11,023 lb (5000 kg); maximum loaded 16,535 lb (7500 kg).
**Performance:** maximum speed 120 mph (193 km/h); service ceiling, about 11,000 ft (3350 m); range, about 400 miles (650 km).
**Armament:** one or two 400 mm AS torpedoes, nuclear or conventional depth charges or other stores, carried in internal weapon bay.
**History:** first flight (Ka-20) probably 1960; service delivery of initial production version, probably 1965.

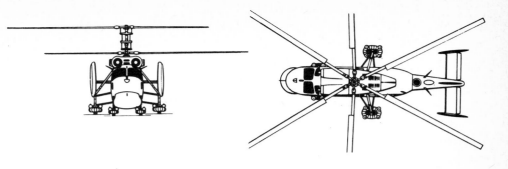

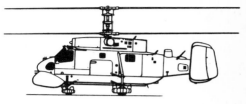

Nikolai Kamov, who died in 1973, was one of the leaders of rotorcraft in the Soviet Union, a characteristic of nearly all his designs being the use of superimposed co-axial rotors to give greater lift in a vehicle of smaller overall size. Large numbers of Ka-15 and -18 piston-engined machines were used by Soviet armed forces, but in 1961 the Aviation Day fly-past at Tushino included a completely new machine designated Ka-20 and carrying a guided missile on each side. It was allotted the NATO code-name of "Harp". Clearly powered by gas turbines, it looked formidable. Later in the 1960s it became clear that from this helicopter Kamov's bureau, under chief engineer Barshevsky, had developed the standard ship-based machine of the Soviet fleets, replacing the Mi-4. Designated Ka-25 and allotted the new Western code name of "Hormone", it is in service in at least five major versions, with numerous sub-types. Whereas the "missiles" displayed in 1961 have never been seen since, and are thought to have been dummies, the Ka-25 is extremely fully equipped with all-weather anti-submarine sensing and attack equipment. The four landing wheels are each surrounded by a buoyancy bag ring which can be swiftly inflated by the gas bottles just above it. Ka-25s are used aboard the carriers *Moskva* and *Leningrad*, *Kresta* and *Kara* class cruisers and from shore bases.

**Above: Ka-25 (ship-based ASW version). Below: A Kamov Ka-25 from the Kresta II-class cruiser, *Admiral Isachenkov*, overflies a Buccaneer and a Phantom on the deck of the Royal Navy's HMS *Ark Royal* during Nato exercise 'Ocean Safari 1975'**

# Mikoyan MiG-15

**MiG-15 and -15bis (Lim-2, S-103), MiG-15UTI (SBLim-1, CS-102, F-2)**
**Type:** (-15) single-seat fighter; (-15UTI) dual-control trainer.

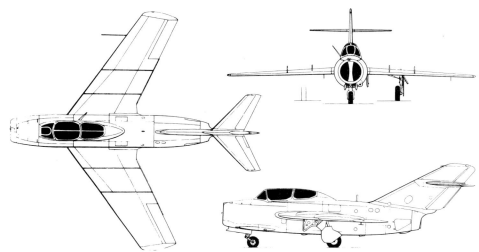

Above: MiG-15bis (People's Republic of China AF). Below: MiG-15 (early production, North Korea AF).

**Engine:** (-15) one 5,005 lb (2270 kg) thrust RD-45F single-shaft centrifugal turbojet; (-15bis and most -15UTI) one 5,952 lb (2700 kg) VK-1 of same layout; (later -15bis) 6,990 lb (wet rating) VK-1A.
**Dimensions:** span 33 ft 0¾ in (10·08 m); length (-15, -15bis) 36 ft 3¼ in (11·05 m); (-15UTI) 32 ft 11¼ in (10·04 m); height (-15, -15bis) 11 ft 1¾ in (3·4 m); (-15UTI) 12 ft 1½ in (3·7 m).
**Weights:** empty (all) close to 8,820 lb (4000 kg); maximum loaded (-15) 12,566 lb (5700 kg), (11,270 lb clean); (-15UTI) 11,905 lb (5400 kg), (10,692 lb clean).
**Performance:** maximum speed (-15) 668 mph (1075 km/h); (-15bis) 684 mph (1100 km/h); (-15UTI) 630 mph (1015 km/h); initial climb (-15, -15UTI) 10,500 ft (3200 m)/min; (-15bis) 11,480 ft (3500 m)/min; service ceiling (-15, -15bis) 51,000 ft (15,545 m); (-15UTI) 47,980 ft (14,625 m); range (at height, with slipper tanks) 885 miles (1424 km).
**Armament:** (-15, as first issued) one 37 mm N cannon under right side of nose and one 23 mm NS under left side; (-15, -15bis and variants) one 37 mm with 40 rounds under right and two 23 mm each with 80 rounds under left, with two underwing hardpoints for slipper tanks or stores of up to 1,102 lb (500 kg); (-15UTI) single 23 mm with 80 rounds or 12·7 mm UBK-E with 150 rounds under left side, plus same underwing options.
**History:** first flight 30 December 1947; (MiG-15UTI) 1948; service delivery August 1948; final delivery, probably 1953 (USSR) and about 1954 in Poland and Czechoslovakia.

No combat aircraft in history has had a bigger impact on the world scene than the MiG-15. Its existence was unsuspected in the West until American fighter pilots suddenly found themselves confronted by all-swept silver fighters which could fly faster, climb and dive faster and turn more tightly. Gradually the whole story, and the start of the world pre-eminence of the Mikoyan-Gurevich bureau, could be traced back to the decision of the British government to send to the Soviet Union the latest British turbojet, the Rolls-Royce Nene (long before the Nene was used in any British service aircraft). At one stroke this removed the very serious lack of a suitable engine for the advanced fighter the bureau were planning, and within eight months the prototype MiG-15 had flown and the Nene was frantically being put into production (without a licence) in slightly modified form as the RD-45. The original MiG-15 owed a lot to the Ta-183 and other German designs, but the production machine had a lower tailplane, anhedral, wing fences and other changes. Notable features were the extensive use of high-quality welding and the quick-detach package housing the two (later three) heavy cannon. Production rapidly outstripped that of any other aircraft in the world, at least 8,000 being built in the Soviet Union in about five years, plus a further substantial number at Mielec, Poland, as the Lim-2, and at the newly established Vodochody works near Prague as the S-103 (S = stihac, fighter). The two satellite countries also made the UTI trainer under an extension of their original licences, finally producing several thousand trainers by rebuilding MiG-15 fighters phased out of front-line service after 1954. In 1958 the Chinese plant at Shenyang began licence-production of the MiG-15UTI as the F-2. Most MiG-15 fighters were of the more powerful 15bis type with perforated flaps and redesigned rear-fuselage airbrakes; small numbers were made of a night fighter version with simple AI radar and of a ground-attack version with large ordnance carriers inboard of the drop tanks (the latter being originally of the slipper type but after 1952 often being carried below the wing on braced pylons). Known to NATO as "Fagot" (the trainer being "Mongol"), the MiG-15 saw considerable combat in Korea but suffered from the inexperience of its hastily trained Chinese and Korean pilots. As late as 1960 it was still used as a fighter by 15 countries and in 1975 the UTI trainer was still a standard type in the Soviet Union, Czechoslovakia, Poland, East Germany, Egypt, North Korea, Syria, Iraq, Cuba, Guinea, Somalia, Uganda, Mali, Khmer, S. Yemen, Algeria and Afghanistan, while the F-2 is used by China, Pakistan and Vietnam.

Above: MiG-15UTI trainer. Below: Ejection training exercise from MiG-15.

# Mikoyan MiG-17

F-4 (Khmer [Cambodia] AF)

MiG-17F (Syrian AF, Federation of Arab Republics insignia)

**MiG-17, -17P, -17F (Lim-5P and -5M, S-104, F-4), -17PF and -17PFU (NATO name "Fresco")**
**Type:** single-seat fighter; (PF, PFU) limited all-weather interceptor.
**Engine:** (-17, -17P) one 5,952 lb (2700 kg) thrust Klimov VK-1 single-shaft centrifugal turbojet; (later versions) one 4,732/7,452 lb (3380 kg) VK-1F with afterburner.
**Dimensions:** span 31 ft (9·45 m); length (all) 36 ft 3 in (11·05 m); height 11 ft (3·35 m).
**Weights:** empty (all) about 9,040 lb (4100 kg); loaded (F, clean) 11,773 lb (5340 kg); maximum (all) 14,770 lb (6700 kg).
**Performance:** maximum speed (F, clean at best height of 9,840 ft) 711 mph (1145 km/h); initial climb 12,795 ft (3900 m)/min; service ceiling 54,460 ft (16,600 m); range (high, two drop tanks) 913 miles (1470 km).
**Armament:** (-17) as MiG-15, one 37 mm and two 23 mm NS-23; (all later versions) three 23 mm Nudelmann-Rikter NR-23 cannon, one under right side of nose and two under left; four wing hardpoints for tanks, total of 1,102 lb (500 kg) of bombs, packs of eight 55 mm air-to-air rockets or various air-to-ground missiles.
**History:** first flight (prototype) January 1950; service delivery, 1952; service delivery (F-4) January 1956; final delivery (Soviet Union) probably 1959.
Only gradually did Western observers recognise the MiG-17 as not merely a slightly modified MiG-15 but a completely different aircraft. Even then it was generally believed it had been hastily designed to rectify deficiencies shown in the MiG-15's performance in Korea, but in fact the design began at the beginning of 1949, long before the Korean war. This was because from the first the MiG-15 had shown bad behaviour at high speeds, and though the earlier fighter was eventually made completely safe (partly by arranging for the air brakes to open automatically at Mach 0·92) it was still a difficult gun platform due to its tendency to snake and pitch. The MiG-17 – which was probably the last fighter in which Gurevich played a direct personal role – had a new wing with thickness reduced from 11 per cent to about 9 per cent, a different section and planform and no fewer than three fences. Without taper and with inboard sweep of 47° this made a big difference to high-Mach behaviour, and in fact there are reasons to believe the MiG-17 can be dived to make a sonic bang. With a new tail on a longer rear fuselage the transformation was completed by considerable revision of systems and equipment, though at first the VK-1 engine was unchanged. In 1958 the first limited all-weather version, the -17P, went into modest production with longer nose housing the same Izumrud ("Scan Odd") AI radar and ranging avionics as was also in production for the MiG-19. With the introduction of an afterburning engine the airbrakes were moved aft of the wing, away from the hot back end, but this was not a good position and they were returned (in enlarged rectangular form) to the tail in the most important sub-type the -17F. This was made in Poland as the Lim-5P (the -5M being a rough-field close-support version with larger tyres and drag chute), in Czechoslovakia as the S-104 and in China as the F-4. The PF was the afterburning all-weather version, and the final model was the PFU with guns removed and wing pylons for four beam-riding "Alkali" air-to-air missiles. Total production for at least 22 air forces must have considerably exceeded 5,000 exports from China alone exceeding 1,000. Many 17F remained in use in the mid-1970s.

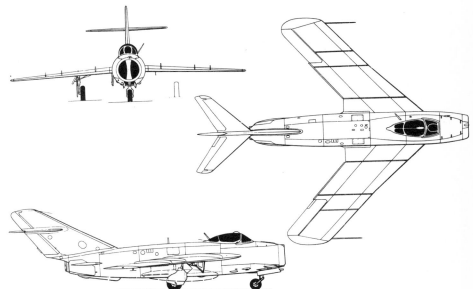

# Mikoyan MiG-19

F-6, Chinese-built MiG-19SF (Peoples' Republic of China AF)

F-6 (Pakistani AF, with camouflage which became standard during 1973 war).

MiG-19PM (Polish AF, showing radar and four "Alkali" missiles)

**MiG-19, -19S, -19SF (Lim-7, S-105, F-6), -19PF and -19PM; NATO code name "Farmer".**
**Type:** single-seat fighter (PF, PM, all-weather interceptor).
**Engines:** (-19, -19S) two 6,700 lb (3,040 kg) thrust (afterburner rating) Mikulin AM-5 single-shaft afterburning turbojets; (-19SF, PF, PM) two 7,165 lb (3250 kg) thrust (afterburner) Klimov RD-9B afterburning turbojets (probably single-shaft engines).
**Dimensions:** span 29 ft 6½ in (9 m); length (S, SF, excluding pitot boom) 42 ft 11¼ in (13·08 m); (-19PF, PM) 44 ft 7 in; height 13 ft 2¼ in (4·02 m).
**Weights:** empty (SF) 12,698 lb (5760 kg); loaded (SF, clean) 16,755 lb (7600 kg); (maximum, SF) 19,180 lb (8700 kg); (PM) 20,944 lb (9500 kg).
**Performance:** maximum speed (typical) 920 mph at 20,000 ft (1480 km/h, Mach 1·3); initial climb (SF) 22,640 ft (6900 m)/min; service ceiling (SF) 58,725 ft (17,900 m); maximum range (high, with two drop tanks) 1,367 miles (2200 km).
**Armament:** see text.
**History:** first flight, September 1953; service delivery early 1955; first flight (F-6) December 1961.

With the MiG-19 the Mikoyan-Gurevich bureau established itself right in the front rank of the world's fighter design teams. The new fighter was on the drawing board as the I-350 before even the MiG-15 had been encountered in Korea, the five prototypes being ordered on 30 July 1951. Maj Grigori Sedov flew the first aircraft on 18 September 1953 on the power of two non-afterburning AM-5 engines giving only 4,410 lb thrust each. Nevertheless, despite the high wing loading and bold sweep angle of 55° (at 25% chord), the MiG-19 handled well, large fences and Fowler flaps giving satisfactory low-speed control. With afterburning engines the MiG-19 became the first Russian supersonic fighter and it was put into production on a very large scale, rivalling that of the MiG-15 and -17, despite a 100 per cent increase in price. After about 500 had been delivered the MiG-19S (*stabilizator*) supplanted the early model with the fixed tailplane and manual elevators replaced by a fully powered slab. At the same time the old armament (unchanged since MiG-15 and -17) was replaced by three of the new 30 mm NR-30 guns, one in each wing root and one under the right side of the nose. A large ventral airbrake was also added. In 1956 the AM-5 engine was replaced by the newer and more powerful RD-9, increasing peak Mach number from 1·1 to 1·3. The new fighter was designated MiG-19SF (*forsirovanni*, increased power), and has been built in very large numbers. Total production possibly exceeds 10,000, including licence-manufacture as the Lim-7 in Poland, S-105 in Czechoslovakia and F-6 in China. The corresponding MiG-19PF (*perekhvatchik*, interceptor) has an Izumrud AI radar (called "Scan Odd" by NATO) in a bullet carried on the inlet duct splitter, with the ranging unit in the upper inlet lip, changing

The final production version was the MiG-19PM (*modifikatsirovanni*), with guns removed and pylons for four early beam-rider air-to-air missiles (called "Alkali" by NATO). All MiG-19s can carry the simple K-13A missile (the copy of Sidewinder, called "Atoll" by NATO) and underwing pylons can carry two 176 gal drop tanks plus two 551 lb weapons or dispensers. Perhaps surprisingly, there has been no evidence of a two-seat trainer version of this fine fighter, which in 1960 was judged obsolescent and in 1970 was fast being reappraised as an extremely potent dogfighter.

Part of the understanding of the MiG-19's qualities has resulted from its purchase in large numbers by Pakistan as the F-6 from the Chinese factory at Shenyang. The notable features of the F-6 were its superb finish, outstanding dogfight manoeuvrability and tremendous hitting power of the NR-30 guns, each projectile having more than twice the kinetic energy of those of the Aden or DEFA of similar calibre. F-6 or MiG-19 fighters remain in use with Pakistan, Tanzania, Indonesia and many Warsaw Pact countries.

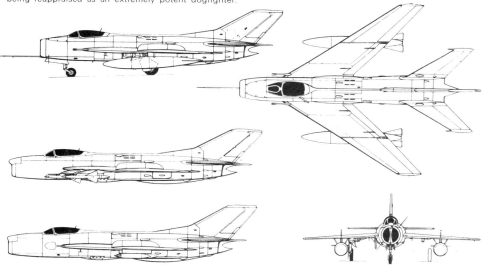

**Below: MiG-19SF in Pakistani AF markings**

# Mikoyan MiG-21

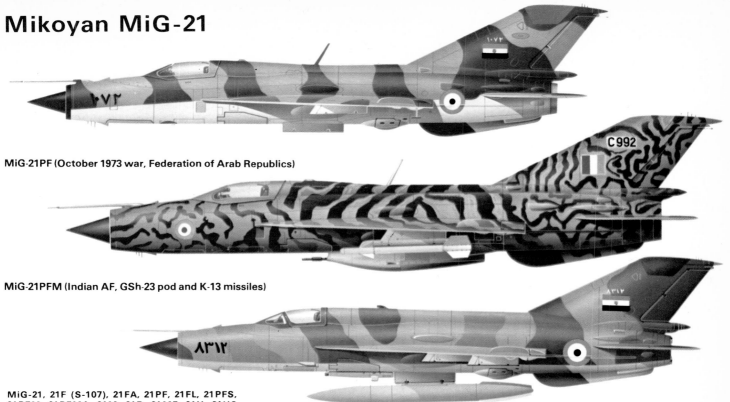

**MiG-21PF (October 1973 war, Federation of Arab Republics)**

**MiG-21PFM (Indian AF, GSh-23 pod and K-13 missiles)**

**MiG-21, 21F (S-107), 21FA, 21PF, 21FL, 21PFS, 21PFM, 21PFMA, 21M, 21R, 21MF, 21U, 21US and 21UM, plus countless special versions. Several versions made in China as F-8.**

**Type:** single-seat fighter; (PFMA and MF) limited all-weather multi-role; (R) reconnaissance; (U) two-seat trainer.

**Engine:** in all versions, one Tumansky single-shaft turbojet with afterburner; (-21) R-11 rated at 11,240 lb (5100 kg) with afterburner; (-21F) R-11-F2-300 rated at 13,120 lb (5950 kg); (-21FL, PFS, PFM and PFMA) R-11-G2S-300 rated at 13,668 lb (6200 kg); (-21MF and derivatives) R-13-300 rated at 14,550 lb (6600 kg).

**Dimensions:** span 23 ft 5½ in (7·15 m); length (excluding probe) (-21) 46 ft 11 in; (-21MF) 48 ft 0½ in (14·6 m); height (little variation, but figure for MF) 14 ft 9 in (4·5 m).

**Weights:** empty (-21) 11,464 lb (5200 kg); (-21MF) 12,346 lb (5600 kg); maximum loaded (-21) 18,740 lb (8500 kg); (-21MF) 21,605 lb (9800 kg) (weight with three tanks and two K-13A, 20,725 lb).

**Performance:** maximum speed (MF, but typical of all) 1,285 mph (2070 km/h, Mach 2·1); initial climb (MF, clean) 36,090 ft (11,000 m)/min; service ceiling 59,050 ft (18,000 m); range (high, internal fuel) 683 miles (1100 km); maximum range (MF, high, three tanks) 1,118 miles (1800 km).

**Armament:** see text.

**History:** first flight (E-5 prototype) late 1955; (production -21F) late 1957; service delivery early 1958.

**MiG-21MF (Egyptian AF, Federation of Arab Republics insignia)**

Undoubtedly the most widely used combat aircraft in the world in the 1970s, this trim little delta has established a superb reputation for cost effectiveness and in its later versions it also packs a formidable multi-role punch. It was designed in the 18 months following the Korean War. While Sukhoi developed large supersonic fighters to rival the American F-100, the Mikoyan-Gurevich bureau, by now led only by Col-Gen Mikoyan (who died in 1970), concentrated on a small day interceptor of the highest possible performance. Prototypes were built with both swept and delta wings, both having powered slab tailplanes, and the delta was chosen for production. At least 30 pre-production aircraft had flown by the time service delivery started and the development effort was obviously considerable. The initial MiG-21 abounded in interesting features including Fowler flaps, fully powered controls, upward ejection seat fixed to the rear of the front-hinged canopy (which incorporated the whole front of the cockpit enclosure except the bullet-proof windshield) to act as a pilot blast-shield, and internal fuel capacity of only 410 gal. Armament was two 30 mm NR-30 in long fairings under the fuselage, the left gun usually being replaced by avionics. Part of these avionics served the two K-13 ("Atol") missiles carried on wing pylons on the slightly more powerful 21F. This had radar ranging, 515 gal

fuel, broader fin, upward-hinged pitot boom attached under the nose (to prevent people walking into it) and two dorsal blade aerials. Czech-built aircraft (still called 21F) did not have the rear-view windows in the front of the dorsal spine. The F was called "Fishbed C" by NATO and Type 74 by the Indian Air Force; it was also the type supplied to China in 1959 and used as the pattern for the Chinese-built F-8. As the oldest active variant it was also the first exported or seen in the West, the Finnish AF receiving the 21F-12 in April 1963.

At Tushino in 1961 the prototype was displayed of what became the 21PF, with inlet diameter increased from 27 in to 36 in, completely changing the nose shape and providing room for a large movable centre-body housing the scanner of the R1L (NATO "Spin Scan") AI radar. Other changes included deletion of guns (allowing simpler forward airbrakes), bigger mainwheels (causing large fuselage bulges above the wing), pitot boom moved above the inlet, fatter dorsal spine (partly responsible for fuel capacity of 627 gal) and many electronic changes. All PF had an uprated engine, late models had take-off rocket latches and final batches had completely new blown flaps (SPS) which cut landing speed by 25 mph and reduced nose-up attitude for better pilot view. The FL was the export PF (L = *lokator*, denoting R2L radar) with even more powerful engine. Like the F models rebuilt in 1963–4, this can carry the GP-9 gunpack housing the excellent GSh-23 23 mm twin-barrel gun, has a still further

broadened vertical tail and drag-chute repositioned above the jetpipe. The PFS was the PF with SPS blown flaps, while the PFM was a definitive improved version with another 19 in added to the fin (final fillet eliminated), a conventional seat and side-hinged canopy, and large flush aerials in the fin. One-off versions were built to prove STOL with lift jets and to fly a scaled "analogue" of the wing of the Tu-144 SST. The very important PFMA, made in huge numbers, was the first multi-role version, with straight top line from much deeper spine (housing equipment and not fuel and holding tankage to 572 gal), and four pylons for two 1,100 lb and two 551 lb bombs, four S-24 missiles and/or tanks or K-13A missiles. The 21M has an internal GSh-23 and since 1973 has been built in India as Type 88. The 21R has multi-sensor reconnaissance internally and in pods and wing-tip ECM fairings, as do late models of the 21MF, the first to have the new R-13 engine. The RF is the R-13-powered reconnaissance version.

Code-named "Mongol" and called Type 66 in India, the U is the tandem trainer; the US has SPS flaps and UM the R-13 engine and four pylons. Many other versions have been used to set world records. About 10,000 MiG-21s have been built, and among users are Afghanistan, Algeria, Bangladesh, Bulgaria, China, Cuba, Czechoslovakia, Egypt, Finland, East Germany, Hungary, India, Indonesia, Iraq, North Korea, Poland, Romania, Syria, Vietnam and Yugoslavia.

# Mikoyan
# MiG-23

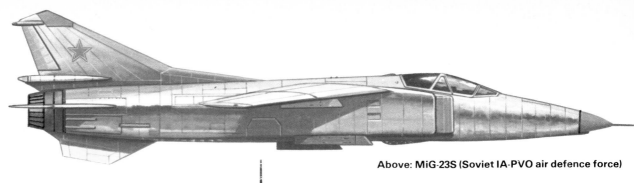

**Above: MiG-23S (Soviet IA-PVO air defence force)**

**Left: MiG-23B (FA, frontal aviation)**

**MiG-23, -23B, -23S and -23U ("Flogger")**
**Type:** (-23B) single-seat tactical attack; (-23S) single-seat all-weather interceptor; (-23U) dual-control trainer.
**Engine:** one Tumansky afterburning turbofan of unknown type, with maximum rating of about 21,000 lb (9525 kg) (-23S, 24,000 lb).
**Dimensions:** (estimated) span (21° sweep) 46 ft 9 in (14·25 m), (72°) 26 ft 9½ in (8·17 m); length 55 ft 1½ in (16·8 m), (-23U may be slightly longer); height 15 ft 9 in (4·8 m).
**Weights:** (estimated) empty 20,000 lb (9070 kg); loaded (clean) 30,000 lb (13,600 kg); maximum loaded 40,000 lb (18,145 kg).
**Performance:** maximum speed, clean, 840 mph (1350 km/h, Mach 1·1) at sea level, 1,520 mph (2445 km/h, Mach 2·3) at altitude; maximum speed at altitude with two air-to-air missiles, about Mach 2; service ceiling, over 60,000 ft (18,290 m); combat radius (hi-lo-hi mission) 600 miles (966 km); ferry range, 2,000 miles (3220 km).
**Armament:** (-23B attack version) one 23 mm "Gatling" five-barrel gun in belly pack projecting below centre-line; two body pylons and two pylons on fixed inboard wings, each rated at about 2,000 lb (907 kg) and used for variety of weapons or tanks including AS-7 "Kerry" missile; (-23S) one 23 mm GSh twin-barrel gun, two AA-7 "Apex" (one radar, one infra-red) under wing gloves, two AA-8 "Aphid" dogfight missiles on belly pylons.

**History:** first flight, probably 1965; (first production aircraft) believed 1970; service delivery, believed 1971. Revealed at the 1967 Moscow Aviation Day, the prototype swing-wing MiG-23 was at first thought to be a Yakovlev design, though it appeared in company with a jet-lift STOL fighter having an identical rear fuselage and tail and strong MiG-21-like features (though much bigger than a MiG-21). Over the next four years the Mikoyan bureau greatly developed this aircraft, which originally owed something to the F-111 and Mirage G. By 1971 the radically different production versions, the -23B attack and -23U trainer, were entering service in quantity, and by 1975 several hundred had been delivered to Warsaw Pact air forces and also to Egypt, Iraq, Libya, Syria and possibly other countries. Though there is no doubt its technology is older than that of MRCA, the MiG-23 is a versatile and formidable aircraft; the variable-sweep wing strongly suggests multi-role use. There are at least three versions in service: fighter, attack and trainer. The attack machine has a pointed nose (no radar), fixed inlets and simpler engine nozzle. In 1973 the then Secretary of the US Air Force stated the official view that the fighter version carried radar and missile systems comparable with the latest Phantom, and most MiG-23 versions seem well equipped with ECM (countermeasures).

**Below MiG-23 prototype**

# Mikoyan MiG-25

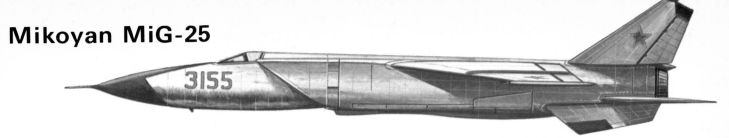

**MiG-25 ("Foxbat A"), MiG-25R and MiG-25U**

**Type:** "Foxbat A" (believed to be MiG-25S), all-weather long-range interceptor; MiG-25R, reconnaissance; MiG-25U, tandem-seat dual trainer with stepped cockpits.

**Engines:** two afterburning turbofans or turbojets, believed to be of Tumansky design and each rated at an estimated 31,000 lb (14,100 kg) thrust.

**Dimensions:** (estimated) span 46 ft (14.0 m); length (A) 72 ft 6 in (22.1 m), (R) 74 ft 6 in (22.7 m); height 19 ft (5.8 m).

**Weights:** (estimated) empty 34,000 lb (15,425 kg); maximum, loaded 75,000 lb (34,050 kg).

**Performance:** (estimated) maximum speed at altitude 2,100 mph (3380 km/h, Mach 3·2); initial climb, about 50,000 ft (15,240 m)/min; service ceiling 80,000 ft (24,400 m); high-altitude combat radius without external fuel, 700 miles (1130 km).

**Armament:** ("-A") four underwing pylons each carrying one AA-6 air-to-air missile (two radar, two infra-red) or other store; no guns; ("-B") none.

**History:** first flight (E-266 prototype) probably 1964; (production reconnaissance version) before 1969; (production interceptor) probably 1969; service delivery (both) 1970 or earlier.

This large and powerful aircraft set a totally new level in combat-aircraft performance. The prototypes blazed a trail of world records in 1965–67 including closed-circuit speeds, payload-to-height and rate of climb records. The impact of what NATO quickly christened "Foxbat" was unprecedented. Especially in the Pentagon, Western policymakers recognised that here was a combat aircraft that outclassed everything else, and urgent studies were put in hand for a new US Air Force fighter (F-15 Eagle) to counter it. By 1971 at least two pairs of "Foxbat-B" reconnaissance aircraft were flying with impunity over Israel, too high and fas-

## MiG-25 ("Foxbat A", without 21 foot AA-6 missiles)

for Phantoms to catch, while others have made over-flights deep into Iran. This version is different in many respects, the nose having cameras instead of a large "Fox Fire" pulse-doppler radar, and other sensors being carried under the large body. Both versions have

twin outward-sloping vertical tails, single mainwheels and a flush canopy shaped for speed rather than pilot view. In speed and altitude the MiG-25 still far outclasses all Western aircraft, and both versions appear to carry comprehensive ECM (countermeasures).

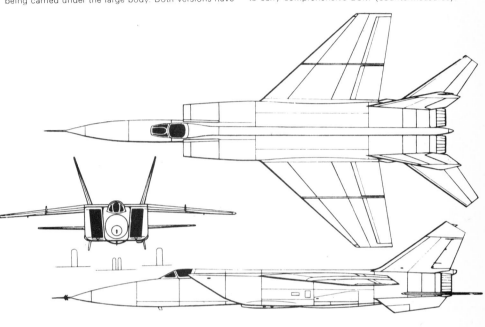

# Mil Mi-6 and -10

**Mi-6, Mi-10 and -10K**

**Type:** -6, heavy transport helicopter; -10, crane helicopter for bulky loads; -10K, crane helicopter.

**Engines:** (-6, -10) two 5,500 shp Soloviev D-25V single-shaft free-turbine engines driving common R-7 gearbox; (-10K) two 6,500 shp D-25VF.

**Dimensions:** Main rotor diameter 114 ft 10 in (35 m); overall length (rotors turning) (-6) 136 ft 11½ in (41·74 m); (-10, -10K) 137 ft 5½ in (41·89 m); fuselage length (-6) 108 ft 10½ in (33·18 m); (10, -10K) 107 ft 9¾ in (32·86 m); height (-6) 32 ft 4 in (9·86 m); (-10) 32 ft 2 in (9·8 m); (-10K) 25 ft 7 in (7·8 m).

**Weights:** empty (-6, typical) 60,055 lb (27,240 kg); (-10) 60,185 lb (27,300 kg); (-10K) 54,410 lb (24,680 kg); maximum loaded (-6) 93,700 lb (42,500 kg); (-10) 96,340 lb (43,700 kg); (-10K) 83,776 lb (38,000 kg) with 5,500 shp engines (90,390 lb, 41,000 kg expected with D-25VF engines).

**Performance:** maximum speed (-6) 186 mph (300 km/h) (set 100 km circuit record at 211·36 mph, beyond flight manual limit); (-10) 124 mph (200 km/h); service ceiling (-6) 14,750 ft (4500 m); (-10, -10K, limited) 9,842 ft (3000 m); range (-6 with half payload) 404 miles (650 km); (-10 with 12,000 kg platform load) 155 miles (250 km); (-10K with 11,000 kg payload, 6,500 shp engines) over 280 miles (450 km).

**Armament:** normally none, but Mi-6 often seen with manually aimed nose gun of about 12·7 mm calibre.

**History:** first flight (-6) probably early 1957; (-10) 1960; (-10K) prior to 1965.

Development by Mikhail L. Mil's design bureau at Zaporozhye of the dynamic system (rotors and shafting) of the Mi-6 was a task matched only by Soloviev's development of the huge R-7 gearbox, which weighs 7,054 lb (much more than the pair of engines). By far the biggest rotor system yet flown, this served to lift by far the biggest helicopter, the Mi-6 (NATO code name "Hook"), which quickly set world records for speed and payload, though the normal load is limited to 26,450 lb (12,000 kg) internally, loaded via huge clamshell rear doors, or 19,840 lb (9000 kg) externally slung. About 500 have been built, possibly half being in military use with the Soviet Union, and the armed forces of Bulgaria, Egypt, Indonesia, Iraq, Syria and Vietnam. Most have the rotor unloaded in cruising flight (typically 150 mph) by a fixed wing of 50 ft 2½ in span. These huge helicopters have played an active role in field exercises carrying troops (typically 68) and

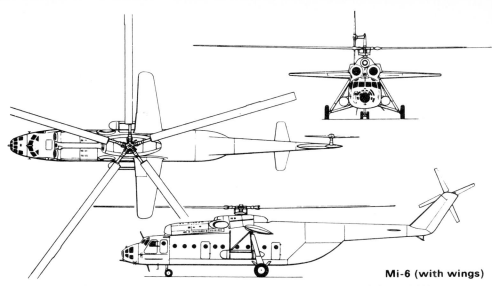

**Mi-6 (with wings)**

tactical missiles or vehicles in the class of the BRDM. The Mi-10 (code name "Harke") has lofty landing gears which enable it to straddle a load, such as a bus or prefabricated building, 3·75 m (12 ft 3½ in) high;

heavy loads weighing 33,070 lb (15,000 kg) and up to over 65 ft in length have been flown. It uses a TV viewing system for load control, but the short-legged Mi-10K has an under-nose gondola.

**Above: The Mi-10 'Harke' which can straddle heavy loads. Below: Colour photo of the Mi-6 transport helicopter on a recent exercise**

# Mil Mi-8

**Mi-8 (Egyptian AF, Federation of Arab Republics insignia)**

## Mi-8, Mi-8T

**Type:** general utility helicopter for internal loads and externally mounted weapons.

**Engines:** two 1,500 shp Isotov TV2-117A single-shaft free-turbine engines driving common VR-8A gearbox.

**Dimensions:** main rotor diameter 69 ft $10\frac{1}{2}$ in (21·29 m); overall length, rotors turning 82 ft $9\frac{3}{4}$ in (25·24 m); fuselage length 60 ft $0\frac{3}{4}$ in (18·31 m); height 18 ft $6\frac{1}{2}$ in (5·65 m).

**Weights:** empty (-8T) 15,026 lb (6816 kg); maximum loaded (all) 26,455 lb (12,000 kg) (heavier weights for non-VTO operation).

**Performance:** maximum speed 161 mph (260 km/h); service ceiling 14,760 ft (4500 m); range (-8T, full payload, 5 per cent reserve at 3,280 ft) 298 miles (480 km).

**Armament:** optional fitting for external pylons for up to eight stores carried outboard of fuel tanks (always fitted); typical loads eight pods of 57 mm rockets, or mix of gun pods and anti-tank missiles (Mi-8 not normally used in anti-tank role).

**History:** first flight 1960 or earlier; service delivery of military versions, before 1967.

Originally powered by a single 2,700 shp Soloviev engine, the Mi-8 soon appeared with its present engines and in 1964 added a fifth blade to its main rotor. It has since been the chief general utility helicopter of the Warsaw Pact powers and many other nations. By mid-1974 it was announced that more

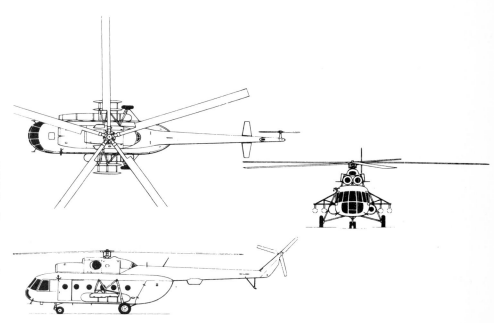

**Above: Three-view of standard V-Vs assault transport Mi-8 with radome under tailboom and missile pod pylons. Left: Czechoslovak standard Mi-8. Below: Pakistani Army Mi-8**

than 1,000 had been built, the majority for military use, with about 300 having been exported to Bangladesh, Bulgaria, Czechoslovakia, Egypt, Ethiopia, Finland, East Germany, Hungary, India, Iraq, Pakistan, the Sudan, Syria and Vietnam. The Mi-8 is a passenger and troop carrier normally furnished with quickly removable seats for 28 in the main cabin. The -8T is the utility version without furnishing and with circular windows, weapon pylons, cargo rings, a winch/pulley block system for loading and optional electric hoist by the front doorway. All versions have large rear clamshell doors (the passenger version having airstairs incorporated) through which a BRDM and other small vehicles can be loaded.

# Mil Mi-24

**Mi-24 versions with NATO names Hind-A and -B.**
**Type:** Tactical multi-role helicopter.
**Engines:** almost certainly two 1,500 shp Isotov TV2-117A free-turbine turboshaft.
**Dimensions:** (estimated) diameter of five-blade main rotor 55 ft 9 in (17 m); length overall (ignoring rotors) 55 ft 9 in (17 m); height overall 14 ft (4·25 m).
**Weights:** (estimated) empty 14,300 lb (6500 kg); maximum loaded 25,400 lb (11,500 kg).
**Performance:** maximum speed 170 mph (275 km/h); general performance, higher than Mi-8.
**Armament:** (Hind-A) usually one 12·7 mm gun aimed from nose; two stub wings providing rails for four wire-guided anti-tank missiles and four other stores (bombs, missiles, rocket or gun pods). (Hind-B) two stub wings of different type with four weapon pylons.
**History:** first flight, before 1972; service delivery, before 1974.

Few details are yet known of this attractive-looking battlefield helicopter, though in 1974 many were seen in service in East Germany and two versions were disclosed to the West in photographs. It appears to be based on the Mi-8, though the engines look smaller and the main rotor has blades of considerably shorter length but increased chord. The nosewheel-type landing gear is fully retractable, and the cabin is large enough for a crew of two and 12 to 14 troops. The exterior is well streamlined, broken only by avionic aerials and the prominent weapon stub-wings. The Mi-24 is much larger than the British Lynx, yet smaller than the Mi-8. One reason may be that it is the smallest machine capable of using the well-tried Mi-8 dynamic components, and in the anti-tank role the surplus payload could be used for spare missiles or infantry teams that could be dropped and then recovered later. Maximum slung load is estimated at 8,000 lb (3630 kg).

**Mi-24 ("Hind A")**

**Above: Mi-24 Hind A gunship and assault helicopter. Below: Colour picture of the Mi-24**

# Myasishchev Mya-4

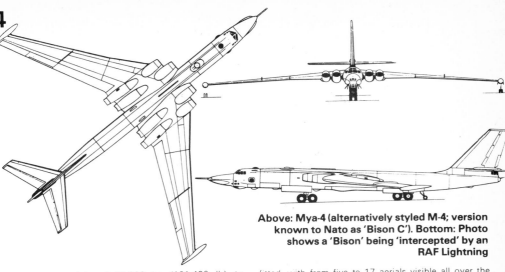

**Mya-4 (three versions, known to West as "Bison A, B and C)**

**Type:** (A) heavy bomber; (B) strategic reconnaissance and ECM; (C) multi-role reconnaissance bomber.

**Engines:** (A) four 19,180 lb (8700 kg) Mikulin AM-3D single-shaft turbojets; (B and C) four 28,660 lb (13,000 kg) D-15 engines (design bureau unknown, probably two-shaft turbojets, not turbofans).

**Dimensions:** (A) estimated, span 165 ft 7½ in (50.48 m); length 154 ft 10 in (47.2 m); height 46 ft (14.1 m).

**Weights:** estimated, empty (A) 154,000 lb (70,000 kg); (B, C) 176,400 lb (80,000 kg); maximum loaded (A) 352,740 lb (160,000 kg); (B, C) 375,000 lb (170,000 kg).

**Performance:** (estimated) maximum speed (all) 560 mph (900 km/h); service ceiling (A) 42,650 ft (13,000 m); (B, C) 49,200 ft (15,000 m); range (all) 6,835 miles (11,000 km) with 9,920 lb. (4500 kg) of bombs or electronic equipment.

**Armament:** (A) ten 23 mm NR-23 cannon in manned turret in tail and four remotely controlled turrets above and below front and rear fuselage (two guns in each turret); internal bomb bays in tandem for at least 22,050 lb (10,000 kg) stores; (B, C) six 23 mm cannon in two forward turrets and tail turret; internal bay for at least 10,000 lb (4500 kg) stores. In many versions a single 23 mm gun is fixed on the right side of the nose, firing ahead.

**History:** first flight, probably 1953; service delivery, probably 1955; final delivery, probably about 1958. A single example of this large aircraft took part in the 1954 May Day parade fly past over Moscow, its size being gauged from the escorting MiG fighters. It was expected to appear in large numbers, but little was heard of it for years. In fact a useful run of about 150 had been delivered, at first being used as bombers ("Bison A"). In 1959 a re-engined aircraft, called Type 201-M, set up world records by lifting a payload of 10,000 kg (22,046 lb) to 50,253 ft (15,317 m) and the formidable weight of 55,220 kg (121,480 lb) to 2000 m (6,561 ft). By this time the Mya-4 bombers were being likewise fitted with more powerful engines, and their role changed from bomber to long-range oversea reconnaissance, ECM and, in some cases, flight-refuelling tanker. All aircraft were given large fixed FR probes, the rear turrets were removed and a vast amount of special reconnaissance equipment fitted, with from five to 17 aerials visible all over the aircraft. In the "Bison C" sub-type a large search radar fills the entire nose, lengthening the nose by about 6 ft and changing its shape. Since 1967 these now obsolescent aircraft have been frequently encountered on probing missions far over the Arctic, Atlantic, Pacific and elsewhere, at both high and very low levels, the C-model having been seen most frequently.

**Above: Mya-4 (alternatively styled M-4; version known to Nato as 'Bison C'). Bottom: Photo shows a 'Bison' being 'intercepted' by an RAF Lightning**

# Sukhoi Su-7/11

Su-7BM (Indian AF)

Su-7BM (Egyptian AF)

Su-7B (Frontal Aviation, Czech AF)

**Su-7B, -7BM, -7U, -9, -11, -17 and -20.**
**Type:** (-7B and BM) single-seat close-support and attack; (-7U and -9U) dual-control trainer; (-9 and -11) single-seat all-weather interceptor.
**Engine:** one 22,046 lb (10,000 kg) thrust Lyulka AL-7F single-shaft afterburning turbojet.
**Dimensions:** span (-7) 29 ft 3½ in (8·93 m); (-9, -11) 27 ft (8·23 m); length (including pitot boom) (-7) 57 ft (17·37 m); (-9, -11) about 58 ft (17·68 m); height (-7) 15 ft 5 in (4·70 m); (-9, -11) 16 ft (4·88 m).
**Weights:** empty (-7BM) 19,000 lb (8620 kg); (-11) about 20,000 lb (9072 kg); maximum loaded (-7BM) 29,750 lb (13,500 kg); (-11) about 30,000 lb (13,610 kg).
**Performance:** maximum speed at altitude, clean (-7BM) 1055 mph (1700 km/h, Mach 1·6); (-11, estimated) 1,190 mph (1915 km/h, Mach 1·8); initial climb (-7BM) 29,900 ft (9120 m)/min; (-11) 27,000 ft (8230 m)/min; service ceiling (-7BM)

49,700 ft (15,150 m); (-11) 55,000 ft (16,765 m); range with twin drop tanks (all) 900 miles (1450 km).
**Armament:** (-7) two 30 mm NR-30 cannon, each with 70 rounds, in wing roots; four wing pylons, inners rated at 1,653 lb (750 kg) and outers at 1,102 lb (500 kg), but when two tanks are carried on fuselage pylons total external weapon load is reduced to 2,205 lb (1000 kg); (-9) four "Alkali" air-to-air missiles on wing pylons; no guns. (-11) two "Anab" air-to-air missiles, one radar-homing and one infra-red, on wing pylons; no guns.
**History:** first flight (-7 prototype) not later than 1955; (-9 prototype) before mid-1956; service delivery (-7B) 1959; (-9) 1959; (-11) probably 1968.

Two of the wealth of previously unknown Soviet air-

craft revealed at the 1956 Aviation Day at Tushino were large Sukhoi fighters, one with a swept wing (called "Fitter" by NATO) and the other a tailed delta (called "Fishpot"). Both were refined into operational types, losing some of their commonality in the process. The highly swept Su-7B became the standard Soviet bloc attack aircraft, some thousands being supplied to all Warsaw Pact nations and to Egypt, Cuba, India, Syria, Hungary, Iraq and North Vietnam. There are many sub-variants, the -7BM being a STOL rough-field version. The delta -9 fighter was used in large numbers as a standard Soviet (P-VO Strany) defensive fighter, replaced from 1968 by the Su-11 with long nose, large radar and inlet and new missiles. Code names of tandem trainers are Su-7U Moujik and Su-9U Maiden. In 1971–72 deliveries began of the Su-17 ("Fitter C") with slatted variable-sweep wings, and the Su-20 export version operated by the Polish Air Force with large drop tanks on pylons under the wing pivots.

# Sukhoi Su-15

**Versions known to the West are code-named "Flagon-A to -E"**

**Type:** most versions, all-weather interceptor.

**Engines:** two afterburning engines, believed to be 14,550 lb (6600 kg) Tumansky RD-13-300 single-shaft turbojets.

**Dimensions:** (estimated) span 30 ft (9·15 m); length 68 ft (20·5 m); height 19 ft (5·79 m).

**Weights:** ("Flagon-A", estimated) empty 23,000 lb (10,435 kg); maximum loaded 35,275 lb (16,000 lb).

**Performance:** (estimated) maximum speed at altitude, with two missiles, 1,520 mph (2445 km/h, Mach 2·3); initial climb 35,000 ft (10,670 m)/min; service ceiling 65,000 ft (19,800 m); combat radius 450 miles (725 km); ferry range about 1,400 miles (2250 km).

**Armament:** two underwing pylons normally carry one radar "Anab" and one infra-red "Anab"; two fuselage pylons normally carry drop tanks.

**History:** first flight (Su-15 prototype) probably 1964; (production Su-15) probably 1967.

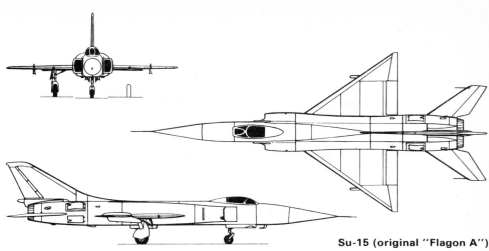

**Su-15 (original "Flagon A")**

Following naturally on from the Su-11, and strongly resembling the earlier aircraft in wings and tail, the Su-15 has two engines which not only confer increased performance but also leave the nose free for a large AI radar. The initial "Flagon-A" version entered IA-PVO Strany service in 1969. "Flagon-B" is a STOL rough-field version with three lift jets in the fuselage and a revised "double delta" wing. "Flagon-C" is the Su-15U dual trainer, "-D" is basically a "-B" without lift jets, and "-E" has completely updated electronics and more powerful engines. In 1971 a US official estimated that 400 Su-15 were in service, with production at about 15 monthly. Small batches have served overseas, notably in Egypt in 1973.

**Three photos of the Sukhoi Su-15, probably the most important combat aircraft of the Soviet Air Defence forces (PVO-Strany)**

# Sukhoi Su-19

**Su-19 versions known to NATO as "Fencer"**
**Type:** two-seat multi-role combat aircraft.
**Engines:** two afterburning turbofan or turbojet engines, each in the 21,000 lb (9525 kg) thrust class (possibly same as engine of MiG-23).
**Dimensions:** (estimated) span (spread, about 22°) 56 ft 3 in (17·15 m), swept (about 72°) 31 ft 3 in (9·53 m); length 69 ft 10 in (21·29 m); height 21 ft (6·4 m).
**Weights:** (estimated) empty 35,000 lb (15,875 kg); maximum loaded 70,000 lb (31,750 kg).
**Performance:** (estimated) maximum speed, clean, 950 mph (1530 km/h, Mach 1·25) at sea level, about 1,650 mph (2655 km/h, Mach 2·5) at altitude; initial climb, over 40,000 ft (12,200 m)/min; service ceiling, about 60,000 ft (18,290 m); combat radius with maximum weapons, about 500 miles (805 km); ferry range, over 2,500 miles (4025 km).
**Armament:** one 23 mm GSh-23 twin-barrel cannon in lower centreline; at least six pylons on fuselage, fixed and swinging wings, for wide range of stores included guided and unguided air-to-ground or air-to-air missiles.
**History:** first flight, probably about 1970; service delivery, 1974 or earlier.
First identified publicly in the West by the Chairman of the US Joint Chiefs of Staff, who described the Su-19 as "the first modern Soviet fighter to be developed specifically as a fighter-bomber for the ground-attack

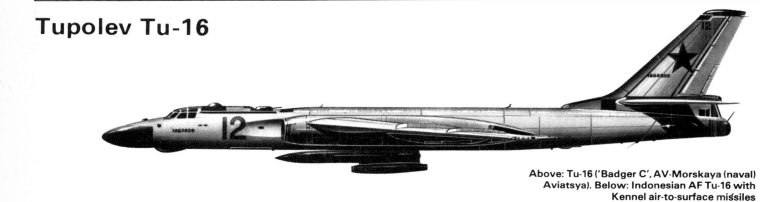

Provisional three-view and side profile of original Su-19, the former showing the range of wing sweep.

mission", this aircraft will probably be the chief tactical attack aircraft of the Soviet V-VS in 1980. Like the rival but much smaller MiG-23, the Su-19 is an extremely clean machine strongly reminiscent of the F-111 and Mirage G, having side-by-side seats and wing and tailplane at the same level, as in the US

machine, yet following the French aircraft in general layout. In general capability the nearest Western equivalent is the F-14 Tomcat, which shows just how formidable this aircraft is. Whereas "Foxbat" was on many Western lips in the 1960s, so is "Fencer" a big scare-word in the 1970s.

# Tupolev Tu-16

Above: Tu-16 ('Badger C', AV-Morskaya (naval) Aviatsya). Below: Indonesian AF Tu-16 with Kennel air-to-surface missiles

**Sub-types known to West as "Badger A" to "Badger G"; Tupolev bureau, Tu-88**
**Type:** designed as strategic bomber; see text.

**Engines:** believed in all versions, two Mikulin AM-3M single-shaft turbojets each rated at about 20,950 lb (9500 kg).

**Dimensions:** span (basic) 110 ft (33·5 m), (varies with FR system. ECM and other features); length (basic) 120 ft (36·5 m), (varies with radar or glazed

nose); height 35 ft 6 in (10·8 m).

**Weights:** empty, typically about 72,750 lb (33,000 kg) in early versions, about 82,680 lb (37,500 kg) in maritime/ECM roles; maximum loaded, about 150,000 lb (68,000 kg).

**Performance:** maximum speed, clean at height, 587 mph (945 km/h); initial climb, clean, about 4,100 ft (1250 m)/min; service ceiling 42,650 ft (13,000 m); range with maximum weapon load, no missiles, 3,000 miles (4,800 km); extreme reconnaissance range, about 4,500 miles (7250 km).

**Armament:** in most variants, six 23 mm NR-23 cannon in radar-directed manned tail turret and remote-aimed upper dorsal· and rear ventral barbettes; versions without nose radar usually have seventh NR-23 fixed firing ahead on right side of nose. Internal weapon bay for load of 19,800 lb (9000 kg), with certain versions equipped to launch missiles (see text).

**History:** first flight (Tu-88), believed 1952; service delivery 1954; final delivery (USSR) about 1959, (China) after 1975.

Representing a simple and low-risk approach to the strategic jet-bomber requirement, the Tu-88 prototype was generally in the class of the Valiant but incorporated heavy defensive arament. Technology throughout was derived directly from the Boeing B-29, which Tupolev's bureau had in 1945-53 built in large

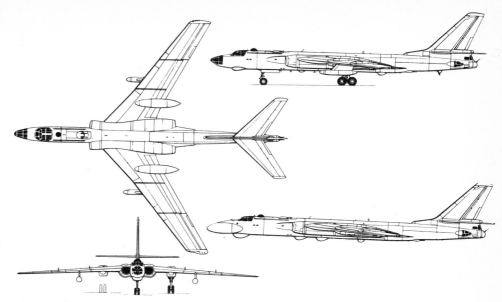

**Above: drawings of two current versions of the Tu-16 side, plan and front views of the "Badger F," and side view of the "Badger D" with larger nose radar. Below: "Badger F" snapped as it wheels low over the Atlantic.**

numbers as the Tu-4. The first ("Badger A") version had blind-bombing radar and glazed nose, and a few were supplied to Egypt and Iraq. The B carried two "Kennel" cruise missiles on underwing pylons and served the AV-MF (Navy) and Indonesian AF. C carried the large "Kipper" stand-off missile on the centreline, with panoramic nose radar for ship search and missile guidance. D is a maritime reconnaissance type, with comprehensive radars and ECM. E is a photo and multi-sensor reconnaissance type, F is an E with major new ECM and ESM installations, and G is an updated B which launched many missiles against Israel in 1973. Total production exceeded 2,000, and production (without Soviet aid) continues in China.

# Tupolev Tu-20

**Tu-95 (Tupolev bureau designation) in versions known to West as "Bear A" to "Bear F" and "Moss" (Tu-126)**
**Type:** designed as strategic bomber; see text.
**Engines:** four 14,795 ehp Kuznetsov NK-12M single-shaft turboprops.

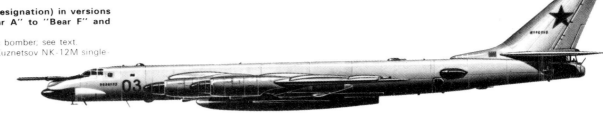

**Dimensions:** span 159 ft (48·5 m); (Moss) 167 ft 8 in (51·10 m); length 155 ft 10 in (47·50 m), (certain versions differ by up to 6 ft. and Moss is much bigger); height 38 ft 8 in (11·78 m); (Moss) over 40 ft.
**Weights:** empty, probably about 160,000 lb (72,600 kg); maximum loaded (Bear and Moss, estimate) about 340,000 lb (154,000 kg).
**Performance:** maximum speed (typical Bear, clean) 540 mph (870 km/h); service ceiling, about 44,000 ft (13,400 m); range with 25,000 lb (11,340 kg) bomb load, 7,800 miles (12,550 km).
**Armament:** normally six 23 mm NS-23 in radar-directed manned tail turret and remote-aimed dorsal and ventral barbettes (defensive guns often absent from late conversions and from Moss); internal weapon bay for load of about 25,000 lb (11,340 kg); (Moss) no weapons.
**History:** first flight (prototype) mid-1954; service delivery, 1956; final delivery, probably about 1962.

Making use of identical systems, techniques and even similar airframe structures as the Tu-16, the Tu-95 (service designation, Tu-20) is much larger and has roughly double the range of its turbojet predecessor. The huge swept wing, forming integral tanks, was a major accomplishment in 1952–54, as were the monster turboprop engines and their eight blade 18 ft 4½ in (5·6 m) contraprops. The basic bomber called "Bear A" had a glazed nose, chin radar and gun-sight blisters on the rear fuselage. First seen in 1961, "Bear B" featured a solid nose with enormous radome, refuelling probe and centreline attachment for a large cruise missile ("Kangaroo"). C appeared in 1964 with a large new blister on each side of the fuselage (on one side only on B), while D was obviously a major ECM/ESM reconnaissance type with chin radar, very large belly radar, and from 12 to 21 avionic features visible from stem to stern. E is a multi-sensor reconnaissance conversion of A, while F is a recent further conversion with an array of ventral radars and stores bays in place of the ventral guns. "Moss" is an AWACS (Airborne Warning And Control System) with giant "saucer" radome and the larger airframe of the Tu-114 transport.

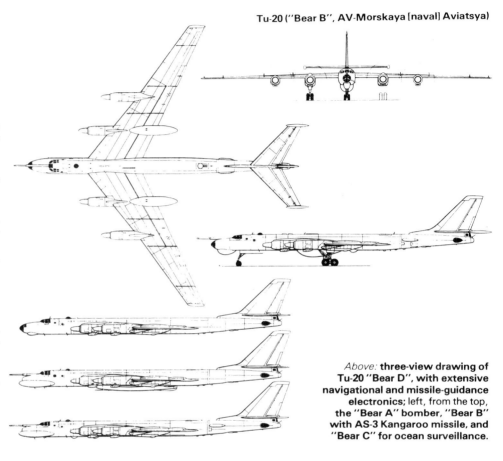

**Tu-20 ("Bear B", AV-Morskaya [naval] Aviatsya)**

*Above:* **three-view drawing of Tu-20 "Bear D", with extensive navigational and missile-guidance electronics;** left, from the top, the "Bear A" bomber, "Bear B" with AS-3 Kangaroo missile, and "Bear C" for ocean surveillance.

Colour view of Tu-20 underside, photographed from a RAF Lightning.

# Tupolev Tu-22

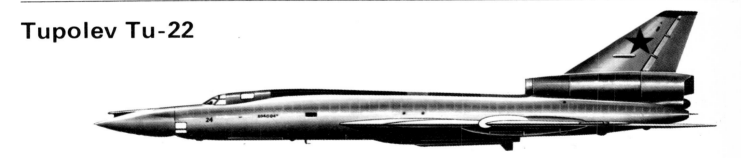

Tu-22 ("Blinder B", operator believed to be V-VS strategic aviation)

**Tu-22 in versions known to West as "Blinder A"
to "Blinder D"; Tupolev bureau, Tu-105**
**Type:** originally bomber; see text.
**Engines:** two afterburning turbojets, of unknown
type, each with maximum rating estimated at 27,000 lb
(12,250 kg).
**Dimensions:** span 90 ft 10½ in (27·70 m); length
(most versions) 132 ft 11½ in (40·53 m); height
17 ft (5·18 m).
**Weights:** empty, about 85,000 lb (38,600 kg);
maximum loaded, about 185,200 lb (84,000 kg).
**Performance:** maximum speed (clean, at height)
920 mph (1480 km/h, Mach 1·4); initial climb, about
11,500 ft (3500 m)/min; service ceiling 59,000 ft
(18,000 m); range (high, internal fuel only) 1,400 miles
(2250 km).
**Armament:** one 23 mm NS-23 in radar-directed
barbette in tail; internal weapon bay for at least
20,000 lb (9070 kg) of free-fall bombs or other stores.

*Continued on next page*

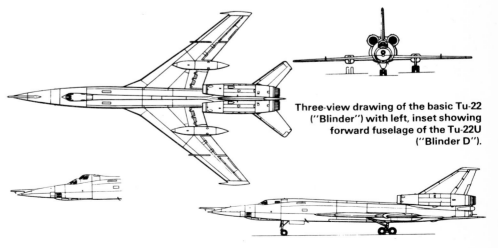

**Three-view drawing of the basic Tu-22
("Blinder") with left, inset showing
forward fuselage of the Tu-22U
("Blinder D").**

or (Blinder B) one "Kitchen" stand-off cruise missile semi-recessed under centreline.

**History:** first flight, well before public display in 1961; service delivery, probably 1960.

Having an efficient wing closely related to that of the Tu-28P, this supersonic bomber is a large aircraft with a bigger body and higher gross weight than the USAF B-58 Hustler. Typical crew appears to be a pilot, upward-ejecting, and two more members in tandem at a lower level who eject downwards. "Blinder A" was a reconnaissance bomber, seen in small numbers. B carried the stand-off missile, had a larger nose radar and semi-flush FR probe. C is the main variant, used by Naval Aviation for oversea ECM/ESM surveillance, multi-sensor reconnaissance and with limited weapon capability. D is a dual trainer with stepped cockpits. Recent versions appear to have later engines (probably turbofans) with greater airflow.

**Though an extremely impressive aircraft, the Tu-22 suffered from the penalties of supersonic performance (especially in having limited range), while reaping few benefits. The Blinders left and below were photographed during exercises over the Soviet Union. In real missions a close formation would be unlikely.**

# Tupolev Tu-28P

**Tu-28P (IA-PVO air defence forces)**

**Tu-28 versions of unknown designation; Tupolev bureau, Tu-102**

**Type:** long-range all-weather interceptor.

**Engines:** originally, two large axial turbojets of unknown type, each with afterburning rating of about 27,000 lb (12,250 kg), probably similar to those of Tu-22; later versions, afterburning turbofans of about 30,000 lb (13,610 kg) each, as in later Tu-22.

**Dimensions:** (estimated) span 65 ft (20 m); length 85 ft (26 m); height 23 ft (7 m).

**Weights:** (estimated) empty 55,000 lb (25,000 kg); maximum loaded 100,000 lb (45,000 kg).

**Performance:** (estimated) maximum speed (with missiles, at height) 1,150 mph (1850 km/h, Mach 1·75); initial climb, 25,000 ft (7500 m)/min; service ceiling (not gross weight) about 60,000 ft (18,000 m); range on internal fuel (high patrol) about 1,800 miles (2900 km).

**Armament:** no guns seen in any version; mix of infra-red homing and radar-homing "Ash" air-to-air guided missiles, originally one of each and since 1965 two of each.

**History:** first flight, believed 1957; service delivery, probably 1961.

Largest fighter known to be in service in the world, this formidable machine is essentially conventional yet has a interception radar known to exist. It was one of a number of supersonic types produced by the Tupolev bureau with technology explored with the family of aircraft of the late 1950s known to NATO as "Backfin" (another is the Tu-22). Like the others the Tu-28P has

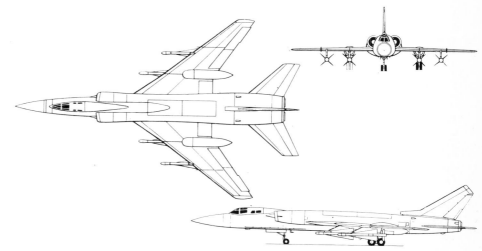

**Three-view of Tu-28P carrying four AA-5 Ash air-to-air missiles, seen in the dramatic photo below being "rippled" in a full salvo.**

a distinctive wing with sharply kinked trailing edge, the outer 45° panels being outboard of large fairings extending behind the trailing edge accommodating the four-wheel bogie landing gears. Two crew sit in tandem under upward-hinged canopies, and all armament is carried on wing pylons. Early versions had twin ventral fins and usually large belly fairings, but these features are absent from aircraft in current service. The Tu-28P would be an ideal strategic patrol fighter to operate in conjunction with the "Moss" AWACS.

# Tupolev V-G bomber

**Two main versions with NATO code names "Backfire-A" and "-B"**
**Type:** long-range bomber and missile platform with probable crew of four.
**Engines:** two afterburning turbofans, probably Kuznetsov NK-144 two-shaft engines each with maximum rating of 48,500 lb (22,000 kg).
**Dimensions:** (estimated) span (spread, about 20°) 110 ft (33·5 m), (swept, about 55°) 88 ft (26·8 m); length 135 ft (41·2 m); height 39 ft (11·9 m).
**Weights:** (estimated) empty 121, 250 lb (55,000 kg); maximum loaded 272,000 lb (123,350 kg).
**Performance:** (estimated, "Backfire B") maximum speed at altitude 1,520 mph (2445 km/h, Mach 2·3); speed at sea level, over Mach 1; service ceiling over 60,000 ft (18,290 m); maximum combat radius on internal fuel 3,570 miles (5745 km); ferry range, about 8,000 miles (12,875 km).
**Armament:** internal weapon bay(s) for free-fall bombs up to largest thermonuclear sizes, with provision for carrying two AS-6 stand-off missiles.
**History:** first flight ("Backfire A" prototype) not later than 1969; ("Backfire-B") probably 1973; entry to service, probably 1974.
Owing to the obvious inability of the Tu-22 to fly strategic missions the Tupolev bureau designed this far more formidable aircraft, larger in size and fitted with a swing-wing. "Backfire-A" was apparently not a very successful design, with multi-wheel main gears folding into large fairings projecting in typical Tupolev fashion behind the only moderately swept wing. About half the gross wing area was fixed, just the outer portions swinging through a modest arc. Today's 'Backfire-B" has no landing-gear boxes and is improved in other ways, though the side view is still largely a matter for conjecture. The large engines are fed through wide inlet ducts which probably pass above the wing; a flight refuelling probe is fitted above the nose, but even without this "Backfire-B" has an endurance of some ten hours. The Chairman of the US

### Tu "Backfire A" (provisional in all respects)

### Backfire B

Joint Chiefs of Staff said in 1974 "It is expected to replace some of both the current medium and heavy bombers and, when deployed with a compatible tanker force, constitutes a potential threat to the continental United States." The speed of development is also disquieting to the West, because these aircraft were being encountered on long oversea missions in early 1975.

---

# Yakovlev Yak-26

**Yak-26, -27P and "Mandrake"**
**Type:** two-seat reconnaissance (27P, interceptor).
**Engines:** (26, 27P) two Tumansky RD-9B or other RD-9 versions rated at from 7,165 lb (3250 kg) to 8,820 lb (4000 kg) with maximum afterburner; ("Mandrake") two non-afterburning turbojets, probably RD-9 rated at about 6,000 lb.
**Dimensions:** span (26 and 27P) 38 ft 6 in (11·75 m); (original 27) 36 ft 1 in; ("Mandrake") estimated at 71 ft (22 m); length (26) 62 ft (18·90 m); (27P) about 55 ft (16·75 m); ("Mandrake") about 51 ft (15·5 m); height (26, 27P) 14 ft 6 in (4·40 m); ("Mandrake") about 13 ft (4 m).
**Weights:** empty (all) about 18,000 lb (8165 kg); maximum loaded (26) about 26,000 lb (11,800 kg); (27P) about 24,000 lb (10,900 kg); ("Mandrake") possibly nearly 30,000 lb (13,600 kg).
**Performance:** maximum speed (26, 27P, at altitude) 686 mph (1104 km/h, Mach 0·95); ("Mandrake") about 470 mph (755 km/h); initial climb, about 15,000 ft (4600 m)/min ("Mandrake", less); service ceiling (26, 27P) 49,200 ft (15,000 m); ("Mandrake") about 62,000 ft (19,000 m); range at altitude (26) about 1,675 miles (2700 km); (27P) 1,000 miles (1600 km); ("Mandrake") possibly 2,500 miles (4000 km).
**Armament:** (26) one 30 mm NR-30 cannon in fairing low on right side of forward fuselage, small batches with cannon and rockets then small batches with two missile pylons; ("Mandrake") none.
**History:** first flight (26) before mid-1956; (27P) before mid-1956; ("Mandrake") possibly 1957.

Stemming directly from the Yak-25, these aircraft introduced various changes, of which the most significant was afterburning engines in the Yak-26 and 27P. The leading edge was swept very sharply at

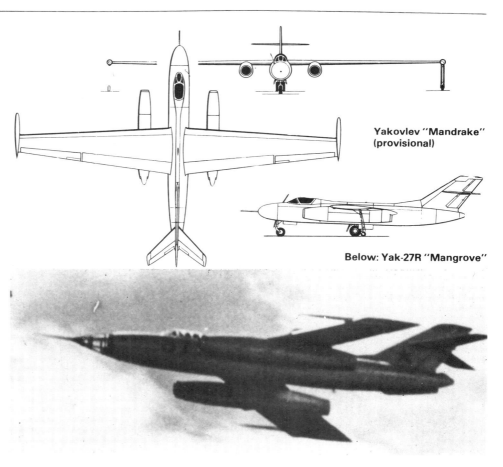

### Yakovlev "Mandrake" (provisional)

### Below: Yak-27R "Mangrove"

longer nacelles to meet the body at 90° and give much greater root chord. The nose was pointed (glazed on the 26 and a radome on the 27P) and in the production aircraft the outer wings were extended beyond the outrigger gear and fitted with drooped extended-chord leading edges. Only the 26 was built in large numbers

(NATO name "Mangrove"). The 27P was called "Flashlight C". The high-altitude, unswept "Mandrake", whose proper designation is not known, made overflights in Eastern Asia, the Middle East and along the borders of Communist territory in Europe before being retired in 1972 or 1973.

# Yakovlev Yak-28

**Yak-28 attack versions, -28P, -28R and -28U**
**Type:** 28 (unknown designations) two-seat attack; (P) all-weather interceptor; (R) multi-sensor reconnaissance; (U) dual-control trainer.

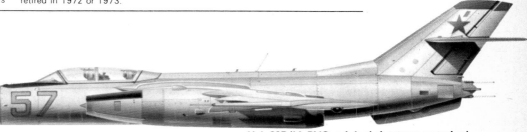

Yak-28P (IA-PVO, original short-nose version)

**Engines:** two Tumansky RD-11 single-shaft afterburning turbojets each with maximum rating of 13,120 lb (5950 kg); certain sub-types have RD-11-300 rated at 13,670 lb (6200 kg).
**Dimensions:** (estimated) span 42 ft 6 in (12·95 m), (some versions have span slightly less than standard); length (except late P) 71 ft 0½ in (21·65 m); (late 28P) 74 ft (22·56 m); height 12 ft 11½ in (3·95 m).
**Weights:** empty (estimated, typical) 24,250 lb (11,000 kg); maximum loaded (U) 30,000 lb (13,600 kg); (others) 35,300–41,000 lb (16,000–18,600 kg).
**Performance:** (estimated) maximum speed at altitude 735 mph (1180 km/h, Mach 1·13); initial climb 27,900 ft (8500 m)/min; service ceiling 55,000 ft (16,750 m); range (clean, at altitude) 1,200–1,600 miles (1930–2575 km).
**Armament:** (attack versions) one 30 mm NR-30 cannon on both sides of fuselage or on right side only, fuselage weapon bay for internal load of free-fall bombs (estimated maximum, 4,400 lb, 2000 kg), hardpoints or pylons between drop-tank attachments and outrigger gears for light loads (usually pod of 55 mm rockets); (28P) two "Anab" air-to-air guided missiles, one radar and the other infra-red; in some aircraft, two additional pylons for two K-13A ("Atoll") missiles, both "Anab" then being radar homers; (R) believed none; (U) retains weapon bay and single gun.
**History:** first flight, before 1961; (production attack and interceptor versions) before 1961; service delivery, not later than mid-1962; final delivery, before 1970.

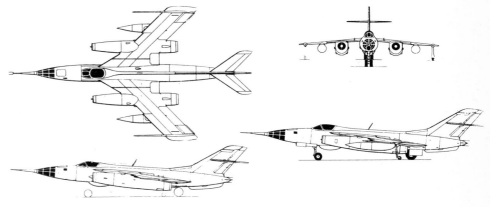

These drawings show main versions of the Yak-28 other than the -28P Interceptor: plan, front and side views of the Yak-28I "Brewer C;" side view of -28L "Brewer B" (Immediately above) and of—28U "Maestro" (right).

Obviously derived from the Yak-25/26/27, the Yak-28 is a completely new aircraft, with high wing of different form, new engines, steerable twin-wheel nose gear and considerably greater weight. Early attack versions had slightly shorter fuselage and shorter nacelles ahead of the wing; many hundreds (possibly thousands) of glazed-nose attack 28s (code name "Brewer") were built, most having been rebuilt as ECM and other specialist tactical machines. The Yak-28P (code name "Firebar") remains 'a leading interceptor, its "Skip Spin" radar being enclosed in a much longer and more pointed nose from 1967. The 28U trainer (code name "Maestro") has a separate front (pupil) cockpit with canopy hinged to the right. Many 28R versions ("Brewer D"), with cameras and various non-optical sensors, may be converted attack aircraft. Flight refuelling is not fitted.

# The Soviet Navy

**Captain J. E. Moore, RN**

Although the main focus of interest today is upon the astonishing rise of the Soviet Navy's capabilities and power in the last 20 years, this must be viewed as part of a lengthy and, at times, painful evolution. Unlike the German navy of Kaiser Wilhelm II and Tirpitz, which was created from virtually nothing, the history and tradition of the Russian fleet stretches back over 250 years, a period during which operations

against Sweden, Turkey, France and Great Britain brought such names as Apraksin, Ushakov, Senyavin and Makarov to the fore. In common with other navies the Russian fleet suffered from contraction and neglect in times of peace. Imaginative ideas were stultified by bureaucracy. By the time of the outbreak of the Russo–Japanese War in 1904 the Russian fleet was fourth in the world in numbers, but ill-led and poorly trained,

with its morale sapped by the wide gulf between officers and men. The geographical position of Russia also caused wide dispersion of the available forces and these were soundly defeated by the Japanese.

New building programmes were slow in realisation and thus, by the outbreak of World War I in 1914, the navy was sadly lacking in modern ships. Its performance during the war with Germany was inadequate

A 'Kashin' class destroyer. These ships are now being converted to carry four surface-to-surface missiles as well as existing anti-aircraft armament.

and the Revolution of October 1917 (November 1917 in the revised calendar) found it of poor quality, with its ratings only too ready to join with the revolutionaries.

The foundation of the Workers' and Peasants' Red Navy dates from Lenin's decree of 11 February 1918, but little was done to provide modern ships. Small groups operated against the Allied and White Russian forces, but the manpower was much diluted by the purge which followed the sailors' demands for free elections in February 1921. War damage to Russian shipyards delayed the building and refitting of ships, and by 1924 this meagre fleet consisted of two battleships, a cruiser, 18 destroyers and nine submarines. Two years later the Defence Council authorised the construction of 12 submarines, 18 escorts and a number of light forces, a decision which was built into the first 5-year plan in 1928. Although there is no evidence that the escort vessels were built, the submarine programme continued at an increased rate until, by the time of the German invasion of Russia in June 1941, 180 submarines had been completed, with another 90 on the slips. Meanwhile Stalin, impelled in the later years by the lessons of the Spanish Civil War, had set his sights on an impressive surface fleet. In addition to the three old battleships, 10 cruisers and 60 destroyers, a further three battleships, 12 cruisers and 45 destroyers were on the building slips in 1941. Few of them were, however, to be completed.

Although the ships available to the USSR were considerably more numerous than those of the German navy when hostilities began in 1941, the performance of the Soviet Navy was inefficient and ineffective. This was due in large measure to the fact that a great number of the experienced officers in the fleet had been removed and executed in the purges started by Stalin in 1934. The standard of material efficiency in the fleet was low, training had suffered and only when Allied ships were transferred on loan did the Soviet Navy learn of new sensors such as sonar and radar.

In July 1945 Stalin ordered that a fleet 'still stronger and more powerful' should be provided but, as after the previous war, the destruction of the main surface-ship building yards hampered the fulfilment of this instruction. As the yards were repaired so did construction begin, but the designs remained basically those of the prewar years. At the same time, though, new classes were being laid out on the drawing-board. These benefited from the lessons learned from the recent war and were indications of new and advanced attitudes among Soviet naval constructors. The last stage of the Stalinist period (1945–1953) saw radical changes under way. The very numerous 'Whisky' class submarines and their larger companions of the 'Zulu' class were, at the time, equalled by very few Western boats; the naval air force reached a strength of 4,000 aircraft; and research into missiles for maritime purposes was well advanced.

The interregnum which came between Stalin's death and the accession to power of Khrushchev saw a dramatic change in the Soviet naval programmes. In January 1956 Admiral Sergei Gorshkov was appointed as Commander-in-Chief of the Navy at the age of 45. This post, which has no equivalent in Western navies, combines the duties once vested in the British First Lord of the Admiralty and the First Sea Lord, and 20 years later Admiral Gorshkov still holds the reins. These 20 years have seen the totally dramatic renaissance of the Soviet fleet. Fourth in strength the Russian navy may have been in 1904 – today it challenges the power of the United States Navy, is a fleet which leads the world in certain aspects and has learned lessons of tactics, seamanship and worldwide operations in a period which would have been thought absurdly short a quarter of a century ago.

Admiral Gorshkov inherited a number of advantages when he assumed command. The first submarine-oriented ballistic missile had been test-launched in the previous year, two years before the USA laid down a ballistic-missile submarine. Within months of his appointment the first 'Zulu V' class was at sea, mounting two SSN-4 'Sark' missiles with a range of 350 miles. At the same time plans were in hand for the building of the new 'Krupny' class, the world's first destroyers armed with surface-to-surface missiles (SSMs), aimed at defence against Western aircraft-carriers. Also in hand were the 'Kildin' class destroyers with

*Above left:* 'Kresta II', cruiser: **(A)** MBU 2500 anti-submarine rocket launcher (12-barrelled). **(B)** Surface-to-air missiles, SA-N-3 type. **(C)** Surface-to-surface missiles (SS-N-10). **(D)** Head Light radar for SA-N-3. **(E)** Top Sail radar for long-range surveillance. **(F)** Muff Cob radar for 57mm guns. **(G)** 57mm guns. **(H)** Torpedo tubes. **(J)** Gatling-type guns. **(K)** Bass Tilt radar for Gatlings. **(L)** Helicopter pad and hangar. **(M)** MBU 4500 anti-submarine rocket launcher (six-barrelled).

*Above:* 'Knivak' destroyer: **(A)** Surface-to-surface missiles (SS-N-10). **(B)** MBU 2500 anti-submarine rocket launcher (12-barrelled). **(C)** 76mm guns. **(D)** SA-N-4 surface-to-air point defence missiles in covered mountings. **(E)** Torpedo tubes. **(F)** Variable depth sonar. **(G)** Owl Screech radar for 76mm guns. **(H)** Pop Group radar for SA-N-4. **(J)** Head Net C radar for long-range surveillance. **(K)** Eye Bowl radar (modification of Head Light) for SS-N-10.

*Right:* **Provorny and Kavkaz**, two of the 'Kashin' class destroyers first completed in 1962. These were the first all gas-turbine warships in the world.

*Left:* A long-range SS-N-3 surface-to-surface missile being launched by a surfaced submarine, one of several methods of attack used by the Soviet Fleet.

a missile armament similar to the 'Krupnys' and the 'Whisky Twin Cylinder' submarines armed with twin SSN-3 launchers – all aimed at the prevention of seaborne attacks on the USSR.

Programmes in the immediate future were similarly reactive to the possibility of external assault – missile-firing fast attack craft of the 'Osa' and 'Komar' classes, cruisers of the 'Kynda' class with SSMs and then ships with surface-to-air missiles as the naval air force lost its own fighter squadrons and the fleet was planned to operate further from Russia's coasts.

The final phase has come in the last 10 years with the 'Moskva' helicopter cruisers, the all-purpose cruisers of the 'Kresta I', 'Kresta II' and 'Kara' classes, and the multiple-armed destroyers of the 'Krivak' class. With the completion of the first aircraft-carrier of the 'Kuril' class Admiral Gorshkov has achieved his aim of the creation of a balanced fleet, 'a powerful ocean-going navy' in his own words.

**Submarine development**

Since the first major building programme of 1926 the Soviet Navy has laid great em-

phasis on submarine construction. This was originally due to the defensive role planned for the fleet and, later, because the widely dispersed submarine yards were the only ones to survive the German attacks between 1941 and 1945. The first boats were little more than improved editions of World War I designs and this tendency continued until 1950. In this period of 24 years huge numbers of submarines were completed, a programme equalled only by that of Germany in the war years. Thus, in the immediate postwar period, the boats included in the Soviet order-of-battle were well behind modern developments. But in 1951 the first of a class which was eventually to number 240 in the next six years joined the fleet. This was the 'Whisky' class, a design which had clearly profited greatly from German experience. Of some 1,350 tons dived displacement, with six torpedo-tubes and a submerged speed of 15 knots, they looked not unlike the German Type XXI boats, and were to be the basic hulls for no less than eight variants. These ranged from the original type with twin guns, to the 'Canvas Bag' radar pickets and the 'Long Bin' fitted with four SSN-3 cruise-missile launchers. At the same time a larger version, the 'Zulu' class, began to appear and this submarine was chosen as the first conversion for ballistic missile operations. The first of six was completed in 1956 and carried two 350-mile SSN-4 missiles.

By then the forerunners of the present

nuclear submarine fleet were under construction, in the form of the 'November' class. Displacing over 4,000 tons, they were fast but noisy, characteristics shared by the 'Echo I' and 'II' classes of nuclear boats which followed them and which were armed with six and eight SSN-3 cruise-missiles respectively. These were clearly aimed at the forward defence of the USSR, as also were the 16 'Juliet' class of diesel submarines with four SSN-3 tubes. Not only cruise-missile boats joined the fleet – the diesel-propelled 'Golf' class and the nuclear 'Hotel' class followed rapidly in the early 1960s, both originally carrying SSN-4 missiles which were later replaced in many cases by the 700-mile SSN-5 'Serb' missiles.

There was now a pause before the next three major classes were reported – the 'Victor' fleet submarine, the 'Charlie' cruise-missile submarine and the 'Yankee' ballistic-missile submarine. All included improved hull and reactor designs, and were faster and better armed. 'Victor' had eight torpedo-tubes, 'Charlie' eight tubes for the 30-mile SSN-7 missile which could, for the first time, be launched under water, and 'Yankee' carried 16 tubes for the new 1,300-mile SSN-6 'Sawfly' ballistic missiles. Improvements to all three have been launched, the 'Victor II', 'Papa' and 'Delta' classes, but it is the last which has caused the greatest change in today's balance of naval power. Armed with 12 4,200-mile SSN-8 missiles, this class can cover targets throughout

Canada, the USA and the whole of Asia without leaving the Barents or Greenland Seas. The final monster, the 'Delta II', carries probably 16 of these missiles in a hull of 16,000 tons, the largest class of submarine ever built. They are an impressive addition to today's fleet of some 340 submarines.

### Aircraft-carrier development

Although the Russian and Soviet navies have, since 1910, recognised the place of aircraft in maritime warfare, it was not until 1937 that plans were laid for the building of true aircraft-carriers. This intention was

*Above:* **Kotlin-SAM class destroyer with her SA-N-3 surface-to-air missiles passing close under the stern of HMS Ark Royal**

*Above, right:* **Soviet frigates firing rockets from their MBU launchers during an anti-submarine action. These launchers are usually 6 or 12 barrelled.**

*Right:* **A gun crew mans the forward twin-37mm mounting on a fast attack craft.**

overtaken by the war with Germany and, in the postwar years, there was much difference of opinion in Soviet naval circles about the value of this type of ship. However, in 1967 the *Moskva* was produced, first of a pair of 17,000-ton helicopter-carriers. With a flight-deck occupying the after half of the ship and with a complement of 18 Kamov Ka-25 'Hormone' helicopters, these were clearly intended for anti-submarine operations.

Five years after *Moskva*'s appearance came reports of the first of the 35,000-ton 'Kuril' class aircraft-carriers. With an angled flight-deck these new ships, of which in 1976 the first is in commission, one is fitting out and possibly two more building, are apparently designed to operate VTOL aircraft and helicopters. As such they are the logical advance towards the achievement of a balanced fleet capable of worldwide operations.

## Cruiser development

The cruiser strength of the Soviet Navy during the early post-Revolutionary days was confined to two ships completed and three building. In 1935 the first pair of the 9,000-ton 'Kirov' class, a new design to meet the needs of the second 5-year plan, joined the fleet. Six of these were eventually built, to be followed by the larger 'Frunze' or 'Chapaev' class. Five of these were finished and gave place in the yards to the 18,000-ton 'Sverdlov' class with 6-inch guns. Twenty-four of these were planned but, as their construction coincided with the end of the Stalin era and the subsequent eruption of new thoughts on naval programmes, only 14 were completed. The last commissioned in 1956, six years before the first of the 'Kynda' class appeared.

The ships of the 'Kynda' class were apparently the first guided-missile vessels designed from scratch – the preceding

missile destroyers were conversions of earlier hull designs. Armed with two quadruple SSN-3 cruise-missile mountings and a twin SAN-1 mount on a 6,000-ton hull, they had no helicopter and a light gun armament. In 1967 the 'Kresta I' class appeared – larger at 8,000 tons, with an embarked helicopter but carrying only half the number of missiles and with smaller guns. However, she did carry two twin SAN-1 mountings for aircraft defence, and these were replaced by twin SAN-3s in the next class, 'Kresta II'. The main change in this class was in the replacement of the long range SSN-3s by two quadruple launchers for SSN-10 missiles with a 29-mile range. This evidence of new tactical thought was continued in the 'Kara' class of 10,000 tons. The first of these appeared in March 1973 with a missile armament similar to that of 'Kresta II' and with the addition of two twin SAN-14 launchers, the new 'Gatling'

*Above:* **A test-firing from one of the Soviet Navy's 80 ballistic missile-equipped submarines.**

*Left:* **A 'Krupny' class destroyer launching an SS-N-1 'Scrubber' missile, an outdated model now replaced by surface-to-air missiles.**

*Below, left:* **A decontamination monitoring of the forward 30mm gun mounting in a fast attack craft, a frequent exercise in detecting nuclear fall-out.**

anti-aircraft mounting, larger guns and an increased anti-submarine armament. This class is now (1976) in series production in addition to continued building of 'Kresta IIs'.

## Destroyer development

The considerable force of destroyers in the Tsarist navy was reduced to 15 by 1924 and by June 1941 had reached a total of only 70–80. Four years later the total, including lend/lease ships, a few captured from the Germans and the small number completed during the war, was down to 52. These were, on the whole, inefficient ships by Western standards. Their numbers were augmented by new construction, but these were also ships of prewar design.

It was not until 1949 that there appeared the first postwar destroyers, the 3,100-ton 'Skory' class, of which 70 were eventually completed. These were conventional all-gun ships, as were their successors of the 'Tallin' and 'Kotlin' classes of 1954–1955. At this point the Soviet Navy produced its first missile-armed destroyers: four 'Kotlin' hulls were converted to 'Kildins' with a single SSN-1 (130-mile) surface-to-surface missile-launcher and eight more into 'SAM Kotlins' with a twin SAN-1 surface-to-air launcher. These conversions of 1957–1962 were among the first ships so fitted, and were followed by the 4,650-ton 'Krupny' class of eight ships, the lead ship appearing in 1960. They had originally been designed as large all-gun destroyers and some underwent a further conversion in 1967–1971 when their two SSN-1 launchers were replaced by a twin SAN-1 mounting and more anti-submarine (A/S) weapons. Since then three of the remainder have been similarly changed, the whole group being known as the 'Kanin' class. The emphasis on surface-to-air missiles in destroyers was continued in the 'Kashin' class of 4,500 tons with two twin SAN-1 mountings, first seen in 1962.

These were the world's first all-gas-turbine major warships and have become a numerous and effective group. So successful have they been, in fact, that their successors, the 1971 'Krivak' class, continued this method of propulsion. The latter's armament was, however, totally different: a quadruple launcher for the new SSN-10 29-mile surface-to-surface missile and two 'pop-up' SAN-4 launchers were backed by four 76-mm guns, eight torpedo-tubes and the advantage of a variable depth sonar. The lack of a helicopter, a deficiency partially rectified in the new conversion of the 'Kashins', may need attention in the future. All-in-all, though, the Soviet destroyer force consists of powerful ships with good sea-keeping qualities and all capable of speeds of some 35 knots.

## Frigate and corvette development

In 1945 there was a motley group of escort ships available, but it was not until 1950 that the early ships of the 1,900-ton 'Kola' class appeared. This was a postwar design and was closely followed by the 'Rigas' of 1,600 tons and capable of 28 knots. Both these classes were conventional ships capable of escort duties, and the production of 'Rigas' continued until 1959. After a pause of two years came the 'Petya' class of 1,150 tons fitted with gas-turbines and diesels, an ideal combination for A/S ships. This task was further assisted by the provision of a heavier A/S armament of torpedoes and rocket-launchers, a layout continued in the succeeding 'Mirka' class. Sixty-five of these two classes were completed by 1969, a powerful group which has not been further augmented.

The corvette type was first represented by the 380-ton 'Kronstadt' class, 230 of which were built between 1948 and 1956. Smaller at 250 tons were the 'SO Is', about 100 being built between 1957 and 1961 before the gas-turbine/diesel propulsion form appeared in the 600-ton 'Poti' class. Seventy of these were followed by the im-pressive 'Nanuchka' class in 1969. Of 850 tons, their design provided a really sea-worthy hull for the very powerful armament of six 150-mile SSN-9 surface-to-surface missiles, a twin SAN-4 cylinder as well as A/S rocket launchers and a twin 57-mm gun mounting. This class is designed as part of a strike-force, while the contemporary 'Grisha' class is clearly an A/S design. Slightly smaller than 'Nanuchka', these have an A/S armament, an SSN-4 mounting (replaced by an additional twin 57-mm gun mounting in later ships) and a gas-turbine/diesel layout. Once again this group shows variety, innovation and provides a valuable force for any commander.

## Amphibious forces development

The 12,000-strong Soviet Naval Infantry was re-established in 1961–1962 and was, at that time, provided with a number of Landing Craft (Utility), only one class being of any notable size. But in 1963–1964 a pattern of new construction appeared – the 800-ton 'Polnocny' class Landing Craft (Tank) (LCT) and the 5,800-ton 'Alligator' class Landing Ship (Tank) (LST). Both have proved to be successful designs, 60 of the former and 12 of the latter now being in service. The first ships of the replacement class of LCTs, the 'Ropucha' class, have recently been completed in Poland. In considering amphibious affairs the backing available from the very large Soviet merchant navy must always be remembered, as must the increasing Soviet emphasis on hovercraft.

## Mine warfare development

Russia has always been interested in the use

*Right:* **An SA-N-3 anti-aircraft missile leaves a twin launcher.**

*Below:* **A 'Kara' class cruiser, one of the latest type of ships which are currently building. Very heavily armed with four types of missile, and powered by gas turbines**

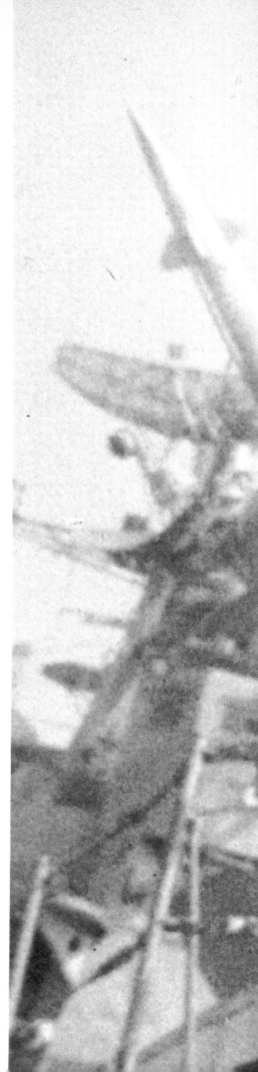

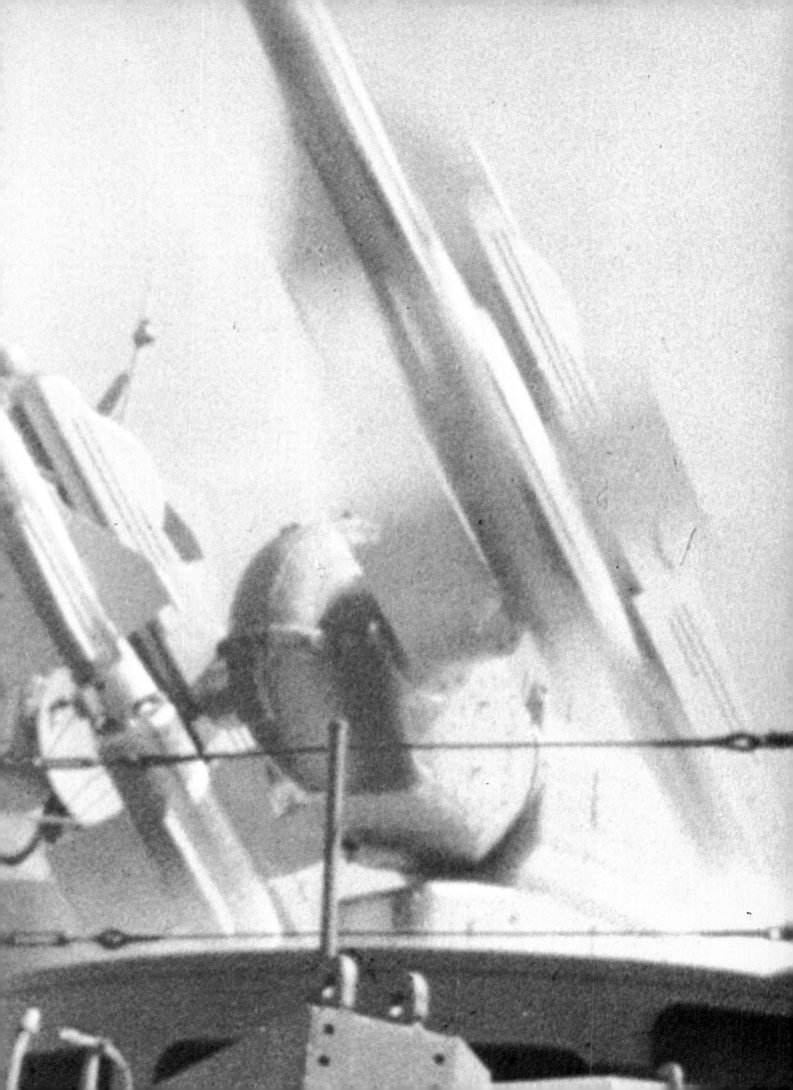

of the moored or bottom mine. All the earlier surface ships had a minelaying capability, as do all modern submarines and many aircraft. Very few specialised minelayers exist in the Soviet Navy today, but a considerable force of some 180 ocean minesweepers and 120 coastal minesweepers are kept in commission. All forms of minesweeping are available, although there is no clear sign of a minehunting capability. The forces are kept well up-to-date, the latest coastal sweepers of the 'Zhenya' and 'Sonya' classes being reported as having GRP (glass-reinforced plastic) hulls.

## Light forces development

Soviet interest in fast attack craft dates from 1927, when two coastal motor boats

*Right:* Leningrad is one of two 'Moskva' class helicopter cruisers. She carries 18 helicopters as well as a considerable armament of missiles and guns.

*Below:* 'Poti' class corvettes firing their MBU anti-submarine rockets. The Soviet Navy has 70 of these 650-ton ships in service.

*Far right:* Fast attack craft manoeuvring. Well over 300 such craft are available.

(CMBs) were bought from John I. Thorny-croft & Co Ltd. These were followed by several Italian designs, and by 1941 about 140 such craft were in commission. In the postwar years indigenous designs were used for the small 'P2' and 'P4' classes, which were followed by the 600 craft of the 'P6', '8' and '10' classes. These were 66-ton boats, with 21-inch torpedoes, some having hydrofoils, some gas-turbines. The main variant of this hull-design was the 'Komar', carrying two 'Styx' missiles. At the same time in 1960 there appeared the first of the 'Osa' class, with four 'Styx' launchers on a 200-ton hull. These craft have remained the main strike force since then, while considerable numbers of both torpedo and patrol craft, including hydrofoils, have been added to the inventory. In addition some 100 craft are employed on patrol duties on the Danube, Amur and Ussuri rivers as well as the Caspian Sea.

### Support forces

In the earlier stages of the build-up of the Soviet fleet, the main emphasis in this sphere was on depot and repair ships. Twelve classes, varying from the 7,000-ton 'Ugra' and 'Don' submarine depot ships to the 3,000-ton 'Oskol' repair ships, provide a total of 61 vessels designed for duties as diverse as submarine maintenance and the provision of missiles. The provision of afloat replenishment of both fuel and stores 20 years ago was entirely confined to tankers and store-ships taken from trade. In 1971 the first custom-built fleet replenishment ship, *Boris Chilikin*, appeared and was soon followed by two more 23,000-ton ships and one smaller edition.

### Survey, research and intelligence ships

The past 20 years have seen the growth of an enormous fleet of these various types of ships. Today 120 survey ships, 25 so-called 'Space Associated' ships, 30 major and many minor ships on research duties and 193 fishery research ships provide a vast flow of data on the world's oceans. While much of this is basic scientific information, there is little that is not to some extent of military value. The intelligence-gatherers (AGIs) have increased their numbers from four in 1963 to 54 today. Their duty is to monitor Western naval movements and exercises, an activity from which a great fund of both communications and tactical knowledge has been built up, materially assisting in the training of the Soviet Navy.

### Naval aviation

Despite a reduction from 4,000 aircraft in 1956 to 1,200 today, the Soviet naval air force is a very important part of the fleet. A considerable part of the cut resulted from the transfer of air-defence duties to the Air Force but the Soviet naval air force has retained maritime reconnaissance and strike tasks and ASW duties. These are carried out by a wide range of aircraft from the huge Tu-95 'Bear' to the 'Hormone' helicopter and include the variable-geometry 'Backfire' bomber. The operation of these aircraft worldwide has been greatly assisted by the increasing availability of foreign airfields in such places as Cuba, Guinea, Somalia and Aden. (A fuller discussion of Soviet naval aviation will be found in the

*Above left:* **A 'Foxtrot' class patrol submarine, one of the best types of diesel-propelled boats available. Armed with 21-inch torpedoes.**

*Left:* **A 'Victor' class nuclear-propelled submarine capable of over 30 knots submerged. Armed with eight 21-inch torpedo tubes.**

*Above:* **A 'Whisky' class submarine. Currently being phased out, 240 vessels of this class were built between 1951 and 1957.**

*Right:* **A fully-enclosed floating dock used for servicing submarines in the very cold conditions experienced in the Soviet Northern Fleet area.**

chapter on the Soviet Air Forces.)

## Command and control

In considering this aspect of Soviet naval affairs it must be remembered that these are far more interwoven with the political organisation than in any Western navy. This is true at all levels from the Central Committee and the Defence Ministry down to the political officer in an individual ship. Partly as a result of this there is far more centralised control of fleets and ships than in the West. The C-in-C of the Navy exercises this control on the instructions of the Central Committee, with the assistance of six deputies and a large naval staff, the whole being under the eye of the General Staff. His is an organisation which is reflected in the various fleet commands. These, the Northern, Baltic, Black Sea and Pacific Fleets, are each controlled by staffs of a similar pattern to that found in Moscow. Autonomy is not a word welcome in the Soviet Union except at the most senior levels, and this is the second fact to be remembered in considering the operations of the Soviet Navy.

## Entry and training

With a little under 500,000 people involved, the Soviet Navy has an enormous training task. In a fleet manned entirely by conscripted junior ratings, a great weight of responsibility rests on the officers and senior rates. Both are drawn from volunteers and the first receive a highly technical training in one of 11 establishments. During this period they are given an efficient indoctrination, both professional and political, into their future life. Some of this time is now spent at sea and when they receive their first appointments they may expect a long period in the same ship, sometimes moving from a junior position to command. This, in a number of cases, is achieved at an early age,

although the more sensitive ships and submarines are reserved for the very senior.

The reason that so much depends on the officers is that the ratings are conscripted at 18 and after six months training serve for $2\frac{1}{2}$ years with the fleet. At 21 they may have become petty officers and, at this age and if they volunteer, will be signed on as chief petty officers. As they lack experience it is not surprising that they rely largely on their seniors for direction. The biannual intake of junior ratings, earning some £50 per year, is 60,000 and this means a continual state of flux in all ships, a situation which is not conducive to efficiency.

**Bases and shipbuilding**
Each of the four fleets has a main shore-base – the Northern Fleet at Severomorsk, the Baltic at Baltiysk, the Black Sea at Sevastopol and the Pacific at Vladivostok. All four fleets have large local exercise areas and when their ships are deployed beyond these wide boundaries they are described as 'out-of-area'. However, within the local commands a number of minor bases provide support and repair services for the ships of their fleet. There are also numerous commercial ports which have naval facilities.

In some cases these bases coincide with the areas where naval ship-building takes place. In the west these ports suffered great damage in both world wars but all were brought rapidly back to full production. The north, virtually unharried in the past, has a major submarine yard at Severodvinsk, there are five yards in the Leningrad area

and four smaller yards on the Baltic. While major submarine building takes place at Gorkiy on the Volga, the main big-ship building base is at Nikolayev close to the Black Sea. In the east the yards at Komsomolsk and Khabarovsk on the Amur river produce destroyers and submarines, and there are other fitting-out yards in the area. With nearly 20 yards available for naval construction the Soviets thus have a very major capability in this field.

**Deployment**
Admiral Gorshkov has shown very clearly that he understands the mission of the Soviet Navy abroad. While claiming in 1967 that his fleet was fully capable of offensive operations, he has recently stated that 'The Soviet Navy is a powerful factor in the creation of favourable conditions for the building of Socialism and Communism, for the active defence of peace and for strengthening international security.' With the worldwide deployments that have become the standard method of operation of the Soviet Navy, this statement can only be construed as an intention to use that fleet for political purposes.

With this in mind it is interesting to observe the areas to which these ships have been despatched since 10 years ago. At this time the first signs of a permanent Soviet presence in the Mediterranean were seen, a presence which was rapidly reinforced to a total of some 100 ships during the Arab–Israeli war of 1973, when these could have inhibited any action by the US 6th Fleet in that area.

This is possibly the best-known area of Soviet naval expansion but is by no means the only one needing consideration. In the Caribbean, the scene of Soviet humiliation off Cuba in 1962, their survey ships continue to operate and a large fishery base has been built at Havana. By 1969 confidence had been restored sufficiently for a Soviet naval squadron to visit the area. Since then frequent similar visits have taken place and 'Bear' reconnaissance aircraft are now welcome in that island.

Similar facilities exist in Conakry, the capital of Guinea in West Africa, where Soviet ships responded rapidly to President Sekou Touré's call for help after an abortive invasion. Further east, fishing interest in Somalia has been built up until it has yielded a missile support base at Berbera. This, with facilities at Aden and Hodeida, provides the Soviet squadron, which has been in the Indian Ocean since 1968, with valuable base support as well as a forward airfield for both reconnaissance and strike aircraft of the Soviet naval air force.

As Soviet interest in Mauritius, Vietnam, Mozambique and Angola continues, their ships are ever-present in a worldwide deployment impossible only 10 years ago.

**The future**
Once its new aircraft-carriers are in commission, the Soviet Navy will have a well-balanced fleet deficient only in embarked high-performance aircraft. The numbers of ships in the fleet are clearly limited by the manpower available and, although this is a variable governed by the Central Com-

*Far left:* **A Soviet naval conscript, entered for three years service at the age of 18. Conscription is probably the weakest link in the Soviet fleet organisation.**

*Above:* **An artist's impression of the 'Kiev' class aircraft carrier, the first of which started trials in 1975. Other carriers are under construction at Nikolayev.**

*Left:* **Admiral of the Fleet Sergei Gorshkov, C in C of the Soviet Navy since January 1956 and architect of its present strength and deployment.**

mittee, it has possibly now reached a level unlikely to be exceeded in the near future. While the ships themselves possess increasingly efficient weapons and are capable of worldwide operations, there are many other factors which must be considered in assessing a country's capability at sea. Chief of these is training and the capability of those who man the ship. Present indications are that the officer corps of the Soviet Navy is both self-reliant and efficient despite centralised control. The same is not true of the junior conscripted ratings, and these must remain the weakest link, as will always be true under such a system. But it is wrong either to over- or under-estimate this navy. It is perfectly capable of remaining an efficient political weapon for many years to come, although its capabilities in drawn-out hostilities might be questionable.

# Soviet Warships

**Bill Gunston**

## Kiev class V/STOL cruisers

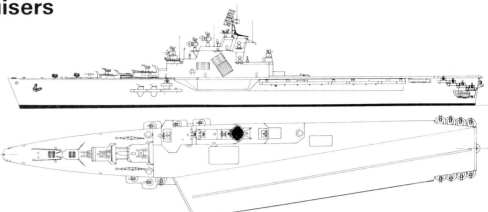

**Displacement:** About 40,000 tons (45,000 full load)
**Dimensions:** Estimated length overall 920ft (280m), deck width overall about 200ft (61m); beam 92ft (28m).
**Aircraft:** Estimated 35, mix of jet V/STOLs and helicopters. Another estimate suggests 35 of each type simultaneously.
**Armament:** Two twin SA-N-3 installations; 1 un-identified twin missile launcher; 14 twin 57mm dual-purpose guns; two 12-barrel MBU (AS rocket) launchers.
**Propulsion:** Believed mainly gas turbines, speed at least 30kt.

Easily the biggest warship ever built in the Soviet Union, Kiev was built in 1968–73, spent 1973–75 fitting out at the Nikolayev yard and in late 1975 was working up in the Black Sea. Before this volume appears she may be in the Mediterranean. Like all modern Soviet warships she is extremely bold, modern, ingenious and formidable. Her fore part is a missile cruiser packed with AA and AS (anti-submarine) weapons; her stern is a simple V/STOL carrier with angled deck for V/STOL aircraft and AS helicopters (initially Mi-8 or Ka-25). Extremely versatile, the Kiev class are expected eventually to number up to 20. Two more were under construction at Nikolayev in 1976. In contrast, the US Navy has delayed its Sea Control Ships and the Royal Navy Harrier Carrier remains a paper project.

## Moskva, Leningrad helicopter cruisers

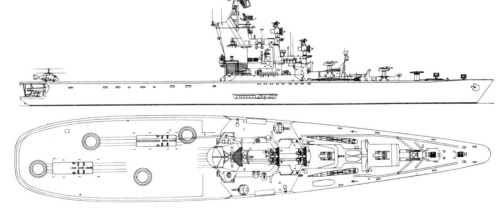

**Displacement:** 15,000 tons (18,000 full load)
**Dimensions:** Length overall 645ft (197m); deck width overall 115ft (35m); beam 76ft (23m); draught 25ft (7·6m).
**Aircraft:** Typically 18 Ka-25/Mi-8 helicopters.
**Armament:** Two twin SA-N-3 installations; 1 un-identified twin launcher; two twin 57mm dual-purpose guns; two 12-barrel MBU (AS rocket) launchers; two quintuple 21in (533mm) torpedo tubes.
**Propulsion:** Steam turbines, 50,000shp on each of two shafts, 30kt.

When the Moskva appeared in 1967 it took some time to be assessed by the West, because a vessel that was half a cruiser, bristling with electronics and weapons, and half an operating platform for helicopters, was then quite novel. Now it is concluded that these ships were the Soviet Union's answer to the Polaris submarines. With their ability rapidly to deploy more than a dozen potent ASW helicopters over a wide area, they would have been formidable to the submarines armed with Polaris A-1, but less effective against Polaris A-3 and Poseidon carriers. The second of these 'helicopter cruisers' was finished in 1969, and no more were built their place in the vast Nikolayev yards being taken by the much bigger Kiev class. They operate in the Atlantic, Mediterranean, Red Sea and Barents Sea. In 1974 Leningrad used Mi-8 helicopters to help sweep the Suez canal free from mines, but their main complement is of the Ka-25 type.

# Echo II class missile submarines

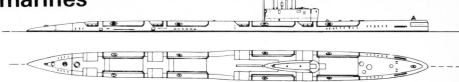

**Displacement:** 5,600 tons (Echo I, about 5,000 tons) submerged; 5,000 surface (Echo I, 4,600).
**Dimensions:** Length overall 388ft (118m) (Echo I, 381ft, 116m); beam 28ft 5in (8·6m); draught 26ft (7·9m).
**Armament:** Eight launch tubes for SS-N-3 cruise missiles (Echo I, only six); six 21in (533mm) torpedo tubes in bow, four 16in (406mm) AS tubes in stern.
**Propulsion:** Nuclear (pressurized water reactor); twin steam turbines, total 22,500shp, two shafts each with 11,250shp steam turbine, submerged speed 20kt.

These large and probably formidable vessels have for many years formed an important part of the Soviet Navy's offensive firepower at sea. Forming a natural follow-on to the Juliet class, they have bigger hulls generally similar to those of the November class, and doubtless powered by the same nuclear installation (the first to be developed in the Soviet Union). The first three were equipped with three pairs of N-3 launch tubes. Then the decision was taken to lengthen the hull and incorporate a fourth pair, resulting in the impressive E-II class. The first of these appeared in 1962 or 1963, and the considerable total of 27 was built by 1967. The Echo II class have since been seen in many parts of the world, operating with both the Northern and Pacific fleets. They still constitute a great threat to Allied surface ships of all kinds.

# Golf class missile submarines

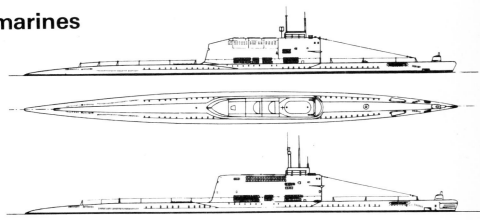

**Displacement:** 2,800 tons submerged; 2,350 surface.
**Dimensions:** Length overall 320ft (97·5m); beam 25ft (7·6m); draught 22ft (6·7m).
**Armament:** Three launch installations for ballistic missiles, with vertical expulsion tubes in line extending from keel to top of conning tower (see text for missile types); in bows, ten 21in (533mm) torpedo tubes.
**Propulsion:** Diesel-electric, with 2,000shp electric motor on each of three shafts, submerged speed about 17kt.

The first Soviet ballistic-missile submarines were the seven of the Zulu class converted to launch the SS-N-4 missile in 1955–57. These boats, called Zulu V class, were rebuilt with enormous conning towers incorporating launch tubes for two missiles, and though not a very cost/effective or attractive solution did at least get ballistic missiles to sea at an early date and enable operational experience to be acquired. By 1957 work had begun on the Golf class, for fully operational deployment. Rather larger than the ZV, they went to sea with three tubes for the N-4 missile. No fewer than 22 were built, all being at sea by 1962. Quite late, from 1967, all 22 were converted to launch the N-5 missile. These submarines were judged likely to be withdrawn from operational duty in 1976–78.

# Juliet class missile submarines

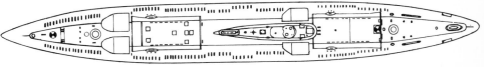

**Displacement:** 2,500 tons; 2,200 surface.
**Dimensions:** Length overall 281ft (85·5m); beam 31ft 5in (9·5m); draught 20ft (6m).
**Armament:** Four launch tubes for SS-N-3 cruise missiles; six 21in (533mm) torpedo tubes in bow, two or four 16in (406mm) AS tubes in stern.
**Propulsion:** Diesel-electric; three shafts, each with 2,000shp, speed about 16kt surface or submerged.

Though representing a tremendous advance over the crude missile conversions of the Whisky class, the excellent Juliets were in turn overtaken by the bigger and heavier-armed Echo series. Nevertheless they are nimble and much cheaper than an Echo, and 16 were commissioned in 1962–66. They are well equipped with sonar and communications, and have proved very successful. They are essentially Foxtrots with enlarged hulls equipped with the hydraulically elevated missile tubes. The latter were derived from the crude system proved on Whisky class vessels. Normally stowed horizontally, flush with the tall deck casing, they are elevated to a firing angle of just under 20°. Many submarines of this class, nearly all having small individual differences in equipment, have been seen in the Mediterranean and Atlantic.

# Victor class submarines

**Displacement:** 4,200 tons submerged; 3,600 surface.
**Dimensions:** Length overall 285ft 5in (87m); beam 32ft 10in (10m); draught 26ft 3in (8m).
**Armament:** Eight 21in (533mm) torpedo tubes.
**Propulsion:** Nuclear (pressurized water reactor); single shaft with 24,000shp, submerged speed about 33 knots.

This class is the one significant exception, and carries only the submarine's traditional armament of anti-ship torpedoes. Thus, the Victors are attack submarines, and they are extremely fast and dangerous craft, able to sink virtually any kind of surface vessel. They carry the latest and most lethal Soviet torpedoes, which are continually being updated and improved and appear to have overtaken even the latest Freedom, Tigerfish and Alcatel torpedoes used in the West. Victors have fat, streamlined hulls, but retain a traditional upper deck casing with free flood holes (which make them noisier to underwater sonics sensors than corresponding Western boats). About 20 were in use by early 1976, on patrol in all parts of the world.

# Zulu class submarines

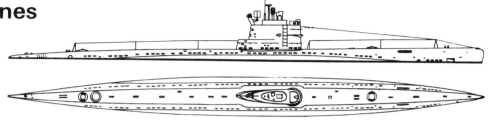

**Displacement:** 2,200 tons submerged; 1,900 surface.
**Dimensions:** Length overall 295ft 4in (90m); beam 23ft 10in (7.3m); draught 19ft (5.8m).
**Armament:** Originally built with ten 21in (533mm) torpedo tubes (six bow, four stern); some converted to other weapons.
**Propulsion:** Three diesels, with total output 10,000shp; three electric motors with total output 3,500hp; speed 18kt on surface, 15kt submerged.

Considerably larger than the Whisky class, these long-range patrol submarines were likewise designed (possibly with the help of German engineers) immediately after World War II to incorporate all the lessons that could be learned from the German Type XXI. They were larger than the famed German boat, enabling radius of action to be extended to about 25,000 miles, despite having the large complement of six officers and 64 ratings and room for 24 torpedoes or ten torpedoes and 40 mines. About 35 were built in 1951–55. At least seven were converted in 1955–57 to carry and fire three SS-N-4 ballistic missiles (Zulu V class). The rest have been modified in various ways, and those remaining are mostly described as Zulu IV boats, with extended conning towers.

# Whisky class submarines

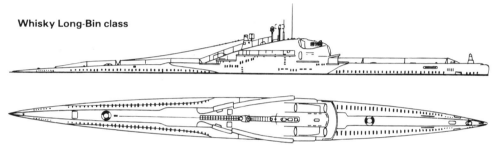

**Displacement:** Typically, 1,180/1,200 tons submerged; 1,030 tons surface.
**Dimensions:** Length overall 240ft (73·2m); beam 22ft (6·7m); draught 15ft (4·6m).
**Armament:** As originally built, six 21in (533mm) torpedo tubes in the bow, with 18 torpedoes (or 40 mines in lieu of all torpedoes).
**Propulsion:** Two 2,000hp diesels and two 1,250hp electric motors on two shafts; speed 17kt on surface, 15kt submerged.

**Whisky class**

**Whisky Long-Bin class**

Designed shortly after World War II to incorporate the full technology developed with the German Type XXI U-boats, this medium-range patrol class was put into volume production on a scale never before seen in peacetime and seldom equalled in war. About 40 were delivered each year from 1951, and the final total was between 240 and 276. They were efficient and useful boats, and were at one time seen over huge stretches of ocean. From 1955 many were converted to serve as radar-equipped aircraft direction ships and early-warning pickets (Whisky Canvas Bag), as experimental carriers of the then-new SS-N-3 missile (W-Twin-Cylinder) or as operational carriers with four N-3 launch tubes (W-Long Bin, with greater length and 1,800 ton displacement). Today only a few of this vast class remain, though large numbers serve with other navies.

*Below:* **Whisky class submarine in the English Channel in 1975.**
*Bottom:* **Whisky-Long-Bin entering port**

# Delta class missile submarines

**Displacement:** About 10,000 tons submerged; 8,400 surface. (Delta II, about 16,000 tons).
**Dimensions:** Length overall 427ft (130m); beam 35ft (10·7m); draught 33ft (10·2m).
**Armament:** Twelve missile launch systems for SS-N-8, with vertical expulsion tubes each about 48ft long and faired into hull by large casing aft of conning-tower sail; believed to be eight 21 in torpedo tubes in bow. Delta II, sixteen missiles.
**Propulsion:** Nuclear (pressurized-water reactor), about 24,000shp, submerged speed about 25kt.

Largest submarines in service in the world, the for-midable Delta class (the name is simply a NATO code, in the absence of a known Soviet designation) have been in quantity production since 1971. Though only one delivery system for Soviet strategic thermonuclear warheads, they already outstrip in number the strategic missile forces of the Western nations, and continue in production at the rate of about seven per year. All these monster ships are being built at the vast complex at Severodvinsk, which has a greater construction potential than all the submarine yards in the USA combined. The Deltas are in most respects the most potent warships ever operated, with missiles having a range of 4,200 nautical miles (4,830 miles). As this book went to press the Soviet Union had about 875 ballistic missiles at sea.

# Yankee class missile submarines

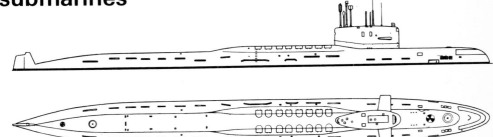

**Displacement:** About 9,000 tons submerged; 8,200 surface.
**Dimensions:** Length overall 427ft (130m); beam 35ft (10·7m); draught 32ft (9·75m).
**Armament:** Sixteen missile launch systems for SS-N-6, with vertical expulsion tubes extending just above the circular hull and faired inside a flat-topped upper deck. In the bows, eight 21in (533mm) torpedo tubes.
**Propulsion:** Nuclear (pressurized-water reactor), about 24,000shp, submerged speed about 27kt.

With a general arrangement identical to that of the US Polaris submarines, the Yankee class were designed in the early 1960s, put into high-rate production and first reported by the Western nations in 1968. Four boats were delivered in that year, and output then climbed to eight in 1971, the final total being 32, reached in 1973. Far more formidable than the earlier Golf and Hotel classes, the Yankee was deficient only in its missiles, which were still somewhat large in bulk and short in range compared with the US counterparts. Thus, on their first deployment the Yankees had to stand close in to the US coast to get coverage over most of the United States, and there was still a band between the Rockies and Mississippi that could not be reached. Later the N-6 missiles were updated, and today they may be being progressively replaced by the much more formidable N-8.

# Hotel class missile submarines

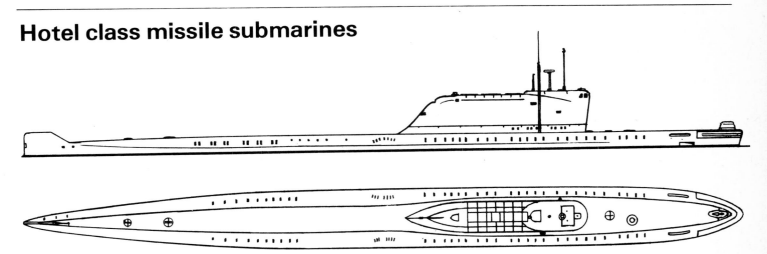

**Displacement:** 4,100 tons submerged; 3,700 surface.
**Dimensions:** Length overall 377ft (115m); beam 28ft (8·6m); draught 25ft (7·6m).
**Armament:** Three missile launch systems for SS-N-5, with the vertical expulsion tubes extending from the keel to near the top of the conning tower. In the bow, six 21in (533mm) torpedo tubes; in the stern, four 16in (406mm) anti-submarine torpedo tubes.
**Propulsion:** Nuclear (pressurized water reactor); two shafts each with 11,250shp steam turbines, submerged speed about 24kt.

The Soviet wish to pour out armaments, regardless of cost, is well illustrated by this class, built in 1958–62. By the time the first was on the slipway it was known to be obsolete, yet nine were subsequently commissioned, at the maximum output rate. Originally fitted with the N-4 missile, they were only marginally useful vessels, though retaining full torpedo armament and capable of secondary employment in the attack role. From 1963 all nine Hotel submarines were converted to launch the N-5 missile, and subsequently spent almost their whole operational career off the coasts of North America (including northern Canada). By 1980 these costly and not especially effective vessels are expected to be transferred to reserve status.

# November class submarines

**Displacement:** About 4,000 tons submerged; 3,500 surface.
**Dimensions:** Length overall 361ft (110m); beam 32ft 1in (9·8m); draught 24ft 4in (7·4m).
**Armament:** Bow, six 21in (533mm) torpedo tubes; stern, four 16in (406mm) anti-submarine torpedo tubes.
**Propulsion:** Nuclear (pressurized water reactor); twin steam turbines, 11,250shp on each of two shafts, submerged speed about 25kt.

These large and generally conservatively designed boats

were the first Soviet submarines to have nuclear propulsion. To a considerable degree the technology was based upon intelligence information from the United States in 1955, though at that time the Soviet Union had not appreciated the advantages of the streamlined 'spindle' hull first seen in the US Navy Albacore. Accordingly the Novembers were given long conventional hulls with two screws. By 1963 a total of

13 had been commissioned, despite the fact that they had long since been overtaken by later technology, showing yet again how indifferent the Soviet Union is to heavy arms expenditure. In any case, anti-ship Attack and Fleet submarines never had the same priority as the purely offensive missile submarines, once the latter had been brought to the operational stage in the late 1950s.

# Foxtrot class submarines

**Displacement:** 2,300 tons submerged; 2,000 surface.
**Dimensions:** Length overall 297ft (90·5m); beam 24ft 1in (7·3m); draught 19ft (5·8m).
**Armament:** Bow, six 21in (533mm) torpedo tubes; stern four 21in (533mm) tubes.
**Propulsion:** Diesel-electric; three shafts, each with 2,000hp set, speed about 20kt surface and 15kt submerged.

Though they are only patrol submarines, with traditional diesel-electric propulsion and torpedo armament, the Foxtrots have been built in greater numbers than any other single class of submarine in the world since

the preceding Soviet patrol class known to the West as Whisky vessels. The first Foxtrots appeared about 1958, and they stayed in production at the rate of seven a year for eight years, a total of 56, all delivered from the long-established yards of Sudomekh and at Leningrad. Though bigger than the Zulu class, and

with less-powerful diesels, they actually have marginally better performance. By all accounts the Foxtrots have been extremely successful, and they have been frequently encountered by Western patrol aircraft all over the world. Since 1968 many units of this class have been sold or given to other countries.

# Romeo class submarines

**Displacement:** 1,600 tons submerged; 1,100 tons surface.
**Dimensions:** Length overall 246ft (75m); beam 24ft (7·3m); draught 14ft 6in (4·4m).
**Armament:** Six 21in (533mm) torpedo tubes (bow).
**Propulsion:** Diesel-electric; two shafts, each with 2,000 hp set; speed about 17kt on surface, 14kt submerged.

These patrol submarines were a direct development of the mass-produced Whisky class, rather more than 20 being built between 1958 and 1960. It is especially significant that they were built as new submarines, at a time when over 200 Whiskys were available for

modernization. They have hulls slightly longer and with fractionally greater beam than the Whisky class, improved electric propulsion, new conning towers, and — most important of all — a much later and more comprehensive suite of sonar sensor and communications equipment. They are medium-range

vessels, which tend to stay relatively close to Soviet shores (though similar submarines are in production in China, and six were sold or given to the Egyptian Navy in 1966). It is expected that the Romeo class will be withdrawn from front-line duty by 1980, thereafter being used mainly for training and research.

# Quebec class submarines

**Displacement:** 740 tons submerged; 650 surface.
**Dimensions:** Length overall 185ft (56·4m); beam 18ft (5·5m); draught 13ft 3in (4·0m).
**Armament:** Four 21in (533mm) torpedo tubes, in bow.
**Propulsion:** One 3,000shp diesel; three shafts each with 800/900hp electric motor, speed about 18kt on surface, 16kt submerged.

These are the only small submarines built in the Soviet Union since World War II (denoting a sharp contrast with the pre-war policy, when coastal short-range types strongly predominated). About 25 were built

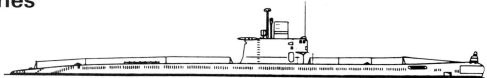

in the early 1950s, one batch believed to number 13 having been delivered in 1955 from the Sudomekh yard at Leningrad. They are believed to have been efficient and successful craft, and some are still in operational service. Probably the chief reason for their relatively small number is their limited cruising range of about 7,000 miles, which severely hampers their

deployment in the context of the vast size of the Soviet Union and its growing interest in dominating all parts of the world. One of their attractive features was that they could be built at dispersed plants and transported in prefabricated sections to a final assembly yard, which is no longer possible with the much larger submarines of today.

# Charlie class cruise-missile submarines

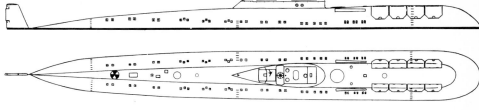

**Displacement:** 4,300 tons (surface), 5,100 tons (submerged).
**Dimensions:** Length overall 295ft 7in (90m); beam 32ft 10in (10m); draught 24ft 7in (7.5m).
**Armament:** eight tubes for launching SS-N-7 missiles (see comments below); eight 533mm (21in) torpedo tubes.
**Propulsion:** Nuclear reactor, steam turbine of about 24,000shp, single screw at tip of hull; submerged speed 33 knots.

First seen in 1968, this class of submarine is still something of an enigma. The basic vessel is fast and streamlined, having a fat spindle-type hull with the most powerful (second-generation) Soviet naval reactor installation. The conning tower is squat and well profiled, and altogether these vessels probably have the highest performance of any Soviet submarines (though their free-flood holes under the separate deck casing make them noisier than Western boats). They have become common in the Mediterranean and in many other areas, though their modest production rate of about three per year means that the total number is still only about 20. The puzzle concerns their armament. They appear to have a deck installation for a new type of cruise missile, appreciably smaller than the N-3 but similar in concept. Called N-7 by NATO, these missiles are thought to have a range of 56km (30 miles) and to be capable of being fired from below the surface. Little is known of N-7/'Charlie' fire control and guidance.

# Sverdlov class cruisers

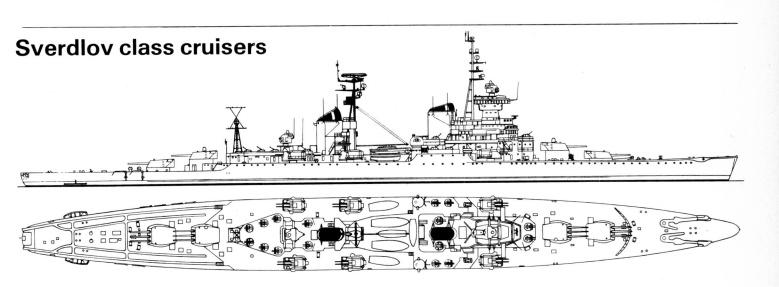

**Displacement:** As built, about 19,200 tons (full load); as converted, usually fractionally less.
**Dimensions:** Length overall 689ft (210m); beam 72ft 3in (22m); draught 24ft 6in (7·5m).
**Armament:** See text.
**Propulsion:** Geared steam turbines with 130,000shp on two shafts, maximum speed 34kt.

During World War II these fine cruisers were designed to have four triple 6in gun turrets and dozens of smaller dual-purpose guns, plus two quintuple 21in (533mm) torpedo tubes. A class of 24 was planned, 20 keels were laid, 17 hulls launched and, by 1956, 14 cruisers commissioned. About five have now been passed to other navies or placed in reserve, and the remainder have been rebuilt in contrasting ways. The first four conversions, in 1969–71, were of Dzerzhinski, Admiral Senyavin, Mikhail Kutuzov and Zhdanov. In general, the rebuild programmes have involved reduction in the number of 6in turrets, addition of a vast amount of radar and electronics, surface-to-air and other missile systems, helicopters (with pads and hangars) and other equipment of which some is still not identified. Torpedo tubes are being removed, but minelaying installations usually remain. Some of these large cruisers are serving as strategic command ships (including Zhdanov and Senyavin), with communications, radars, displays, computers and other installations to direct the whole operations in a theatre.

# Kara class cruisers

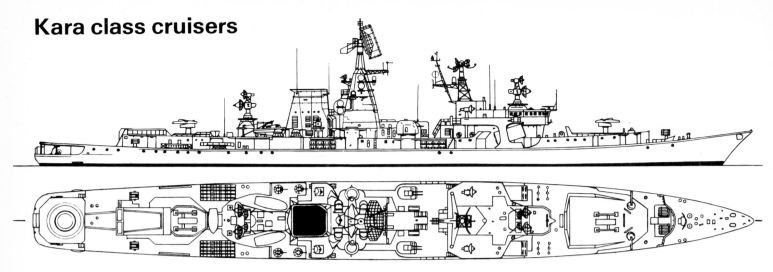

**Displacement:** About 9,000 tons (10,000 full load).
**Dimensions:** Length overall, about 560ft (171m); beam 62ft (19m); draught 20ft (6·2m).
**Armament:** Bombardment missiles, two quadruple launcher boxes for SS-N-10 (each side of bridge); surface-to-air missiles, two twin launch installations for SA-N-3 (fore and aft) and two retractable silo installations of SA-N-4 (each side of mainmast); AS weapons, two 16-barrel MBU launchers (foredeck) and two 6-barrel MBU launchers (aft); guns, two twin 3in (76mm) each side between bridge and mast, four twin 30mm abeam funnel; torpedoes, two sets quintuple 533mm tubes each side between funnel and hangar.
**Propulsion:** Eight sets gas turbines, probably two shafts, maximum speed about 34kt.

When the lead-ship of this class, Nikolayev, steamed into the Mediterranean on 2 March 1973 she cast yet a further mantle of gloom over naval defence observers in the West. She was like previous Soviet cruisers only more so'. In other words she fairly bristled with an array of weapons and electronics that no ship in any Western navy can even remotely begin to match. On top of this, she has proved to be a good sea-boat, with excellent reliability and fine all-round performance. Compared with immediate predecessors, such as the Kresta II ships, the Kara class escape from squeezing too many quarts into a pint pot. Their hulls are larger, the propulsion system more compact and their interior design apparently outstanding. On the small fantail at the stern is a platform for a Ka-25 'Hormone A' helicopter for AS use. Below the platform is a variable-depth sonar (VDS), and all-round AS capability of these big cruisers is formidable. So also is their missile/gun AA firepower. Deficiencies are conspicuously absent.

# Kresta I class cruisers

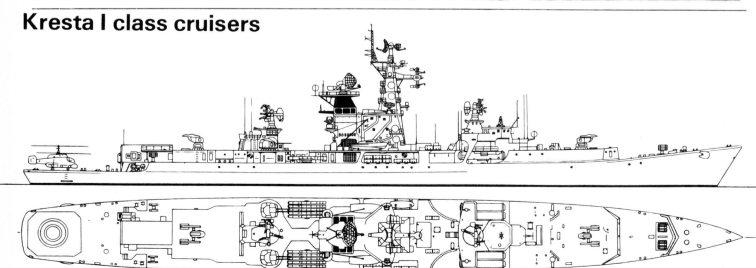

**Displacement:** 5,140 tons (6,500 full load).
**Dimensions:** Length overall 510ft (155·5m); beam 55ft (16·8m); draught 18ft 8in (5·7m).

**Armament:** Bombardment missiles, two twin launchers for SS-N-3 abeam of bridge; surface-to-air missiles, two twin installations for SA-N-1 ahead of bridge and ahead of hangar (B and X positions); AS weapons, two 12-barrel MBU launchers (foredeck) and two 6-barrel MBU launchers (each side of hangar); guns, two pairs 57mm (abeam rear radar tower); torpedoes, two sets quintuple 21in (533mm) aft of funnel

**Propulsion:** Two sets steam turbines, 100,000shp, maximum speed 34kt.
Though overtaken by swiftly galloping technology, these four ships marked the turning point in Soviet naval construction, together with the contemporary Kashin class. Prior to 1960 Soviet surface vessels were not exceptional; afterwards, largely through the forceful direction of Admiral Gorshkov, they became the fear and envy of other navies. The Kresta class set designers and constructors firmly on the road towards packing incredible arrays of weapons and electronics into modest hulls. The drawing on p. 135 underlines the visible and identified equipment installed in the K-I class, and additional items are still appearing each time these far-ranging ships are seen in Western waters. They are unusual in carrying the Ka-25 helicopter in its 'Hormone B' form for over-the-horizon targeting of the N-3 long-range missiles. These were the last surface ships to carry the N-3 missile, which was superseded by the smaller, multiple-reload N-10. It was the need to provide for over-the-horizon target guidance for N-3 that led to the K-I class carrying a helicopter, for the first time in a Soviet warship.

# Kresta II class cruisers

An annotated photograph of this class appears on page 114.

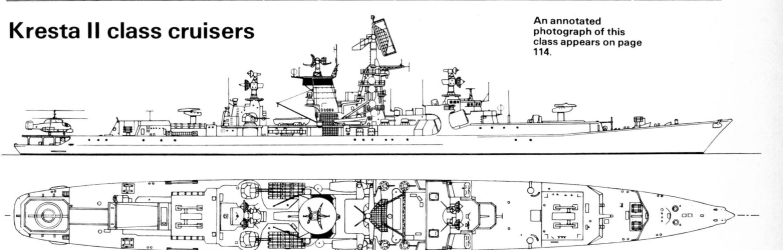

**Displacement:** About 6,000 tons (7,500 full load).
**Dimensions:** Length overall 520ft (158m); beam 55ft (16·8m); draught 18ft 8in (5·7m).
**Armament:** Bombardment missiles, two quadruple launchers for SS-N-10 abeam of bridge; surface-to-air missiles, twin installation for SA-N-3 ahead of bridge and ahead of hangar (the traditional B and X positions); AS weapons, two 12-barrel MBU launchers (foredeck) and two 6-barrel MBU launchers (aft); guns, two pairs 57mm (each side of 'mainmast', rear radar tower), four pairs 30mm (abeam 'foremast', main radar tower); torpedoes, two sets quintuple 21in (533mm) tubes aft of funnel.
**Propulsion:** Two sets steam turbines, 100,000shp, maximum speed about 34 knots.

With these ships the Soviet naval designers went considerably further than in the Kresta I class and demonstrated their amazing ability to fit the weapons and electronics of the largest modern 'capital ship' into a hull not much bigger than a destroyer. Put another way, there are many Western naval vessels of similar size, but all have a much smaller range of weapons and electronics. Especial emphasis must be laid on the electronics, because radar, ECM and communications are the most vital installations in any combat platform and the Soviet Union has leapt in a decade from inferiority to superiority in such matters. The K-II ships positively bristle with a wealth of installations indicative of the most lavish funding, and they are extremely formidable in a wide range of roles. They remain in production alongside the Karas.

# Krivak class destroyers

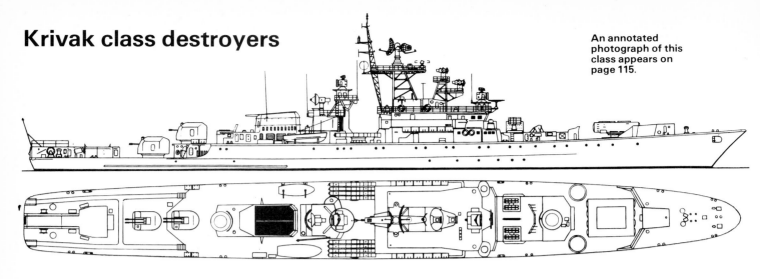

An annotated photograph of this class appears on page 115.

**Displacement:** 3,800 tons (4,200 full load).
**Dimensions:** Length overall 405ft (123·4m); beam 46ft (14m); draught 16ft 5in (5m).
**Armament:** Bombardment missiles, quadruple launch tubes for SS-N-10 on foredeck; surface-to-air missiles, two silos for SA-N-4 (one abaft N-10 launch tubes, the other between funnel and guns); AS weapons, two 12-barrel MBU launchers (forward of bridge); guns, two twin 76mm (aft, in X and Y positions), two twin 30mm (each side abeam bridge);

torpedoes, two quadruple sets of 21in (533mm) tubes amidships.
**Propulsion:** Eight sets of gas turbines, total 112,000shp on two shafts, maximum speed 38kt.

These splendid ships perfectly typify the modern Soviet philosophy with surface ships: big on weapons, electronics and power, small on hull. Though classed as destroyers, they pack a bigger punch than almost any Western cruiser, and as well as four multi-reload

bombardment missiles have very considerable gun power, SAM capability and outstanding AS effectiveness with VDS (variable-depth sonar) and a large hull-mounted sonar. The Krivaks were among the first ships to appear with the SA-N-4 missile. Not least of their capabilities is unsurpassed speed, plus good seakeeping. There are at least six with the Baltic Fleet, two with the Black Sea Fleet and one with the Northern Fleet.

# Kynda class cruisers

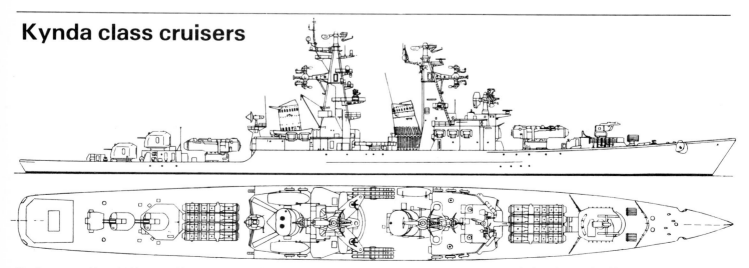

**Displacement:** About 4,500 tons (6,000 full load).
**Dimensions:** Length overall 465ft 9in (142m);

beam 51ft 10in (15·8m); draught 17ft 5in (5·3m).
**Armament:** Bombardment missiles, two sets quad-

ruple launch tubes for SS-N-3 (ahead of bridge and ahead of gun turrets); surface-to-air missiles, twin

installation for SA-N-1 on foredeck; AS weapons, two 12-barrel MBU launchers on foredeck ahead of SA-N-1 launcher; guns, two twin 76mm turrets (at rear, in X, Y positions); torpedoes, two triple 21in (533mm) tubes abaft forefunnel.
**Propulsion:** Two sets steam turbines, 100,000shp, maximum speed 35kt.

These were the last 'traditional' cruisers built in the Soviet Union; even so, they were redesigned while under construction to carry fewer guns and instead have the huge launch tubes for the N-3 missile. Associated with these long-range weapons are the prominent 'Scoop Pair' search/guidance radars, on the foremast and mainmast. These, however, cannot

see beyond the radar horizon, and so to use N-missiles at extreme range the Kynda cruisers have to operate in partnership with friendly aircraft, such as the missile-guidance versions of the Tu-95 called 'Bear D'. The next cruiser design, the Kresta I, carried a helicopter for this purpose.

# Kashin class destroyers

Beginning with the Ognevoi and Sdergyannyi, Kashins are being refitted with four SS-N-11 SSM boxes and four 30mm turrets, as shown in this drawing.

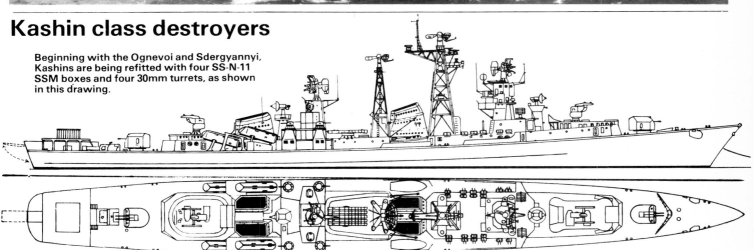

**Displacement:** 4,300 tons (5,200 full load).
**Dimensions:** Length overall 471ft (143m); beam 52ft 6in (15·9m); draught 19ft (5·8m).
**Armament:** Surface-to-air missiles, two twin installations for SA-N-1 on upper deck at front and rear (B and X positions); AS weapons, two 12-barrel MBU launchers (high in front of bridge), two 6-barrel MBU launchers aft; guns, two twin 76mm (fore and aft, in A and Y positions); torpedoes, single set of

quintuple 21in (533mm) torpedo tubes amidships (on centreline). (See caption above.)
**Propulsion:** Eight sets of gas turbines, 96,000shp on two shafts, maximum speed 35kt.

When the Kashins appeared in 1962 they were dramatically new and impressive; in particular, they were the first large warships in the world to be powered solely by gas turbines. It is eloquent testi-

mony to the awesome pace of Soviet warship development that within ten years these important ships have been rendered obsolescent. Probably the whole class (believed to number 19) are now being refitted with later SAM installations, long-range SSMs, a helicopter, VDS and even more elaborate electronics. A major refit would group the eight exhaust trunks into a single stack, as in the Krivak and Kara class ships, instead of four stacks arranged in inclined pairs.

# Krupny class destroyers

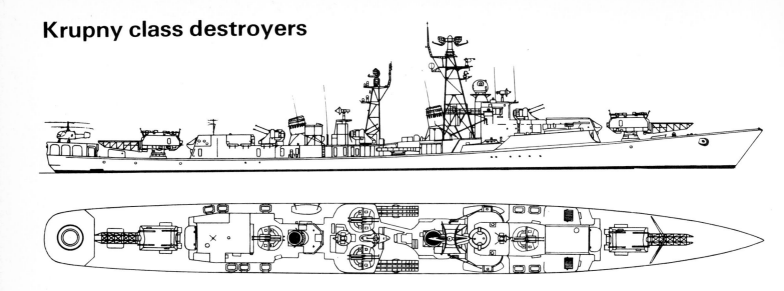

**Displacement:** 3,650 tons (4,650 full load).
**Dimensions:** Length overall 452ft (137·8m); beam 48ft 2in (14·7m); draught 16ft 5in (5m).
**Armament:** Bombardment missiles, single launch system at front and rear for SS-N-1; guns, sixteen 57mm (four quads, one ahead of bridge, one behind second funnel and two abeam amidships); torpedoes, two sets triple 21in (533mm) tubes amidships (immediately ahead of side guns).
**Propulsion:** Two sets steam turbines, 80,000shp on two shafts, maximum speed 34kt.

Built at Leningrad in 1958–62 this was a substantial class of conventional destroyers distinguished only by the clumsy SS-N-1 installations. Most have now been converted into the Kanin SAM destroyers, leaving only two Krupnys — named Gordii and Gnevnii — which have been updated in more minor ways. They carry a Ka-25 helicopter in AS form on a very restricted fantail platform immediately astern of the aft N-1 missile launcher. As related in the section on the N-1 this missile is little known in the West, but is clearly obsolescent.

All Krupny class vessels have now been converted to Kanin class vessels *(July 1976)*.

# Kanin class destroyers

**Displacement:** 3,700 tons (4,650 full load).
**Dimensions:** Length overall 457ft (139·3m); beam 48ft 2in (14·7m); draught 16ft 5in (5m).
**Armament:** Surface-to-air missiles, one twin installation for SA-N-1 (aft, in X position); AS weapons, three 12-barrel MBU launchers (foredeck and each side abeam 'mainmast'); guns, eight 57mm (two quads, in A and B positions) and eight 30mm (four twins); torpedoes, two sets quintuple 21in (533mm) tubes amidships.

**Propulsion:** Two sets steam turbines, 80,000shp on two shafts, maximum speed 34 knots.

Built as Krupny-class destroyers, the six Kanins dispense with the outmoded SS-N-1 installations and instead have completely revised electronics, SAMs, AS weapons, sonar and better helicopter installation.

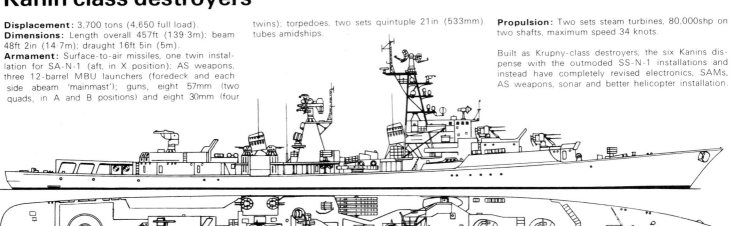

Conversions were all carried out at the Zhdanov Yard at Leningrad where the Krupnys were built in the late 1950s. Though outmoded by today's Soviet ships, in any other Navy the Kanins would be judged large, versatile and extremely effective. They continue to be active in Western waters.

**Kanin class destroyer shadowing HMS Hermes**

---

# Kildin class destroyers

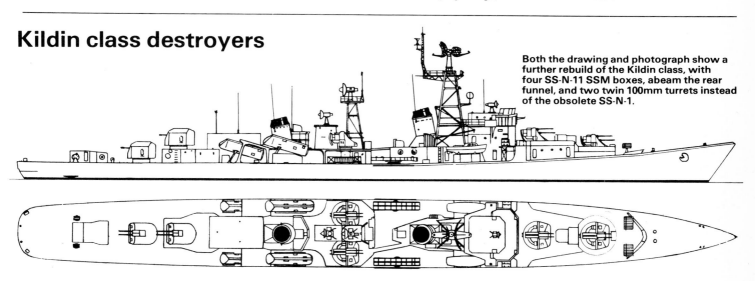

**Both the drawing and photograph show a further rebuild of the Kildin class, with four SS-N-11 SSM boxes, abeam the rear funnel, and two twin 100mm turrets instead of the obsolete SS-N-1.**

**Displacement:** 3,000 tons (4,000 full load).
**Dimensions:** Length overall 415ft (126·5m); beam 42ft 7in (13m); draught 16ft 6in (5·03m).
**Armament:** Bombardment missiles, single launcher for SS-N-1 (aft, on flush deck); AS weapons, two 16-barrel AS rocket launchers (not MBU type, foredeck); guns, four quad 57mm (two front, A, B positions, two abeam of mainmast) or (one ship) four quad 45mm;

torpedoes, two sets twin 21in (533mm) tubes (each side amidships). (See caption above.)
**Propulsion:** Two sets steam turbines, 72,000shp, maximum speed 36kt.
Originally laid down in 1955 as units of the Kotlin class, these four vessels were completed as the first carriers of the large SS-N-1 cruise missile, carried in a hangar behind the rear funnel and launched from a

rather clumsy system riding on a trainable and elevatable rail on the quarterdeck. Compared with the Kotlins these ships also have different electronic aerials, and instead of depth-charge projectors have the 16-barrel rocket launcher on the foredeck with two horizontal rows of tubes. One ship, Bedovy, differs in many respects (45mm guns, masts and funnels alter her appearance).

# Kotlin class destroyers

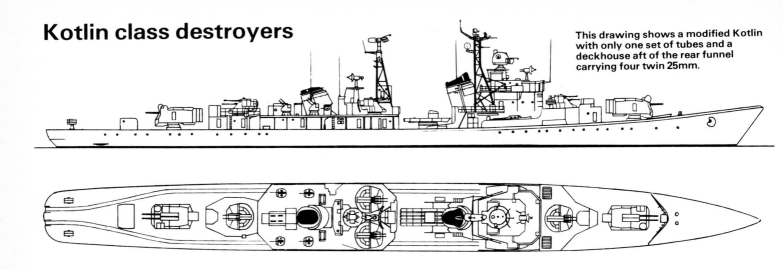

This drawing shows a modified Kotlin with only one set of tubes and a deckhouse aft of the rear funnel carrying four twin 25mm.

**Displacement:** Typically about 2,850 tons (3,885 full load).

**Dimensions:** Length overall 415ft (126·5m); beam 42ft 7in (13m); draught 16ft 1in (4·9m).

**Armament:** Missiles, none; AS weapons, originally six depth-charge projectors, but replaced progressively by two 16-barrel rocket launchers, guns, originally two twin 5.1in (130mm) at front and rear on flush deck, plus four quad 45mm (front and rear in B and X positions and abeam amidships), but progressively being modified; torpedoes, originally two sets quin-tuple 21in (533mm) tubes on centreline amidships and behind rear funnel, but rear set often replaced by deckhouse; mines, 80 as originally built.

**Propulsion:** Two sets steam turbines, 72,000shp, maximum speed 36kt.

Immediate successors to the prolific Skory class in the early post-war years, the Kotlins were likewise designed for rapid mass-production and were probably intended to number at least 50. Eventually only about 30 were completed, the last four being modified into the Kildin class. They proved to be seaworthy and reliable, but by later standards are completely outdated. About 15–18 remain in commission, nearly all with significant modifications. A few have a Ka-25 helicopter for AS duty (so-called 'Kotlin Helo' class, with raised platform immediately below 5·1in gun level at the stern). Electronics, especially radar and communications, have been progressively updated, and AS gear has been improved by removing TT and DC-projectors and adding the MBU rocket installations. At least eight have been converted to the Kotlin SAM class.

# Kotlin-SAM class destroyers

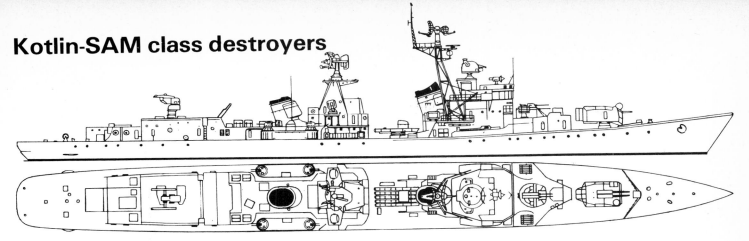

**Displacement:** 2,850 tons (3,885 full load).
**Dimensions:** Length overall 415ft (126·5m); beam 42ft 7in (13m); draught 16ft 1in (4·9m).
**Armament:** Surface-to-air missiles, one twin installation for SA-N-1 aft (X position); AS weapons, two 12-barrel MBU launchers (each side ahead of bridge); guns, one twin 100mm (foredeck, A position), one quad 57mm (ahead of bridge, B position) and, in most, four 30mm (singles abeam rear funnel); torpedoes, one set quintuple 21in (533mm) amidships.
**Propulsion:** Two sets steam turbines, 72,000shp, maximum speed 36kt.

Eight of the useful Kotlin class destroyers were rebuilt in 1960–68 so extensively as to warrant classification as a new class. The four quad 45mm guns were replaced by a single quad 57mm, and an SA-N-1 installation was added together with the Peel Group radar fire control on new electronics towers. The 130mm guns were replaced by a single quick-fire 100mm turret, and the entire interior and deck area was rearranged for greater efficiency with updated equipment. Most of these destroyers have the 30mm guns with associated Drum Tilt radars, further augmenting their capability against aircraft and soft-skinned targets.

# Skory class destroyers

**Displacement:** 2,600 tons (3,500 full load).
**Dimensions:** Length overall 395ft 2in (120·5m); beam 38ft 10in (11·8m); draught 15ft 1in (4·6m).
**Armament:** Various: nearly all retain two twin 5·1in (130mm), guns, four depth-charge projectors and two sets of quintuple 21in (533mm) torpedo tubes (centre-line amidships and aft of rear funnel); many modified to have five single 57mm guns or other schemes with one quad 57mm, and two 16-barrel AS rocket launchers; some retain pair of 3·4in (85mm) guns, many have arrangements of 37mm in single and twin mountings, and some have only one set of torpedo tubes.
**Propulsion:** Two sets steam turbines, 60,000shp, maximum speed 33kt.

Designed in the late 1940s as a standard class for mass-production, about 75 were finally completed in the early 1950s. In the past 20 years this number has been whittled down to about 40 (still no mean total), partly by transfers to other navies. The remaining ships in Soviet service incorporate many modification programmes, most of which affect their appearance. It is doubtful they will be subjected to further major refit or rebuild.

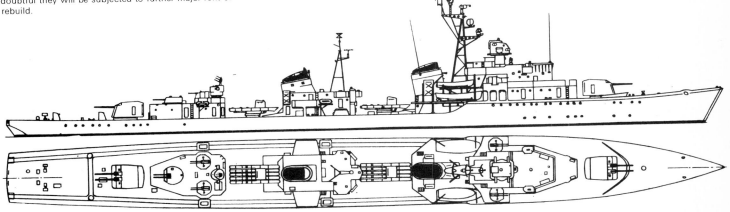

# Riga class frigates

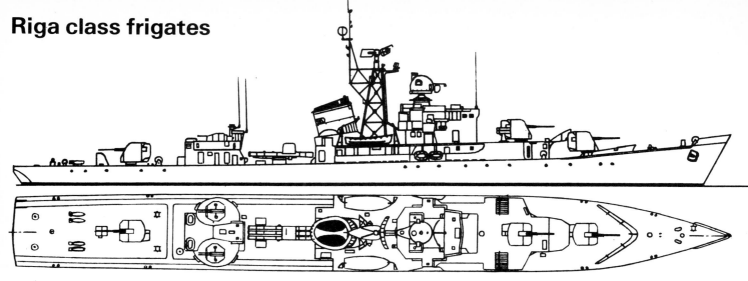

**Displacement:** 1,200 tons (1,600 full load).
**Dimensions:** Length overall 299ft (91m); beam 33ft 8in (10·2m); draught 11ft (3·4m).
**Armament:** AS weapons, two 16-barrel AS rocket launchers, four depth-charge projectors; guns, three 3·9in (100mm) (single turrets, in A, B and Y positions) and two twin 37mm; torpedoes, one set triple 21in (533mm) tubes.

**Propulsion:** Steam turbines, 25,000shp on two shafts, maximum speed 28kt.
About 65 of this trim class were built in the 1950s, to replace the bigger Kola series. Flush-decked, they are relatively conventional, and can carry mines for laying along rails at the stern. Considerable numbers of these vessels have been transferred to other navies, and it is doubtful if the number in Soviet service now exceeds 40. They carry the usual Slim Net search radar, but their overall equipment with electronics is modest in comparison with later vessels in the same category.

# Petya class frigates

**This drawing shows a Petya I with four 16-tube rocket launchers and only one set of torpedo tubes.**

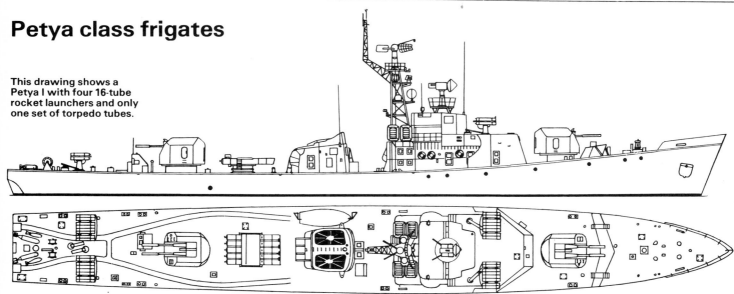

**Displacement:** 950 tons (1,150 full load).
**Dimensions:** Length overall 270ft (82·3m); beam 29ft 11in (9·1m); draught 10ft 6in (3·2m).

**Armament:** AS weapons, two standards, either (Petya I) four 16-barrel AS rocket launchers or (Petya II) two 12-barrel MBU launchers ahead of bridge; guns, usually two twin 76mm (some ships, VDS instead of rear turret); torpedoes, two sets quintuple 16in (406mm) AS tubes (some ships, including most

Petya I, only one set).

**Propulsion:** Combined diesel and gas turbine (CODOG), with two 3,000shp diesels and two 15,000shp gas turbines, giving total of 36,000shp on two shafts, maximum speed 34kt.

The first Petyas were built at Kaliningrad (formerly Königsberg) in 1960, and were among the first production ships with CODOG propulsion in the world. Their extremely squat square funnel was a portent of shapes to come with much bigger ships, but their armament is traditional. Compared with

previous frigates their electronic equipment is comprehensive, and Slim Net and Hawk Screech radars are backed up by much other gear. Probably all will eventually have the MBU launchers and VDS (variable-depth sonar) instead of the aft turret.

# Mirka class frigates

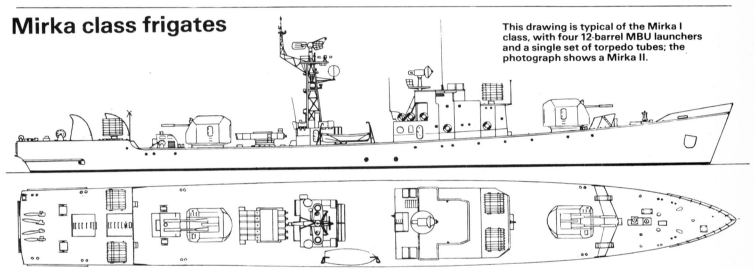

This drawing is typical of the Mirka I class, with four 12-barrel MBU launchers and a single set of torpedo tubes; the photograph shows a Mirka II.

**Displacement:** 950 tons (1,100 full load).
**Dimensions:** Length overall 270ft (82·3m); beam 29ft 11in (9·1m); draught 9ft 10in (3m).
**Armament:** AS weapons, two or four 12-barrel MBU launchers (some, two 16-barrel AS rocket launchers); guns, two twin 76mm; torpedoes, one or two sets of quintuple 16in (406mm) AS tubes.
**Propulsion:** CODOG, two 3,000shp diesels and two

15,500shp gas turbines, total 37,000shp on two shafts, maximum speed 33 knots.

Improved Petyas, these neat frigates were built during the 1960s. Their appearance was at first sight unusual, because (like the prolific Poti corvettes and several other Soviet classes) they have no conventional funnel. In the West they are commonly divided into two

groups, Mirka I having a single set of torpedo tubes aft of the single mast and Mirka II having a second set ahead of it. Nearly all Mirkas seem to use the 12-barrel MBU launcher, but there are variations in equipment and some ships carry VDS (variable-depth sonar) at the stern. The speed of 33kt is almost certainly a conservative estimate.

# Grisha class corvettes

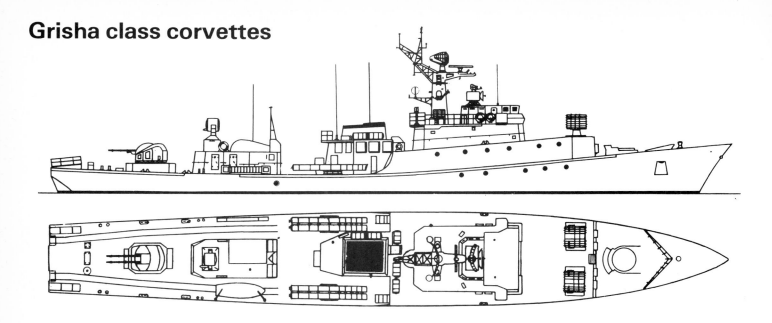

**Displacement:** 750 tons full load.
**Dimensions:** Length overall 234ft 10in (71·6m); beam 32ft 10in (10m); draught 9ft 2in (2·8m).
**Armament:** AS weapons, two 12-barrel MBU launchers; surface-to-air missiles, single silo for SA-N-4 in bow; guns, one twin 57mm (stern); torpedoes, two pairs 16in (406mm) tubes at sides amidships.
**Propulsion** CODOG, two diesels and two gas tur-

bines, total about 20,000shp on two shafts, maximum speed 30kt.

Newest corvettes in the Soviet navy, these remarkable vessels show that the brilliance in modern Soviet ship design is not confined to big warships. They have proved to be outstanding sea boats, and to be able to maintain very high speeds even in rough weather. Their versatility is considerable, and they are well

equipped with electronic equipment of all kinds. They retain a funnel, a square casing around the combined CODOG uptakes. About three or four of these craft are being delivered each year, the total by 1976 being about 20. It is difficult to see how these corvettes could be improved, but one may be certain that new designs, with even more advanced weapon systems, are on the drawing board.

# Nanuchka class small missile boats

**Displacement:** 800 tons (about 900 full load).
**Dimensions:** Length overall 196ft 10in (60m); beam 39ft 7in (12m); draught 9ft 11in (3m).
**Armament:** Bombardment missiles, two triple boxes for launching SS-N-9 missiles; surface-to-air missiles, single silo for SA-N-4 in bow; AS weapons, one (sometimes two) 12 barrel MBU launcher; guns, one twin 57mm (aft).
**Propulsion:** Diesel (though CODOG more likely and would tally better with the reported performance), two shafts, maximum speed 32kt.

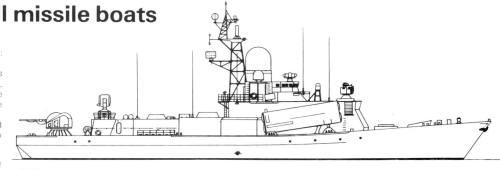

These broad-beamed missile carriers pose a number of enigmas, not least of which is the N-9 missile. The latter is briefly referred to on another page, but appears to be different from the missiles used in all other Soviet naval vessels. They are apparently guided during the initial part of their flight by the large radar housed in a dome on the superstructure, which again was new when it appeared on the first Nanuchka in 1969. Other radars include Slim Net for search, Hawk Screech for the 57mm guns and Skin Head on each side of the large dome. They are markedly larger than previous inshore SSM carriers such as the Osa and Komar classes.

# Poti class corvettes

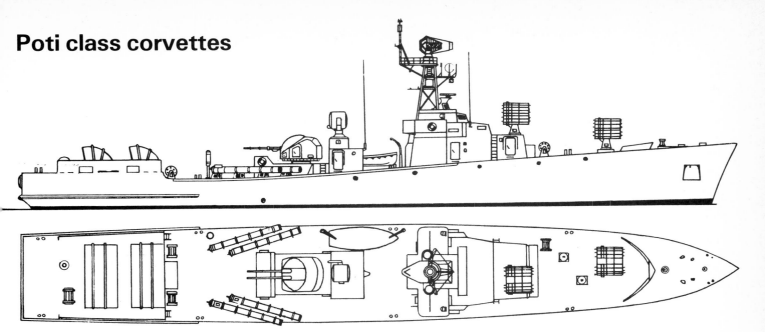

**Displacement:** 550 tons (650 full load).
**Dimensions:** Length overall 195ft 6in (59·5m); beam 26ft 2in (8m); draught 9ft 2in (2·8m).
**Armament:** AS weapons, two 12-barrel MBU launchers (foredeck and ahead of bridge, A and B positions); guns, one twin 57mm (high, amidships); torpedoes, two pairs 16in (406mm) AS tubes (at sides, just aft of guns).

**Propulsion:** CODOG, two diesels on two outer shafts, two gas turbines on two inner shafts, total believed to be 20,000shp on four shafts, maximum speed about 30kt.
At least 70 of these trim craft have been commissioned since 1961. They were the first CODOG-powered corvettes, and are in consequence markedly faster than their all-diesel predecessors (indeed they

virtually began a new class of small high-speed multi-role craft). They have no conventional funnel (stack) and, like the Grisha class which succeeded them, have high freeboard at the bows falling away with a sloping deck. Standard radars include Strut Curve surveillance atop the mast and Muff Cob amidships for gunfire direction.

# Osa class small missile boats

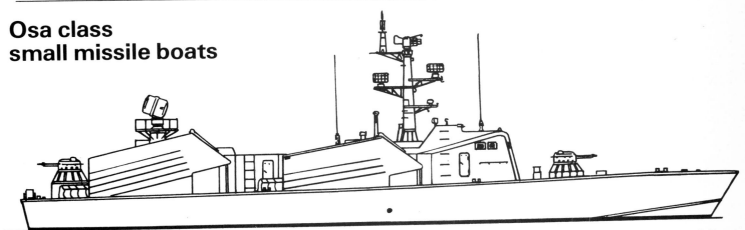

**Displacement:** 165 tons (200 full load).
**Dimensions:** Length overall 128ft 8in (39·2m); beam 25ft 1in (7·65m); draught 5ft 11in (1·8m).
**Armament:** Surface-to-surface missiles, two pairs of launchers for SS-N-2A (in tandem on left and right, reloadable only in port); guns, two twin 30mm (front and rear). Osa II class, four tubular launchers for SS-N-11.
**Propulsion:** Three diesels, 13,000shp on three shafts,

maximum speed 32 knots.

Though the prior existence of the remarkable Komar class blunted the impact of these boats on the world naval scene, the sheer number of some 220 of the Osa class have made them a force to be reckoned with. Of these, about 100 have been sold or transferred to other navies, where several have seen action (for example,

Indian Osa boats wrought havoc among Pakistani shipping in the war of 1971). Compared with the Komars they are considerably bigger, and better equipped for all-weather operations. Targets are sought on the Square Tie surveillance radar on the masthead, while gunfire is directed by the Drum Tilt on a pylon between the rear missile tubes. In later Osas the missile launchers are tubes, rather than boxes, they are called 'Osa II' class, numbering about 55.

# Komar class small missile boats

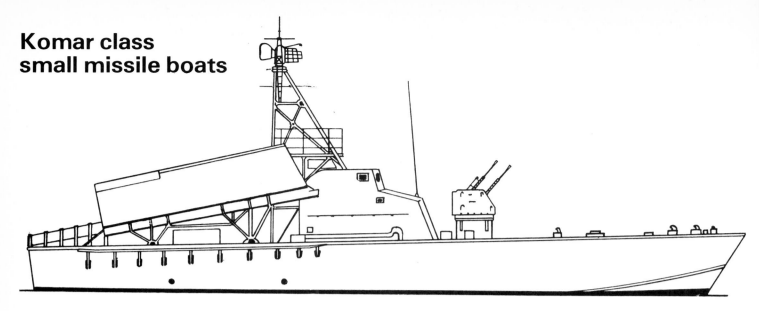

**Displacement:** 70 tons (80 full load).
**Dimensions:** Length 83ft 8in (25·5m); beam 19ft 10in (6m); draught 5ft (1·52m).
**Armament:** Surface-to-surface missiles, two shrouded cylindrical launchers for SS-N-2A (on deck, toed outwards on each side); guns, one twin 25mm (foredeck).
**Propulsion:** Four 1,200shp diesels, total 4,800shp on four shafts, maximum speed reputedly 40kt.

These small craft did not burst like a bombshell over the world's navies; for several years after their appearance in 1961 they were regarded as odd curiosities. Nobody in any Western navy did anything to counter their menace, nor was any move made to emulate them by developing a similar annihilating bombardment missile that could be carried by small craft in the West. Not until the Egyptians fired N-2As at the Israeli destroyer *Eilat* on 21 October 1967, sinking it with three direct hits, did the rest of the world suddenly recognise that here was a craft as nimble and hard to hit as the traditional MTB or PT-boat which could destroy the largest ships from ranges greater than the biggest gun. About 70 Komars were converted from P6 class patrol boats, most having now been transferred to other navies.

# Stenka class torpedo boats

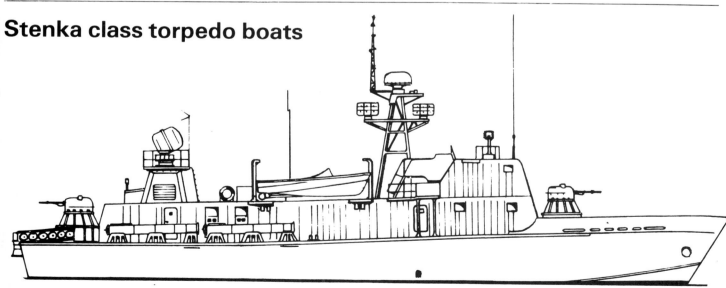

**Displacement:** 170 tons (210 full load).
**Dimensions:** Length overall 130ft 8in (39·8m); beam 25ft 1in (7·65m); draught 6ft (1·82m).
**Armament:** Torpedoes, four 16in (406mm) AS tubes, two in tandem on each side; guns, two twin 30mm (front and rear); AS weapons, depth charge racks at stern.

**Propulsion:** Three diesels, total 10,000shp on three shafts, maximum speed reputedly 40kt.

The 30-plus boats of this class were based on the Osa, but carry torpedoes instead of missiles. Correctly described as inshore multi-role boats, they are well equipped with electronics and have Square Tie sur-

veillance radar at the masthead. Drum Tilt for gunfire control and a Pot Drum small surveillance scanner atop the lattice tower mast. Extremely fast, the Stenkas have entered service since 1968, and the only unexplained fact about them is how they can be so much faster than the smaller Osas, on less power.

# Pchela class patrol hydrofoils

**Displacement:** (When buoyant) 70 tons (80 full load).
**Dimensions:** Length overall 82ft (25m); beam 19ft 8in (6m); draught, not relevant when running on foils.
**Armament:** Two twin 12·7 or 13mm machine guns; depth charge projectors.
**Propulsion:** Two 3,000shp diesels, total 6,000shp on two shafts, maximum speed 50kt.

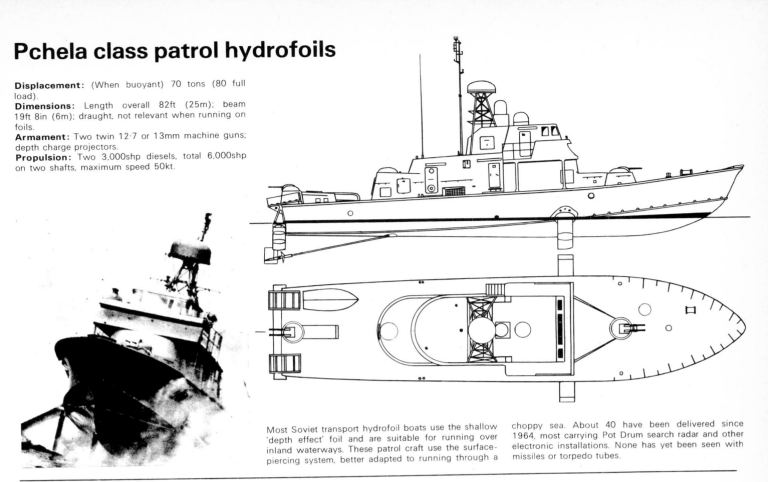

Most Soviet transport hydrofoil boats use the shallow 'depth effect' foil and are suitable for running over inland waterways. These patrol craft use the surface-piercing system, better adapted to running through a choppy sea. About 40 have been delivered since 1964, most carrying Pot Drum search radar and other electronic installations. None has yet been seen with missiles or torpedo tubes.

# Turya class patrol hydrofoils

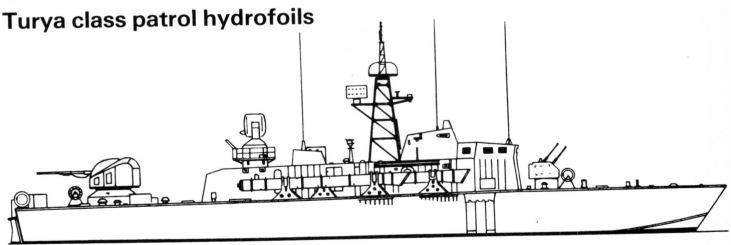

**Displacement (or mass):** 165 tons (maximum 190 tons).
**Dimensions:** Length overall 123ft 1in (37.5m), beam 27ft 10½in (8.5m); draught (foilborne) 5ft 11in (1.8m).
**Armament:** Four 21in (533mm) torpedo tubes, or various missile installations; twin 57mm guns (aft); twin 25mm guns (forward).
**Propulsion:** Not known (believed to be three 4,300hp diesels); foilborne, up to 45kt.

Produced at yards at both ends of the Soviet Union, this refined patrol hydrofoil is in service in considerable numbers (probably 120 by mid-1976) and is appearing with different equipment fits. Most carry 'Pot Drum' and 'Drum Tilt' radars, and appear to be used mainly for ASW roles, cruising as displacement vessels.

# Shershen class torpedo boats

**Displacement:** 150 tons (160 full load).
**Dimensions:** Length overall 115ft 6in (35·2m); beam 23ft 1in (7m); draught 5ft (1·52m).
**Armament:** Torpedoes, four 21in (533mm) in tandem on left and right; AS weapons, 12 depth charges; guns, two twin 30mm (front and rear).
**Propulsion:** Three diesels, total 13,000shp on three shafts, maximum speed 41kt.

Another class based on the hull of the Osa missile boats, the Shershens are effective torpedo boats with the most modern electronics and the new automatic 30mm gun turrets. About 100 have been built since 1962, of which about half have been sold or transferred to other navies. The torpedoes used in these boats are the large 21in type, not the 406mm species used for AS work. Radars include Drum Tilt for gunfire and Pot Drum for search.

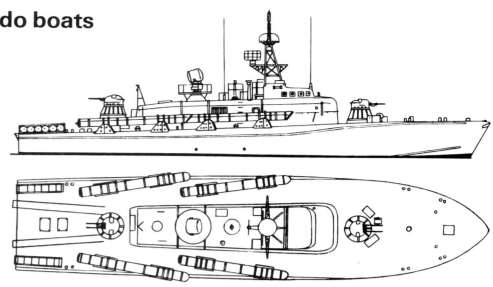

# P-classes of torpedo boats

**Displacement:** Typically 66 tons (75 full load).
**Dimensions:** Length overall 84ft 2in (25·7m); beam 20ft (6·1m); draught 6ft (1·83m).
**Armament:** Torpedoes, usually two 21in (533mm) tubes, left and right; guns, two twin 25mm (front and rear); some boats carry AS weapons or mines instead of torpedo tubes.
**Propulsion:** P6 class, four 1,200shp diesels, four shafts, maximum speed 43kt; P8 and P10 classes, two or four gas turbines, total over 6,000shp, maximum speed about 45kt.

Designed in the late 1940s, the P6 class went into production in 1951 and at least 200 were built (some were converted, for example into Komar missile craft). The more powerful P8 and P10 series can be distinguished by the exhaust stack (funnel) behind the changed superstructure. All have Pot Drum search radar, and many other electronic systems. About 130 of all classes are in Soviet use, and about 200 in other countries (at least 80 were built in China).

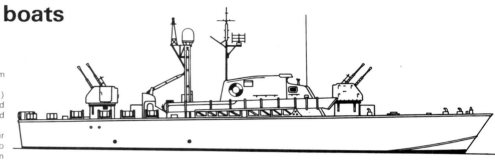

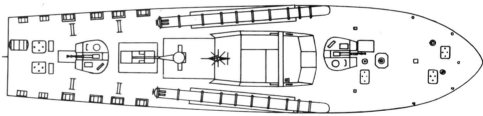

# Natya class minesweepers

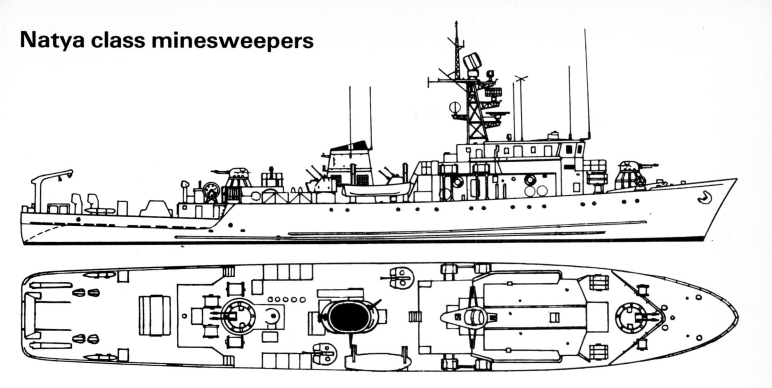

**Displacement:** 650 tons.
**Dimensions:** Length overall 200ft 1in (61m); beam 34ft 1in (10·4m); draught 7ft 2in (2·2m).
**Armament:** AS weapons, two six-barrel MBU launchers; guns, two twin 30mm, two twin 25mm.

**Propulsion:** Two 2,500shp diesels, two shafts, maximum speed 18kt.

Currently being produced at the rate of 3–4 per year, the Natyas are standard mine-warfare vessels and about 16 are in commission so far. As might be expected, they are extremely well equipped with MCM (mine countermeasures) gear, and have a large lattice mast bristling from base to tip with electronics. Hull material is not known.

# Yurka class minesweepers

**Displacement:** 500 tons (550 full load).
**Dimensions:** Length overall 171ft 11in (52·4m); beam 31ft 4in (9·5m); draught 8ft 11in (2·7m).
**Armament:** Two twin 30mm gun turrets.
**Propulsion:** Two 2,000shp diesels, two shafts, maximum speed 18kt.

During the 1960s about 45 of these neat MCM (mine counter-measures) ships were commissioned, and they are likely to stay in service for another decade. Hulls are known to be steel.

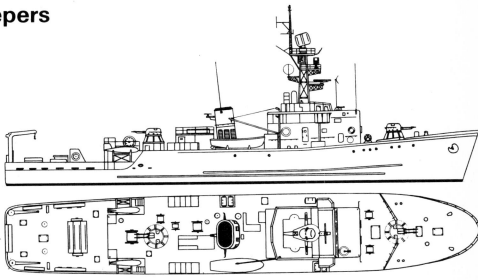

# Alligator class landing ships

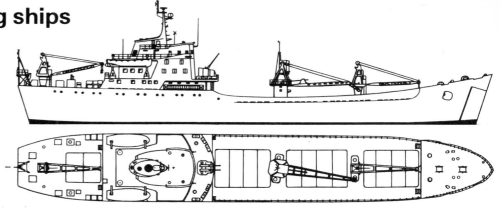

**Displacement:** 4,100 tons (5,800 full load).
**Dimensions:** Length overall 374ft (114m); beam 50ft 11in (15·5m); draught 12ft 1in (3·7m).
**Armament:** One twin 57mm gun turret.
**Propulsion:** Diesel, total 8,000shp, maximum speed 15kt.

First commissioned in 1966, at least 12 of these vessels had entered service by 1974, and more are thought to have been built since. They are the largest Soviet amphibious assault vessels, with carrying capacity of 1,500 tons and large ramps at both bow and stern. Examples are in use with either one, two or three cranes, the newer one-crane type being predominant.

# Polnocny class landing ships

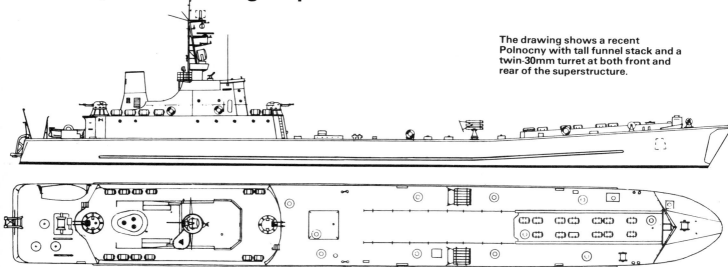

The drawing shows a recent Polnocny with tall funnel stack and a twin-30mm turret at both front and rear of the superstructure.

**Displacement:** 780 tons (1,000 full load, and see text for Polnocny 'Type IX').
**Dimensions:** Length overall 246ft (75m), except Type IX 265ft (80·7m); beam 29ft 6in (9m) (Type IX, 27ft 8in, 8·44m); draught 9ft 10in (3m).
**Armament:** Two 18-barrel rocket launchers (left and right, on foredeck) for bombarding hostile shores; in nearly all, one twin 30mm gun turret.
**Propulsion:** Two 2,500shp diesels. maximum speed 18kt.

By far the most numerous Soviet amphibious assault ships, the Polnocnys now number about 70, in ten classes. The only significantly different group is the 'Type IX', which has a longer but slightly slimmer hull of greater displacement. Cargo is loaded and unloaded through the full section bow doors, a typical load including six battle tanks. Gun-equipped ships, which are almost standard, have Muff Cob radar atop the superstructure.

# Ugra class submarine support ships

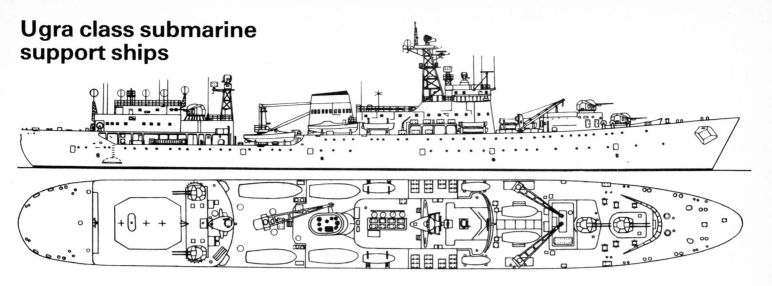

**Displacement:** 6,750 tons (9,500 full load).
**Dimensions:** Length overall 463ft 10in (141·5m); beam 57ft 7in (17·6m); draught 22ft 6in (6·9m).
**Armament:** Usually four twin 57mm, with two Hawk Screech fire-control radars.
**Propulsion:** Four diesels, 16,000shp, maximum speed 21kt.

These ships are packed with equipment and facilities and are virtually floating dockyards. About ten have been built at Nikolayev since 1961, one being sold to India. They contain elaborate workshops, stores and test facilities for ship systems, weapons and electronics, as well as accommodation for several sub-marine crews. Among their electronics are Slim Net search radar, Strut Curve and Muff Cob. Still in service are six older Don-class ships. Only two (called Don Helo class) have helicopter provision, which is standard in the Ugras. Type of helicopter varies, but is often a Ka-25 transport version.

# Primorye class intelligence ships

**Displacement:** 5,000 tons.
**Dimensions:** Length overall 274ft (83·5m); beam 47ft 2in (14·4m); draught 26ft 6in (8m).
**Propulsion:** Probably two 2,500shp diesels, about 14kt.

The Soviet Union has more intelligence-gathering ships than the rest of the world combined, a known total of more than 70 vessels. Some are similar to large oceangoing trawlers, many are large and carefully planned, and the six ships of this class are unlike any-thing else afloat. Their names are Primorye, Kavkaz, Krym, Zabaikalye, Zakarpatye and Zaporozhye. Each is a huge floating intelligence station, linked by the most elaborate communications systems with sensors in smaller ships, in aircraft and probably in the great number of Soviet military satellites which constantly overfly Western territories. The interiors, of course, are unknown, but there seems every likelihood that com-plete processing (for example, of photographs and electronic signatures) and analysis are performed on board. The results are doubtless transmitted by a secure (satellite) link to Moscow.

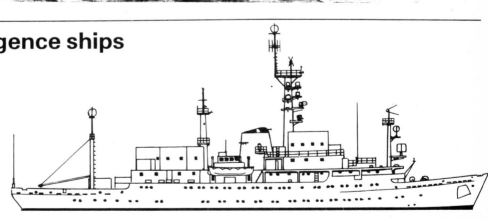

# Kosmonaut Yuryi Gagarin

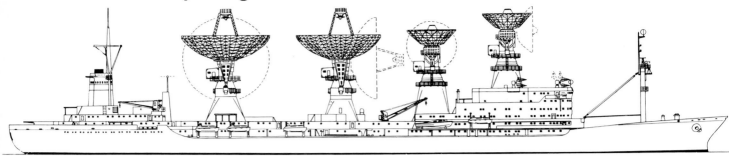

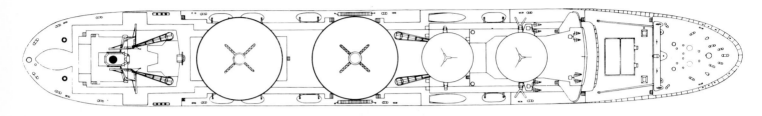

**Displacement:** 45,000 tons.
**Dimensions:** Length overall 773ft 4in (235·7m); beam 101ft 8in (31m); draught 30ft (9·14m).
**Propulsion:** Single set geared steam turbines, 19,000shp, maximum speed 17kt.

Largest Soviet research ship, and almost certainly the largest in the world, this striking vessel was built at Leningrad in 1970–71, with a hull based on an established Soviet tanker design. She carries two pairs of steerable receiver aerial dishes, and their signals are processed in large laboratories. Her purpose is research into the control of space vehicles, space communications, upper-atmospheric conditions and other phenomena. Based at Odessa, she has made several long voyages. To facilitate accurate positioning (not necessarily at berthing) she has front and rear lateral thrusters.

# Kosmonaut Vladimir Komarov

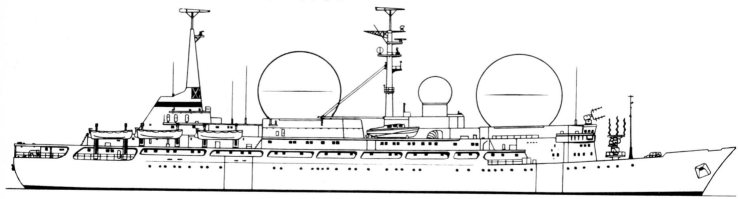

**Displacement:** 17,500 tons.
**Dimensions:** Length overall 510ft 10in (155·7m); beam 75ft 6in (23m); draught 29ft 6in (9m).
**Propulsion:** Two sets of diesels, total 24,000shp, maximum speed 22kt.

Another of the remarkable Soviet 'space ships', Komarov was built in 1966 at Leningrad for the Academy of Sciences ostensibly to study the upper atmosphere in the Western Atlantic. Her hull is bulged along each side into huge overhanging sponsons (not clearly visible in a side view such as the photograph on this page) and she has appeared in different paint schemes and with slightly different electronic fits. The two large and one small radomes are self-evident; the larger ones could enclose 50ft dishes.

# Soviet Naval Strengths

*Following are approximate Fleet strengths at June, 1976 and vary with out-of-area deployments.*

## Submarines

| Class | North | Baltic | Black Sea & Caspian | Pacific | Total |
|---|---|---|---|---|---|
| Delta II | 2 | — | — | — | 2 |
| Delta | 10 | — | — | — | 10 |
| Yankee | 26 | — | — | 8 | 34 |
| Hotel III | 1 | — | — | — | 1 |
| Hotel II | 5 | — | — | 3 | 8 |
| Papa | 1 | — | — | — | 1 |
| Charlie | 12 | — | — | ← | 12 |
| Echo II | 15 | — | — | 12 | 27 |
| Echo I | 4 | — | — | — | 4 |
| Charlie II | 2 | — | — | — | 2 |
| November | 9 | — | — | 4 | 13 |
| Victor | 15 | — | — | 2 | 17 |
| Victor II | 1 | — | — | — | 1 |
| Golf I & II | 14 | — | — | 8 | 22 |
| Zulu V | 1 | — | — | — | 1 |
| Juliet | 11 | — | — | 5 | 16 |
| W Twin Cylinder } | 5 | 2 | 1 | 4 | { 5 |
| W Long Bin } | | | | | { 7 |
| Alpha | 1 | 1 | — | — | 2 |
| Bravo | 1 | 1 | 1 | 1 | 4 |
| Tango | — | 1 | 2 | — | 3 |
| Foxtrot | 31 | 14 | — | 11 | 56 |
| Romeo | — | 5 | 9 | — | 14 |
| Quebec | — | 6 | 11 | — | 17 |
| Zulu IV | 9 | 3 | 3 | 4 | 19 |
| Whisky | 10 | 40 | 22 | 28 | 100 |
| Whisky Canvas Bag | 1 | — | — | 2 | 3 |

## Surface Ships

| Class | North | Baltic | Black Sea & Caspian | Pacific | Total |
|---|---|---|---|---|---|
| Kiev | — | — | 1+2 | — | 1+2 |
| Kara | 2 | — | 2 | — | 4+1 |
| Moskova | — | — | 2 | — | 2 |
| Sverdlov | 2 | 3 | 4 | 3 | 12 |
| Chapaev | 1 | 1 | — | — | 2 |
| Kresta II | 4 | 2+1 | 0 | 2 | 8+1 |
| Kresta I | 3 | — | — | 1 | 4 |
| Kynda | — | — | 2 | 2 | 4 |
| Krivak | 2 | 6 | 1 | 2 | 11 |
| Kashin | 2 | 2 | 11 | 4 | 19 (5 mod.) |
| Kanin | 4 | 1 | — | 2 | 7 |
| SAM Kotlin | 2 | 1 | 3 | 2 | 8 |
| Kildin | — | 2 | 2 | — | 4 |
| Kotlin | 3 | 3 | 4 | 8 | 18 |
| Skory | 10 | 10 | 10 | 10 | 40 |
| Mirka I and II | 4 | 8 | 8 | — | 20 |
| Petya I and II | 12 | 10 | 12 | 11 | 45 |
| Kola | 1 | — | 3 | 1 | 5 |
| Riga | 9 | 10 | 12 | 9 | 40 |
| Ugra | 4 | 3 | — | 2 | 9 |
| Lama | 1 | 1 | 2 | 2 | 6 |
| Don | 1 | — | 3 | 2 | 6 |
| Nanuchka | 3 | 6 | 5 | — | 14+2 |
| Grisha | 8 | 4 | 5 | 4 | 21 (3 Gresha II) |
| Poti | 25 | 25 | 5 | 15 | 70 |
| Kronstadt | 5 | 4 | 4 | 4 | 17 |
| Purga | — | 1 | — | — | 1 |
| Amga | 1 | — | — | — | 1 |
| Alesha | 1 | 1 | — | 1 | 3 |
| W. Bauer | 1 | 1 | — | — | 2 |
| Amur | 4 | 4 | 2 | 4 | 14 |
| Oskol | 3 | 3 | 1 | 3 | 10 |
| Atrek | 4 | 1 | — | 1 | 6 |
| Dnepr | 4 | 1 | — | — | 5 |
| Tovda | — | 1 | — | — | 1 |
| Fleet Sweepers | 40 | 61 | 40 | 50 | 185 (20 Natya, 45 Yurka, 20 T 58, 100 T 43) |
| Coastal Sweepers | 25 | 46 | 25 | 25 | 121 (3 Sonya, 3 Zhenya, 70 Vanya, 40 Sasha, 5 T 301) |
| Inshore Sweepers | 25 | 25 | 25 | 25 | 100 |
| Pchela | — | 10 | 15 | — | 25 |
| Turya | 1 | 6 | 4 | 6 | 17 |

| Class | North | Baltic | Black Sea & Caspian | Pacific | Total |
|---|---|---|---|---|---|
| Osa | 25 | 35 | 25 | 35 | 120 (65 Type I, 55 Type II) |
| Stenka | 5 | 24 | 4 | 17 | 50 |
| SO 1 | — | 40 | 30 | 10 | 80 |
| MO VI | — | 15 | — | — | 15 |
| FAC—Torpedo | 15 | 55 | 15 | 40 | 125 (45 Shershen, 80 P6, 8, 10) |
| River Patrol Craft | — | 10 | 40 | 40 | 90 (40 Schmel, 30 BK III, 20 BKL IV) |
| Ropucha | 0 | 2+1 | 0 | 2 | 4+1 |
| Alligator | 2 | 3 | 4 | 5 | 14 |
| Polnocny | 12 | 15 | 18 | 15 | 60 |
| Landing Craft | 15 | 16 | 30 | 20 | 81 (10 MP 10, 5 MP 8, 8 MP 6, 15 MP 4, 8 MP 2, 35 Vydra) |
| Intelligence Ships (AGIs) | 16 | 8 | 15 | 15 | 54 |

## Overall Totals

*(Figures in italic indicate ships being built and are approximate)*

| | |
|---|---|
| Aircraft Carriers | 1+2 |
| Helicopter Cruisers | 2 |
| Submarines (SSBN) | 55+10 |
| Submarines (SSB) | 23 |
| Submarines (SSGN) | 40 |
| Submarines (SSG) | 28 |
| Submarines (SSN) | 37+3 |
| Submarines (SS) | 216 |
| Cruisers (CLG) | 20+2 |
| Cruisers (Gun) | 11 |
| Destroyers (DDG) | 45+2 |
| Destroyers (Gun) | 58 |
| Frigates | 110 |
| Corvettes (Missile) | 32+2 |
| Corvettes | 170 |
| Fast Attack Craft (Missile) | 120 |
| Fast Attack Craft (Patrol) | 65 |
| Fast Attack Craft (Hydrofoil) | 42 |
| Fast Attack Craft (Torpedo) | 125 |
| River Patrol Craft | 90 |
| Minesweepers—Ocean | 185 |
| Minesweepers—Coastal | 121 |
| Minesweepers—Inshore | 100 |
| LSTs | 18+1 |
| LCTs | 60 |
| LCUs | 81 |
| Depot and Repair Ships | 63 |
| Intelligence Collectors (AGI) | 54 |
| Survey Ships | 97 |
| Research Ships | 32 |
| Fishery Research Ships | 192 |
| Space Associated Ships | 23 |
| Fleet Replenishment Ships | 4 |
| Tankers | 24 |
| Harbour Tankers | 18 |
| Salvage Vessels | 19 |
| Rescue Ships | 15 |
| Training Ships | 27 |
| Lifting Ships | 15 |
| Icebreakers (Nuclear) | 4 |
| Icebreakers | 38 |
| Cable Ships | 6 |
| Large Tugs | 120 |

*Information derived from "The Soviet Navy Today" by Captain John E. Moore, RN (published by Macdonald and Jane's, 1976)*

# The Soviet Ground Forces

**Christopher Donnelly**

The Soviet Ground Forces constitute a separate arm of service in the Soviet Union, second in importance only to the Strategic Rocket Forces. The 1,825,000 men under the command of General of the Army I. G. Pavlovskii form the very foundation of the Soviet Army; and although in the Khrushchev period their importance was in fact diminished as a result of that politician's belief that any major war would inevitably be waged with strategic nuclear weapons, today the Ground Forces' importance is fully recognised by the leaders of the USSR.

As a result the Ground Forces are being constantly strengthened and modernised, to improve their capability to fight either a conventional or a nuclear war.

The various types of troops that go to make up the Ground Forces fall into four broad categories: the teeth arms – motor-rifle (motorised infantry), tank and airborne troops; the artillery – missile troops, air-defence and field artillery; the special troops – engineer, signals and chemical troops; and supporting arms and rear services – transport, medical, traffic control and police etc.

A division is the basic all-arms formation, and the Soviets class their divisions as either Motor-Rifle, Tank or Airborne according to the identity of the major fighting arm in the division. The basic unit of the Soviet Ground Forces is the regiment, which is made up of three or four battalions plus support elements.

**T-55 Tanks photographed during a large-scale Soviet Army exercise**

## Motor-Rifle Battalion organisation

The probable composition of the motor-rifle battalion, the basic motorised infantry sub-unit, is given in a table. The battalion's teeth are its three motor-rifle companies, each of three platoons, each of three sections. A section travels in an armoured personnel carrier (APC) which may be of the BTR-50, BTR-60 or BMP series. The tracked BTR-50, used to carry infantry in tank divisions, and the wheeled BTR-60, used to carry infantry in motor-rifle divisions, are both in the process of being replaced by the modern BMP combat vehicle, which has better mobility and firepower. The battalion's artillery support is provided by six 120-mm mortars and, in battalions not equipped with the BMP (which carries an anti-tank missile on each vehicle), an anti-tank platoon of two recoilless anti-tank guns and two anti-tank guided weapons (ATGWs). Battalion logistic support is contained in a tail of only seven or eight vehicles, for, as will be explained below, logistics are cut to a minimum to increase flexibility. A battalion will be supplied from the vehicles held by its parent regiment.

A tank battalion, the basic armoured sub-unit, is organised on similar lines, but has no mortars or anti-tank support, and has a slightly larger tail. The tank platoons in the tank battalions of a tank regiment have ten tanks per company, i.e. 31 per battalion. The tank platoons in the tank battalion organic to motor-rifle regiments have four tanks per

platoon, i.e. 40 per battalion.

The basis of a motor-rifle regiment is three motor-rifle battalions plus one tank battalion of 40 tanks. In addition a regiment has strong support elements: a strong reconnaissance company equipped with PT-76 light amphibious tanks (now being replaced by BMPs), BRDM heavy armoured reconnaissance vehicles and motorcycles for reconnaissance and liaison. At least two of the BRDMs will be equipped for reconnaissance in a nuclear, biological and chemical warfare (NBC) environment. Artillery support is provided by an anti-tank company, equipped with 'Sagger' or 'Swatter' ATGWs mounted on BRDM vehicles; an anti-aircraft battery of four ZSU-23-4 multi-barrelled AA tanks, and four SA-9 infra-red homing missiles mounted in packs of four on BRDM (twin 23-mm cannon, trolley-mounted, are available in some regiments in addition to or instead of the new SA-9); and a field battery of six 122-mm D-30 towed gun-howitzers. These will probably be replaced eventually by 122-mm self-propelled (SP) guns (some regiments may be allotted as many as 18 towed 122-mm guns for field artillery support as the new SP guns are introduced.

A tank regiment is a considerably smaller organisation, with only 1,300 officers and men at the most. Its basis is three tank battalions, 95 tanks in all. In the past, tank regiments had no organic motor-rifle troops; but it is now thought that, in the front-line units, at least a company, and in some cases

*Above:* **The Soviets use mortar fire for suppression of enemy defensive positions to cover an attack. There are six 120-mm mortars in every motor rifle battalion**

*Above right:* **The BM-21 is the latest in a long line of 'Katyusha' type rocket launchers. A battalion of eighteen weapons can fire 720 rounds in 30 seconds**

*Right:* **'Sagger' ATGW is launched from a BRDM1 AFV. This missile is reasonably effective up to nearly 2 miles and was responsible for destroying many Israeli tanks during the Yom Kippur war**

a battalion, of motor-rifle troops is included in the regiment. Artillery support is also absent – the tank regiment has only anti-aircraft artillery for protection, utilising the ZSU-23-4 and the older ZSU-57-2 twin-barrelled anti-aircraft tank, although this is gradually being replaced by SA-9.

Both tank and motor-rifle regiments have engineer mine-clearing and river-crossing support, and decontamination equipment. The light regimental tail provides scanty field recovery and repair facilities and a small medical post as well as cargo and fuel vehicles to resupply the sub-units.

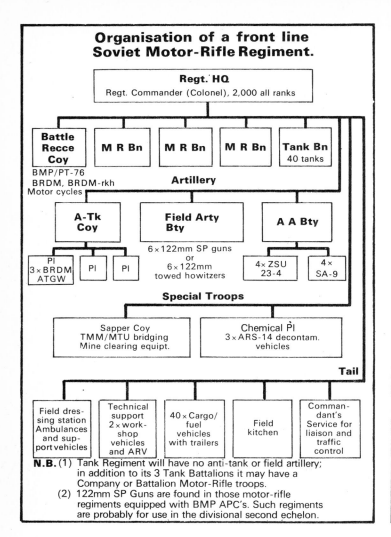

**Organisation of a front line Soviet Motor-Rifle Regiment.**

**Regt. HQ**
Regt. Commander (Colonel), 2,000 all ranks

- **Battle Recce Coy**
  BMP/PT-76 BRDM, BRDM-rkh Motor cycles
- **M R Bn**
- **M R Bn**
- **M R Bn**
- **Tank Bn** 40 tanks

**Artillery**

- **A-Tk Coy**
  - PI 3 × BRDM ATGW
  - PI
  - PI
- **Field Arty Bty**
  6 × 122mm SP guns or 6 × 122mm towed howitzers
- **A A Bty**
  - 4 × ZSU 23-4
  - 4 × SA-9

**Special Troops**

- **Sapper Coy** TMM/MTU bridging Mine clearing equipt.
- **Chemical PI** 3 × ARS-14 decontam. vehicles

**Tail**

- Field dressing station Ambulances and support vehicles
- Technical support 2 × workshop vehicles and ARV
- 40 × Cargo/fuel vehicles with trailers
- Field kitchen
- Commandant's Service for liaison and traffic control

**N.B.** (1) Tank Regiment will have no anti-tank or field artillery; in addition to its 3 Tank Battalions it may have a Company or Battalion Motor-Rifle troops.
(2) 122mm SP Guns are found in those motor-rifle regiments equipped with BMP APC's. Such regiments are probably for use in the divisional second echelon.

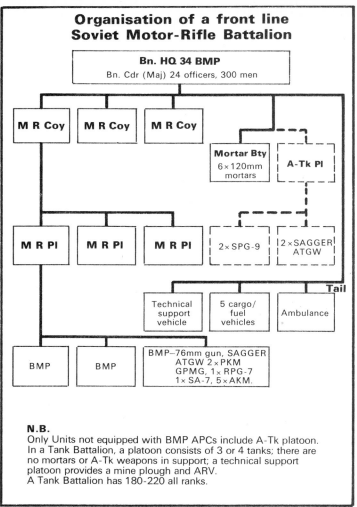

**Organisation of a front line Soviet Motor-Rifle Battalion**

**Bn. HQ 34 BMP**
Bn. Cdr (Maj) 24 officers, 300 men

- **M R Coy**
- **M R Coy**
- **M R Coy**
- **Mortar Bty** 6 × 120mm mortars
- **A-Tk PI**

- **M R PI**
- **M R PI**
- **M R PI**
- 2 × SPG-9
- 2 × SAGGER ATGW

**Tail**

- Technical support vehicle
- 5 cargo/fuel vehicles
- Ambulance

- BMP
- BMP
- BMP–76mm gun, SAGGER ATGW 2 × PKM GPMG, 1 × RPG-7 1 × SA-7, 5 × AKM.

**N.B.**
Only Units not equipped with BMP APCs include A-Tk platoon. In a Tank Battalion, a platoon consists of 3 or 4 tanks; there are no mortars or A-Tk weapons in support; a technical support platoon provides a mine plough and ARV. A Tank Battalion has 180-220 all ranks.

The organisation of the basic all-arms formation, the division, is founded upon three motor-rifle regiments and one tank regiment for motor-rifle divisions, and three tank and one motor-rifle regiment for tank divisions. Recent increases in the numbers of tanks in motor-rifle regiments and divisions have, however, tended to make the motor-rifle division an equally balanced tank and infantry formation, while the tank division remains an armour-heavy formation. Both divisions have strong reconnaissance battalions with a commando-type parachute company for deep penetration; they also have effective battlefield radar and direction-finding equipment, as well as armoured vehicles for ground reconnaissance in conventional and nuclear war. A motor-rifle division alone has an extra tank reserve of some 40–50 tanks.

Both motor-rifle and tank divisions have a considerable amount of artillery in addition to that held by their regiments. Air cover is provided by 24 57-mm towed AA guns and a battalion of SA-6 AA missiles. A motor-rifle division alone has 18 100-mm towed anti-tank guns. Field artillery support is provided by three battalions, each of 18 122-mm guns; in motor-rifle divisions only, one battalion is equipped with 152-mm guns, which are beginning to be replaced by a new 152-mm SP gun.

Eighteen 40-round multi-barrelled rocket launchers and four free-flight surface-to-surface missile (SSM) launchers complete the division's formidable artillery support. The former weapon is ideal for delivering a chemical strike, and the latter a nuclear

strike. A division has particularly strong mine-clearing and river-crossing support, much of the equipment it uses having been tried and proven in the Yom Kippur Israeli–Arab war of 1973. The engineers also have fair obstacle-creating ability in the way of mine-laying vehicles and trench-diggers; and chemical defence troops provide good decontamination ability with personnel and vehicle decontaminating equipment.

The division's logistic tail is true to the principle of lightness and flexibility. The recovery and repair facilities of the technical support battalion are not extensive and not designed for repairing heavily damaged vehicles. The medical battalion's field hospital is designed to treat 60 bed cases at any time, but provides light treatment or immediate evacuation for many more. The divisional supply transport battalion has the task of carrying fuel and supplies forward to the regiments. Divisional movement is controlled by a strong detachment of traffic police (the so-called 'Commandant's Service') who organise routes and deployment areas and site depots etc.

The organisation of a Soviet army is flexible, with a variable number of divisions of all types. A typical combination might be three tank divisions plus two motor-rifle divisions. An army would dispose of a large amount of artillery, some of which in war would probably be retained for army use, and some of which would be allocated to whichever divisions the army commander thought to be in most need of it. As well as a large number of 122- and 152-mm gun-howitzers, army artillery includes such

excellent pieces as the M1943 130-mm field gun with a range of 17 miles, the 180-mm heavy gun with an even greater range, the 160-mm heavy mortar and a variety of multi-barrelled rocket-launchers. An army commander would be extremely unlikely to allot any of his medium-range SS-1C 'Scud' nuclear missiles to a division. An army commander would also have a tank reserve which could be used to strengthen an important axis, and a large amount of engineer equipment to construct more permanent river-crossing sites.

Most of the soft-skinned transport vehicles which will be needed to supply divisions in time of war are under army control. They are not, however, held on strength in peacetime, but in event of war will be mobilised, together with their drivers, from the civilian economy. To diversify his means of fuel supply in an offensive war, the army commander might have units capable of laying tactical fuel pipelines from strategic railheads to forward depots.

In time of war, Soviet Ground Force formations, now organised into Groups of Forces (outside the USSR) and Military Districts (inside the USSR), would be organised as 'Fronts', and several Fronts together would probably be combined in a Theatre of Military Action. For example, the 20 Soviet divisions now forming the Group of Soviet Forces Germany (GSFG) would probably become a Front in war, and along with the Northern (Poland) and Central (Czechoslovakia) Group of Forces might be classed as the Central European

*Above:* **Traditional Soviet use of artillery demands rapid deployment by battery in open positions, but as a result of the low survival rate of such positions in the 1973 Yom Kippur war, new Soviet Army artillery tactics are being duscussed**

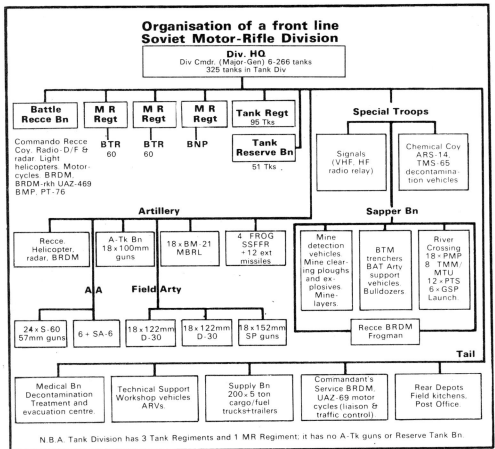

### Organisation of a front line Soviet Motor-Rifle Division

**Div. HQ**
Div Cmdr. (Major-Gen) 6-266 tanks
325 tanks in Tank Div

| **Battle Recce Bn** | **M R Regt** | **M R Regt** | **M R Regt** | **Tank Regt** 95 Tks |
|---|---|---|---|---|

Commando Recce Coy. Radio-D/F & radar Light helicopters. Motorcycles. BRDM, BRDM-rkh UAZ-469 BMP, PT-76

BTR 60 — BTR 60 — BNP

**Tank Reserve Bn** 51 Tks

**Special Troops**

| Signals (VHF, HF radio relay) | Chemical Coy ARS-14, TMS-65 decontamination vehicles |
|---|---|

**Artillery**

| Recce. Helicopter, radar, BRDM | A-Tk Bn 18 x 100mm guns | 18 x BM-21 MBRL | 4 FROG SSFFR + 12 ext missiles |
|---|---|---|---|

**Sapper Bn**

| Mine detection vehicles. Mine clearing ploughs and explosives. Minelayers. | BTM trenchers BAT Arty support vehicles. Bulldozers | River Crossing 18 x PMP 8 TMM/ MTU 12 x PTS 6 x GSP Launch. |
|---|---|---|

**A A**   **Field Arty**

| 24 x S-60 57mm guns | 6 + SA-6 | 18 x 122mm D-30 | 18 x 122mm D-30 | 18 x 152mm SP guns |
|---|---|---|---|---|

Recce BRDM Frogman

**Tail**

| Medical Bn Decontamination Treatment and evacuation centre. | Technical Support Workshop vehicles ARVs. | Supply Bn 200 x 5 ton cargo/fuel trucks+trailers | Commandant's Service BRDM, UAZ-69 motor cycles (liaison & traffic control). | Rear Depots Field kitchens, Post Office. |
|---|---|---|---|---|

N.B.A. Tank Division has 3 Tank Regiments and 1 MR Regiment; it has no A-Tk guns or Reserve Tank Bn.

Theatre.

It is to the Front commander that the Soviet tactical air force (Frontal Aviation) would be subordinated. The Front commander would deploy his air power in coordination with his ground forces, allotting it to whichever sector of the battlefield he considered most important. The Front commander has in addition medium-range nuclear missiles ('Shaddock' and 'Scaleboard') which he can deploy as he wishes.

The airborne forces would also come under Front control; but, as a result of the very limited amount of air transport available to drop or air-land troops, and the great vulnerability of large-scale assault groups, the Front commander would probably detach a proportion of the airborne troops allotted to him to armies under his control.

The airborne forces are the elite of the Soviet Ground Forces. There are only seven or eight divisions, and all are stationed inside the territory of the USSR. A conscious effort is made by the Soviet authorities to maintain an elitist spirit among these troops by means of a constant propaganda campaign, a special distinctive uniform and a hard and exciting training programme. The airborne forces get the pick of the con-

scripts, many of whom will have practised parachuting or other military sports with the *DOSAAF* organisation (see Chapter 3) before their conscription.

The Soviet airborne forces are trained to operate in several roles. They could be dropped in small teams by advanced parachuting techniques to operate secretly as reconnaissance and sabotage groups in the enemy rear. Considerably larger units, up to a battalion or larger, might be deployed deep in the enemy rear on suicide missions of strategic importance, such as the destruction of a communications centre or government buildings in a city.

The airborne forces would also be used in the traditional role: they might be landed by aeroplane, parachute or helicopter in the enemy rear to fight conventionally until relieved by the advancing main forces. When used in this manner, there would be no limit to the size of the airborne force deployed; but it is unlikely that the Soviets would fly their men in in more than battalion-size groups because of their vulnerability to counter-strike, especially in nuclear war. The Soviets do insist that to mount any airborne operation of a significant size, local command of the air is essential.

An airborne battalion is organised on similar lines to a motor-rifle battalion: three companies, mortars, anti-tank support and a light tail. However, its equipment scales will vary enormously depending on its role, means of transport and means of landing. Long-range reconnaissance teams of up to a platoon in size would have only the lightest scale of issue: as they would hope to remain undetected, vehicles and heavy kit would be merely an embarrassment. However, battalion groups operating independently in the enemy rear, to exploit rapidly the effect of a nuclear strike or to seize and hold a strategic position in advance of the main forces, would be heavily equipped. The 82-mm mortars, SPG-9 recoilless anti-tank guns and portable 'Sagger' ATGWs and SA-7 AA missiles which are standard equipment in airborne battalions, could be dropped by parachute, followed by 120-mm mortars, ZU-23 twin AA cannon and 85-mm anti-tank field-guns for heavier fire support.

The battalion could also be provided with the BMD – the new air-droppable version of the BMP – which would give it a significant offensive capability and extra protection in an NBC environment. This vehicle replaces or supplements the old but effective ASU-57 self-propelled anti-tank gun.

A battalion group equipped with these weapons, operating in the enemy rear, would be quite a formidable force. It could be strengthened still further by helicopter-borne and air-landed equipment, if local mastery of the air could be maintained, and if, in the case of transport aeroplanes, a suitable landing field could be found.

The great increase in the number of

*Above:* **An ASU-57 anti-tank gun just unloaded from an Mi-6 Hook helicopter. The gun gives airborne forces extra hitting power during assault landings. It is being replaced by the BMD**

*Above right:* **The air-portable ASU 85 provides an airborne force operating in the enemy's rear with an effective armoured anti-tank capability**

*Right:* **A T-62 tank company of the Transbaikal Military District. Low ground pressure and good power to weight ratio enable the T-62 to operate over very soft ground**

helicopters in the Soviet Army in recent years now gives a senior Soviet commander the capability to lift several battalion groups with light scales at any one time. The great advantage of helicopters is that ordinary motor-rifle troops can be used with minimal training. This makes it more likely that helicopters would be deployed under divisional control to enable tactical landings to be made in very close support of the leading formations and at very short notice. The equipping of helicopters with heavy armament has made them capable of lending a considerable amount of fire support to any landing party.

Airborne forces, however transported, would have only a limited amount of

supplies and ammunition, and would not be expected to operate without support or reinforcement for very long.

The exception is long-range strike groups, *reidoviki,* dropped in strength deep in the enemy rear to carry out a mission of strategic importance such as sabotage of a vital installation or the assassination of an important person. Having completed their task, there might be no way for such groups to return or escape. This is just their hard luck; the Soviet High Command is not likely to worry about the loss of 200 or 300 soldiers if they accomplish a mission of sufficient importance.

Formidable though the airborne forces may appear, however, their role is only subsidiary to, and in support of, the operations of the motor-rifle and tank formations; for it is on the ground that the Soviets consider the war will be lost or won.

A study of the deployment of units and formations brings one to a conclusion that the Soviet High Command envisages two major roles for the Ground Forces, in addition to the responsibility for internal security in the Soviet Union and Eastern Europe, a responsibility which they share with the para-military KGB and MOOP troops. Firstly, they must defend the USSR from invasion by land from Western Europe, the Middle East or China, and secondly, they must prosecute a war beyond the Socialist *bloc* with the aim of extending Soviet communist influence to other countries. A closer study of troop dispositions will quickly show that the force level which the Soviet High Command maintains facing China, while adequate to repel any Chinese invasion of the Asiatic USSR, is nothing like sufficient to ensure success in a major invasion of that country. The force level maintained in the European USSR and Eastern Europe, however, is certainly much higher than at present necessary to deter NATO from invading the Soviet Union, and may well be thought sufficient, under the right conditions, to invade Western Europe, defeat the forces of NATO and bring most of Western Europe under Soviet domination.

The principles of Soviet military doctrine, and therefore the shape and form of the Ground Forces, are heavily influenced by the geography and economics of the USSR. The country is so vast and the population density (even in European Russia) so low, that the state simply could not bear the cost of Maginot Line-type fortifications along its entire borders, even assuming that this kind of fortification could be made effective today. Another problem with such defensive fortifications is where to site them. Almost the whole of the European USSR is a vast plain, bounded by the Baltic Sea to the north and the Black Sea to the south, while to the west the plain stretches unbroken to Holland. Eastwards, only the rolling hills of the southern Urals lie between Moscow and the Tien Shan mountains, where the border with China runs.

The only real natural obstacles to any military operations in the USSR are the very size of the country and the large rivers which dissect it. Consequently, Soviet military thinking is bound to reckon with these factors, which affect attacker and defender alike, and plan the development of the

Ground Forces accordingly.

The size of the army is limited by the level of the Soviet economy; and although the figure of 166 divisions appears enormous, it must be related to the area of land to be fought over. It is in the light of such geographic and economic considerations that Soviet military doctrine emphasises the primacy of the offensive as a means of warfare. This lays great value on the seizure of the initiative, the ability to cover large distances at great speed and the achievement of the maximum of effect by manoeuvre, concentration and surprise, together with vigorous fighting to the very depths of the enemy's position.

These principles of military doctrine the Soviets consider to be equally applicable to strategic defence or offence. Thus whether their role is strategically defensive or offensive is of less importance for the training and equipping of the Soviet Ground Forces than might have been thought. Whatever their strategic role, the Soviet Ground Forces are trained and equipped to fight any campaign by offensive means – to seize the initiative by attack or counter-attack and to carry the action to the depths of the enemy's position, so as to bring about his defeat in the shortest possible time. Only in the offensive (or counter-offensive) lies the way to victory; and in event of any major war – certainly in the event of war between capitalist and communist states – the Soviets will aim for nothing less than complete and total victory, irrespective of whether or not they start the war.

The Ground Forces are, therefore, organised, trained and equipped on one overall basic standard pattern to fight one type of war, no matter where and for what they are located; though of course those units stationed in areas where special geographic or climatic conditions appertain will be additionally trained to fight in those particular conditions.

The requirement of mobility and manoeuvrability affects organisation of units and formations, and design of equipment alike. Soviet military doctrine demands that units and formations up to divisional level are not burdened with a cumbersome, mobility-hampering logistic train. The combat vehicles themselves must carry as much as possible in the way of essential fuel and ammunition, and units have organic to them merely a flexible tail, receiving further logistic support from transport and equipment held by higher formations. The design of Soviet combat vehicles shows clearly that considerations of range, mobility and fire-power are given priority over those of protection and crew comfort.

One advantage that highly mobile forces bring is the possibility of concentrating them at chosen points to achieve overwhelming local superiority over an enemy, thus giving them the chance to break

*Left:* **The T-62 is the most modern Russian tank in widespread service. Although equipped with a very powerful 115-mm gun it is rather cramped and tiring to drive. The T-72 is now replacing it.**

through into the depths of his position. Soviet doctrine is to exploit this by firm, centralised control at high level, with stricter subordination of formations than is common in the armies of the Western alliance. This characteristic is regarded by the Soviet High Command as one of its main strengths, permitting as it does the greatest strategic value to be obtained from a concerted effort.

It might be useful at this point to list the principles of Soviet military art – the means by which doctrine is to be put into practice – as defined by contemporary Soviet strategists and tacticians. As principles, they are equally applicable at all levels of military involvement: strategic, i.e. the overall involvement from military action at theatre

*Right:* **T-54/55 is by far the most numerous tank in the world today and is the mainstay of the Warsaw Pact forces. In the Soviet Army, it is currently being supplemented by the T-62 and the new T-72**

*Below:* **The BMP is a vehicle specially designed for rapid and mass exploitation of a breakthrough of a lightly-defended point and is particularly well designed for NBC warfare**

*Far right:* **The RPG-7 is probably one of the best infantry anti-tank weapons currently available. It is light, accurate and relatively effective against a tank's side armour**

(1) an encirclement: the delivery of two main attacks, or one main and one subsidiary attack, to converge on and encircle the enemy forces, subjecting these encircled forces to assault and bombardment from all directions and preventing their reinforcement while continuing the main offensive deep into the enemy's rear;

(2) an attack along axes: the delivery of one or more frontal attacks on the enemy's defensive position and advancing deep into his rear, to destroy rear installations and reserves moving up, at the same time developing the attack sideways to attack defending forces from the flank or rear; and

(3) single concerted thrust to push the enemy back along the whole front and squash him against a natural obstacle such as the sea or a mountain range.

The Soviets accept that in modern war a superiority in the order of 3 or 4:1 at least is desirable if an attacker is to have a good likelihood of success, and that a 7 or 8:1 superiority is even better because it doubles the chance of a quick victory. However, in key areas where the Soviet Army might be employed, e.g. Western Europe or Soviet Central Asia, the USSR cannot at present achieve even a 3:1 superiority in men and equipment over the whole front. (While such a superiority is possible on, for example, the flanks of NATO, these areas would not be of major strategic importance to the USSR in the event of a general war, and therefore they are not discussed in detail at this point).

As the third example of an 'operation' above, involving as it does a push along the whole front, would therefore require overall superiority of at least 3:1 and desirably double that, it is unlikely to be the operation chosen under present conditions for a campaign against China or the central front of NATO.

The other operations, both the encirclement and the attack along axes, do not require overall superiority, but achieve their effectiveness by the attainment of overwhelming local superiority in the order of 8 or 10:1 to smash through or around the enemy defences, and break through into his 'soft' rear area where they can do a disproportionate amount of damage. While overall superiority in men and equipment is highly desirable for these operations, Soviet strategists do emphasise that if the operations are carried out skilfully, using the proper tactics, success can be achieved by an attacking force equal in size to the defending force or, in extreme cases, even inferior in terms of manpower. (It does seem extremely unlikely that the Soviet Army should even have to consider the likelihood of fighting a European enemy which has superior numbers of men.)

By the speed of the advance into enemy territory that both these operations entail, they do offer the best possible medium for a successful offensive force to penetrate to the economic heart of an enemy nation and occupy or neutralise it, thus bringing the war to a speedy conclusion.

The key to the success of the operations is an effective break-through of the main enemy positions, either directly or around the flank, and it is particularly interesting to

level up to national economic and political considerations; operational, which term the Soviets use to describe military action at army or more usually at Front level; and tactical – actions at divisional level.

In order of priority these principles are given as:
(1) the achievement of mobility and the maintenance of a high tempo of combat operations;
(2) the concentration of the main effort and the creation thereby of superiority of men and *materiel* over the enemy at the decisive place and time;
(3) surprise;
(4) aggressiveness in battle – no let-up in the attack, break-through and pursuit;
(5) preservation of the combat-effectiveness of one's own troops by
    (a) being properly prepared and efficiently organised,
    (b) maintaining at all times efficient command and control over one's forces and
    (c) maintaining morale and the will to fight in one's troops;
(6) ensuring that the aim and plan of any operation conform with the realities of the situation, so that neither too much nor too little is attempted;
(7) ensuring the co-operation of all arms of service and ensuring the co-ordination of effort towards achieving the main objectives; and
(8) attempting simultaneous action upon the enemy to the entire depth of his deployment and upon objectives deep in his rear.

There are three basic types of 'operation' by which the Ground Forces might seek to implement the requirements of Soviet military art to defeat an enemy such as the NATO forces in Western Europe;

*Above:* **The retro-rocket para-braking system is clearly seen in this photograph. It enables heavy loads to be air-dropped without damage**

*Left:* **A Soviet 130-mm field gun taking part in Exercise Dniepr in 1967. Originally a long-range naval weapon, it is mainly used by the army for counter battery work**

# SOVIET BATTLE TACTICS

## AN ENCIRCLEMENT OPERATION

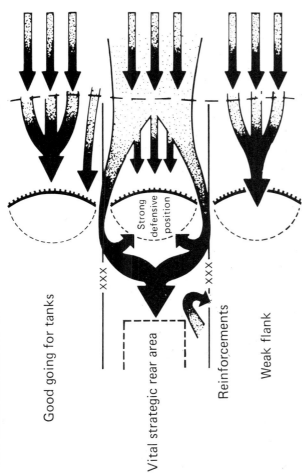

Good going for tanks

Strong defensive position

— xxx —

Vital strategic rear area

— xxx —

Reinforcements

Weak flank

## AN OPERATION BY FRONTAL ATTACK ALONG PARALLEL AXES

## CONCENTRATION

Though a division might advance on a frontage of 3–5 miles, it would concentrate to 1/3 this at the point of break-through of an enemy defensive position.

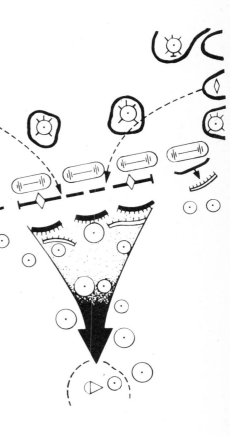

| | |
|---|---|
| ☼ | Tactical missile |
| ⊞ | Artillery group |
| ◇ | Armoured formation |
| ⌒ | Defensive position |
| ⊙ | Tactical nuclear strike |
| ⊣ | Attacking units |

*Above:* **The BTR 60PB APC is used to carry troops of the Motor Rifle Divisions, whereas tank divisions use the BTR 50P or BMP**

*Left:* **Soviet parachutists on exercise. Drops are seldom made from below 1,500 feet and, in war, it is unlikely that more than a battalion of paratroops would be dropped at a time**

study the Soviet principles of military art enumerated above in the light of such a break-through.

A diagrammatic representation of such a break-through, taken from Soviet sources, is given. From a study of information supplied by the many means of reconnaissance available to him, the Front commander will select the area or areas for concentration and break-through, paying particular attention to finding suitable terrain for the movement of large armoured forces. Making every effort to conceal his intentions, he will attempt to achieve surprise, and if possible to catch the enemy before they have even taken up their defensive positions. The four or five divisions of the army allotted the task of accomplishing the break-through, or at least of acting as the first wave of the assault, would approach the appointed area well dispersed in extended march column to concentrate only on the objective itself. As the leading elements of the army reach the enemy positions, they will immediately engage them to test their strength, and to give cover to the following main forces, approaching rapidly, a heavy air and artillery bombardment into the very depths of the enemy's defensive position (with either conventional or nuclear and chemical shells depending on a political decision at higher level) would be laid down very rapidly. On the heels of this the main forces of the army would advance at speed on a width of front of perhaps only $12\frac{1}{2}$–20 miles, to overwhelm the defences and break through into the flanks or rear of the enemy position.

So as to lessen their vulnerability to enemy counter-strikes, especially under nuclear conditions, the Soviet divisions would deploy in balanced or armour-heavy battle groups of regimental size. These would themselves be divided into three or four battalion groups with a high degree of linear separation – a division might advance on one or two axes on a front of only five or six miles but extended to a depth of up to 30 or more miles. Concentration would be achieved as each successive regimental group was fed into the battle, advancing rapidly in march columns and only deploying when approaching the area of fighting. At every tactical and operational level it is Soviet practice to make attacks in two echelons. The task of the first echelon, normally one-half to two-thirds of the force involved, with all the armour available and all artillery support, is to break through the enemy defences. The second echelon forces then exploit this breach and pass on into the depths of the enemy position to complete the destruction

and engage the enemy reserves before they can reinforce the defenders or organise a second line of defence.

When we study the pattern of deployment in greater detail, we see that within the battalion, vehicles would move 25–50 yards apart in a long crocodile.

The divisional commander commands his long crocodile by a complex radio net from a forward command and observation post well up with the first regiments. This command element will be a fairly small organisation, composed of only the commander, a few assistants and his communications vehicles (with, of course, the ubiquitous AA defence). The division is controlled by the HQ, under the command of the chief-of-staff, who has a large number of deputies to assist him. His job is to organise and control the division in accordance with the commander's orders, leaving the divisional commander free to plan the battle. This HQ is a large organisation; and, being both essential and vulnerable, will not travel so far forward as the commander himself does, but probably will move ahead with the second echelon regiments. Organisation of the rear, and logistic supply, is done from a rear HQ element, commanded by the deputy commander for the tail. This HQ element moves behind the fighting troops. Command and control does not pass from one element of the HQ to the other; but all elements exercise their function continuosly, so some provision must presumably be made for shadow command and main HQ elements to take over if the commander and staff are knocked out.

Speed of advance is achieved by march in column, when not in direct contact with enemy troops. The axes of the advance will be planned to make the best possible use of good ground for rapid movement and good road networks. A division would advance probably on two axes, up to two miles apart. Although the divisional front of responsibility might be up to 10 miles wide, the division would not be spread out over the whole distance, but concentrated over perhaps only one-third of this, with reconnaissance and flank protection sub-units covering the extra ground.

The division would march in regimental groups (motor-rifle or tank regiments plus elements of divisional artillery and engineers), each of which would deploy a strong battalion as an advance guard, and even further forward or on threatened flanks strong companies as march security patrols. Reconnaissance patrols would scout the area in front of and between the marching units. Each marching battalion would attempt to keep just over one mile distant from its neighbour to avoid presenting a juicy nuclear target.

Having located the enemy and ascertained their strengths and positions, by battle if necessary, the strong reconnaissance elements would pass the information back to the divisional advance guard before attempting to push on into the enemy rear, and then continue their advance with the special task of locating subsequent enemy reserves. The advance guard will engage the enemy with the purpose either of destroying him and thus obviating the need for the main forces of the division to deploy unnecessarily and thereby waste valuable time; or, if the enemy is in great strength, of sacrificing itself in a delaying or diversionary action to give the divisional commander time to deploy his forces from the line of march into battle formation. The regimental groups will normally deploy with two battalion groups of mixed armour and infantry in the first echelon and one battalion group in the second echelon, with engineers and artillery in close support. The task of the first echelon is to defeat the enemy's main forces, whereupon the second echelon will exploit their success, break through into the enemy rear and engage the enemy reserves.

Soviet tactical doctrine lays great stress on the desirability of speed and rapid manoeuvre, and emphasises that it far preferable not to have to attack a prepared enemy defence, where the attacker needs superiority of forces, but rather to attack his troops while the latter are still on the march. This tactic is known as the encounter battle. When the reconnaissance units of the advancing Soviet forces give warning of an enemy force advancing towards them, the Soviet advance guard will engage the enemy advance guard, and the Soviet main forces would then hope to manoeuvre and, deployed in platoon columns 100 yards apart, to attack the advancing enemy in the flank while still on the move, giving him no chance to prepare a defence. Thus the odds would be even in a very fluid battle, and by dint of careful planning, surprise and the attacking of the enemy along the whole depth of his formation at the same moment, the Soviet forces would hope to wrest a victory without numerical superiority.

Although the Soviet Ground Forces consider fighting a war only by means of the offensive and counter-offensive, they by no means ignore the tactics of defence, accepting that enemy counter-attacks might well throw them on to the defensive at very short notice. A diagram of a classic Soviet defensive position is also shown. Of particular significance is the positioning of the defence in two echelons, with good communication and flank cover, and the massing of a mobile counter-offensive force to meet the enemy should he break through, and to seize the initiative and counter-attack at the first possible moment.

Such tactics as are described above are extremely demanding of an army, and necessitate not only a high degree of co-ordination and control and well trained officers and men, but also first-class units and formations suitably organised and equipped to fight such highly intensive mobile engagements. As our study of the Soviet Ground Forces has shown, in organisation, equipment and training they do indeed attempt to fulfil these operational requirements and this is why they differ in several marked respects from the armies of many NATO states.

All the tactics and operations discussed so far are seen by the Soviets as being equally applicable to wars fought in a conventional environment or using weapons of mass destruction (the Soviet term for nuclear and chemical weapons). In conventional conditions, greater concentration is possible than in conditions where nuclear weapons might be used, and a slower overall rate of advance would be expected on a non-nuclear battlefield: 15–20 miles per day instead of 25–30 miles.

The Soviets have a very significant cap-

*Below:* **Rail communications are essential to Soviet stretegic re-supply plans in a prolonged war. This pontoon bridge can be constructed in a few hours.**

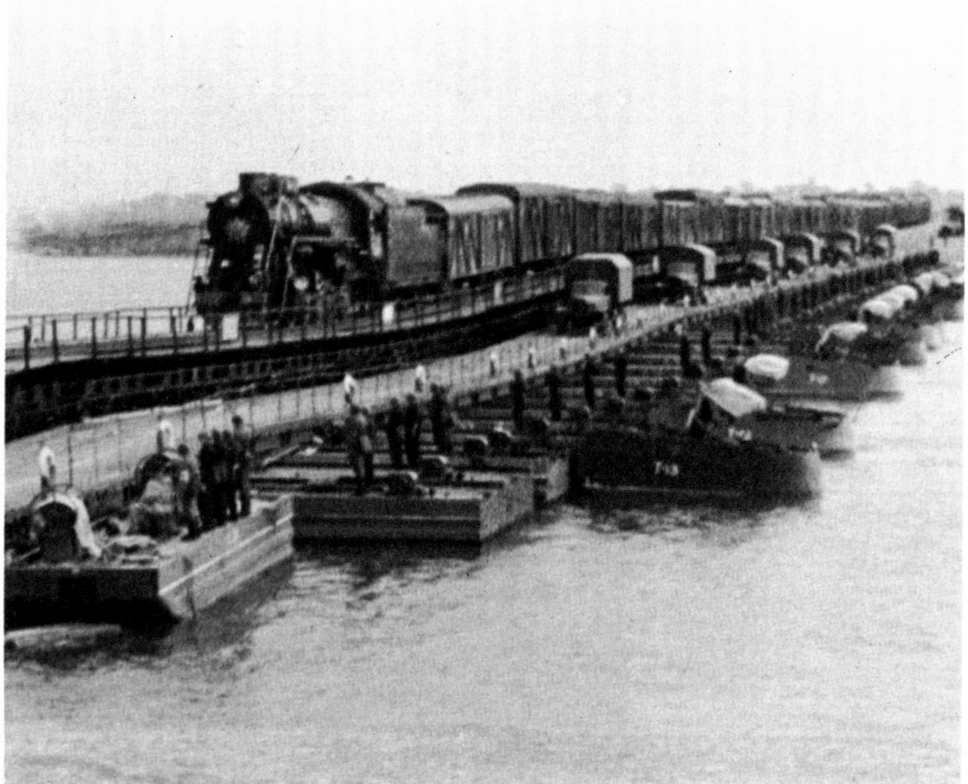

# SOVIET BATTLE T

**KEY**

An apc or apc unit (eg. motor rifle company)

A tank or a tank unit

A gun or artillery unit

Anti-aircraft artillery

(a) Strong recce patrol eg. BRDM BMP T62 motorcycle
(b) & (c) The Vanguard
(b) Recce vehicle (BRDM)
(c) Vanguard consisting of a Motor rifle coy (10 apcs) plus a tank platoon (4 tanks)
(d) – (p) Main Forces
(d) Recce vehicle
(e) Bn HQ
(f) SP anti-aircraft guns (2 x ZSU 23-4)
(g) Tank platoon
(h) Tank platoon
(i) Motor rifle coy (10 BMP)
(j) Motor rifle coy (10 BMP)
(k) Engineer vehicle
(l) Artillery platoon 2-3 SP guns
(m) Artillery platoon 2-3 SP guns
(n) Rear service vehicles
(p) Flank guard – (BMP or BRDI
(q) Rearguard – (BMP or BRDM)

## BATTALION DEFENSIVE POSITION

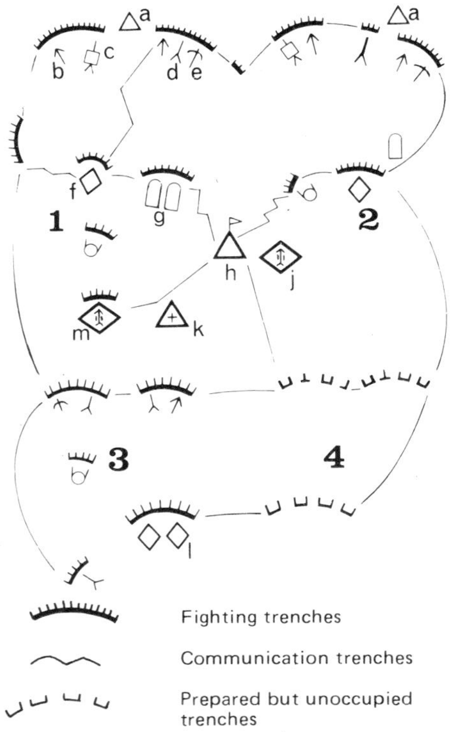
a
a
b
c
d
e
f
g
h
j
k
m
l
1
2
3
4
Fighting trenches
Communication trenches
Prepared but unoccupied trenches

(a) Observation post
(b) Machine gun
(c) Anti-tank missile launcher (Sagger)
(d) Anti-tank grenade launcher (RPG-7)
(e) Heavy machine gun
(f) Dug in tank
(g) APCs giving fire support
(h) Bn HQ
(j) Anti-aircraft tank (ZSU 23-4)
(k) Medical post
(l) Tanks for counter attack
(m) Mortars

1 & 2 – Company positions – 1st echelon of defence

3 – Company posi tion – 2nd echelo an expected (left flank) axis of enem attack

4 – Reserve positi in case main attack is on right flank

## MARCH ORDER

Soviet military map symbols depicting a motor-rifle battalion group on the march. This march order is adopted when an encounter battle is anticipated and rapid deployment will be necessary.

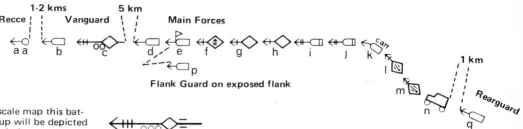

On small scale map this battalion group will be depicted by the symbol

## A BATTALION'S DEPLOYMENT FROM THE MARCH TO THE ATTACK -- BASIC DRILL

A Battalion group would normally attack in one line (or echelon) as indicated here, with another battalion group of the same regiment close behind the second wave of the attack.

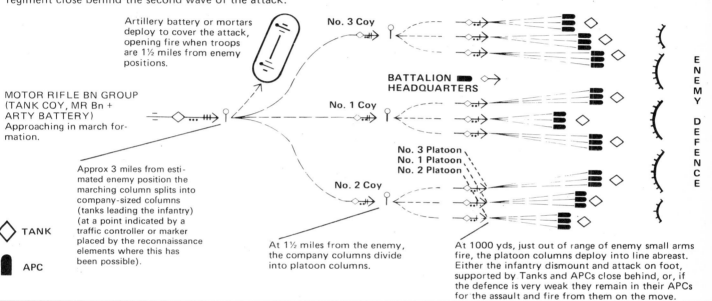

Artillery battery or mortars deploy to cover the attack, opening fire when troops are 1½ miles from enemy positions.

MOTOR RIFLE BN GROUP (TANK COY, MR Bn + ARTY BATTERY) Approaching in march formation.

Approx 3 miles from estimated enemy position the marching column splits into company-sized columns (tanks leading the infantry) (at a point indicated by a traffic controller or marker placed by the reconnaissance elements where this has been possible).

◇ TANK

▮ APC

BATTALION HEADQUARTERS

No. 3 Coy

No. 1 Coy

No. 2 Coy

No. 3 Platoon
No. 1 Platoon
No. 2 Platoon

At 1½ miles from the enemy, the company columns divide into platoon columns.

At 1000 yds, just out of range of enemy small arms fire, the platoon columns deploy into line abreast. Either the infantry dismount and attack on foot, supported by Tanks and APCs close behind, or, if the defence is very weak they remain in their APCs for the assault and fire from them on the move.

ENEMY DEFENCE

---

The **encounter battle** is a tactic much favoured by the Soviet Army. When the enemy is occupying a prepared defensive position, superiority in the order of 5:1 will probably be needed to destroy him. An encounter battle occurs when Soviet forces, moving forward rapidly, meet an enemy force advancing in a counter move. In such a case it is clearly in the interests of the Soviets, in the role of attacker, to engage the enemy whilst he is still on the move. Thus, battle is between two totally mobile forces, and no time is available for defensive positions to be occupied. This effectively evens the odds, and the Soviets believe that by careful manoeuvre they should be able to overwhelm an opponent of equal size very quickly. This is particularly true if the opponent is equipped with British or US AFVs which are much less suited to this type of battle on the move than are the Soviet vehicles. The stages of an encounter battle are as follows:

The recce elements of the advancing Soviet column locate an advancing enemy and the Soviet advance guard engages the enemy vanguard. As the enemy main forces advance to assist their hard-pressed van, the Soviet main forces abandon their advance guard and execute a flanking manoeuvre under the guidance of their own recce. They are thus able to attack the marching enemy column from the flank, following a short artillery barrage from their attached battery (which would deploy at first contact). Travelling at high speed, the deployed Soviet unit will drive right into the enemy column, and a fierce fire fight at pointblank range will ensue.

The Soviets consider that such an encounter battle is the most decisive means of achieving tactical victory, as the side which is defeated will be totally destroyed; so much so that there is no Soviet drill for recovery from defeat in an encounter battle!

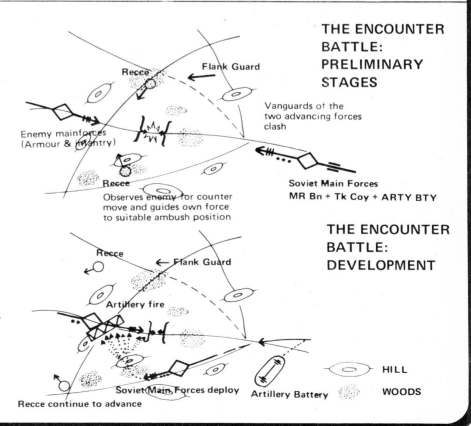

## THE ENCOUNTER BATTLE: PRELIMINARY STAGES

Vanguards of the two advancing forces clash

Soviet Main Forces
MR Bn + Tk Coy + ARTY BTY

Enemy mainforces (Armour & Infantry)

Observes enemy for counter move and guides own force to suitable ambush position

## THE ENCOUNTER BATTLE: DEVELOPMENT

Artillery fire

⬯ HILL

WOODS

Soviet Main Forces deploy

Artillery Battery

Recce continue to advance

acity for fighting with weapons of mass destruction. They are known to hold stocks of persistent and non-persistent chemical agents for their artillery. The BM-21 multi-barrelled rocket-launcher is an ideal weapon for rapid delivery of a non-persistent chemical agent, for example hydrogen cyanide or a nerve gas such as sarin. Persistent chemical agents could be delivered by air strike or long-range artillery to targets such as airfields which the Soviets might want to deny to the enemy but not to destroy. Soviet commanders at field level and above are taught to regard the use of chemical weapons as a matter of course – simply a weapon available to them which will be used when tactical and meteorological conditions permit.

Although political considerations are likely to determine whether or not battlefield nuclear weapons are used, if they are released, then they too are simply regarded for tactical terms as replacing a large artillery barrage; and commanders must expect to take their use in their stride. Whether their battlefield systems will in fact be capable of dealing with nuclear devastation on a large scale is impossible to say, but the Soviets certainly pay more than lip service to the necessity for planning for such an eventuality. All reconnaissance units in the Ground Forces have elements specially equipped for duty in contaminated areas. Each soldier has protective clothing, a respirator and a personal decontamination kit. Decontamination sprays are held at company level and above, and divisions have complex mass decontamination equipment such as the TMS 65 – a jet engine mounted on a lorry which sprays activated bleach slurry to decontaminate armoured fighting vehicles (AFVs).

The Soviet Ground Forces are also widely equipped with passive and infra-red night-vision devices and battlefield surveillance radar, although many Western specialists consider these to be less effective than some possessed by NATO forces. Soviet doctrine insists that pressure on the enemy must be maintained at night, but it is unlikely that the advance would be continued at daytime pace. Cover of darkness would be used for the consolidation of positions, moving up of supplies and preparation for resumption of the advance at first light. River crossings would probably be attempted at last light, and bridges built and crossed at night wherever possible to enable attacks to be launched from bridgeheads before dawn. Certain operations, such as deep-penetration paratroop or heliborne assaults, might, of course, wait for darkness because the protection it affords outweighs the difficulties of operating in the dark.

As rivers and canals constitute perhaps the major geographic obstacle to any attack on Western Europe, it is not surprising that the Soviets have equipped their army with extremely effective river-crossing equipment. Moreover, with the minimum of preparation, their tanks can be prepared for schnorkelling where the river banks and bed are suitable. All their APCs are fully amphibious, and divisions are well supported with amphibious cargo vehicles

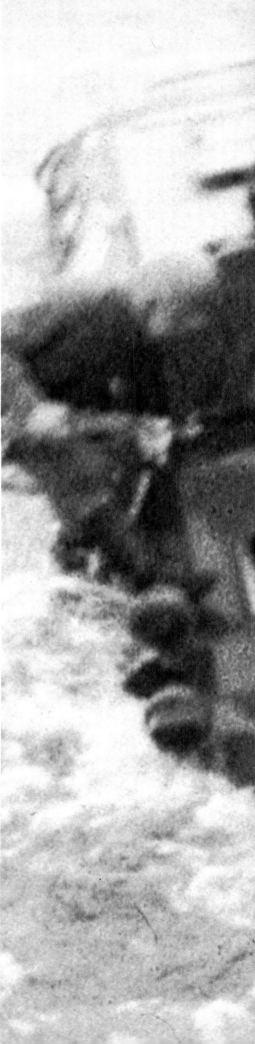

*Right:* **A BTR 60P in difficulties. Although it has good swimming characteristics, this wheeled vehicle needs a very gentle slope if it is to climb out of the water when loaded**

*Below:* **The Mi-24 Hind is the first Soviet helicopter gunship. Fire support during assault landings is its primary role.
(1) Pitot head. (2) 12.7-mm machine gun.
(3) Perspex bullet-proof shield. (4) Engine exhaust. (5) Laser rangefinder on gun camera mount. (6) Pods holding 32 57-mm unguided rockets. (7) Rails for Swatter semi-automatic ATGW**

capable of carrying supplies and weapons.

The Soviets do not maintain units solely for warfare in special conditions such as desert, mountain and snow. The entire army is expected to be able to fight in all climatic conditions – and in view of the extremes of climate in the USSR this is hardly surprising. Those units stationed in mountainous or desert areas practise the same tactics and operations with the same equipment as does the army as a whole. Tactics will be adapted to accommodate the difficult conditions where necessary, but in practice Soviet units seem to make few concessions to difficult terrain.

## Chemical warfare

One area in which, it is generally agreed, Soviet military technology leads the West is chemical warfare. From the establishment in the 1920s, with German help, of a gas war-

fare school, the USSR has continued to develop her CW capability. Chemical weapons are considered a most effective means of waging war; indeed, the USSR sees herself as being particularly vulnerable to their strategic use.

Along with nuclear weapons, chemical and bacteriological weapons are classed by the Soviets as "weapons of mass destruction". Although bacteriological warfare is under international interdict, there is no doubt that the USSR has conducted a great deal of research in this sphere too.

The Soviet Armed Forces of today are trained to accept the use of chemical weapons as a matter of course. Soviet officers make an intensive study of the special conditions of chemical warfare on their Staff courses. Chemical phases are included in all large Ground Forces exercises and many Naval ones, and are a major feature of most Civil Defence exercises.

## Civil Defence

With the possible exception of China, the USSR maintains the largest and most active Civil Defence organisation in the world.

Under the control of Deputy Minister of Defence, the Civil Defence organisation reaches every sector and age-group of the population. Its objectives are, in event of an attack, to prevent panic, to maintain law and order, to maintain agricultural and industrial production, and to ensure organised decontamination to eradicate the effects of any attack.

To these ends, the organisation sets out to teach the Soviet citizen how to protect himself from nuclear, chemical and bacteriological weapons. Instruction is given in schools and universities, in factories and on farms. Large-scale compulsory exercises are organised regularly, involving hospital staff and local government officials as well as thousands of members of the public.

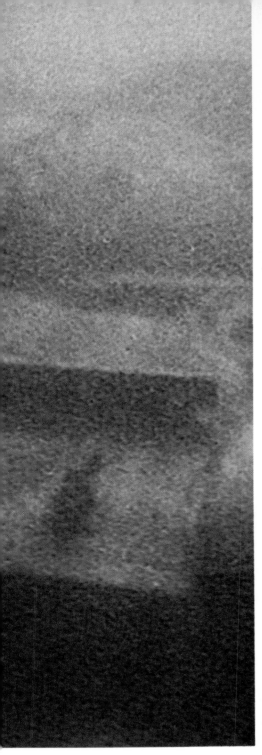

*Above left:* **All modern Soviet tanks can schnorkel across rivers with firm beds and banks. It takes only 30 minutes to waterproof the tank for wading in this manner**

*Above:* **A soldier of an NBC defence unit monitors contaminated equipment. The Russians use radio-active material in exercises to provide realistic training**

*Left:* **Chemical defence troops practise decontamination of a road during Exercise Neman in 1968, in preparation for the invasion of Czechoslovakia**

The Civil Defence organisation is responsible for organising the construction of shelters in factories, schools, public buildings and blocks of flats, the evacuation of urban areas and the organisation of emergency services. Naturally the Communist Party plays a major role in the co-ordination of Civil Defence activities, and co-opts the young party organs—the Pioneers and the Komsomol—and the DOSAAF into assisting with their organisation.

It is argued by some that Civil Defence will not be effective in a future war. The Soviet General Staff refute this idea totally, and urge the Party and Government to give the organisation all possible support. Moreover, the Civil Defence organisation provides yet another means of involving the Soviet population in disciplined activity and serves to maintain an awareness of the ever-present "Capitalist Threat" and the need for defence against it.

# Army Weapons

**Bill Gunston**

## The Soviet Union

| | |
|---|---|
| Total armed forces | Active 4.4 million; reserve 6.8 million |
| Ground Forces Command | 1.9 million active regular and conscripted troops (KGB troops 375,000, including border guards, Ministry of Interior and Construction troops 290,000). The USSR is divided into 16 military districts and Soviet troops abroad are formed into 4 'groups of forces'. |
| | In peace time, teeth arms are organised in divisions of 3 types: 110 Motor Rifle Divisions, 50 Tank Divisions, 8 Airborne Divisions. |
| There are 3 stages of combat readiness | |
| First category | over 75 per cent manned with full equipment scales |
| Second category | 50-75 per cent manned with full scales of fighting vehicles but not necessarily of the latest type |
| Third category | 35-50 per cent manned with 50-75 per cent equipment scales plus 'mothballed' obsolescent equipment. |
| First category equipment scales | *Tank Divs:* 325 tanks; 170 combat APCs; 98 battle reconnaissance vehicles; 96 guns, rocket launcher vehicles or heavy mortars, plus 60 AA missile vehicles or radar controlled gun systems; 4 FFR (FROGs) 21 heavy anti-tank weapons. |
| | *Motor Rifle Divs:* 260 tanks; up to 372 combat APCs; 125 battle reconnaissance vehicles; 144 field guns; rocket launcher vehicles or heavy mortars; 60 AA missile vehicles or radar-controlled gun systems; 4 FFR (Frogs); 81 heavy anti-tank weapons. |
| | *Airborne Divs:* 126 BMD combat vehicles; 18 ASU 85 SP guns; 81 field guns, plus medium or heavy mortars and rocket launchers; 138 heavy anti-tank guns/missiles; 18 battle reconnaissance vehicles. |
| Second category equipment scales | *Tank Divs:* 310 tanks, less AA defence. |
| | *Motor Rifle Divs:* 215 tanks; 312 combat APCs; less AA and anti-tank weapons. |
| Third category equipment scales | These vary to accommodate stockpiling requirements. Combat ready vehicles usually comprise 75 per cent of Second Category scales. |

### Deployment

| Divisions | Tank | M.R. | Air | |
|---|---|---|---|---|
| Group of Soviet Forces (Germany) | 10 | 10 | — | All Category 1 |
| Central Group of Forces (Czechoslovakia) | 2 | 3 | — | All Cateogry 1 |
| Northern Group of Forces (Poland) | 2 | — | — | All Category 1 |
| Southern Group of Forces (Hungary) | 2 | ·2 | — | All Category 1 |
| European USSR (Moscow, Leningrad, Kiev, Odessa, Belorussian, Baltic, Carpathian Military Districts) | 23 | 36 | 40 | All airborne: Cat 1 <br> Tank and MR: 35% Cat 1 <br> 35% Cat 2 <br> 30% Cat 3 |
| Southern USSR (N. Caucasus, Trans-Caucasus and Turkestan Military Districts) | 3 | 19 | 2 | All airborne: Cat 1 <br> Tank and MR: 35% Cat 1 <br> 35% Cat 2 <br> 35% Cat 3 |
| Central USSR (Volga and Ural Military Districts) | 1 | 5 | — | All Cat 3 |
| Eastern USSR (Central Asian, Siberian, Transbaikal and Far Eastern Military Districts and Mongolian Peoples Republic) | 7 | 5 | 1 or 2 | Airborne div(s): Cat 1 <br> Tank and MR: 35% Cat 1 <br> 30% Cat 2 <br> 35% Cat 3 |

### Major Weapons and Equipment

| | | *Estimated Totals* |
|---|---|---|
| Tanks: | T-72, T-62, T-55, T-54, T-10(m) | 42,000 |
| APC'S and AAICUs: | BMP, BMD, GTTM1970, PT-76, BRDM, BTR 60, BTR 50, BTR 40, BTR 152 | 41,000 |
| Artillery: | 152 and 122mm SP guns, 180mm, 152mm, 130mm, 122mm field guns; 122mm, 140mm, 200mm, 240mm, multi-barrelled rocket launchers; | 20,000 |
| | 120mm, 160mm, 240mm, heavy mortars; | 8 to 10,000 |
| | 57mm, 73mm, 82mm, 85mm, 100mm, 107mm anti-tank guns and Snapper, Sagger and Swatter anti-tank guided weapons. | |
| AA Artillery: | 23mm, 57mm; tower AA guns; ZSU57-2 and ZSU 23-4 AA SP guns; | 6 to 7,000 |
| | 85mm, 100mm, 130mm emplaced guns; SA-7 (hand held), SA-9, SA-6, SA-4, SA-8 and SA-2 mobile AA missiles. | (excluding SA-7) |

| | | | |
|---|---|---|---|
| Per Annum Production Rates 1974-75 (USSR only) | Tanks 2,600 | Artillery 1,400 | APC/AAICV 3,700 |
| Frontal Aviation (Under Ground Forces Control) | Helicopters: | Hind, Hip, Hook, Hound (under Divisional and Army Control) | 1,800 |
| | Fixed wing aircraft | Total: 6,000 aircraft — 1,000 fighters, 2,000 fighter bombers — 3,000 strike aircraft. Grouped in Tactical Air Armies, one with each of 12 border Military Districts and European Military Districts in USSR, and one with each Group of Forces abroad. Largest is 16 TAA with GSFG. Approx. 4,200 aircraft in Europe and European USSR and 1,800 in Central and Eastern USSR. | |
| | Aircraft: | MiG 25, MiG 23, Su 17/20, Su 19, MiG 21, Su 7, MiG 19, MiG 17, Yak 28, Il 28, An 12 EW. | |

## Non-Soviet Warsaw Pact Countries

In recent years the improvement in the quality of equipment supplied by the USSR to her Warsaw Pact Allies has been tremendous. In addition, several Warsaw Pact Nations, most notably Czechoslovakia, have developed their own armaments industries. The table below shows the priority allotted to Non-Soviet Warsaw Pact (NSWP) armies for quality/quantity of equipment supplied by the USSR. (The figures indicate total equipment to date, not during year in question.)

| | 1963 | 1967 | 1971 | 1975 |
|---|---|---|---|---|
| 1 | POLAND } equally | CZECH | POLAND | POLAND |
| 2 | CZECH | POLAND | CZECH | E. GERMANY |
| 3 | BULGARIA | HUNGARY | HUNGARY | CZECH |
| 4 | HUNGARY | BULGARIA | E. GERMANY | BULGARIA } equally |
| 5 | ROMANIA | E. GERMANY | BULGARIA | HUNGARY |
| 6 | E. GERMANY | ROMANIA | ROMANIA | ROMANIA |

The low positions of Czechoslovakia and Hungary on the list reflect the large amount of equipment produced for these armies in Eastern European arms factories. In effect, of all East European armies, only Romania's was not fully modernised by early 1976. The improvement in the East German Army's equipment holdings was most marked of all the Warsaw Pact Armies.

## East Germany (DDR)

| | |
|---|---|
| Total Armed Forces | 140,000 MOD troops, 48,000 Border troops, 25,000 Ministry of the Interior troops, 500,000 Territorial Workers Militia, 250,000 Reserves (active), |
| Ground Forces | 102,000 |
| | Along with Romania, E. Germany is the only Warsaw Pact country in the short (18 months) conscription period (usually 2 years) 4 Motor Rifle Divs; 2 Tank Divs. organised into Northern (V), Southern (III) Military Districts, the Tank Divs in each case being located close to the Polish border (see maps); 2 airborne battalions. All at full or 75 per cent strength. |
| Weapons and Equipment | Tanks T-62, T-55, T-54, T-34 |
| | OT-65, PT-76, BRDM, BTR 40 Recce vehicles |

2,500
220

| | | |
|---|---|---|
| *APCs/AAICVs* | BMP, BTR 60, BTR 50, BTR 152, APCs | |
| *Artillery* | 76mm, 85mm, 100mm, 122mm, 130mm, 152mm, Czech RL-70, MBRL, 120mm mortars; | |

Snapper, Swatter, Sagger, ATGM; and 57, 82, 85, and 100mm A-Tk guns
Frog-7 and Scud B Tactical Surface-to-Surface missiles (SSMs);
ZSU 57-2 and ZSU 23-4 SPAA guns and S60 57mm AA guns; SA-7 missiles
Recently, East Germany has begun to buy equipment from Czechoslovakia, in addition to heavy equipment made in the GDR under licence. There are, however, no AFVs of native design.

*Frontal Aviation*  90 Mi-1, Mi-4, Mi-8 helicopters, 500 FGA aircraft (MiG-17, MiG-21, MiG-23 and Su-7), 34 Transport aircraft
The airborne battalions rely on Soviet aircraft or Civil aviation for transport.

## Poland

**Total Armed Forces**  298,000 MOD troops, 80,000 Territorial Defence Troops (inc. Border Guards), 350,000 Volunteer Militia, 500,000 Reserves
**Ground Forces**  212,000
5 Tank Divs.; 8 M.R. Divs.; 1 Airborne Div.; 1 Marine Div.; a large percentage at full strength. Qualitatively and quantatively the strongest Non-Soviet Warsaw Pact Army.

| **Weapons and Equipment** | *Tanks:* | T-62, T-55, T-54, JS-III | 4,200 |
|---|---|---|---|
| | *Battle Recce Vehicles* | PT-76, BRDM, FUG | 800 + |
| | *APCs* | OT-62, TOPAZ, OT-64, SKOT | |
| | *Artillery* | 76mm, 85mm, 100mm, 122mm, 152mm, guns; 85 and 100mm SP assault guns; 122 and 152mm modern SP guns; 122mm and 140mm MBRL; 120mm mortars. | |
| | | 80 Frog 7 and Scud B SSMU. | |
| | | 76, 82, 85, 100mm A-Tk guns. | Total 2,000 |
| | | ASU-57 and ASU-85. | |
| | | Snapper, Sagger, ATGW. | |
| | | ZSU 57-2 and ZSU 23-4 AA guns. | |
| | | 57, 85mm and 100mm AA guns. | |
| | | SA-6, SA-7, SA-9 AA missiles. | |
| | *Frontal Aviation* | 130 Mi 2, 4, 8, helicopters, 645 FGA aircraft — Mig 17/19/21/23, Su-7, Su-20, 60 Transport aircraft can transport about ¼ of Airborne strength. Almost all APCs are domestically produced with Czechoslovakia. Many other items of equipment are bought from Czechoslovakia or licence-built in Poland. | |

## Hungary

**Total Armed Forces**  103,000 MOD Troops, 20,000 Border Guards, 60,000 Volunteer Militia, 110,000 Reserves
**Ground Forces**  88,000 conscript and regular
1 Tank Div., 5 Motor Rifle Divs.

| **Weapons and Equipment** | *Tanks:* | T-62, T-55/54, T-34 | 1,700 |
|---|---|---|---|
| | *Battle Recce Vehicles:* | BTR 40, PT-76, OT-65, FUG | 2,200 |
| | *APCs* | BTR 50, BTR 60, OT62 | |
| | *Artillery:* | 76, 85, 100, 122 and 152mm guns; 122mm and 140mm MBRC; 120mm and 160mm heavy mortars; 57, 82, 85 and 107mm A-tk guns; Snapper and Sagger ATGW. | 700 |
| | | Frog 3/4/5 and Scud A SSM; S60 and ZSU 57-2 AA guns; 85 and 100mm AA guns and SA-7. | |
| | *Danube flotilla:* | 10 gunboats; 6 landing craft. | |
| | *Frontal Avaition* | 30 Hook and Hound helicopters; 120 FGA Aircraft — MiG 15/17/19/21; A large percentage of Hungary's AFVs are the light domestically produced battle/recce vehicles such as the OT-65 and FUG. | |

## Bulgaria

**Total Armed Forces**  150,000 MOD troops, 20,000 Ministry of Interior troops and Border Guards, 12,000 Construction troops, 150,000 Volunteer militia, 280,000 Reserves
**Ground Forces**  120,000 conscript and regular
8 Motor Rifle Divs.; 5 Tank regiments; 1 Airborne regiment; 35 per cent at cadre strength (20 to 30 per cent manned and all equipment). Due to the mountainous terrain, Bulgaria does not deploy Tank Divisions, but alone amongst Warsaw Pact Armies deploys her armour with her infantry.

| **Weapons and Equipment** | *Main tank force:* | T-55/T-54 — approx 2,000. A few training units with T-62 plus approx 150 T-34 tanks; 600 PT-76 and BRDM and BTR-40 Recce vehicles; 2,000 BTR-60, BTR-50 and OT-62 (Topaz) APCs. |
|---|---|---|
| | | 1,000 Artillery pieces, rocket launchers and mortars, inc. 100mm, 122mm, 130mm, 152mm towed guns and 120mm mortars; 30 Frog 3/4/5 and 20 Scud A missiles; 57mm, 76mm, 85mm anti-tank guns; Snapper and Sagger ATGW; ZSU 23-4, S-60 AA guns and SA-7; plus a large stockpile of older artillery pieces. |
| | *Frontal Aviation* | 36 Mi-4 Hound helicopters; 72 MiG-17 FGA aircraft; 12 MiG-21; 12 MiG 15; 12 Il-28 reece aircraft; approx 20 older type transport aircraft. |

The army relies on the Soviet air forces or its own civil air fleet to transport its Parachute Regiment.

## Czechoslovakia

**Total Armed Forces**  210,000 MOD troops, 20,000 Ministry of the Interior Border Guards, 120,000 Voluntary militia/CD, 305,000 Army reserves
**Ground Forces**  161,000 Conscript and regular
5 motor Rifle Divs.; 5 Tank Divs.; 1 Airborne Regiment; (35 per cent at Cadre strength).

| **Weapons and Equipment** | *Tanks:* | T-62, T-55/54 | 3,300 |
|---|---|---|---|
| | *APCs:* | OT-65 O/FUG Recce; OT-62 Topaz OT-64 Skot APCs. | 2,000 |
| | *Artillery:* | 85mm, 100mm, 122mm, 130mm, 152mm towed guns; 122 SP; RM-70, RM 132 multiple rocket launchers; 120mm mortars; 72 tactical SSM (Frog 4/5, Scud); Snapper, Sagger and Swatter ATGW; 57mm, 82mm, 85mm SP, 100mm, 107mm anti-tank guns; 23mm, 30mm, 57mm, 85mm AA guns; 30mm and ZSU SP AA guns; SA-7. | |
| | *Frontal Aviation* | 220 Hook, Hound, Harc helicopters; 370 FGA aircraft, inc. MiG 15, MiG 21, SU-7 and domestically produced trainers/close support aircraft. | |

Almost all the Czech Army's APCs are domestically produced (and in conjunction with Poland and Hungary), as is much of her artillery. Other heavy equipment is built under licence, including the 122mm SP gun. The RM-70 40 barrelled rocket launcher is an improvement on the Soviet BM-21. There is also a complete range of excellent Czech small arms and infantry anti-tank weapons.

## Romania

**Total Armed Forces**  167,000 MOD troops, 45,000 Border troops and Ministry of Interior troops, 700,000 Volunteer militia, 500,000 Reserves
**Ground Forces**  139,000
(16-months National Service Period)

Romania is the only Warsaw Pact country to have reduced its defence expenditure over the past 5 years, and her army is deficient in many items of modern equipment. There is little domestic production of AFVs. The BTR-60 has recently been produced under licence.
2 Tank Divs.; 8 Motor Rifle Divs.; 2 mountain regiments; 1 Airborne battalion (40 per cent at full strength; 60 per cent at 50 to 30 per cent strength.)

| **Weapons Equipment** | *Tanks:* | T-55/T-54, T-34 | 1,800 |
|---|---|---|---|
| | *Battle Recce vehicles:* | BTR-40, PT-76, OT-65 | 300 |
| | *APCs:* | BTR-50, 60, 152; OT-810, 62. | |
| | *Artillery:* | 76mm, 85mm, 100mm, 122mm, 130mm, 152mm guns; 85mm and 100mm obsolescent SP guns; 120mm mortars; 132mm Czech MBRL; Frog 4, Scud A SSM; 57mm, 85mm, 100mm A-Tk guns; Snapper and Sagger ATGW; ZSU 57-2 SPAA guns; 37, 57 and 100mm AA guns. | |
| | *Frontal Aviation* | 12 Hound helicopters; 180 FGA aircraft — MiG 15/17/19/21; 30 Transport aircraft (Il-14 and Il-18). | |

# T-64 or T-72

**New battle tank**
**Combat weight:** Estimated at 39·3 tons (40,000kg).
**Length:** (Gun to front) about 32ft (10m).
**Length:** (Gun to rear) about 23ft (7m).
**Width:** About 11ft 6in (3·5m).
**Height:** Estimated at 7ft 2in (2200mm).
**Engine:** New engine of unknown type, but expected to be water-cooled diesel of about 900hp.
**Armament:** New gun reported variously as having calibre of 122mm and of 125mm, with bore rifled at start and smooth thereafter, firing fin-stabilized APDS ammunition from 28-round automatic loader; probably one 7·62mm (co-axial) with large quantity of ammunition.
**Speed:** Up to 50mph (80km/h).
**Range:** Probably about 310 miles (500km).
**Armour:** Probably up to 120mm (more on mantlet), possibly of modern type resistant to shaped charges.

Observers in the West have suggested that the new turret of the T-62 was probably intended to be fitted to a new chassis which was not ready in time. Continued progressive development led, by way of a reported T-67 with the T-62 turret, to today's new main battle tank now equipping armoured divisions of the Soviet and other Warsaw Pact forces. Its designation has been reported to be T-64 and also T-72 (the latter was accepted in the UK and USA at the time of writing), and it is certainly an extremely formidable tank able to outgun and out-fight any Western tank except the British Chieftain. The completely new chassis has small wheels and return rollers, a new engine and transmission, and low-flash fuel stowage as protection on each side. The heavily armoured turret incorporates a superb new gun with mechanical loading. This has allowed the crew to be reduced from

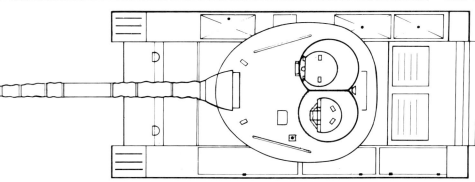

*Above:* **Drawings represent 'development' T-64 (T-72) with different guns**

four to three, with the commander and gunner seated high in the turret with no need to attend to the main gun. The very latest IR, laser-ranging and NBC equipment are certain to be fitted, and it is reported that driver fatigue has been greatly eased by reducing engine vibration and driving work-load. Road speed is remarkable.

# T-62

**Main battle tank**
**Combat weight:** (Fully stowed, no crew) 36·93 tons (37,500 kg).
**Length:** (Gun to front) about 30ft 8in (9488 or 9770mm).
**Length:** (Gun to rear) 22ft (6705mm).
**Width:** Close to 11ft (3352mm).
**Height:** 7ft 11in (2400mm).
**Engine:** V-2-62 vee-12 water-cooled diesel, 700hp.
**Armament:** U-5TS 115mm smooth-bore gun, 40 rounds; one 7·62mm (co-axial) with 2,000 or 3,500 rounds.
**Speed:** Up to 34mph (55km/h).
**Range:** Typically 310 miles (500km).
**Armour:** Up to 100mm, mantlet up to 170mm.

Again the Soviet designers found the existing (T-55) design almost impossible to better. The T-62 follows exactly the same formula but with a slightly bigger hull housing more power and some extra equipment, and with an outstanding smooth-bore gun firing fin-stabilized ammunition. The bigger gun, with evacuator

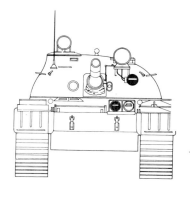

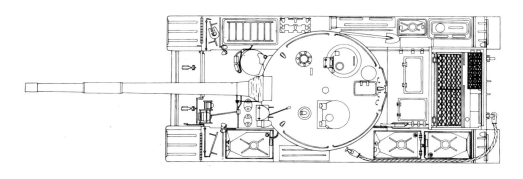

well back from the muzzle, is an identification feature, as are the close-spaced three front pairs of road wheels (the opposite of the T-54 and -55 chassis). The commander's cupola is cast integral with the turret, and equipment includes full IR, NBC protection and deep snorkel for wading. Since 1973, eight years after the T-62 entered service, these tanks have appeared with laser ranging and a 12·7mm AA gun. Numerous examples of these formidable tanks have been supplied to at least six countries outside the Warsaw Pact. It will remain the principal Soviet battle tank until about 1978, when T-64 (T-72) numbers are likely to overtake it.

**T-62 tanks on a recent exercise in the Soviet Union**

# T-54, T-55

**Main battle tank and derived vehicles**
**Combat weight** (fully stowed, no crew): About 35·9 tons (36,500kg).
**Length:** (Gun to front) 29ft 7in (9020mm).
**Length:** (Gun to rear) 21ft 7in (6570mm).
**Width:** 10ft 9½in (3265mm).
**Height:** 7ft 10in (2380mm).
**Engine:** V-2-54 vee-12 water-cooled diesel, 520hp; T-55, V-55, 580hp.
**Armament:** D-10T, D-10TG or D-10T2S 100mm gun (T-54, 34 rounds, T-55, 43 rounds); two 7·62mm SGMT or PKT machine guns (co-axial and bow) with 3,000 rounds; T-54 also one 12·7mm DShK with 500 rounds for AA use.
**Speed:** 30mph (48km/h).
**Range:** 250 miles (400km); T-55, 310 miles (500km).
**Armour:** Up to 100mm, mantlet up to 170mm.

The Soviet tank designers found it hard to improve on the T-34/85, the T-44 of 1945 introducing an improved chassis but having the old turret. In 1947 the T-44 chassis reappeared with a new elliptical turret

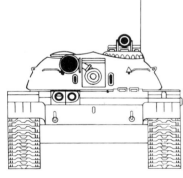

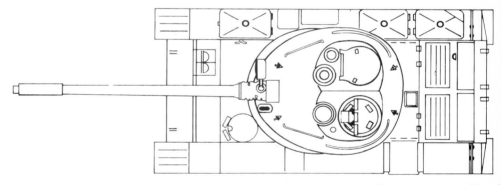

mounting a 100mm gun, and the resulting T-54 became the standard Soviet-bloc battle tank (much faster and more compact than Western tanks, but cramped inside). There were seven main production versions, some built in Poland, Czechoslovakia and China. The T-55, built in even greater numbers, appeared in 1961. This has slightly more power, a revised turret with more ammunition and no AA gun, and very tall snorkel tube for deep wading. Most tanks of this series have been progressively fitted with IR night equipment, stabilized gun and provision for NBC-contaminated environments. They are used by all Warsaw Pact armies, in tank, bridgelayer, flame-thrower, mine-clearing, recovery and dozer versions, and also by about 25 other countries.

# T-34/85

**Medium tank and many derived vehicles**
**Combat weight:** (Fully stowed, no crew) 32 tons (31,500kg).
**Length:** (Gun to front) 26ft 6in (8076mm).
**Length:** (Gun to rear) 20ft 4in (6190mm).
**Width:** About 10ft (2997–3050mm).
**Height:** About 8ft 6in (2680–2743mm).
**Engine:** Usually V-2-34 or -34M vee-12 water-cooled diesel, 500hp.
**Armament:** M-1944 85mm gun, 56 rounds; DT or DTM 7·62mm machine guns (co-axial and bow) with total of 2,394 rounds.
**Speed:** Up to 34mph (55km/h).
**Range:** Up to 190 miles (300km).
**Armour:** Up to 75mm (2·95in).

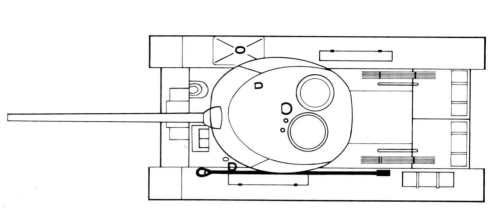

The original T-34 tank, derived by way of the BT Cruiser from the American Christie T.3 of 1931, is widely regarded as the best all-round tank of its age,

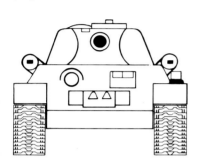

with great speed, firepower and armour. In 1941, when it had been in production just a year, it proved a severe shock to the invading Germans, who discussed the possibility of making a copy themselves. In December 1943 the T-34/85 appeared, with a hard-hitting 85mm gun (instead of 76mm) in a larger three-man turret. Production continued long after 1945, the total possibly rivalling the astronomic numbers of the original T-34/76. Even today many thousand of these excellent tanks and their chassis continue in service in many nations. The chassis is used for the SU-85 and SU-100 (p.188), and other special purpose vehicles for engineering, recovery, minelaying, mine-clearing, bulldozing, crane and bridgelaying. At least 20 nations still use the T-34/85 as a medium tank.

# T-10

**T-10, T-10M heavy tanks**
**Combat weight:** (T-10M, no crew) 48·23 tons (49,000kg), 54 US tons.
**Length:** (Gun to front) 34ft 9in (10,490mm typical).
**Length:** (Gun to rear) 23ft 1in (7400mm).
**Width:** 11ft 8in (3440mm).
**Height:** (Excl. AA gun) 7ft 5in (2260mm).
**Engine:** V-10 vee-12 water-cooled diesel, 700hp.
**Armament:** M-1955 122mm gun, 30 rounds; (T-10M) two 14·5mm KPV (co-axial and AA), 1,000 rounds; (T-10) two 12·7mm DShK, 1,000 rounds.
**Speed:** 26mph (42km/h).
**Range:** 155 miles (250km).
**Armour:** Up to 210mm.

Last of the Soviet 'heavy' tanks, the T-10 family were natural improvements of the IS-III, with a new engine and gun, seven road wheels each side in a revised suspension, new hull with better armour, and a bigger and less cramped turret. The improved 122mm gun has a bore evacuator, and in the T-10M (possibly in the T-10 also) is stabilized. The T-10M has augmented equipment including IR, and its gun has a large muzzle brake. Deep wading is possible with the tall snorkel stack. Some of these tanks have a large container welded around the rear of the turret. They are in use in several countries outside the Warsaw Pact, and all chassis of this type seem to be still serving as tanks and not as missile carriers or in other roles.

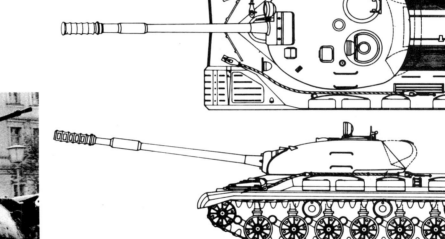

# IS (JS)

**IS-II, -III and -IV heavy tanks**
**Combat weight:** (Fully stowed, no crew) 45·2–45·8 tons (46,000–46,500kg).
**Length:** (Gun to front) 32ft 9in (9980mm).
**Length:** (Gun to rear) 22ft 4in (6800mm).
**Width:** 10ft (3050mm).
**Height:** (Excl. AA gun) 9ft (2740mm).
**Engine:** V-2-IS vee-12 water-cooled diesel, 520hp.
**Armament:** M1943 (D-25) 122mm gun, 28 rounds; DTM 7·62mm co-axial, 2,000 rounds (JS-2, three DTM, bow, co-ax and rear); 12·7mm DShK for AA use.
**Speed:** 23mph (37km/h).
**Range:** 112 miles (180km).
**Armour:** Up to 120mm (JS-2, 132mm).

The standard heavy tank of the ground forces in June 1941 was the KV-1 (Klimenti Voroshilov), first used in Finland in 1939. Though heavily armoured it lacked the T-34's good shape, and had only the same 76mm gun. By late 1941 lead-designer Kotin had transformed this into the JS-1 (Josef Stalin), with 85mm gun, followed in early 1944 by the JS-2 (now called IS-II) with 122mm gun, and in January 1945 by the excellent JS-3 (IS-III) with squat sloping profile. Small numbers were built in the late 1940s of the JS-4 with even heavier armour and more power, and with a co-axial 12·7mm gun. Large numbers of IS-type tanks and derived vehicles remain in service, the chassis being used in the 'Scud A' and 'Scud B' missile systems, the 'Scamp' and 'Scrooge' ICBM systems, the ISU-122 and -152 assault guns, the 'Frog 1' tactical rocket system, several obsolescent SP guns and large mortars, and a variety of recovery and other engineer vehicles.

# PT-76

**PT-76 (three models) amphibious light tank and derivatives**
**Combat weight:** (No crew) 13·78 tons (14,000kg).
**Length:** (Gun to front) 25ft 0in (7625mm).
**Length:** (Gun to rear) 22ft 7in (6910mm).
**Width:** 10ft 5in (3180mm).
**Height:** 7ft 5in (2260mm) (early models, 2195mm).
**Engine:** V-6 six-in-line water-cooled diesel, 240hp.
**Armament:** 76mm gun (D-56T, multi-slotted muzzle brake, PT-76-I; D-56TM, double-baffle brake plus bore evacuator, Model II; unknown gun designation, plain barrel, Model III), 40 rounds; 7·62mm SGMT (co-axial), 1,000 rounds.
**Speed:** 27mph (44km/h) on land, 6¼mph (10km/h) on water.
**Range:** 155 miles (250km) on land, 62½ miles (100km) on water.
**Armour:** Usually 11–14mm.

Since it appeared in 1952 this large, lightly armoured but highly mobile vehicle has appeared in at least 15 different guises, and been built in very large numbers. The basic PT-76 (PT-76B when fitted with stabilized gun) is still the most numerous reconnaissance tank of the Warsaw Pact armies. To swim, the twin hydrojets at the rear are uncovered and clutched-in, and a trim board is folded down at the front. Smokelaying equipment is standard. The 76mm ammunition is the same as for the M-1942 (ZIS-3), SU-76 and T-34/76. The PT-76 is used by at least 17 countries outside the Warsaw Pact. Its basic design of chassis is used in the ASU-85, SA-6 Gainful SAM vehicle, BTR-50, FROG-2/-3/-4/-5, GSP bridger, M-1970, OT-62 APC, Pinguin, PVA and ZSU-23-4

# BMD

**Air-portable APC**

**Combat weight:** (without crew): Estimated 8.86 tons (9000kg).
**Length overall:** Estimated 17ft 4½ in (5300mm).
**Width overall:** Estimated 8ft 8in (2640mm).
**Height overall:** (excl. crew or aerials) 6ft 0in (1850mm).
**Engine:** Possibly a V-6, of about 280hp.
**Armament:** Turret identical to BMP, with 73mm low-pressure smooth-bore gun with auto-loading, from 30-round magazine, 7·62mm PKT co-axial, and 'Sagger' missile on launch rail. In addition, at least two 7·62mm PKT in mounts in front corners of hull.
**Speed:** Estimated at least 40mph (65kh/h) on land, 6mph (10km/h) in water.
**Cruising range:** Estimated 250 miles (400km) on land.
**Armour:** Probably 20mm.

First seen in November 1973, this trim little APC (armoured personnel carrier) is another of the 'quart in a pint pot' vehicles developed primarily for the large and important Soviet airborne forces. Though such aircraft as the An-22 could easily carry the BMP, it was judged the same capability could be built into a smaller and lighter APC capable of being airlifted in greater numbers and more readily dropped by parachute. At first styled 'M-1970' in the West, the BMD (Boyevaya Machine Desantnaya) has a crew of three and carries six airborne infantry. Unlike the bigger BMP it has a hydrojet for water propulsion, but its interior is obviously cramped and it is doubtful if there is NBC protection for nine occupants. It has the BMP turret, possibly with fewer reload missiles, but cannot be classed as an MICV (mechanised infantry combat vehicle.

# BTR-40/BRDM

**BTR-40 family, BTR-40P (BRDM) family and BTR-40PB (BRDM-2)**
**Combat weight:** -40, 5·2 tons (5300kg); -40P, 5·5 tons (5600kg); -40PB, 6·89 tons (7000kg).
**Length:** -40, 16ft 8in (5000mm); -40P, 18ft 8in (5700mm); -40PB, 18ft (5750mm)
**Width:** -40, 6ft 3in (1900mm); -40P, 7ft 6in (2285mm); -40PB, 7ft 8½ in (2350mm).
**Height:** -40, 5ft 8½ in (1750mm); -40P, 6ft 3in (1900mm); -40PB, 7ft 7in (2310mm).
**Engine:** -40, GAZ-40, six-in-line water-cooled gasoline, 80hp; -40P, GAZ-40P, 90hp; -40PB, GAZ-41, vee-eight, 140hp.
**Armament:** Most, 7·62mm SGMB, 1,250 rounds; PB has 14·5mm KPVT turret, 500 rounds.
**Speed:** -40, 50mph (80km/h); -40P, land 50mph (80km/h), water 6mph (9km/h); -40PB, land 62mph (100km/h), water 6¼ mph (10km/h).
**Range:** -40, 404 miles (650km); -40P, 310 miles (500km); -40PB, 465 miles (750km/h).
**Armour:** All ·10mm.

The wartime GAZ-63A 4×4 truck was developed into the BTR-40 scout car which went into production in 1951. Large numbers of many versions are still serving, but from 1959 many were replaced by the amphibious BTR-40P (BRDM), which has central tire-pressure control and two pairs of retractable mid-

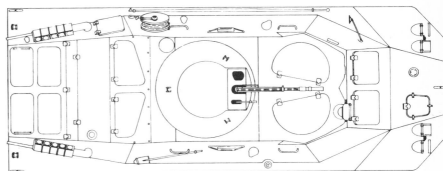

*Top:* **Colour side view shows BTR-40PB (BRDM-2); below it is top view of similar version.**

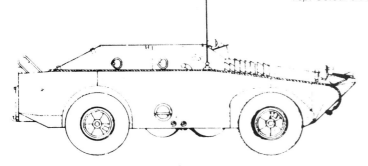

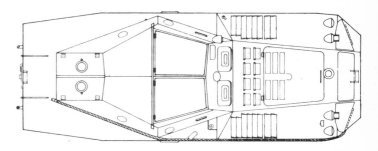

*Above:* **Side and top views of the BTR-40 (BRDM) reconnaissance vehicle**

wheels for rough ground and trench-crossing. Again there are many versions, some carrying either 'Snapper', 'Swatter' or 'Sagger' ATGW (anti-tank guided weapons). All have hydrojet water propulsion. In 1966 appeared BTR-40PB, also called BTR-40P-2 and BRDM-2, which has a modified hull, more power, gun turret (same as on the BTR-60PB) and advanced overland navigation system. Unlike similar designs of other Warsaw Pact forces it has a single waterjet (not twin). Two important versions respectively mount six AT-3 'Sagger' ATGWs and quad or octuple launchers for the SA-7 surface-to-air missile.

# BTR-60

**Armoured personnel carriers and derivatives**
**Combat weight:** Loaded: -60PK, 9·82 tons (9980kg);
-60PB, 10·14 tons (10,300kg).
**Length:** 24ft 10in (7560mm).
**Width:** 9ft 3in (2818mm).
**Height:** -60PK, 6ft 9in (2055mm); -60PB, 7ft 7in
(2310mm).
**Engine:** Two GAZ-49B six-in-line water-cooled
gasoline, 90hp each.
**Armament:** See text.
**Speed:** Land, 50mph (80km/h); water, 6¼mph
(10km/h).
**Range:** 310 miles (500km).
**Armour:** -60PK, 10mm; -60PB, 14mm.

First seen in November 1961, the BTR-60 family is
impressive, and is widely used in Warsaw Pact forces
(it is the standard APC of the Soviet Marines) and has
been exported to at least ten other countries. The large
hull is boat-shaped for good swimming and to deflect
hostile fire. It runs on eight land wheels, all powered
and with power steering on the front four. Tire pressures
are centrally controlled at all times. The twin rear
engines can be switched to drive waterjets. The basic
BTR-60P has an open top or canvas hood, and carries
two crew plus 16 troops. Typical armament is a
12·7mm and from one to three 7·62mm SGMB or PK.
The -60PK (often called BTR-60PA) has an armoured
roof, carries 16 passengers and has a single 12·7 or
7·62mm gun. The PB has a turret with co-axial 14·5mm
KPVT and 7·62 PKT (the same turret as on the BTR-
40P-2) and carries 14 troops. There are special
versions for platoon and other commanders, with
extra communications.

*Above:* **BTR-60PA.** *Below:* **Top and side views of BTR-60PB which has conical turret, mounting 14.5mm and 7.62mm machine guns.** *Photo* **below shows interior of BTR-60 APC**

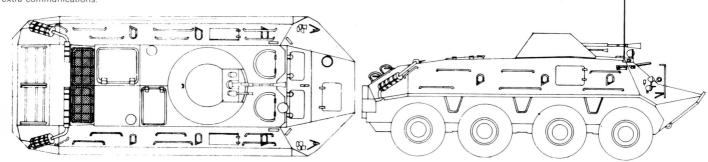

# BMP

## Infantry combat vehicle and derivatives

**Weight:** Empty, 11·32 tons (11,500kg); laden in combat, 12·3 tons (12,500kg).
**Length:** 22ft 2in (6750mm) (incorrectly judged at first by Western observers to be 6300mm).
**Width:** 9ft 9in (2970mm).
**Height:** Over hull, 4ft 10in (1470mm); over turret IR light, 6ft 6in (1980mm).
**Engine:** New model of V-6 six-in-line water-cooled diesel, 280hp.
**Armament:** 73mm (not 76mm) gun, 40 rounds; AT-3 ('Sagger') ATGW launcher; 7·62mm PKT (co-axial), 1,000 rounds.
**Speed:** Land, 34mph (55km/h); deep snow, 25mph (40km/h); water 5mph (8km/h).
**Range:** 186 miles (300km).
**Armour:** Mainly 14mm.

When it appeared in 1967 the BMP was recognised in the West as just what the West's own armies desperately needed: a true MICV (mechanized infantry combat vehicle). Significantly smaller than Western APCs (armoured personnel carriers), it has considerably greater firepower. The eight troops have multiple periscopes and can fire on the move; like the crew of three (the commander is also leader of the troop squad), they have NBC protection in the pressurized and filtered hull. The new 73mm gun has a smooth bore and fires fin-stabilized boosted HEAT ammunition at eight rounds per minute with the aid of an automatic loader. The missile launcher above the gun carries one round, with three more loaded manually from racks inside. The BMP is amphibious, with scoops on the tracks and rear water-deflector plates to give thrust. Since 1970 the sharp bow has been made more prominent, which with other changes has improved swimming behaviour. In 1975 a variant was seen with the troop compartment replaced by a rear-positioned turret carrying a battlefield radar.

The BMP's extreme vulnerability in the face of a strong defence was amply demonstrated in the 1973 Arab-Israeli war. Consequently, there is a fierce debate in the Soviet Army at present (1976) as to how this vehicle should be used in battle.

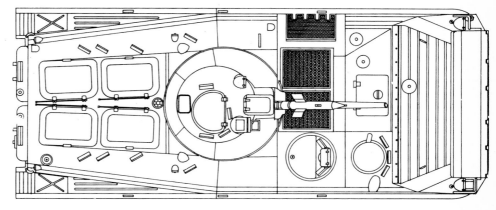

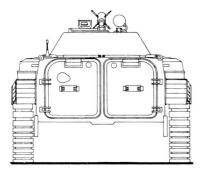

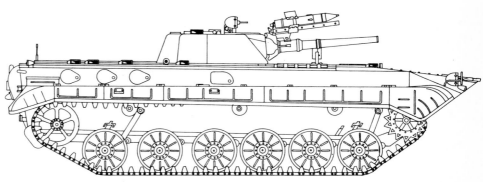

# BTR-152

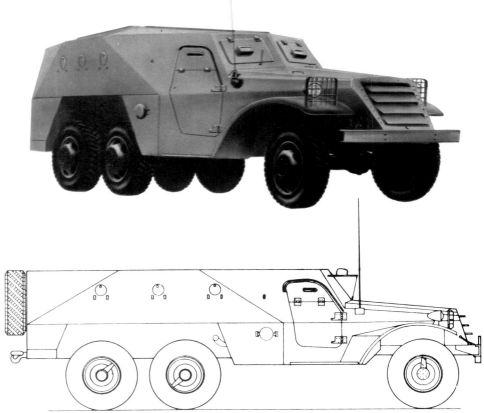

**BTR-152 family of APCs and derivatives**
**Combat weight:** Basic 152, loaded: 8·8 tons (8950kg).
**Length:** 22ft 3in (6830mm).
**Width:** 7ft 7½in (2320mm).
**Height:** (Excl. gun) 6ft 6in (1980mm).
**Engine:** ZIL-123 six-in-line water-cooled gasoline, 110hp.
**Armament:** usual standard, 7·62mm SGMB, 1,250 rounds; (-152V-2) ZPU-2 twin 14·5mm AA, 300 or 600 rounds.
**Speed:** 41mph (65km/h).
**Range:** 405 miles (650km).
**Armour:** Up to 12mm.

This 6×6 armoured personnel carrier appeared in 1950, and has since been considerably developed. Early versions were based on the ZIL-151 truck, but nearly all in current service use the modified ZIL-157 chassis with larger tires having centralized pressure regulation. These versions are designated -152V, many sub-types differing in equipment and other features. Some have an armoured roof, increasing weight to 9·05 tons (9200kg), while other variations include IR equipment, winch, weapons and the location of tire air piping. The -152U is a command model with extra communications, while the 152V-2 has twin AA guns as noted above. Normal load is a crew of two and 17 troops or almost any light weapons or stores, with additional towed loads. Though being replaced by amphibious vehicles these prolific vehicles still serve at least 30 nations including every Warsaw Pact army except Czechoslovakia.

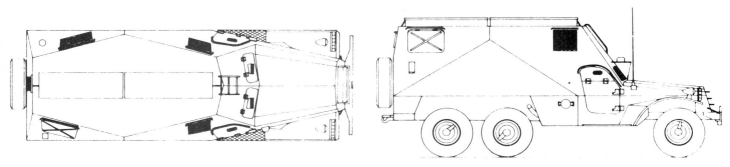

*Top:* **BTR-152 with armoured roof.** *Above:* **Standard version with no roof armour.** *Below:* **Top and side views of 152U command version.**

*Photo* **below shows standard BTR-152 on exercise**

# BTR-50

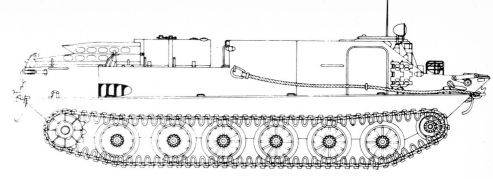

**Amphibious tracked APC and variants (data for PK)**
**Combat weight:** (Loaded) 14·27 tons (14,500kg).
**Length:** 23ft 3in (7080mm) (not 6910mm as commonly reported).
**Width:** 10ft 3in (3140mm).
**Height:** (Excl. gun) 6ft 6in (1980mm).
**Engine:** V-6 six-in-line water-cooled diesel, 240hp.
**Armament:** 7·62mm SGMB, 1,250 rounds (see text for variations).
**Speed:** Land, 27mph (44km/h); water 6¼mph (10km/h).
**Range:** Land 162 miles (260km).
**Armour:** Up to 10mm.

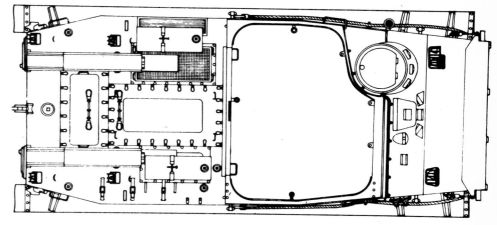

Based on the amphibious PT-76 chassis, the BTR-50 was first seen in 1957 as the open-topped BTR-50P. Today it is still the standard APC of Soviet motor-rifle regiments and serves Soviet and E German forces, and at least 16 other nations, in very large numbers. The most common version is the 50PK with armoured roof, though these cannot transport the artillery (usually 57, 76 or 85mm) transported and fired aboard the original open model. Normal load is two crew and 20 troops. Variants include the -50PA with 14·5mm KPVT or ZPU-1, the -50PU command vehicle with extremely elaborate navigation and communications equipment, and small numbers of special-purpose modifications used for such tasks as carrying ECM (countermeasures).

# ASU-57

**Airborne assault gun**
**Combat weight:** 3·3 tons (3350kg).
**Length:** (Gun to front) 16ft 4½in (4995mm).
**Length:** (Excl. gun) 11ft 5in (3480mm).
**Width:** 6ft 10in (2082mm).
**Height:** (Shield down, no AA) 3ft 10in (1180mm).
**Engine:** M-20E four-in-line water-cooled gasoline, 55hp.
**Armament:** Ch-51M 57mm gun, 30 rounds.
**Speed:** 28mph (45km/h).
**Range:** 155 miles (250km).
**Armour:** 6mm.

The Soviet Union was the pioneer of the modern airborne army which, so far as technology allows, lacks nothing. Great efforts have been made to build up an air-portable capability which includes even self-propelled heavy firepower. The ASU-57 was the first of these purpose-designed vehicles, and since 1957 it has been in large-scale service with Warsaw Pact powers. To get the weight down to a scarcely credible value it is extremely lightly armoured, and is mainly of light alloy. The engine is derived from that of the Pobeda family car. Large transport aircraft or helicopters can carry several, the former delivering via parachutes with retro-rockets ignited just above impact. The gun has the same ammunition as other Soviet ATk 57mm, and traverses 12° with rate of fire up to 10 rds/min. The original Ch-51 had a long 34-slot muzzle brake. Six airborne troops can ride as passengers behind the regular crew of three.

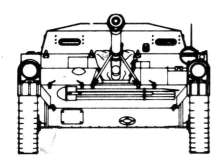

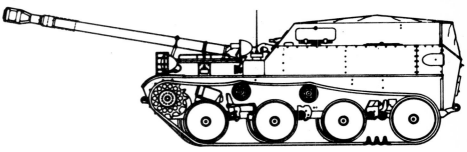

# ASU-85

**Airborne assault gun**
**Combat weight:** Loaded 13·78 tons (14,000kg).
**Length** (Gun horizontal ahead) 27ft 10in (8490mm).
**Width:** 9ft 2½in (2800mm).
**Height:** (Excl. IR etc.) 6ft 11in (2100mm).
**Engine:** V-6 six-in-line water-cooled diesel, 240hp.
**Armament:** Improved SD-44 85mm gun, 40 rounds; 7·62mm PKT (co-axial).
**Speed:** 27mph (44km/h).
**Range:** 162 miles (260km).
**Armour:** Up to 40mm.

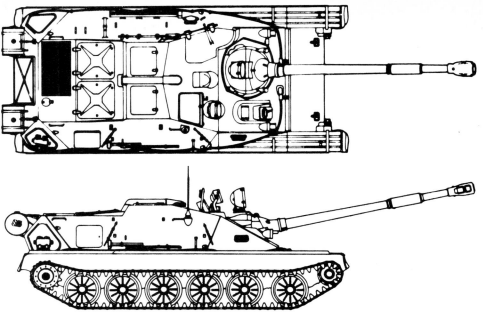

Much tougher and heavier than the ASU-57, this formidable vehicle became possible with the advent of the Mi-6 and Mi-10 helicopters and (for fixed-wing drop) high-capacity multi-chute and retro-rocket systems. The ASU-85 was first seen in 1962 and is widely used by Soviet and Polish airborne divisions. Though the chassis is based on the PT-76 it is not amphibious, having no waterjets. The gun has 12° traverse and fires up to 5 rds/min. Above the NBC-sealed and armoured roof are a large IR night-fighting light for the gunner, aligned with the gun, and a smaller one on the right for the commander. Since 1973 other target-acquisition and ranging aids are reported to have been retrofitted to these useful anti-armour vehicles.

# SU-100

**Assault gun.**
**Weight:** (Loaded, no crew) 31·1 tons (31,611kg).
**Length:** (Incl. gun) 32ft 8in (9960mm).
**Length:** (Excl. gun) 20ft 3½in (6190mm).
**Width:** 10ft 0in (3050mm).
**Height:** (Excl. aerial) 7ft 6in (2300mm).
**Engine:** V-2-34M vee-12 water-cooled diesel, 500hp (or V-2-3411, 520hp).
**Armament:** D-10S (M-1944) 100mm gun, 34 rounds.
**Elevation:** −2° to +17°.
**Traverse:** 17° total.
**Speed:** 35mph (55km/h).
**Armour:** Up to 75mm.

The SU-85 (85mm) assault gun is now seldom seen, most having been converted either into this more formidable vehicle or into training or recovery vehicles. The SU-100 uses the same chassis, based on that of the T-34 tank, but mounts the 100mm gun used in the T-54 and T-55 tanks and uses widely distributed ammunition (the same as for many field and AA guns). A wide range of special-purpose derivatives of the SU-100 are now in use, some having no gun and carrying ECM (countermeasures) and, dozer blades, command communications and other equipment. The basic SU-100 is used by about 18 nations.

# ZSU-23-4

**Quad self-propelled AA gun system**
**Combat weight:** 13·78 tons (14,000kg).
**Length:** 20ft 8in (6300mm).
**Width:** 9ft 8in (2950mm).
**Height:** (Radar stowed) 7ft 4½in (2250mm).
**Engine:** V-6 six-in-line water-cooled diesel, 240hp.
**Armament:** Quadruple ZU-23 23mm anti-aircraft, 1,000 rounds.
**Speed:** 27mph (44km/h).
**Range:** 162 miles (260km).
**Armour:** 10mm.

Extremely dangerous to aircraft out to a slant range of 6,600ft (2000m), the ZSU-23-4 is a neat package of firepower with its own microwave target-acquisition and fire-control radar and crew of four in an NBC-sealed chassis derived from the amphibious PT-76. Each gun has a cyclic firing rate of 800 to 1,000rds/min, and with liquid-cooled barrels can actually sustain this rate. The crew of four comprise commander, driver, radar observer and gunner, and there is plenty of room in the large but thin-skinned turret. Gun travel is unrestricted in traverse, and from —7° to +80°. First seen in 1955, this vehicle is used throughout Warsaw Pact armies where it is popularly named Shilka. The same chassis carries the SA-6 missile.

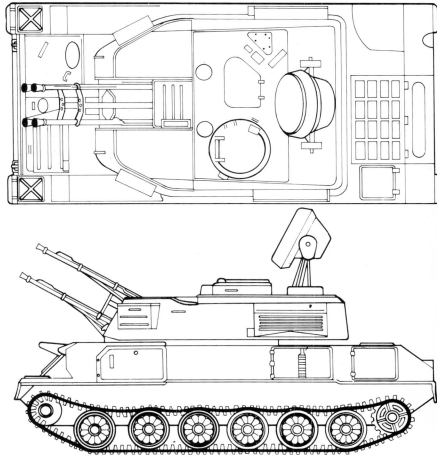

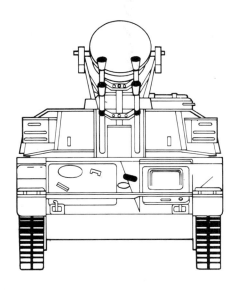

# ZSU-57-2

**Twin self-propelled AA guns.**
**Combat weight:** 27·65 tons (28,100kg).
**Length:** (Guns forward) 27ft 10in (8480mm).
**Length:** (Guns up or to rear) 20ft 6in (6220mm).
**Width:** 10ft 9in (3270mm).
**Height:** (Guns down) 9ft 0in (2750mm).
**Engine:** V-54 vee-12 water-cooled diesel, 520hp.
**Armament:** Twin S-68 57mm AA guns, 316 or 360 rounds.
**Speed:** 30mph (48km/h).
**Range:** 250 miles (400km).
**Armour:** Up to 15mm.

Used in greater numbers than any other SP AA system in the world, the ZSU-57-2 appeared in 1957 and equips all Warsaw Pact forces and at least 11 other nations. The chassis is a shortened version of that used in the T-54 tank, and notable shortcomings are absence of swimming or deep-wading capability, or a radar. On the other hand NBC, IR and a sophisticated optical system are fitted, and the crew of six have a considerable amount of equipment. Turret slewing (360°) and elevation (−5° to + 85°) are hydraulic, and the ammunition (same as the S-60 gun but not the same as 57mm anti-tank and assault guns) is effective out to 13,125ft (4000m) and against armoured vehicles can pierce 4·2in (106mm) at 500m range. Cyclic rate is 105 to 120 rds/min per gun, empty cases being ejected into the wire cage at the rear of the big open turret.

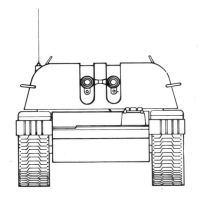

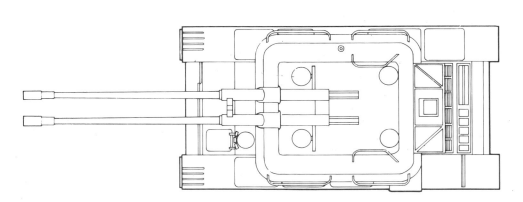

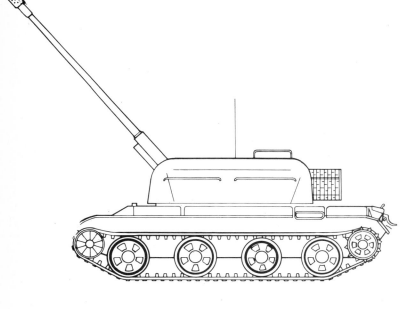

# 203mm M-1955

**Field howitzer.**
**Weight:** Firing 20·07 tons (20,400kg).
**Length:** Travelling 34ft 5in (10,485mm).
**Width:** Travelling 9ft 10in (2996mm).
**Elevation:** −2° to +50°.
**Traverse:** ±22°.
**Projectile mass:** (HE) 225lb (102kg).
**Muzzle velocity:** (HE) 2,600ft/sec (790m/sec).
**Maximum range:** 29,250m.

Largest modern Soviet artillery weapon, this powerful piece has a calibre of 8in and barrel 40 calibres long, giving muzzle velocity and range that really lift it out of the howitzer class. Normally towed by the AT-T, the 415hp tracked monster that carries the gun crew of 14—16, the M-1955 has a screw-type breech and fires separate-loading bagged ammunition with HE, concrete-piercing and (probably) nuclear warheads. Typical rate of fire is one round per minute. When travelling, the barrel is pulled back out of battery over the box-section split trails.

# 122mm D-30

**Field howitzer.**
**Weight:** Firing 3·1 tons (3150kg).
**Length:** Travelling 17ft 8½in (5400mm).
**Width:** Travelling 6ft 5in (1950mm).
**Elevation** −7° to +70°.
**Traverse:** 360°.
**Projectile mass:** (HE) 48·1lb (21·8kg).
**Muzzle velocity:** (HE) 2,264ft/sec (690m/sec).
**Maximum range:** (HE) 15,300m.

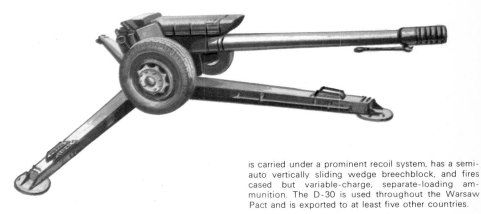

This howitzer, of 121·9mm (4·8in) calibre, typifies the dramatically advanced and effective design of the latest Soviet artillery. It is towed by a large lunette lug under or just behind the muzzle brake, with its trails folded under the barrel. To fire, the crew of seven rapidly unhitch; lower the central firing jack (lifting the wheels off the ground) and swing the outer trails through 120° on each side. The gun can then be aimed immediately to any point of the compass. The barrel is carried under a prominent recoil system, has a semi-auto vertically sliding wedge breechblock, and fires cased but variable-charge, separate-loading ammunition. The D-30 is used throughout the Warsaw Pact and is exported to at least five other countries.

# 122mm D-74

**Field gun.**
**Weight:** Firing 6·49 tons (6600kg).
**Length:** Travelling 32ft 0in (9763mm).
**Width:** Travelling 6ft 7½in (2027mm).
**Elevation:** −2° to +50°.
**Traverse:** ±30°.
**Projectile mass:** (APHE) 55·1lb (25kg).
**Muzzle velocity:** (APHE) 3,116ft/sec (950m/sec).
**Maximum range:** (HE) 21,900m.

Complementing the appreciably bigger and longer-ranged M-1954 and M-1946, which have a calibre of 130mm, the D-74 has a calibre of 121·9mm (4·8in) and uses the same chassis as the 152mm D-20 howitzer. It is similar to the D-20 in firing cased but separately loaded, variable-charge ammunition, and in having a circular firing jack and caster wheels for swiftly rotating the whole gun through 360°. Despite its smaller calibre the barrel (and thus the whole gun) is heavier than that of the D-20, because the length in calibres is 46·3, compared with only 29. Like the 152mm version the barrel is prominently stepped and has a semi-automatic vertically sliding wedge breechblock, and a double-baffle muzzle brake. The D-74 serves throughout the Warsaw Pact ground forces.

# 152mm D-20

**Field howitzer.**
**Weight:** Firing 5·56 tons (5650kg).
**Length:** Travelling 26ft 8½in (8138mm).
**Width:** Travelling 6ft 7½in (2027mm).
**Elevation** −5° to +63°.
**Traverse:** ±45°.
**Projectile mass:** (HE) 96·0lb (43·6kg).
**Muzzle velocity:** (HE) 2,149ft/sec (655m/sec).
**Maximum range:** 17,300m.

Standard heavy artillery in partnership with the D-74 (whose carriage is identical), the D-20 is a powerful 6-inch weapon which replaced the M-1937 (ML-20) of the same calibre used during World War 2. The massive barrel has a large double-baffle muzzle brake and semi-automatic sliding-wedge breech giving a rate of fire up to 4rds/min despite the use of separate-loading, variable-charge case-type ammunition. Essentially the D-20 is a D-74 with shorter barrel, the recoil mechanism being the same, as is the ability to traverse the whole gun swiftly through up to 360°. The D-20 is widely used throughout Warsaw Pact forces and also by several other nations.

# 100mm M-1955 and T-12

**Anti-tank and field guns (data for M-1955).**
**Weight:** Firing 2·95 tons (3000kg).
**Length:** Travelling 28ft 7in (8717mm).
**Width:** Travelling 5ft 2½in (1585mm).
**Elevation:** −5° to +45°
**Traverse:** ±30°
**Projectile mass** (APHE) 35lb (15·9kg).
**Muzzle velocity:** (APHE) 3,280ft/sec (1000m/sec).
**Maximum range:** (HE) 21,000m.

One of the most widely used guns of the Warsaw Pact ground forces, these long-barreled (56 calibres) weapons have high muzzle velocity and can fire HE, APHE or HEAT ammunition. Fixed ammunition is used, which with the semi-automatic, vertical-sliding wedge breechblock gives a practical rate of fire of 7 to 8rds/min. The M-1955 is lighter than the old M-1944 (D-10) and so runs on single tires. It has box-section split trails, twin recoil cylinders behind the shield, and a prominent 'pepperpot' muzzle brake. The later T-12, which has replaced the M-1955 in many Soviet and E. German units since 1968, has a new barrel firing different ammunition with greater muzzle velocity. The most obvious difference is that the muzzle brake does not taper and is only fractionally larger in diameter than the barrel. Usual towing vehicle is the ZIL-131, ZIL-157 or AT-P tracked tug, all of which carry the crew of seven and other personnel.

*Photo:* **T-12 towed by ZIL-157**

# 85mm D-44 and SD-44

**Anti-tank and field guns.**
**Weight firing:** (D-44) 3,804lb (1725kg); (SD-44) 4,961lb (2250kg).
**Length travelling:** (D-44) 27ft 4in (8340mm); (SD-44) 27ft 0in (8220mm).
**Width travelling:** (Both) 5ft 10in (1780mm).
**Elevation:** (Both) —7.° to +35.°.
**Traverse:** ±27°
**Projectile mass:** (HE) 21·0lb (9·5kg); (HVAP) 11·0lb (5kg).
**Muzzle velocity:** (HE) 2,598ft/sec (792m/sec); (HVAP) 3,379ft/sec (1030m/sec).
**Maximum range:** (HE) 15,650m.

Variously designated D-44, D-48 or M-1945, the 85mm divisional gun is one of the most widely used in the Soviet ground forces. The gun is the same as in the T-34/85 tank and M-1944 AA weapons, and is also used in the SU-85 and ASU-85 assault vehicles. It fires various kinds of fixed ammunition at 15 to 20 rds/min, with the usual semi-automatic vertical-sliding wedge-type breech. The muzzle brake is a double baffle. To enable this gun to drive itself about the battlefield it can be fitted with an auxiliary engine, becoming the SD-44. The M-72 two-cylinder 14 hp engine is mounted on the hollow left trail, in which is its fuel; the right trail carries ready-ammunition. The SD-44 is completed by the driver's seat and steering on a large trail wheel.

*Photo:* **SD-44 after landing by Mi-6 helicopter.**

# RPG-7V

**Anti-tank launcher.**
**Weight firing:** (Excluding projectile) 14·4lb (6·5kg)
**Length:** (Without projectile) 37½in (953mm).
**Calibre of tube:** 40mm.
**Calibre of projectile:** 84·5mm.
**Mass of projectile:** 5½lb (2·5kg).
**Muzzle velocity:** 328ft/sec (100m/sec).
**Burn-out velocity:** 984ft/sec (300m/sec).
**Effective range:** (Moving target) 300m.

Standard anti-armour weapon of Soviet infantry, the RPG-7V replaced an earlier weapon derived from the World War 2 German Panzerfaust which merely fired the hollow-charge projectile from a shoulder-rested tube. RPG-7V fires a new projectile which, a few metres beyond the muzzle, ignites an internal rocket to give shorter flight-time, flatter trajectory and better accuracy. The HEAT or HE warhead has improved fuzing, the HEAT round penetrating to 320mm (12·6in) of armour. The optical sight is frequently supplemented by the NSP-2 (IR) night sight.

# 122mm BM-21

**Rocket launcher (40 rounds).**
**Weight:** One rocket, 101lb (45·9kg); launcher, 7,718lb (3500kg); vehicle, launcher and 40 rounds, 11·3 tons (11,500kg).
**Length:** Rocket 8·99ft (2740mm); vehicle, 24ft 1in (7350mm).
**Calibre:** 4·8in (122mm).
**Engine:** (Vehicle) ZIL-375 vee-8 gasoline, 175hp.
**Speed:** (Vehicle) 47mph (75km/h).
**Launcher:** Elevation 0° to +50°.
**Traverse:** ±120°.
**Time to reload:** 10min.
**Maximum range:** (Rocket) over 15,000m.

An important multi-rocket system which first appeared in November 1964, the BM-21 uses a smaller-calibre rocket than any other of its era, and can thus fire a greater quantity (40). It is the first rocket system carried by the outstanding Ural-375 truck, which among other attributes has exceptional cross-country capability. The rockets are fired in salvo, or 'rippled' in sequence or selected individually, always with the vehicle parked obliquely to the target to avoid blast damage to the unprotected cab. The BM-21 is used by the Soviet ground forces and by those of several other Warsaw Pact nations except Czechoslovakia (which uses its rather similar M-51).

# 140mm M-1965

**Rocket launcher.**
**Weight:** One rocket, 87·3lb (39·6kg); launcher (loaded) 2,646lb (1200kg).
**Length:** Rocket, 43in (1092mm); launcher (tubes horizontal) 13·2ft (4·0m).
**Calibre:** 5·5in (140mm).
**Elevation:** 0° to ±45°.
**Traverse:** ±15°.
**Time to reload:** 4min.
**Maximum range:** 10,600m.

The 140mm is one of the most-used artillery rockets in the Soviet forces. Many units fire it in a battery of 16 from the BM-14-16 launcher carried by the ZIL-151 or -157 6×6 trucks, or in a battery of 17 from the BM-14-17 mounted on the light GAZ-63 (the BM-14-17 is used by Soviet Marines, among many other forces). Soviet airborne troops use the light towed M-1965 launcher, first seen in 1967. This has 16 barrels, carried on the same chassis as the M-1943 57mm anti-tank gun. This is also used by some other Warsaw Pact forces, though the Polish army has its own 8-barrel WP-8 firing the same spin-stabilized missiles.

# 240mm BM-24

**Rocket launcher (12 rounds).**
**Weight:** one rocket, 248lb (112·5kg); launcher, 5,995lb (2720kg); loaded launcher on ZIL-157, 9·35 tons (9500kg); loaded launcher on AT-S tractor, 15 tons (15,240kg).
**Length:** Rocket, 46½in (1180mm); ZIL truck, 22ft 4in (6800mm); AT-S tractor, 19ft 2½in (5870mm).
**Calibre:** 9·5in (240mm).
**Elevation:** 0° to ±45°.
**Traverse:** ±105°.
**Time to reload:** 3–4min.
**Maximum range:** 11,000m.

The Soviet 240mm rocket is a spin-stabilized weapon of relatively short and fat shape, packing a tremendous punch but having short range for its calibre. One of its standard carriers is the ZIL-157 truck, on which is mounted an open-frame launcher of welded steel tube, with two rows of six rounds. Another is the AT-S tracked vehicle, found chiefly in armoured units, on which is mounted a different 12-round launcher of the tube type. The truck-mounted frame launcher is used by many countries, but the AT-S installation is believed to be used only by the Soviet Union.

# 240mm M-240 (M-1953)

**Heavy mortar.**
**Weight firing:** 7,960lb (3610kg).
**Length travelling:** 21ft 4in (6510mm).
**Height travelling:** (To top of rim of 2130mm circular baseplate) 7ft 3in (2210mm).
**Length of tube:** 17ft 6in (5340mm).
**Mass of projectile:** (HE) 221lb (100kg).
**Muzzle velocity:** 1,180ft/sec (362m/sec).
**Elevation:** +45° to +65°.
**Traverse:** 17° total.
**Maximum range:** 9700m.

By far the largest mortar in service with any army, this awesome weapon is used by the Soviet Union, certain other Warsaw Pact forces and about four other countries. It is towed muzzle first by an AT-P or other tracked tug in which rides the crew of eight and ammunition. The latter is loaded breech-first, with the tube rotated on a trunnion frame to the horizontal position and the bombs offered up by a trolley or two-man bar-sling. The tube is then returned to its preset aimed position and the round fired by a lanyard. It has been reported that 240mm mortar ammunition includes nuclear rounds, but this is unconfirmed.

# 7.62mm RPK

**Light machine gun.**
**Weight:** With box magazine (loaded) 12·4lb (5·6kg), (unloaded) 11·1lb (5·0kg); with drum magazine (loaded) 15·0lb (6·8kg), (unloaded) 12·4lb (5·6kg).
**Length overall:** 41in (1040mm).
**Ammunition:** Standard M43 (M-1943).
**Muzzle velocity:** 2,411ft/sec (735m/sec).
**Effective range:** 800m.
**Rate of fire:** (Cyclic) 600rds/min.

Standard Soviet LMG, the Kalashnikov RPK is essentially an AK-47 assault rifle with a longer and heavier barrel, bipod, different stock and two larger-capacity magazines, a 40-round curved box and 75-round drum. At any time regular AK or AKM magazines can be clipped on instead. Compared with the Degtyarev RPD of the immediate post-war era the RPK is much lighter and handier, cheaper and more versatile. Like the AK series it is gas-operated, with rotating bolt, and having selection for full or semi-automatic fire. It is often seen fitted with the NSP-2 (IR) night sight.

# 7.62mm PK

**General-purpose machine gun.**
**Weight of basic gun:** (Bipod) 19·8lb (9·0kg);
(tripod) 36·3lb (16·5kg).
**Weight of ammunition box:** With 100-round belt,
8·58lb (3·9kg); 200-rd belt, 17·6lb (8·0kg); 250-rd
belt, 20·6lb (9·4kg).
**Length:** (Gun) 45·7in (1173mm); (on tripod) 49·5in
(1270mm).
**Ammunition:** Soviet 7·62 rimmed Type 54R,
propellant charge 3·11g.
**Muzzle velocity:** 2,755ft/sec (840m/sec).
**Effective range:** 1000m.
**Rate of fire:** (Cyclic) 650 rds/min.

Though a hotch-potch of other weapons (mostly the
Kalashnikov AK-47), the PK family is an excellent
series of weapons which can be described as the first
Soviet GPMGs (general-purpose MGs). Unlike almost
all other Soviet rifle-calibre weapons except the
sniper's rifle it fires the long rimmed cartridge with over

twice the propellant charge of the standard kind. It is
a fully automatic gas-operated gun with Kalashnikov
rotating bolt, Goryunov cartridge extractor and barrel-
change, and Degtyarev feed system and trigger. The
PKS is the PK on a light tripod for sustained or AA
firing. The PKT is a solenoid-operated version without
sights, stock or trigger mechanism for use in armoured
vehicles. The PKM is the latest service version with
unfluted barrel and hinged butt rest, weighing only
8·39kg (18½lb); in a tripod it becomes the PKMS. The

PKB has stock and trigger replaced by a butterfly
trigger for pintle mounting on armoured vehicles (but
the standard PK and PKM can be fired from the ports
of, say, a BMP).

# 12.7mm DShK

**Heavy machine gun.**
**Weight:** (Basic gun) 75lb (34kg).
**Length overall:** 62½in (1588mm).
**Ammunition:** All standard Soviet 12·7mm, in 50-
round metal-link belt (in most installations fed from
box).
**Muzzle velocity:** (API) 2,822ft/sec (860m/sec).
**Effective range:** (Horizontal) 1500m; (slant) 1000m.
**Rate of fire:** (Cyclic) 550–600rds/min.

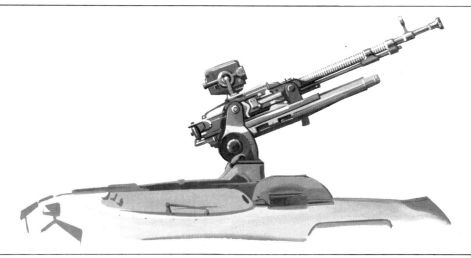

This old gas-operated weapon is still used in great
numbers in many applications. The basic Degtyarev-
Shpagin model is the M-1938/46, of post-war vintage,
but the basic design is earlier. Most DShK guns in land
forces are carried on a two-wheel chassis, which
increases total weight to 368lb (167kg), whose trail
legs can be extended to form a tall tripod for AA use.
Other examples are found on many Soviet armoured
vehicles, including several types of tank and APC,
primarily as an AA weapon with day and night optical
sighting.

# 7.62mm AK and AKM

**Assault rifles.**
**Weight:** AK (loaded magazine) 10·58lb (4·8kg),
(empty magazine) 9·47lb (4·3kg); AKM (loaded magazine) 8·0lb (3·64kg) (early version 8·4lb, 3·8kg),
(empty magazine) 6·93lb (3·14kg) (early version
7·3lb, 3·31kg).
**Length overall (no bayonet):** AK-47 (either butt),
34·25in (870mm); AKM, 34·5in (876mm).
**Ammunition:** Standard M43 (M-1943).
**Muzzle velocity:** 2,345ft/sec (715m/sec).
**Effective range:** (semi-auto) 400m; (auto) 300m.
**Rate of fire:** Cyclic, 600rds/min; auto, 90rds/min;
semi-auto, 40rds/min.

Produced in greater quantity than any other modern
small arms, the Kalashnikov AK and AKM can fairly be
claimed to have set a new standard in infantry weapons.
The original AK-47 came with a wooden stock or (for
AFV crews, paratroopers and motorcyclists) a folding
metal stock. It owed much to German assault rifles, and

like them uses a short cartridge firing a stubby bullet.
A gas-operated weapon with rotating bolt (often
chrome-plated), it can readily be used by troops all
over the world of any standard of education, and gives
extremely reliable results under the most adverse conditions. Versions with different designations have been
licence-produced in at least five countries, and it is
used in about 35. The standard Soviet military weapon
today is the AKM, an amazingly light development
making extensive use of plastics and stampings, and
with a cyclic-rate reducer, compensator and other
improvements. Either rifle can have luminous sights or
the NSP-2 IR sight. Another fitment is a new bayonet
which doubles as a saw and as an insulated wire-
cutter.

# 7.62 SVD

**sniper rifle**
**Weight (with PSO-1 sight):** (Loaded magazine)
9·95lb (4·52kg); (empty magazine) 9·4lb (4·3kg).
**Length (no bayonet):** 48¼in (1225mm).
**Ammunition:** Long 7·62mm rimmed, Type 54R,
3·11g propellant charge.
**Muzzle velocity:** 2,725ft/sec (830m/sec).
**Effective combat range:** 800m.
**Rate of fire, semi-auto:** 20rds/min.

The Dragunov SVD sniper's rifle is a thoroughly
modern, purpose-designed weapon, though it uses the
same 54R ammunition as the old 1891/30 sniper's
rifle and the RK series of GPMGs. It is reported that
users are issued with selected batches of ammunition
to increase accuracy. A gas-operated semi-automatic
rifle, the SVD has the Kalashnikov rotating-bolt breech

but a completely new trigger system, barrel and 10-
round magazine. The muzzle has a flash suppressor and
a recoil compensator to hold the barrel near the target.
The PSO-1 sight is 370mm (14½in) long, and comprises
a ×4 optical telescope with rubber eyepiece, integral
rangefinder, battery-powered reticle illuminator, and
IR sighting for use at night.

# 9mm PM

**pistol**
**Weight:** (Magazine full) 1¾lb (810g).
**Length overall:** 6·3in (160mm).
**Ammunition:** Soviet special pistol 9mm, 244mg charge.
**Muzzle velocity:** 1,035ft/sec (315m/sec).
**Effective range:** 45m.

One of the smallest regular army hand-guns, the familiar Makarov remains widely used throughout many branches of nearly all forces in the Soviet Union, though it is increasingly giving way to the bigger Stechkin. A simple blowback pistol bearing close kinship with the earlier German Walther PP series, the Makarov PM has an 8-round magazine using the special ammunition for Soviet and Polish pistols, and not usable in machine carbines (sub-machine guns) or other Warsaw Pact 9mm weapons. The PM has positive safety on the left side, double-action trigger and external hammer.

# 9mm APS

**pistol**
**Weight:** (Magazine full) 2¾lb (1·22kg).
**Length:** basic gun, 8·9in (225mm); with stock added, 21¼in (540mm).
**Ammunition:** Soviet special pistol 9mm.
**Muzzle velocity:** 1,115ft/sec (340m/sec).
**Effective range:** 200m.

The Stechkin APS is a considerably larger hand-gun than the Makarov, and is a completely different and later design now coming into wide service. It appears to be replacing the Makarov as the usual sidearm of senior field officers, though it is less likely to be seen in the KGB and similar organizations. It has a 20-round magazine, and capability for full automatic fire, with a cyclic rate of 700—750rds/min. A practical rate of fire (auto) is 90rds/min. Like the classic Mauser pistol it can be clipped to its wooden holster/stock for effective use over quite long ranges. The backsight is adjustable to 25, 50, 100 and 200m.

# RDG-5

**hand grenade**
**Weight:** (Fuzed) 0·68lb (310g).
**Length:** 4½in (114mm).
**Diameter of body:** 2¼in (56mm).
**HE charge:** 3·85oz (110g).
**Fuze:** 3—4sec delay.
**Effective fragmentation radius:** 25m.

Probably the most widely used hand grenade of the Warsaw Pact forces, the RGD-5 comprises an HE charge in a serrated frag liner, enclosed in a body of thin sheet steel. The fuze is the same UZRG type used in earlier Soviet grenades, but the RGD-5 is much more compact and can be carried in greater quantity and thrown further.

# RG-42

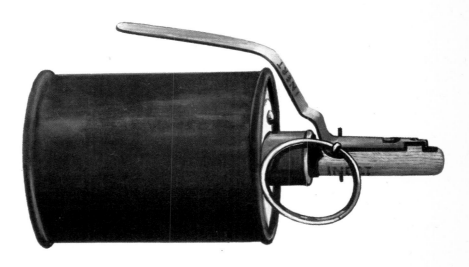

**hand grenade**
**Weight:** (fuzed) 0·88lb (400g).
**Length:** 5·0in (127mm).
**Diameter of body:** 2·13in (54mm).
**HE charge:** 4·16oz (118g).
**Fuze:** 3—4sec delay.
**Effective fragmentation radius:** 20m.

In some respects resembling the German 'potato masher' but without a long throwing handle, this is primarily a blast grenade with a substantial HE filling enclosed in a light serrated liner, which in turn is enclosed in a sheet-steel drum. It uses the standard UZRG percussion fuze.

# F-1 Hand grenade

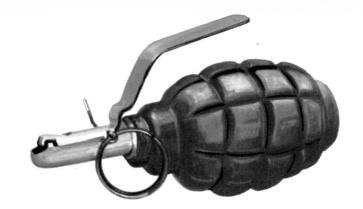

**Weight:** (Fuzed) 1·54lb (700g).
**Length:** 4·9in (124mm).
**Diameter of body:** 2·16in (55mm).
**HE charge:** 1·6oz (45g).
**Fuze:** 3–4sec delay.
**Effective fragmentation radius:** 14·7m.

Though being replaced by the RGD-5, this familiar grenade is still widely distributed among Warsaw Pact forces. Similar to the traditional British No 36 (Mills bomb) and US Mk II, it has a modest charge contained in a heavy body of serrated cast iron, painted olive drab. It uses the UZRG fuze, and the same body and fuze is incorporated in a rifle grenade of the Polish army.

# RKG-3M Anti-tank hand grenade

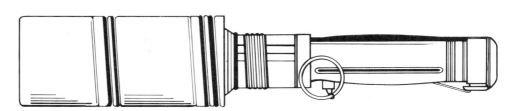

**Weight:** (Fuzed) 2·34lb (1070g).
**Length:** (Before firing) 14½in (362mm).
**Diameter of head:** 2·19in (55·6mm):
**HE charge:** 1¼lb (567g).
**Fuze:** Impact.
**Typical range:** Up to 20m.
**Armour penetration:** 125mm.

Standard hand-thrown anti-armour grenade of the Warsaw Pact forces, the RKG-3M is a stick-type HEAT (high-explosive anti-tank) weapon with a substantial HE charge behind a copper conical lining. This shaped charge can pierce about 5 inches of armour. To ensure that it hits nose-first, a stabilizing drogue parachute deploys as soon as the stick leaves the thrower's hand.

# Nuclear, biological and chemical warfare

NBC warfare, sometimes alternatively called CBR (chemical, biological, radiological), plays a central role in all Soviet planning. As far as published information is concerned, the Soviet ground forces are more fully equipped for such warfare than any other in the world.

**Means of Delivery.**
All Soviet artillery pieces of 122mm calibre and over can be used to deliver persistent and non-persistent chemical agents, but in practice, the most likely weapon for the delivery of non-persistent agents is the BM-21. The density of fire of this area saturation weapon makes it ideal for this purpose. A battery of six such weapons could deliver 240 chemical shells to a target area in a few seconds. Persistent agents would most likely be delivered by the long-range D-74 122mm and M-46 130mm guns. Agents of both types can be delivered by aerial bombs or spray tanks from FGA aircraft of the Tactical Air Armies. Chemical warheads might well be used together with conventional explosives to delude the defender.

**Agents.**
The Soviet Union is known to hold stocks of several kinds of chemical warfare agents. These include:
*Hydrogen cyanide* compounds which cause rapid respiratory failure, but disperse very quickly. One contamination by this agent renders most types of gas mask and vehicle filter useless.
*Nerve agents*, developed from insecticides by German scientists during the last war; the most important of these are known by code letters—GA(Tabun), GB(Sarin), GD(Soman) and VX. Small amounts of these agents inhaled or absorbed through the skin cause malfunction of the nervous system and rapid death. These agents can be used in the persistent and non-persistent forms. Some nerve agents can be countered by antidotes or injections, but it is thought that the latest Soviet compounds may well prove difficult, if not impossible, to counter with present medicines.
*Blistering Agents*—developments of the mustard gas used so effectively in World War I. These are very persistent and produce incapacitating blisters and the vapour, if inhaled, causes death.

It is known that the Soviets maintain stocks of CW agents ready for use, and it is assumed that these would be issued to army formations as the result of a high-level political decision. All army units have the capability of delivery CW attacks, and divisional artillery recce is tasked to provide meteorological data for divisional staffs to plan their employment.

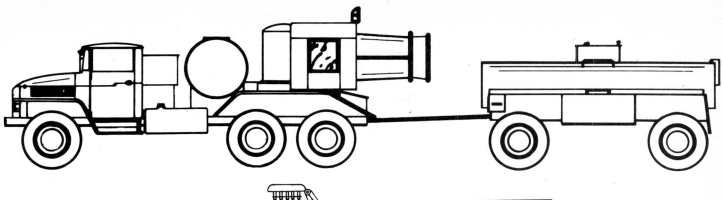

In addition to this offensive capability, all army units and formations, unlike Nato armies, have integral chemical recce and defence elements for detection of contamination and marking of contaminated areas, and for mass decontamination of vehicles and personnel (see diagrams showing structure of motor rifle divisions). Every Soviet soldier has his individual NBC protective clothing and a decontamination kit, and all modern Soviet AFVs are capable of operating in a contaminated environment.

There are several types of Soviet NBC reconnaissance vehicles to detect and warn of contamination, at least 17 types of decontamination vehicle for vehicles, terrain and buildings, and nine types of mobile decontamination station for personnel and clothing. Some of these vehicles carry steam boilers whose output is automatically doped with an additive such as formaldehyde or ammonia. Others are tankers equipped with multiple sprays with special nozzle attachments, discharging alkali or other emulsions or fogs.

The smaller drawing shows the BRDM-rkh reconnaissance vehicle equipped with two sets of automatic emplacers for a total of 40 warning flags. The vehicle explores the boundaries of an infected zone and marks the limits by the 40 bright flags, each automatically driven into the ground by a firing chamber and propulsion cartridge. The larger illustration shows the TMS-65 decontamination vehicle, used for the mass cleansing of vehicles and large items such as radars and missiles. The 6×6 Ural-375E chassis carries a VK-1F turbojet engine and operator cabin, with swivelling and elevation controls. Tanks on the chassis and a towed trailer supply jet fuel and additive decontaminants, delivered by the jet over a line of infected equipment (either the latter or the TMS-65 can be driven past the other).

Whether the Soviets would in fact employ chemical weapons in anything less than total war is hard to predict. Their use is not without disadvantages, not the least of which is that the Soviet protective clothing degrades the soldier's fighting ability more than the equivalent NATO kit. Nevertheless, as the Soviets possess such a formidable offensive and defensive capability and are constantly developing new agents, it would seem prudent to assume that they might be tempted to resort to chemical weapons rather than to the politically more dangerous nuclear weapons if they found themselves in difficulties.

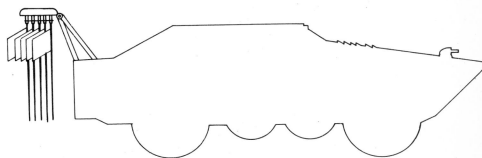

*Top:* **TMS-65 decontamination apparatus for rapid decontamination of vehicles and towed weapons.** *Above:* **BRDM-rkh Radiological-Chemical Reconnaissance vehicle with area warning flag emplacers.** *Below:* **plotting contamination limits for BRDM-tkh.**

# Strategic Rocket Forces

No one today would challenge the assertion that the development and deployment of a substantial strategic nuclear striking force by the Soviet Union constitutes one of the decisive turning points of contemporary international history. The growth of Soviet strategic strength has altered the very structure of world politics, transforming the USSR from a self-proclaimed 'encircled fortress', surrounded by predatory capitalist states, into a global superpower, capable not only of dealing effectively with challenges to immediate Soviet interests but also of projecting its power and influence on a world scale. In the process, the Soviet diplomatic style and the pattern of Soviet behaviour in world politics has been substantially changed as well. The bluff and bluster of the Khrushchev era has been replaced by a new self-confidence and assertiveness, as the USSR manipulates client states in every major strategic region of the world and otherwise behaves as if the world correlation of forces has indeed shifted in its favour. Although the recent massive increases in Soviet strategic strength are a product of the procurement programmes of the last decade – indeed, the Strategic Rocket Forces (*Raketnye Voiska Strategicheskogo Naznacheniya* or Rocket Troops of Strategic Designation) themselves were not created as a separate branch of the Soviet armed forces until 1960 – their origins lie in the Stalinist era, and in particular in the strategic situation by which the USSR was confronted at the close of World War II.

## The origins of strategic power

It is worth recalling at the outset that Soviet military doctrine and practice – unlike, for example, that of the United States – has always stressed the necessary connection between military power and politics, and in particular the impact of Soviet arms upon the course of the world revolution. In the years immediately following the 1917 Revolution, Soviet theorists attempted at length to develop a set of principles for translating military power into political gains, and in particular for profiting from the expected collapse of the capitalist governments in Western Europe. Several prominent writers argued directly that the Red Army itself should be assigned the dual task of defending the Lenin regime and of aiding revolutionary movements abroad. (Among such efforts were those in Persia, Mongolia and Tannu Tuva, all in 1921.) While the wasting effect of the Civil War upon the Soviet economy and Stalin's increasing absorption with domestic politics subsequently led to a de-emphasis of the doctrine of 'revolution by bayonet' in practice, formal Soviet doctrine continued to stress the significance of the military instrument in the revolutionary process. World War II was taken by Soviet thinkers as confirmation of the view that the maintenance of a powerful military capability was essential if the socialist camp was to fend off the forces of counter-revolution and exploit emergent political weaknesses in the capitalist camp.

Nevertheless, after World War II the USSR confronted an entirely new military situation: the need to prepare for a possible conflict with an adversary which was not

**The familiar 'mushroom' cloud looms over a Soviet warhead test site**

accessible by land, as Russia's traditional enemies had been, and which moreover was accustomed – and possessed the capability, most dramatically in the form of nuclear weapons – to utilise power at great distances from its homeland. While the precise manner in which Stalin viewed the world of 1945 remains a matter of scholarly debate, there is general agreement on his specifically military concerns. The USSR faced the need to deter the US from reacting vigorously to hostile political moves emanating from Moscow and from attempting to exploit political unrest in Eastern Europe; more generally, Stalin saw the need to usher the USSR safely through the period in which it would be vulnerable to Western strategic nuclear strength. His immediate solution was to emphasise, both operationally and in his declaratory policy, the continuing significance of land power, represented by mass armies defending a territorial heartland and operating on interior lines of supply and communications – the traditional Russian form of military power. Concretely, he may have consciously decided, as Thomas Wolfe has suggested in his *Soviet Power and Europe, 1945–1970*, to make Western Europe a kind of 'hostage' to ensure US good behaviour by deploying large forces with a substantial offensive capability in the satellite nations and in the Western USSR. In any case, Soviet land power became the counterpoise to US strategic strength.

At the same time, Stalin made substantial efforts to acquire both nuclear weapons and long-range delivery systems. A nuclear weapons research programme had been begun in the USSR as early as 1942. The first Soviet graphite reactor went into operation in December 1946, and, following several public claims that Soviet scientists had solved the problem of the atomic bomb, the first known atomic device was tested on 29 August 1949. Nearly four years later, the USSR exploded its first thermo-nuclear device.

Soviet development of delivery vehicles, although lagging somewhat behind accomplishments in the nuclear weapons field, also proceeded at a steady pace. USSR rocket technology originated in the early 1940s. Short-range tactical rockets were utilised freely in area bombardments during the final campaigns against the Axis in World War II. After the war the USSR took over large stocks of the German V-2 rockets, the type which had been used against London, and put captured German scientists to work on more advanced systems. By 1947 a small number of SS-1 'Scunner' SRBMs (short-range ballistic missiles) – essentially improved V-2s – had been deployed. The initial Soviet nuclear delivery vehicles, however, were aircraft suited mainly for use against European targets: Tu-4 'Bull' piston-engined medium bombers copied from four US B-29s which had made emergency landings in the Far East during World War II, and Il-28 'Beagle' light jet bombers. (The Tu-4 could, of course, have reached the US on a one-way mission or with air refuelling, but the Soviets did not develop a capability for the latter until the late 1950s.) Development of intercontinental bombers was also begun in the late 1940s. Moreover, although the

## SOVIET STRATEGIC MISSILE TEST CENTRES AND RELATED FACILITIES

**A: Kapustin Yar** (48.4°N, 45.8°E). Early test centre for short and medium-range ballistic missiles: Soviet V-2, Shyster/Sandal, Skean. ABM tests with two-stage SL-8 fired towards Sary Shagan. Small Cosmos satellites since 1962.

**B: Tyuratam** (45.8°N, 63.4°E). Test centre for ICBMs launched to target areas Kamchatka Peninsula and central Pacific; small impact area for short/medium range missiles angled

NE. Cosmos photo-reconnaissance (52°, 65° incl.), SIS, ocean surveillance, FOBS, etc.

**C: Plesetek** (62.9°N, 40.1°E). ICBM base (e.g. 65 × SS-13). Military meteorological satellites, Cosmos photo-reconnaissance (63°, 65°, 73°, 81° incl.), military comsats, early warning, ferret, multiple navsats (74° and 83°) SIS target.

**D: Moscow.** Galosh ABM defence site. Four complexes with 16

launchers apiece and associated radars.

**E: Severomorsk.** Major submarine base near Murmansk including Delta class submarines firing SS-N-8 SLBM's.

**F: Barents Sea.** Firings of SS-N-8 SLBM's from submarine to impact central Pacific (stellar-inertial guidance), October 1974.

**G: White Sea.** Firings of SS-N-8 from submarine to impact near Kamchatka

ABM, anti-ballistic missile; SIS, satellite interceptor system; FOBS, fractional orbit bombardment system; ICBM, inter-continental ballistic missile; SLBM, sea-launched ballistic missile.

*Operational ICBM silos have been reported in various sectors of the Soviet Union, e.g. north-west USSR, Ural Mountains, Eastern Siberia; IRBM sites in Western USSR and central Asia covering Europe and Middle East, Eastern Siberia (near the border with Mongolia) covering the whole of the People's Republic of China. Some Scrooge and Scamp mobile launchers in West and East.

### MILITARY DISTRICTS AND MAJOR FLEETS

**1,** Leningrad. **2,** Baltic (Riga). **3,** Belorussian (Minsk). **4,** Moscow. **5,** Carpathian (L'Vov). **6,** Odessa. **7,** Kiev. **8,** N. Causasus (Rostov-on-Don). **9,** Transcaucasus (Tbilisi). **10,** Volga (Kuybyshev). **11,** Urals (Sverdlovsk). **12,** Turkestan (Tashkent). **13,** Central Asian (Alma Ata).

**14,** Siberian (Novosibirsk). **15,** Transbaikal (Chita). **16,** Far Eastern (Khabarovsk). **Fleets:** (I) Northern (Murmansk). (II) Baltic (Kaliningrad). (III) Black Sea (Sevastopol). (IV) Pacific Ocean (Vladivostok).

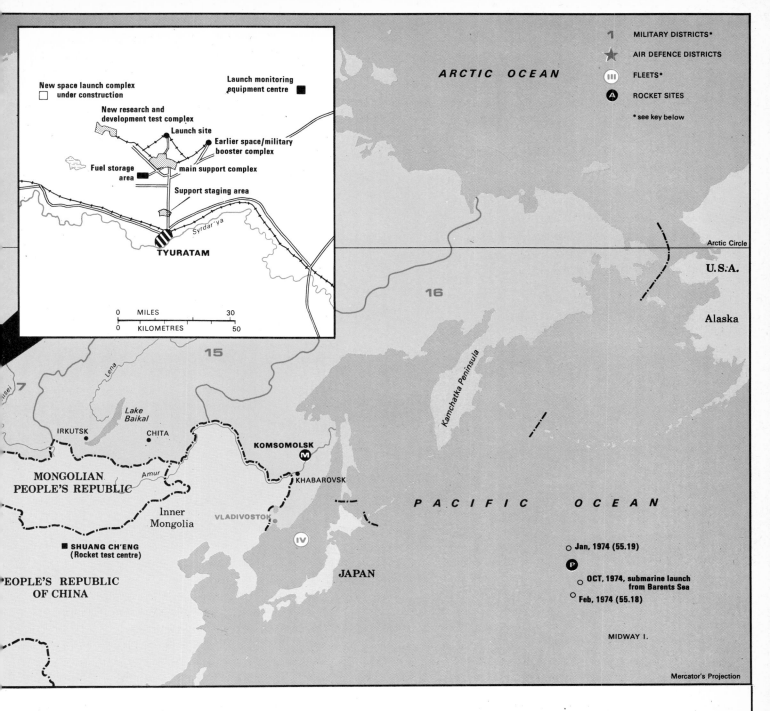

MILITARY DISTRICTS*
AIR DEFENCE DISTRICTS
FLEETS*
ROCKET SITES

* see key below

**ARCTIC OCEAN**

New space launch complex
under construction

Launch monitoring equipment centre

New research and development test complex

Launch site

Earlier space/military booster complex

Fuel storage area

main support complex

Support staging area

*Syrdar'ya*

**TYURATAM**

MILES

KILOMETRES

Arctic Circle

**U.S.A.**

Alaska

16

15

*Lena*

*Yenisei*

Lake Baikal

IRKUTSK

CHITA

**KOMSOMOLSK**

**MONGOLIAN PEOPLE'S REPUBLIC**

*Amur*

KHABAROVSK

Kamchatka Peninsula

**P A C I F I C    O C E A N**

Inner Mongolia

VLADIVOSTOK

**SHUANG CH'ENG**
(Rocket test centre)

**PEOPLE'S REPUBLIC OF CHINA**

**JAPAN**

○ Jan, 1974 (55.19)

**P**

○ OCT, 1974, submarine launch from Barents Sea

○ Feb, 1974 (55.18)

MIDWAY I.

Mercator's Projection

---

Peninsula, February 1974.

**H: Novaya Zemlya.** Major nuclear test centre; impact area for ICBM's launched from Soviet operational silos.

**J: Semipalatinsk.** Underground tests of ABM warheads (20-200 KT); kill mechanisms for ABM and SIS including (?) high-energy lasers and

charged particle beams.

**K: Severodvinsk.** World's largest submarine yard, near Archangel, building Delta-class nuclear-powered submarines.

**L: Gorki.** Submarine yard building nuclear-powered Charlie-class vessels able to launch eight SS-N-7 missiles whilst submerged.

**M: Komsomolsk.** Second major submarine yard, on Amur River in Soviet Far East.

**N: Sary Shagan.** Anti-ballistic missile test centre including long-range ABM SH-4 and never high-acceleration ABM in Sprint class.

**P: Pacific target areas:** (a) SS-19 ICBM Jan. 1974 from Tyuratam; (b)

SS-18 ICBM Feb. 1974; (c) SS-N-8 SLBM Oct. 1974 from Delta 2 class submarine, Barents Sea.

**Chinese facilities**
**a.** Lop Nor nuclear test centre 40°20'N, 90°.10'E.
**b.** Shuang-Ch'eng-tze rocket test centre 41°N, 100°E.

---

creation of the long-range missile force has often been credited in Soviet historiography to Khrushchev, an ICBM (intercontinental ballistic missile) research programme apparently was established at Stalin's direction in 1948 as a follow-on to the work on the V-2 types. (The commander of the Soviet rocket forces, Marshal N. I. Krylov, has stated that research and development on long-range missiles started in the early postwar years.) Only one additional rocket of significance was deployed during the Stalinist years, however; this was the SS-2 'Sibling' SRBM, which embodied some improvements in range and reliability over

the SS-1 and was deployed in small numbers.

Thus although it is probably in the main correct to conclude – as have most Western and Soviet writers – that Stalin did not adequately grasp the strategic and political implications of the new technology, such criticisms should not be pushed too far. Although his stress on the 'permanent operating factors' of war and on old doctrines and strategies generally, as well as the commanding position which he assigned to the army within the Soviet military hierarchy, helped to prolong the pre-eminence of a continental military outlook

in Soviet strategic thinking, Stalin's public depreciation of the significance of nuclear weapons was a reasonable response to Soviet military weakness. And his declaratory policy was in any case belied by his decisions to expend a substantial portion of Soviet R & D (research and development) resources on modern nuclear weapons and delivery systems – decisions which laid the foundation for the Soviet strategic programmes of the Khrushchev and Brezhnev years and the rise of the USSR to a position of no less than strategic parity with the US.

## The Khrushchev period

The death of Stalin and the rise to power of Georgi Malenkov set off a lengthy debate among Soviet theorists about the impact of the new weapons on war and international politics. Several prominent thinkers, including General N. A. Talenski, argued that the nature of war itself had been transformed by nuclear weapons and modern long-range delivery systems, and that the traditional advantages enjoyed by the USSR, stemming from geographic location and physical size, were by themselves no longer sufficient to ensure victory in the event of a major conflict with the West. A new doctrine was needed, in their view, which took into account the now-transcendent importance of strategic surprise; several leaders, including General Talenski, appeared to advocate a pre-emptive attack by the USSR in the event that an assault on the homeland appeared imminent. Above all, the USSR, in the view of Stalin's critics, had to be prepared to fight a nuclear war. Malenkov, on the other hand, in a series of 1954 speeches, appeared to take the position that a new war would mean the destruction of civilization, Soviet as well as Western. He moreover stated that when both sides possessed an adequate strategic nuclear force, there would exist a state of mutual deterrence; under such conditions, local and conventional wars were far more likely than general nuclear war.

The position of Malenkov and his supporters was bitterly opposed by Molotov, Bulganin, Marshal Zhukov and other prominent generals, and ultimately by Khrushchev; and Malenkov was forced from office in February 1955. The new Bulganin–Khrushchev duumvirate immediately set out to shape a new military doctrine and to reorganise the Soviet high command. Generals loyal to Khrushchev were eventually placed in key positions, and the new strategy emphasised preparation for nuclear war. The development of modern weapons continued, and in some areas was accelerated. The SS-3 'Shyster' MRBM (medium-range ballistic missile), like its predecessors essentially an improved V-2, entered service in 1955, and was publicly displayed in Red Square on 7 November 1957. Moreover, the jet Mya-4 'Bison' and the turbo-prop Tu-95 'Bear' long-range strategic bombers had been publicly displayed in 1954 and 1955 respectively, and the Tu-16 'Badger' medium jet bomber was ready to enter the operational inventory. A modest force of the former was eventually deployed, along with some 1,300 'Badgers' assigned to both the strategic and naval air arms. (It was the July 1955 Moscow Air Show which gave rise to the widespread fears in the West that a significant 'bomber gap' had developed, putting the West at a serious strategic disadvantage in dealing with the USSR. But apparently the Soviets flew the same squadrons of 'Bisons' and a few 'Bears' repeatedly past the viewing stand, leading Western observers to conclude that the USSR had embarked on a large-scale build-up of heavy bombers. It has been observed that this air show was 'one of the most successful peacetime military demonstrations of modern times'.)

The technical shortcomings of the 'Bison' and 'Bear' may have influenced Khrushchev's decision not to procure them in large numbers, but in retrospect it seems probable that he simply decided to leap-frog into the missile age. The first full-range test of a Soviet ICBM, involving an early version of the SS-6 'Sapwood', took place on 26 August 1957; production began almost immediately. War-head production had also been proceeding rapidly. (It has also been suggested that war-head production outran that of strategic delivery systems, enabling these war-heads to be deployed in Europe, this in turn making possible the manpower reductions in the Soviet armed forces of the Khrushchev period.) Extensive nuclear weapons tests were carried out in 1958 and again in 1961, when a 58MT (megaton) weapon was exploded. In 1959 a further development of the 'Shyster', the SS-4 'Sandal' MRBM, entered deployment. With its relatively high reliability, a maximum range of 1,200 statute miles, and a 1MT war-head capability, the 'Sandal' quickly became a standard IRBM (intermediate-range ballistic missile) in the Soviet armed forces; 500 or so remain in service at present, deployed both in the western USSR and along the Sino-Soviet border. (Early versions of the SS-4 were radio-command guided, but later models incorporate inertial guidance. The 'Sandal' was one of the two types of Soviet missiles deployed in Cuba late in 1962.) The SS-5 'Skean' IRBM (intermediate range ballistic missile), followed two years later. Similar in appearance

*Above left:* **SS-9 Scarp was Russia's biggest operational ICBM until the SS-18 of the mid-1970s. It can carry a single 25 MT warhead or three multiple re-entry vehicles**

*Above:* **American spy satellites have spotted Scamp launchers near the Chinese border. Set up ready to fire, Scapegoat missiles (the missile portion of the Scamp system) have a range of up to 2,500 miles (4,000 km).**

to the SS-3 and SS-4, but without fins, the 'Skean' has a range of 2,300 miles. About 100 were deployed, some in underground silos; most remain in service. Although generally said to mount a 1MT war-head, the SS-5 has also been reported to carry a large war-head in the 5–10MT range.

The seemingly rapid Soviet progress in the strategic weapons field undoubtedly helped stimulate Khrushchev to undertake another re-examination of Soviet strategic doctrine during the late 1950s. Apparently persuaded by Western behaviour at the Geneva Conference of 1955, by the lack of US action during the Hungarian revolution in 1956, and by the vacillating Western response to his 'rocket diplomacy' during

the Suez crisis and the Turkish-Syrian
tensions of late 1957 that there was little
chance that the West would initiate military
hostilities against the USSR, he decided to
rely on a 'minimum deterrence' posture
both to ensure Soviet security and as the
basis for an adventuresome political strategy
against the West. In his assessment of world
political trends at the 21st Party Congress
in January 1959, he delivered his famous
pronouncement that war was no longer
'fatalistically inevitable', not because the
West had become more kindly disposed
toward the socialist camp, but because a
decisive shift in the world correlation of
forces had occurred in favour of the communist world. In Khrushchev's view, the
West would be increasingly deterred in the
future from offering vigorous resistance to
communist political initiatives. The advance
of socialism was thus assured.

In a subsequent speech on defence issues,
delivered before the Supreme Soviet on 14
January 1960, he developed this theme at
greater length, and also set forth the principal elements of his military doctrine.
Nuclear explosives and rocket weapons, he
stated, had become the decisive factors in
modern war. Under these conditions,
although the USSR would of course be able
to survive and triumph in any future war,
no matter what the circumstances, the first
phase of a future global conflict might well
be crucial. War, he said, 'would start in the
heart of the belligerent countries: there
would not be a single capital, not a single
major industrial or administrative centre,
not a single strategic area which would not
be subjected to attack, not only in the first
days but in the first minutes of the war.'
The USSR, he continued, must therefore
reorganise its military forces to take account
of these factors. In the future, the most
important component of the Soviet armed
forces would be the Strategic Rocket Forces;
research, development and procurement of
the most modern rocket weapons would
consequently be stepped up substantially.
There would be corresponding cuts,
Khrushchev concluded, in conventional
forces, particularly in the army.

On 7 May 1960, when the Strategic
Rocket Forces were elevated to the status of
an Armed Service, on a par with the Ground,
Air, Air Defence and Naval Forces, under the
command of Marshal K. S. Moskalenko,
the shift in Soviet doctrine away from a
purely continental, land power strategy to
one which took fully into account the
revolutionary impact of the new weaponry
was completed. All offensive missiles with a
range of more than 1,000 kilometres (620
statute miles) were assigned to the Strategic
Rocket Forces (missiles of lesser range,
designated as 'operational-tactical' missiles
in Soviet terminology, are assigned to the
Ground, Air, and Naval Forces). Work on
the second generation ICBMs by 1960 was
already far advanced; the first of these, the
SS-7 'Saddler', about which little is known
even today although nearly 200 have been
deployed, began to enter service late in 1961;
the SS-8 'Sasin', like 'Saddler' a two-stage
storable liquid-fuel ICBM with a 5MT
war-head and a range of nearly 7,000 miles,
entered deployment two years later.

Nevertheless, Soviet ICBM progress was
not nearly as rapid as Khrushchev had

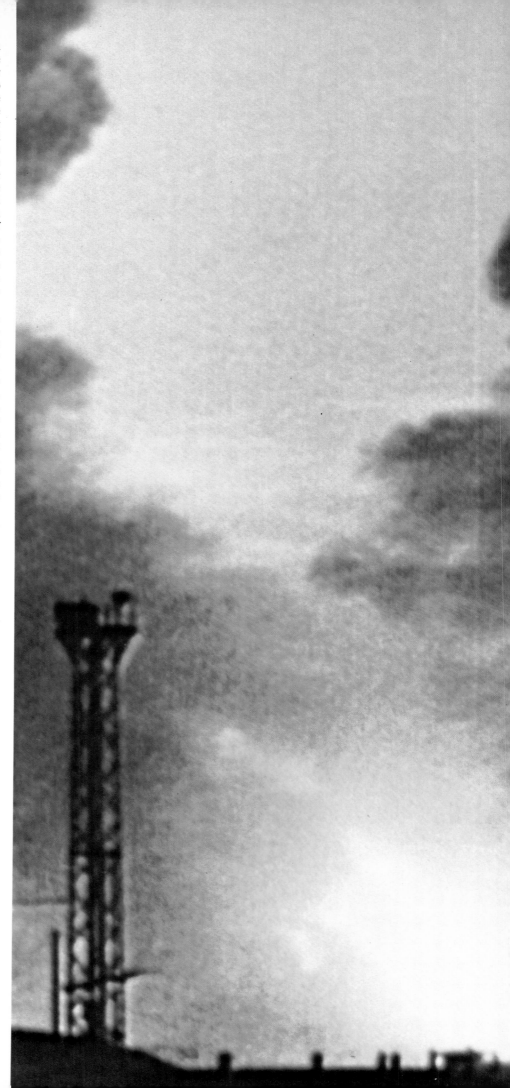

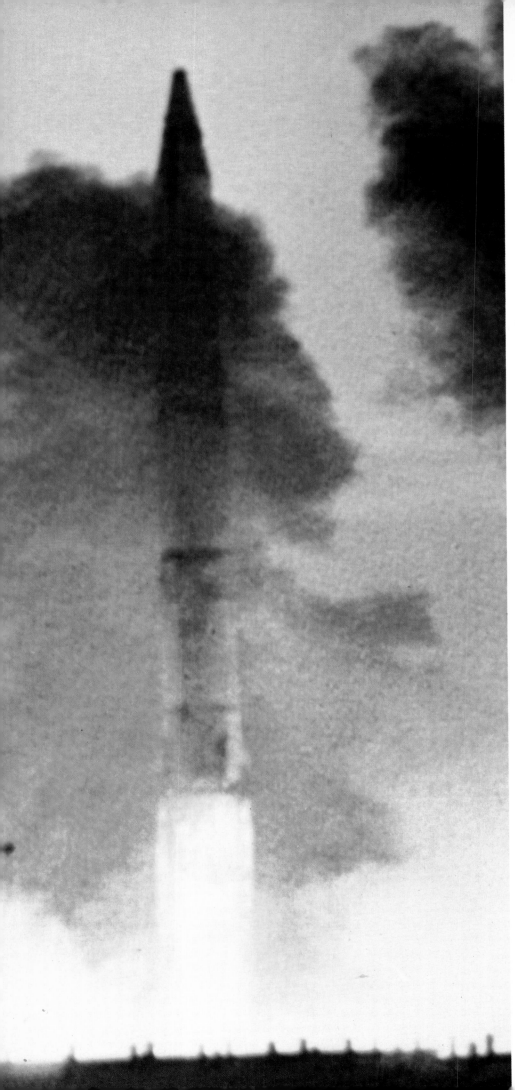

expected during the heady days of the first 'Sputnik' launchings. From the time of the first tests in late 1957 to mid-1961, only a handful of ICBMs was actually deployed; Western intelligence sources credited the USSR with only 10 operational SS-6s as of late 1959. It is now clear that technical complications with the 'Sapwood' were primarily responsible for the slow development rate. Electronics difficulties and problems with the non-storable liquid fuel system led to extremely poor accuracy and low reliability; moreover, the missile required 'soft' emplacement (unprotected against nuclear explosion) in above-ground launching pads and a lengthy pre-launch preparation period. (It has been suggested that one motive for Khrushchev's exaggerated claims for Soviet progress in strategic weaponry during the 1959–1960 period was to conceal from the West his decision not to deploy extensively the first-generation SS-6.)

After the Cuban missile crisis, the deployment pace quickened somewhat. Moskalenko was succeeded by Marshal S. S. Biryuzov in 1962: The Soviet ICBM total had reached 200 by the time of Khrushchev's ousting, with perhaps one-third of these second-generation 'Saddlers' and 'Sasins'. Many of the latter were deployed in dispersed and 'hardened' (protected against nuclear explosion) launchers. An entirely new generation of ICBMs was in the development stage. By this time also MRBM and IRBM deployments had reached their peak of perhaps 750, all of them SS-4 'Sandal' and SS-5 'Skean' types. The Strategic Rocket Forces now consisted of 110,000 men, under the command of Marshal N. I. Krylov, who succeeded Biryuzov in 1963. (Too much is made of the Cuban crisis as a motive for the post-1962 Soviet missile build-up. Khrushchev's retreat in the face of the US ultimatum certainly helped to strengthen Soviet resolve to catch up with the United States as quickly as possible, but it certainly does not by itself explain the size of the Soviet deployments in the late 1960s.) But the unsatisfactory outcomes of the Cuban affair and the campaign against Berlin made it clear that, despite the pronounced shift in doctrine, resources and deployment from conventional to strategic forces which Khrushchev instituted, he had failed to develop a military posture sufficient to support the assertive political strategy he desired. Along with difficulties in the domestic economy for which he was also held accountable, his strategic failures helped bring about his political demise.

### From inferiority to parity plus

Throughout the 1950s and early 1960s there were numerous indications that Khrushchev's ideas on military strategy and on the appropriate force posture for the USSR were encountering opposition within the Soviet military bureaucracy. His decision to accord primacy to nuclear weapons and strategic missiles was one of the issues on which he encountered particularly sharp criticism, and after he was retired his successors once again altered Soviet doc-

*Left:* **A Soviet medium-range ballistic missile blasts into action from a hidden silo. Many such missiles cover targets in Europe from Western parts of the Soviet Union**

trine. His 'single option' strategy was modified, and his apparent belief that all wars between the socialist and capitalist camps must inevitably and quickly escalate to the holocaust level was gradually – if subtly – modified. At the same time, Brezhnev and Kosygin jettisoned the 'minimum deterrence' strategic posture on which Khrushchev, in part out of necessity, based his activist foreign policy between 1958 and 1962.

Generally speaking, the policies of the Brezhnev era have been directed toward improving the global power position of the Soviet Union. This meant that the USSR had to improve substantially its position in the strategic balance *vis-à-vis* the US, and develop the capability to project its military power and political presence into the farthest reaches of the globe. It is of course the former that concerns us here. Shortly after assuming power the regime made the decision to accelerate considerably the missile procurement programme set in motion during Khrushchev's last years, and by late 1966 deployment of two third-generation ICBMs – the SS-9 'Scarp' and the SS-11 'Sego' – was proceeding at the rate of one every two days.

The 'Scarp', the earliest version of which appeared in 1965, is a particularly impressive weapon; it is approximately 35 metres long and 3 metres in diameter, with a throw-weight (payload) of at least 12,000 pounds. The 'Mod 1' and 'Mod 2' versions carry single large war-heads of up to 25MT. The Soviets also begain testing in 1966 a fractional orbital bombardment (FOBS) version of the SS-9, designed to deliver its weapon from a satellite before completing a single orbit; the SS-9 was also tested later in a depressed trajectory mode.

The SS-11 'Sego', which followed in 1966, is, like the 'Scarp', a three-stage missile using a storable liquid propellant; early versions carried a single war-head in the 1–2MT range. Due to unimpressive accuracy the 'Sego' has from the start been regarded as a soft-target, or 'countervalue', weapon. It has been deployed in large numbers – approximately 960 of the 'Mod 1' and 'Mod 2' were in position by 1973, most in underground silos constructed in a broad belt 250 miles wide and 3,000 miles long, beginning east of Moscow and ending near Chita, east of Lake Baikal. The SS-10 'Scrag', another very large ICBM, was shown in Moscow parades beginning in 1965; it was apparently not deployed, however, and may have been a prototype or transition missile presaging the later SS-18. Also in this period the first Soviet solid-fuel missile, the SS-13 'Savage', reached the deployment stage, along with an IRBM variant using the upper two stages, the SS-14 'Scapegoat'. (The SS-14, when considered with its associated erector/transportation system, is known as 'Scamp'.) These missiles were beset with various technical difficulties, however, and were deployed only in small numbers, beginning in 1968. The earliest Soviet multiple re-entry vehicles (MRVs) were also tested in 1968 (unlike the more sophisticated multiple independently-targeted re-entry vehicles, or MIRVs, MRV war-heads cannot be directed at widely separated targets).

By early 1970 the USSR had passed the

US in numbers of operational ICBMs (see Chart 1). By February 1970, 275 SS-9s had been deployed, with a combination of war-head yield and accuracy sufficient to cause concern in the United States and elsewhere that the Soviets were on the verge of acquiring a hard-target capability against the US Minuteman ICBM force. Finally, early in 1970 a 'Mod 2' version of the SS-11, with a more accurate re-entry vehicle, was tested.

The Strategic Rocket Forces by now numbered some 350,000 men. They had become the most widely publicised component of the Soviet armed forces within the USSR. The commander-in-chief of the Strategic Rocket Forces always takes precedence over the other service commanders-in-chief, regardless of actual rank. High position in the Strategic Rocket Forces, in fact, seemed increasingly a path to even greater prominence: after the death of Defence Minister Malinovskiy in 1967, there were rumours that Marshal Krylov was a leading candidate for the position, and in the autumn of 1970 Colonel-General N. N. Alekseyev of the SRF was made a Deputy Defence Minister, and apparently put in charge of co-ordinating all strategic weapons development programmes. When Krylov died in May 1972, his one-time deputy, General V. F. Tolubko, became commander of the Strategic Rocket Forces.

By the time of SALT-1, then, the Brezhnev regime had more than achieved its initial objectives of 1964. The 1972 Interim Agreement on Offensive Weapons permitted the USSR to complete deployment of all

*Above:* Close-up of a Soviet missile silo. Similar sites have been built in birch and fir forests. The heavy covers slide to one side on rails

*Right:* Russia's early lead in space was made possible by a large ICBM tested in August 1957. Developed over the years, it has launched Vostok (seen here), Voskhod and Soyuz manned spacecraft

ICBM (and SLBM, or submarine-launched ballistic missile) launchers under construction as of 1 July 1972; strategic missile-launcher levels were frozen at that level. The Soviets were thus guaranteed a substantial advantage over the United States – no less than 1,408 to 1,054, depending on how many of its older missiles each side chooses to trade in for new SLBMs – in numbers of ICBM launchers. Each side was also allowed to upgrade qualitatively its missile force; thus the long-anticipated Soviet development of MIRV war-heads would not be restricted. Nor were any limits imposed on the USSR's emergent 'cold launch' or 'zero stage' technology, by which ICBMs are propelled from their silos by compressed gas and ignited above ground. The latter development is particularly significant, in that it obviates the need for extensive shielding inside the silo, thus permitting both the deployment of much larger missiles per silo and reasonably rapid re-use of the silo itself. When coupled with continued Soviet progress in the modernisation of their Air, Naval and Ground Forces, the

strategic advantages guaranteed the USSR at SALT-1 meant that they had achieved no less than military parity with the US – a fact which was widely acknowledged by Western experts.

It was the hope of the United States government that the SALT-1 agreement would stabilise the strategic competition between the superpowers. The more advanced technology of the American strategic forces was said to compensate for any disadvantages by the Soviets under the accord. The willingness of the USSR to accept severe constraints on deployment of a missile-type ABM (anti-ballistic missile) system, some commentators argued, indicated that the Soviets might be moving towards acceptance of an 'assured destruction' strategic posture and away from the 'war-fighting' doctrine implicit in much past Soviet military thinking. On this basis, it was suggested, *détente* might over a time become more than a slogan.

It soon became clear, however, that the Soviets intended to exploit fully the opportunities for further force improvements provided them under the SALT-1 accord. Their strategic force build-up since 1972 has proceeded at a pace which former US Defense Secretary Schlesinger termed 'unprecedented in its breadth and depth'. During the past 36 months the Soviets have tested and deployed a 'MRVed' version of the SS-11 'Sego', with more accurate re-entry vehicles. An entire new generation of ICBMs has been tested and is being deployed: the SS-16, a solid-fuel missile designed for deployment in both a fixed and a mobile mode; the SS-17, a soft-target weapon utilising 'cold-launch' technology and deploying four MIRVs; the SS-19, with a volume 56% larger and a throw-weight four times greater than that of the SS-11 and deploying at least four MIRVs; and the giant SS-18, also utilising 'cold-launch' and capable of carrying either a 50MT war-head or eight large hard-target war-heads. All four have new bus-type post-boost vehicles and war-heads with higher re-entry speed coefficients for greater accuracy. (For characteristics of Soviet missiles, see Chart 2.) The silo-hardening programme also continues; some reports indicate that the newest silos can withstand overpressures in excess of 3,000 psi (pounds per square inch). Ten or more additional strategic systems are reported to be under development, including a two-stage mobile version of the SS-19, with a range of 6,335 statute miles, and other longer-range follow-ons to the SS-19. A two-stage IRBM version of the SS-16, designated the SS-20, was extensively tested in 1975. (The USSR tested 371 large rockets in 1973 alone.) There are thus no indications that the Soviets plan to rest content with their fourth-generation ICBMs.

Neither is there any sign that the SALT-2 agreement, if concluded on the basis of the framework agreed upon by President Ford and Mr Brezhnev at Vladivostok in November 1974, will in any way constrain planned Soviet deployments. Under the terms of the agreement each side will be permitted to 'MIRV' up to 1,320 strategic missiles; there are no restrictions on SS-19 deployments or utilisation of 'cold-launch' techniques. Given the greater throw-weight of Soviet ICBMs,

## Chart 1

*Historical Comparison of USSR–US ICBM Strength, 1960–1975*

|        | 1960 | 1961 | 1962 | 1963 | 1964 | 1965 | 1966 | 1967 |
|--------|------|------|------|------|------|------|------|------|
| USSR   | 35   | 50   | 75   | 100  | 200  | 270  | 300  | 460  |
| US     | 18   | 63   | 294  | 424  | 834  | 854  | 904  | 1,054 |

|        | 1968  | 1969  | 1970  | 1971  | 1972  | 1973  | 1974  | 1975   |
|--------|-------|-------|-------|-------|-------|-------|-------|--------|
| USSR   | 800   | 1,050 | 1,300 | 1,510 | 1,550 | 1,575 | 1,590 | 1,599* |
| US     | 1,054 | 1,054 | 1,054 | 1,054 | 1,054 | 1,054 | 1,054 | 1,054  |

*Peaked at 1,618 in mid-year, before phase-out of SS-7 and SS-8s began.
*Source: The Military Balance*, 1969–70 and 1975–76, and Ray S. Cline, *World Power Assessment* (Washington, D.C.: Center for Strategic and International Studies, 1975), p. 57.

## Chart 2

*Characteristics of Soviet Strategic Missiles, 1975*

| Type | Number Deployed | Year Initially Deployed | Max. Range (statute miles) | No. of Warheads | Warhead Yield | Throw-weight in 1,000 lb | Est. CEP (nautical miles)[1] |
|------|-----------------|-------------------------|----------------------------|-----------------|---------------|--------------------------|------------------------------|
| SS-4 Sandal | 500 | 1959 | 1,200 | 1 | 1MT | n.a. | n.a. |
| SS-5 Skean | 100 | 1961 | 2,300 | 1 | 1+MT | n.a. | n.a. |
| SS-7 Saddler | 170[2] | 1961 | 6,900 | 1 | 5MT | 3 | 1+ |
| SS-8 Sasin | 19 | 1963 | 6,900 | 1 | 5MT | 3 | 1+ |
| SS-9 Scarp (Mod. 1 & 2) | 250 | 1965 | 7,500 | 1 | 18–25MT | 12 | .25+ |
| SS-9 Scarp (Mod. 4)[3] | 38 | 1971 | 7,500 | 3 MRV | 5MT | 12 | .25 |
| SS-11 Sego (Mod. 1 and 2) | 926[4] | 1966 | 6,500 | 1 | 1–2MT | 1.5 | .55 |
| SS-11 Sego (Mod. 3) | 66 | 1973 | 6,500 | 3 MRV | 300KT[5] | 1.5 | .5 |
| SS-13 Savage | 60 | 1968 | 5,000 | 1 | 1+MT[6] | 1 | 1.1 |
| SS-14 Scapegoat[7] | unknown | 1968 | 2,500 | 1 | 1MT | n.a. | 1+ |
| SS-16 | n.a. | 1975 | 6,300 | 1 | 1+MT | 2 | n.a. |
| SS-17 | 10 | 1975 | 6,500 | 4 MIRV | 1MT | 4.5 | .25 |
| SS-18 (Mod. 1) | 10 | 1974 | 7,500 | 1 | 25MT[8] | 15[10] | .25 |
| SS-18 (Mod. 2) | n.a. | 1975 | 7,500 | 5–8 MIRV | 2MT[9] | 15 | .25 |
| SS-19 | 50 | 1975 | 6,500 | 4–6 MIRV | 340KT | 6[11] | .25 |
| SS-20[12] | n.a. | — | 2,000+ | 1 | 1+MT | n.a. | n.a. |

*Sources: The Military Balance*, 1975–76; Ray S. Cline, *World Power Assessment* (Washington, D.C. Center for Strategic and International Studies, 1975); other sources as indicated in notes.
[1] Estimated CEPs are drawn from a variety of published sources.
[2] The Soviets have begun phasing out older ICBMs, as specified by SALT I, in order to increase numbers of SLBMs beyond those deployed or under construction as of 1 July 1972.
[3] The SS–9 Mod. 3 is the FOBS.
[4] Includes approximately 100 deployed within MRBM-IRBM fields. A number of SS-11 silos were modified during 1975 to receive SS-17 and SS-19 missiles.
[5] Earlier reports indicated that the SS-11 MRV warhead had a yield of 500KT; see *New York Times* 1 October 1972.
[6] Unconfirmed reports indicate that some SS-13s were deployed with 3 MRVs, probably similar to the SS-11 Mod 3 package.
[7] The SS-14 consists of the upper two stages of the SS-13.
[8] There have been persistent reports that some SS-18 Mod 1 will be deployed with a 50MT warhead see, e.g., Clarence A. Robinson, Jr., 'Soviets Hiding Submarine Work', *Aviation Week and Space Tech nology*, 11 November 1974, p. 14.
[9] The Soviets have recently tested several new large warheads in the 3–6MT range; these could be deployed on the SS-18 or on more advanced missiles.
[10] Other reports indicate a throw-weight of 16,500 lb for the SS-18.
[11] Similarly, some reports indicate a throw-weight of 10,000 lb for the SS-19)
[12] The SS-20, extensively tested during 1975, consists of the upper two stages of the SS-16. One source (Aviation Week and Space Technology, 31 May, 1976) indicated SS-20 consists of first two stages of SS-16, range exceeding 3,000 miles.

*Above:* A launch silo showing the gap between the missile and silo walls required for a 'hot' launch. Latest 'cold launch' techniques allow larger missiles to use the same silo

*Below left:* Forerunner of a new generation of submarine-launched ballistic missiles, SS-N-6 Sawfly has been operational in Yankee class submarines since 1968. Delta-class vessels carry the SS-N-8 with longer range.

*Right:* A test missile of the SS-4/SS-5 family being lifted by its transporter-erector for installation in the launch silo. Fuelled with storable liquids, it can be kept ready to fire

the agreement would thus virtually guarantee that the Soviets will be able, within the next decade, to deploy more war-heads on land-based missiles than the United States. Moreover, these war-heads will be larger and, assuming certain improvements in accuracy, highly counterforce-effective against hardened targets such as US Minuteman silos: a 4MT war-head with a circular error probable (CEP) of 0.29 statute mile would have a 95% kill probability against a silo hardened to withstand 300 psi overpressure. Neither does the agreement restrict deployment of mobile ICBMs, in which the Soviets have exhibited increasing interest in recent years.

It would be idle at this point to speculate on the motives inspiring the continuing expansion in the capabilities of the Strategic Rocket Forces. It can be said with some assurance only that the Soviets show no sign either that they are satisfied with the 'rough parity' with the US which they achieved through SALT-1, or that they view a state of 'mutual assured destruction' as an adequate basis on which to fashion their force posture. It may be, as some commentators have suggested, that the USSR remains obsessed with a 'more is better' approach to weapons procurement, and that neither Soviet political nor military leaders are acting on the basis of a master plan to achieve strategic superiority over the US. Strategic superiority, as has often been pointed out, is in any case both difficult to define and to achieve under contemporary circumstances. But there can be no doubt that the Soviets have acquired a strategic capability not only more than sufficient to deter any attack on the USSR, but one which may also enable them to support the sort of aggressive global political strategy which Khrushchev attempted 15 years ago.

# Soviet Missiles

Kenneth W. Gatland

Although every endeavour has been made to obtain definitive information on missiles included in this survey, many of the figures quoted must be considered provisional in the absence of official data

**Abbreviations: CW** *continuous-wave;* **FOBS** *fractional-orbit bombardment system;* **h.e.** *high explosive;* **IR** *infra-red;* **JATO** *jet-assisted take-off;* **KT** *kiloton;* **MIRV** *multiple, independently targeted re-entry vehicle;* **MRV** *multiple re-entry vehicle;* **MT** *megaton;* **SAR** *semi-active radar;* **CEP** *circular error probable;* **UDMH** *unsymmetrical dimethyl hydrazine.*

# STRATEGIC MISSILES
## Surface-to-Surface

| Designation | Nato Code | Stages | Length metres (ft) | Diameter metres (ft) | Propulsion | Range km (miles) | Notes |
|---|---|---|---|---|---|---|---|
| SS-4 | SANDAL | 1 | 22.4 (73.5) | 1.65 (5.41) | Storable liquid (nitric acid/kerosene) | 1,770 (1,100) | Inertial guidance, formerly radio command. Control by steerable exhaust vanes and aerodynamic rudders. Warhead, 1 MT nuclear or h.e. Service entry 1959. Number in service mid-1975: 500. Being replaced by SS-20(?). |
| SS-5 | SKEAN | 1 | 24.4 + (80 +) | 2.44 (8.0) | Storable liquid | 3,220 (2,000) | Inertial guidance. Probably 2 × RD-216 twin chamber GDL-OKB rocket engines. Warhead 1 MT. Service entry 1961. Number in service mid-1975: 100. Being replaced by SS-20(?). |
| SS-6 | SAPWOOD | 1½ | 30.5 (100) | 2.95 (sustainer only) (9.7) | Liquid oxygen/kerosene | ICBM range | First Soviet ICBM test at long range August 1957. Core of Sputnik/Vostok/Voskhod/Soyuz launchers, etc. Strap-on boosters, 19m (62.3 ft) × 3m (9.85 ft) max diameter. |
| SS-7 | SADDLER | 2 | 31.8 104.5 | 2.74 (9.0) | Storable liquid | 10,460 (6,500) | Inertial guidance. Warhead 1 × 20/25 MT or 1961. Number in service mid-1975: 190. Being replaced by SLBM's under SALT 1. |
| SS-8 | SASIN | 2 | 24.4 + (80 +) | 2.74 (9.0) | Storable liquid | 10,460 (6,500) | Inertial guidance. Warhead 5 MT. Service entry 1963. Number in service mid-1975: 19. Being replaced by SLBM's under SALT 1. |
| SS-9 | SCARP | 2 | 34.6 35.0 (MRV) (113.5) (115.0 MRV) | 3.05 (10.0) | Storable liquid | 12,000 + (7,500 +) | Inertial guidance Warhead 1 × 20/25 MT or 3 × 5 MT MRVs (Mod 4). Service entry 1965. Number in service mid-1975: 288. |
| SS-10 | SCRAG | 3 | 37.8 (124) | 2.74 (9.0) | Liquid | 12,000 + (7,500 +) | Inertial guidance. Developed in parallel with SS-9 but not put into service. |
| SS-11 | SEGO | 2 | 20.0 (65.6) | 2.4 (8.0) | Storable liquid | 10,500 (6,525) | Inertial guidance. Warhead 1 × 20/25 MT or of 500 KT. Service entry 1966. Number in service mid-1975: 990. |
| SS-13 | SAVAGE | 3 | 20.0 (65.6) | 1.7 (5.5) | Solid rocket | 8,000 + (5,000 +) | Inertial guidance. Warhead 1-2 MT or 3 × MRV. Service entry 1968. Number in service mid-1975: 60 (based Plesetsk). |
| SS-14 | SCAPEGOAT | 2 | 10.7 (35) | 1.4 (4.6) | Solid rocket | 3,540 (2,200) | Inertial guidance. Nuclear Warhead. Mobile on Scamp transporter-erector (modified JS III tank chassis). |
| SS-15 | | | 18.3 (60) | 1.7 – 1.8 (5.5 –) (6.0) | Solid rocket | 5,630 (3,500) | Mobile on Scrooge transporter-erector. Possibly related to SS-13 Savage. |
| SS-16 | | 3 | 20.0 (65.6) | 2.0 6.5 | Solid rocket | 9,000 (5,600) | Detected by US space reconnaissance 1972-73. Single re-entry vehicle 1 MT + or MIRV's from post-boost vehicle (bus). Hot-launched from silo. Also mobile role. |
| SS-17 | | 2 | 24.0 + (80) | 2.5 8.2 | Liquid storable | 10,000 + (6,214 +) | Cold launched from modified SS11 silos. Post-boost 'bus' dispensing 4 × KT MIRV's. Seventeen test flights completed April 1974. Number in service mid-1975: 10 SS-17 and SS-19 restricted to 1,036 under SALT 1. |
| SS-18 | | 2 | 37.0 (121.0) | 3.3 11.0 | Liquid storable | 10,500 + mod 1 9,250 + mod 2 (6,525) (Mod 1) (5,750) (mod 2) | Cold launched from silo. Single re-entry vehicle 40-50 MT or up to 8 MIRV's 1MT + each from computerised post-boost 'bus'. Possibly 30 per cent greater throw weight than SS-9 Scarp. Restricted to 310 under SALT 1. Number deployed in mid-1975: 10 Mod 1. |
| SS-19 | | 2 | 24.4 (80) | 2.5 (8.2) | Liquid storable | 10,000 (6,214) | Cold launched from modified SS-11 silos. Post-boost 'bus' dispensing 6 × 400-500 KT MIRV's. Number in service mid-1975: 50. |
| SS-20 | | 2 | 16.8 (55.0) | 2.0 (6.5) | Solid rocket | 2,750-7,400 (1,710-4,600) depending on warhead | Mobile launch system, probably single RV or MRV's. Employs first two stages of SS-16. Replacing SS-4 and SS-5. |

# SUBMARINE-LAUNCHED BALLISTIC MISSILES

| Designation | Nato Code | Stages | Length metres (ft) | Diameter metres (ft) | Propulsion | Range km (miles) | Notes |
|---|---|---|---|---|---|---|---|
| SS-N-4 | SARK | 2 | 15.0 (49) | 1.8 (5.9) | Solid rocket | 580 (360) | Inertial guidance. Launch weight 19,050 kg (42,000 lb). Nuclear warhead. First Soviet submarine-launched ballistic missile, 2 or 3 in extended bridge fin Zulu V, Golf, Hotel. Operational 1958. Surface launched. |

| Designation | Nato Code | Stages | Length metres (ft) | Diameter metres (ft) | Propulsion | Range km (miles) | Notes |
|---|---|---|---|---|---|---|---|
| SS-N-5 | SERB | 2 | 10.7 (35) | 1.5 (4.9) | Solid rocket | 1,200 (750) | Inertial guidance. Launch weight 18,144 kg (40,000 lb). Nuclear MT warhead. Second-generation missile in Golf II and Hotel II submarines, 3 launch tubes apiece. Operational 1963. Number in service mid-1975: 24-33. Warhead IMT? |
| SS-N-6 | SAWFLY | 2 | 12.8 (42) | 1.8 (5.9) | Solid rocket | 2,400 3,000 (Mods 2/3) (1,500) (1,860 (Mods 2/3)) | Inertial guidance. Launch weight 19,050 kg (42,000 lb). Nuclear 1 MT warhead. Third-generation missile in Yankee-class nuclear-powered submarines, 16 per vessel in pressure hull. Mods 2 and 3 improved performance, Mod 3 3 × MRV's. Operational 1967. |
| SS-N-8 | | 2 | 13-14 (42.6-45.9) | | Storable liquid | 7,800 4,847 | Inertial guidance. Nuclear warhead 1-2 MT Advanced missile system in Delta-class nuclear-powered submarines, 12 launch tubes (Delta 1), operational 1972. 16 launch tubes (Delta 2). Launch weight 20,410 kg (4-5,000 lb). |
| SS-NX-13 | | 2 | | | Solid rocket(?) | 1,000 + (620 +) | Submarine launched anti-ship ballistic missile. Nuclear warhead. May be fired from SS-N-6/SS-N-8 launch tubes. Possibly depressed trajectory, apogee 225 km (140 miles); sensor system 'looks down' on distant target and locks on. May operate in conjunction with satellite targeting data. |

# CRUISE OR WINGED MISSILES

| Designation | Nato Code | Length metres (ft) | Diameter cm (in) | Span cm (in) | Propulsion | Range km (miles) | Guidance | Notes |
|---|---|---|---|---|---|---|---|---|
| SSC-1 | SHADDOCK | 13.8 (42) | 100 (39.4) | 210 (82.7) | Turbojet plus two JATO units | 450 (280) | Radio command, mid-course, IR or active radar homing | Coastal defence missile launched from elevating container on eight-wheeled cross-country transporter. Nuclear (1 KT?) or h.e. warhead 1,000 kg (2,205 lb). Launch weight 11,790 kg (26,000 lb). Speed Mach 1.5. |
| SSC-2A | SALISH | | | | Turbojet, solid boost | | Active radar seeker(?) | Tactical use by Soviet Army (land-based version of Samlet). |
| SSC-2B | SAMLET | 7 (23) | | 500 (197) | Turbojet, solid boost | 200 (124) | Autopilot/ radio command, radar homing | Coastal defence missile. Radome larger than on Salish; electronic pod 3 on fin. Weight 3,000 kg (6,614 lb); h.e. warhead. Speed, M0.8-0.9. Developed from AS-1 Kennel. Operated in conjunction with vehicle-mounted Sheet Bend radar. Supplied to Cuba and Egypt. |
| SS-N-1 | SCRUBBER | 6.8-7.6 (23.3-24.9) | 100-150 (39.4-59) | 350-460 (138-181) | Turbojet(?), Solid boost | 110-185 (68-115) | Autopilot/radio command, radar or IR terminal homing | Ship-launched from 'hanger' attached to 17m (56 ft) launch rail on rotatable, elevating, mount. Speed M0.9. Launch weight 4,080 kg (9,000 lb). H.e. warhead. Kildin and Krupny class destroyers. Operational 1958-59. |
| SS-N-2A | STYX | 6.25-6.50 (20.5-21.3) | 75 (29.5) | 275 (108) | Rocket, solid boost | 9-40 (5.7-25) | Autopilot, radio command, active radar homing | On Komar, Osa fast patrol boats. Launch weight 2,495 kg (5,500 lb). Warhead 360 kg (794 lb). Speed M0.9. Operational 1960. |
| SS-N-2B | STYX | | | | | 8.5-40 (5.2-25) | Cruise, autopilot/ radio command, terminal homing | On Komar, Osa fast patrol boats. |
| SS-N-3A | SHADDOCK | 13.8 (42) | 100 (39.4) | 210 (82.7) | Turbojet plus two JATO units | 450 (280) | Autopilot, radio command, terminal homing | Sea-launched version of SSC-1. Entered service 1962. Number in service mid-1975 — 264 in submarines and 48 in surface ships. First on diesel-powered Whisky Twin Cylinder submarines 1958, twin launch canisters elevating from stern. |
| SS-N-7 | | 6.7 (22) | | | | 45-55 (28-34) | Autopilot plus terminal homing | Underwater-launched cruise missile. Autopilot plus terminal homing. Speed M1.5. C-class submarine has eight launchers. Operational 1969-70. Possible surface skimmer in terminal approach to target. |
| SS-N-9 | | 9.1 (30) | | | | 75-275 (47-171) | | Medium-range naval cruise missile intermediate between Styx and Shaddock. Autopilot with radio command link guidance, mid-course by aircraft or helicopter, active radar homing(?). Speed M1.4. H.e. warhead. Triple launches on Nanuchka corvettes. Operational 1968-69. |
| SS-N-10 | | 7.6 (25) | | | | 50 (31) | | Supersonic cruise missile on Kresta II (2 × quad launchers) and Krivak (1 × quad launcher). Radar guidance/anti-radiation passive homing Weight 2,720 kg (6,000 lb). Speed M1.2. Operational 1968. |
| SS-N-11 | | 6.4 (21) | | | Rocket, solid boost | 50 (31) | | On Osa-II fast patrol boat replacing SS-N-2 Styx; also on modified Kildin and Kashin destroyers replacing SS-N-1 Scrubber. Probably active radar homing. Speed M0.9. Operational 1968. |
| SS-NX-12 | | | | | Turbojet | 450-2,500 (280-1,553) | | Shaddock successor. Speed M2-5; altitude 10,670m (35,000 ft). In Echo II submarines, etc. |
| SS-N-14 | | | | | | | | Entering service on Kara, Kresta II, Krivak and Moskva-class vessels. |

# TACTICAL MISSILES
## Anti-Tank

| Designation | Nato Code | Length cm (in) | Diameter cm (in) | Span cm (in) | Propulsion | Range metres (ft) | Notes |
|---|---|---|---|---|---|---|---|
| AT-1 | SNAPPER | 113 (44.5) | 14 (5.5) | 74 (29) | Solid rocket | 500-2,300 (1,640-7,550) | Wire-guided, command line-of-sight. Speed 50m/sec (164 ft/sec). Weight 22.3 kg (49 lb). Warhead 5.25 kg (11.6 lb) hollow charge. Penetrates 35cm (13.7 in) of armour. Carrier VAZ-69, BTR-40P (BRDM). |

| Designation | Nato Code | Length cm (in) | Diameter cm (in) | Span cm (in) | Propulsion | Range metres (ft) | Notes |
|---|---|---|---|---|---|---|---|
| AT-2 | SWATTER A | 90 (35.4) | 15 (5.9) | 66 (26) | Solid rocket | 500-2,300 (1,640-7,550) | Wire-guided, command line-of-sight. Warhead penetrates 40 cm (15.7 in) of armour. Carrier BTR-40P (BRDM). 'B' version of Swatter has second-generation auto-guidance system. |
| AT-3 | SAGGER | 88 (34.6) | 12 (4.7) | 46 (18) | Solid boost, sustainer | 500-2,500 (1,640-7,550) | Wire-guided, command line-of-sight. Speed 120m/sec (394 ft/sec). Weight 11 kg (24.2 lb). Warhead 2.7 (5.95 lb). Penetrates 40 cm (15.7 in) of armour. Carriers, BTR-40P (BRDM), M1967. |

## Short Range (Battlefield Support)

| Designation | Nato Code | Length metres (ft) | Diameter cm (in) | Propulsion | Range km (miles) | Notes |
|---|---|---|---|---|---|---|
| | FROG 1 | 10.2 (33.4) | 61 (24) | Solid rocket | 32 (20) | Spin-stabilised, unguided. Fixed cruciform tail fins. Bulbous warhead, nuclear or h.e. Launch weight 3,000-3,175 kg (6,600-7,000 lb). Entered service 1957. Warhead weight 1,180 kg (2,600 lb); warhead diameter 84 cm (33 in). |
| | FROG 2 | 9.5 (31.2) | 30.5 (12) | Solid rocket | 19 (12) | Spin-stabilised, unguided. Fixed cruciform 1.05m (3.5 ft) span tail fins. Warhead h.e. or chemical. Launch weight 2,450 kg (5,400 lb). Warhead weight 545 kg (1,200 lb). Air-transportable on PT 76 chassis by An-22. |
| | FROG 3 | 10.5 (34.4) | 40 (15.8) | Solid rocket | 36-45 (22-28) | Spin-stabilised, unguided. Fixed cruciform tail fins. Launch weight 2,266 kg (5,000 lb). Cylindrical bulbous warhead, nuclear, chemical or h.e. 454 kg (1,000 lb). On PT 76 chassis, as above. |
| | FROG 4 | 10.2 (33.5) | 40 (15.8) | Solid rocket | 50 (30 + ) | Spin-stabilised, unguided. Fixed cruciform tail fins. Warhead, nuclear, chemical or h.e. On PT 76 chassis, as above. Soviet designation is T-5E. |
| | FROG 5 | 9.5 (31.2) | 40 (15.8) | Solid rocket | 35 (21.7) | Spin-stabilised, unguided. Similar to FROGs 3 and 4 with different warhead, nuclear, chemical or h.e. Warhead weight 454 kg (1,000 lb). |
| | FROG 6 | | | Dummy | | Dummy missile for training purposes. |
| | FROG 7 | 9.1 (29.8) | 55 (21.6) | Solid rocket | 60 (37) | Spin-stabilised, unguided. Fixed cruciform fins. Shorter and fatter than Frog 4. Launch weight 2,300 kg (5,070 lb), warhead, nuclear, chemical or h.e. same diameter as missile body, 450 kg (990 lb). Entered service 1965. On ZIL-135 modernised wheeled transporter. Soviet designation of weapon system is Luna. |

## Medium Range

| Designation | Nato Code | Length metres (ft) | Diameter cm (in) | Propulsion | Range km (miles) | Notes |
|---|---|---|---|---|---|---|
| SS-1B | SCUD A | 10.7 (35.1) | 84 (33) | Single-stage, storable liquid rocket | 80-180 (50-110) | Radio command guidance, rear fins control. Launch weight 4,500 kg (9,920 lb). Warhead, nuclear or h.e., 680 kg (1,500 lb) including nose cone. Entered service 1957. On JS-III chassis. |
| SS-1C | SCUD B | 11.4 (37.4) | 84 (33) | Single-stage, storable liquid rocket | 160-280 (100-170) | Simplified inertial, rear fins control. Launch weight 6,370 kg (14,046 lb). Warhead, nuclear or h.e., 770-860 kg (1,697-1,896 lb). Entered service 1965. On MAZ-543 wheeled transporter, erector/launcher, early models on JS-3 chassis. |
| SS-12 | SCALEBOARD | 11 (36) | | Single-stage, storable liquid rocket | 700-800 (435-497) | Inertial guidance. Warhead, nuclear or h.e. Entered service 1969. On MAZ-543 carrier. |

# ANTI-BALLISTIC MISSILES

| Designation | Nato Code | Length metres (ft) | Diameter cm (in) | Span cm (in) | Propulsion | Slant Range km (miles) | Notes |
|---|---|---|---|---|---|---|---|
| ABM-1 | GALOSH | 18-19 (59-62) | 240-270 (94.5-106) | | Multi-stage rocket; four first-stage nozzles | 300 (186) | Displayed in 20.4m (67 ft) long ribbed-skin cylinder on trailer of enclosed transport vehicle. 64 launchers at four sites defend Moscow. System modified to counter Chinese ICBM. |
| ABM-? | | | | | Multi-stage | | Long range ABM SH-4, exo-atmospheric. Testing began at Sary Sagan in 1974. |
| ABM-? | | | | | Multi-stage | | High-acceleration ABM similar to U.S. Sprint for defence of point targets within the atmosphere. Believed intended for defence against tactical missiles. |

# SURFACE-TO-AIR MISSILES

| Designation | Nato Code | Length metres (ft) | Diameter cm (in) | Span cm (in) | Propulsion | Slant Range km (miles) | Notes |
|---|---|---|---|---|---|---|---|
| SA-1 | GUILD | 12 (39) | 70 (27.6) | 280 (110) | Dual-thrust solid | | Guidance, radio command in conjunction with Yo-Yo radar. Steered by moveable foreplanes and small ailerons on wings. Service entry 1954. No longer produced. |
| SA-2 | GUIDELINE | 10.7 (35) | 70 (27.6) | 170 (67) | Solid boost, liquid sustainer | 40 + (24 + ) | Guidance, automatic radio command with radar tracking of target. Effective ceiling 25,000m (82,020 ft). Launch weight 2,300 kg (5,000 lb); warhead 154 kg (288 lb) h.e. Speed M3.5. |
| SA-3 | GOA | 6.7 (22) | 46 (18) | 120 (47) | Solid boost, solid sustainer | 29 (18) | Guidance, automatic-radio command with radar terminal homing. Effective ceiling 12,000m + (39,370 ft + ). Weight 400 kg (882 lb). H.e. warhead. Speed M2.0. Naval version is SA-N-1. |
| SA-4 | GANEF | 9.2 (30.2) | 80 (31.5) | 230 (90) | Four wrap-round rocket boosts, ramjet sustainer | 70 (43) | Guidance, automatic radio command. Effective ceiling 18,000m + (59,000 ft + ). Weight 1,000 kg + (2,205 lb + ). H.e. warhead. |
| SA-5 | GAMMON | 16.4 (54) | 87.5 (34) | 365 (144) | Solid-boost, solid sustainer | 160 + (100 + ) | Guidance, automatic radio command/SAR homing. Effective ceiling 30,000m (98,425 ft). Operates in conjunction with Square Pair radar. Limited ABM capability. H.e. or nuclear warhead. About 1,100 in service mid-1975. |
| SA-6 | GAINFUL | 6.2 (20.3) | 33.5 (13.2) | 124 (48.8) | Solid fuel, integral ramjet | 59.5 (37) | Guidance, radio command/SAR homing. Weight 550 kg (1,212 lb), warhead 80 kg (176 lb). Effective altitude range 100/18,000m (328/59,055 ft). Proximity/impact fuse. Speed M2.8. |

| Designation | Nato Code | Length metres (ft) | Diameter cm (in) | Span cm (in) | Propulsion | Slant Range km (miles) | Notes |
|---|---|---|---|---|---|---|---|
| SA-7 | GRAIL | 1.35 (4.4) | 7.0 (2.75) | | Solid boost, sustainer | 2.9/4.0 (1.8/2.5) | Man-portable or vehicle-mounted IR-homing missile. Small cruciform (steerable?) wings and tail fins flick out as missile leaves launch tube. Altitude range 45/1,500m (148/4,920 ft). Weight 10 kg + (22 lb + ), warhead 2.5 kg (5.5 lb). Speed M1.5. |
| SA-8 | GECKO | 3.2 (10.5) | 20.2 (8.25) | 64 (25) | Dual-thrust solid? | 12.0 (7.5) | Command guidance. Control by cruciform canard fins. Altitude range 50/6,000m (164/19,685 ft). Can engage one target with two missiles simultaneously on different control frequencies. |
| SA-9 | GASKIN | | | | Solid | 5 (3.1) | Low-level anti-aircraft defence. IR homing. Development of SA-7 with larger warhead and greater range. Twin-quad canister on modified BRDM with radar direction. |
| SA-N-1 | | | | | | | Naval version of SA-3. Entered service 1962. On Kresta I, Kynda, Kashin, Kotlin, Kanin class ships. Operates in conjunction with E/I band Reel radars. |
| SA-N-3 | GOBLET | | | | | | Naval version of Army SA-6 Gainful. Deployed on helicopter carriers and Kresta II class GM cruisers. Operates in conjunction with Headlight acquisition and tracking radar. |
| SA-N-4 | | | | | | | Fast-reacting naval missile possibly related to SA-8 on Krivak class destroyers and other ships. Deck-mounted, retractable twin-round pop-up launcher in weather-protective bin. Operates in conjunction with Pop Group radar. |

# AIR-TO-SURFACE MISSILES

| Designation | Nato Code | Length metres (ft) | Diameter cm (in) | Span metres (ft) | Propulsion | Range km (miles) | Guidance | Notes |
|---|---|---|---|---|---|---|---|---|
| AS-1 | KENNEL | 8.2 (27) | | 4.9 (16) | Turbojet | 100 + (62 + ) | Autopilot, active or passive radar homing | Anti-shipping. Two carried by Tu-16 Badger B on underwing pylons. Beam riding or radio command (two radomes on underside of launch aircraft). Weight 3,000 kg (6,614 lb). Speed M0.9. Surface-to-surface version is Samlet. |
| AS-2 | KIPPER | 9.4 (31) | | 4.6-4.9 (15-16) | Underslung turbojet | 180-210 (112-130) | Autopilot, mid-course radio command(?), radar homing | Anti-shipping. Belly-mounted on Tu-16 Badger C. Weight 6,000 kg + (13,228 lb + ). Speed M1.2. |
| AS-3 | KANGAROO | 15 (49.2) | | 9.0 (29.5) | Turbojet | 185-650 (115-403) | Autopilot, mid-course by radio-command | Largest of Soviet air-to-surface weapons. Belly-mounted on Tu-95 Bear B. Thermonuclear warhead(?). |
| AS-4 | KITCHEN | 11.3 (37) | | 2.4 (8) | Liquid rocket | 300 + (186 + ) | Inertial(?) plus mid-course | Belly-mounted on Tu-22 Blinder B. Weight exceeds 6,000 kg (13,228 lb). Tu-95 Bear D may be mid-course spotter and control platform for this and other long-range missiles. |
| AS-5 | KELT | 9.4 (30.8) | | 4.6 (15) | Liquid rocket | 180 + (112 + ) | Autopilot, active or passive radar homing | Anti-shipping. Two carried by Tu-16 Badger G on underwing pylons. Weight about 4,800 kg (10,580 lb). Well over 1,000 built. Supersedes Kennel. |
| AS-6 | | 9.0 (29.5) | 90 (35.4) | 3.2 (10.5) | Solid rocket(?) | 700-800 (435-497) | Inertial, mid-course(?), homing | Two carried by Tupolev Backfire B for stand-off strike against land targets from high and low-level — possibly also anti-shipping role. Weight about 4,800 kg (10,580 lb). Speed M2.5. Nuclear or h.e. warhead. |
| AS-? | | | | | | | | Carried by Mi-24 Hind A assault helicopter on four wingtip mounts. Swatter derivitive(?). |
| AS-? | | | | | | | | Possible air-launched development of SS-NX-13 for long-range submarine attack in conjunction with satellite sensor targeting. |
| AS-7 | KERRY | | | | | 18 (11) | Anti-radiation or TV command(?) | Tactical missile on close-support aircraft Su-7B Fitter A, Su-17 Fitter C and (?) Su-19 Fencer. |

# AIR-TO-AIR MISSILES

| Designation | Nato Code | Length metres (ft) | Diameter cm (in) | Span cm (in) | Propulsion | Weight kg (lb) | Range km (miles) | Notes |
|---|---|---|---|---|---|---|---|---|
| AA-1 | ALKALI | 2.4 (7.9) 1.86 (6.1) latest version | 18 (7) | 58 (22.8) 32 (12.6) | Solid rocket | 90 (198) | 5.9-8 (3.7-5) | Semi-active homing from launch aircraft fire control radar. Speed M1-2. All-weather MiG-17, MiG-19, Su-9 Fishpot B. Speed, Mach 1-2. *Some reports suggest beam-riding. |
| AA-2 | ATOLL | 2.8 (9.2) | 12 (4.72) | 53 (fins) 45 (wing) (20.8) (17.7) | Solid rocket | 70 (154) | 4.8-6.4 (3-4) | Infra-red homing (resembles US Sidewinder). Soviet designation K13A. MiG-21 Fishbed, MiG-23, MiG-17 Fresco. Also 'Advanced Atoll' with semi-active radar homing. |
| AA-3 | ANAB | 4.1 (13.4) IR 4.0 (13.1) radar | 28 (11) | 130 (51) | Solid rocket | 275 (606) | 8-9.7 (5-6) | Infra-red and radar homing versions. Firebar, Fishpot C, Su-11, Su-15, MiG-23. |
| AA-5 | ASH | 5.5 (IR) 5.2 (SAR) 18 (IR) 17 (SAR) | 30 (11.8) | 130 (51) | Solid rocket | 200 (441) | 22 (13) | IR and radar homing versions. Tu-28P Fiddler, 2 × IR on inboard pylons, 2 × radar on outboard pylons. MiG-25 Foxbat A originally carried two missiles (1972), later four AA-6 Acrid. |
| AA-6 | ACRID | 5.8 (IR) 6.09 (SAR) (19) IR (20) SAR | 40 (15.7) | 225 (88.5) | Solid rocket | 650-850 (1,433-1,874) | 37 (10) | IR and radar homing versions MiG-25 Foxbat A carries two of each on under-wing rails. Aircraft wingtip fairings believed to house continuous wave target illuminating equipment. Launch weight 650-850 kg (1,433-1,874 lb), warhead 100 kg (220 lb) Speed M2.2. |
| AA-7 | APEX | 4.3 (14.1) | 24 (9.45) | 105 (41.3) | Solid rocket | | 28 (17) | MiG-23 Flogger, one under each wing (1 IR homing, 1 SAR). |
| AA-8 | APHID | 2.1 (6.9) | | | Solid rocket | | 5-8 (3.1-5) | MiG Fishbed. Atoll dog-fight development. IR or semi-active radar homing. Two on underbelly pylons MiG-23S Flogger with one IR and one SAR AA-7 on glove pylons. |

# STRATEGIC MISSILES
## Surface-to-surface
### SS-4 Sandal

A medium-range ballistic missile, it was first seen in a Moscow parade in 1961. It followed an earlier missile of the same class, the SS-3 Shyster, which incorporated some of the older V-2 technology. Shyster's engine was a single-chamber RD-103 developed between 1952-53, for which propellants probably were liquid oxygen and a hydrocarbon fuel (kerosene?). Its successor, the SS-4, employed storable liquids which facilitated handling in the field and allowed missiles to be kept at instant readiness. This was the weapon involved in the Cuban crisis of 1962 which threatened south-eastern parts of the United States from sites which had been hastily constructed in Cuba. Its maximum range was about 1,800 km (1,100 miles).

Sandal also differed from Shyster in having a new four-chamber engine, smaller tail fins and a flared skirt over the engine bay. Use of a storable propellant allowed some models to be launched from silos in the USSR. Trials were made from Kapustin Yar.

Sandal was to be adapted as the first stage of the small Cosmos satellite launcher which inaugurated the Cosmos programme at Kapustin Yar in March 1962. It has since been disclosed that the first stage has a four-chamber RD-214 engine of 74 tonnes vacuum thrust, a chamber pressure of 45 atmospheres and a specific impulse of 264 sec. Propellants are nitric acid and kerosene.

### SS-5 Skean

Basically an enlarged Sandal, the SS-5 was first deployed in 1964. Silo-launched, it had a maximum range of 3,200 km (2,000 miles). The missile was deployed with SS-4s in Western parts of the Soviet Union, targeted on Western Europe.

The engine type had not been revealed at the time of writing but its propellant is certainly storable and is possibly nitric acid and kerosene.

Skean, too, has been developed as a satellite launcher by the addition of a second stage.

### SS-6 Sapwood

The SS-6 was Russia's first ICBM. It was tested in great secrecy in August 1957 and announced as having flown "at . . . unprecedented altitude . . . and landed in the target area." It was also responsible for Russia's early space lead. Fuelled with kerosene and liquid oxygen (and requiring immense support facilities) it comprised a central core and four strap-on boosters. Firing at lift-off were no fewer than 20 main thrust chambers and 12 small swivel-mounted verniers — small motors for fine control of speed and direction.

A virtually unmodified SS-6 launched the first Sputnik on 4 October 1957. With an upper stage fitted, on 12 April 1961 it sent Yuri Gagarin, the world's first spaceman, into orbit aboard Vostok 1.

The engine of the central core was the RD-107 of 96 tonnes vacuum thrust; the four boosters had RD-108 engines of 102 tonnes vacuum thrust.

Improved versions of the same basic rocket are still in use for launching Soyuz manned spacecraft and various unmanned Earth satellites and space probes.

### SS-7 Saddler

The mainstay of the Strategic Rocket Forces in the early years, the SS-7 first entered service in 1961. It did not appear in Moscow military parades but is known to be a two-stage, storable liquid ICBM approaching the size of the US Titan II. Although now obsolescent, it has been deployed in both hard and soft sites alongside the SS-8 Sasin. As many as 190 may have seen service over the years (one 1973 report quotes 98) and a large number were launched on test. SS-7s are now being replaced by new-generation ICBMs and a growing family of submarine-launched ballistic missiles (see SS-N-8 entry in table).

# SS-8 Sasin

First seen in a Moscow military parade in November 1964, Sasin is in the ICBM class. The 24 m (80 ft) long two-stage rocket has a maximum range of about 11,000 km (6,800 miles). The transporter is a six-wheeled trailer hauled by a large eight-wheeled fully-enclosed tractor.

The rocket itself, which employs storable liquid propellants, consists of a cylindrical first stage and a top stage of smaller diameter with 'blow-out' interstage fairings. On the example seen in Red Square the engine nozzles were concealed by a disc-like weather cover but four mounting brackets indexed at 90° around the base gave evidence that the flight path was controlled by steerable exhaust vanes. There were no aerodynamic surfaces.

The technology of this missile bore a close resemblance to that applied in the SS-5 Skean.

# SS-9 Scarp

The largest missile in the Soviet armoury before the appearance of the SS-18, the Scarp has been widely deployed in silos. It has two stages, employs liquid storable propellants and was first displayed in Moscow in November 1967. The engine type had not been revealed at the time of writing but the first stage has six fixed thrust chambers and four swivel-mounted verniers for thrust vector control and velocity adjustment.

Four main versions are acknowledged by the US Department of Defense:

*Mod 1.* Entered service in 1965 with a single re-entry vehicle of about 20 MT explosive yield. Principal objectives, Titan and Minuteman ICBM bases within the USA.

*Mod 2.* The standard weapon which carries a single very high yield (25 MT) warhead.

*Mod 3.* Employed for tests of a depressed-trajectory technique, which sacrifices some range, and Fractional Orbit Bombardment System (FOBS). Instead of rising some 1,290 km (800 miles) into space on arching trajectories, as with conventional ICBMs launched over the Northern Hemisphere, FOBS vehicles go into temporary orbit close to the Earth before being cut down by the action of rocket braking. (Example: Cosmos 298, orbit ranged between 127 and 162 km (79 and 101 miles) inclined at 49.6 deg to equator). The test vehicle re-entered the atmosphere at the end of one orbit, presumably under surveillance by Soviet radars at Emba and other centres.

Operationally, such missiles would be aimed to enter the United States through the 'back door' of the South Pole, skirting the BMEWS advance warning radars in England, Greenland and Alaska. However, the advantage of 'surprise' would be offset by reduced target accuracy. US surveillance radars — including the advanced planar radar at Eglin AFB, Florida, which became operational in 1968 and south-looking SLBM radars — now alert the US southern flank.

*Mod 4.* Employed for tests of MRVs (multiple re-entry vehicles) and MIRVs (muliple independently-targetable re-entry vehicles). Early tests ended November 1970; new tests began January 1973.

More recently, a fifth model has been identified with an 'anti-satellite' test programme (SIS, satellite interceptor system) launched from Tyuratam. Some recent 'targets' appear to have been launched from Plesetsk by a missle derived from the SS-5 Skean family. Normally, the 'interceptor' having manoeuvred in orbit achieves a close pass of the 'target' on the descent leg of a wider elliptical orbit. Possible 'kill' techniques include warhead fragmentation, nuclear bursts and, eventually, high-energy pulsed lasers.

# SS-10 Scrag

Developed in parallel with the SS-9, Scrag seems to have been abandoned following successful testing of the former missile. It first appeared in a Moscow parade in 1965.

Not only was the three-stage rocket less advanced than its companion, it had the disadvantage of using cryogenic propellants which meant that it could not be stored for long periods in a ready condition.

First stage control was achieved by swivelling the four thrust chambers. The first stage engine may have been related to the RD-111 which employed liquid oxygen and kerosene (vacuum thrust 166 tonnes, chamber pressure 80 atmospheres, specific impulse 317 sec).

The missile itself was characterised by interstage trusses separating the stages.

# SS-11 Sego

Unlike its solid-propellant SS-13 counterpart, the SS-11 did not appear in a Moscow military parade with other rockets of its day, which marked it out as something special. It has, in fact, been in service with the Soviet Strategic Rocket Forces since 1966 in silos West and East of the Urals.

The US Department of Defense acknowledges three versions:
*Mod 1*, tested over a wide range of distances up to about 10,500 km (6,525 miles) with a single re-entry vehicle.
*Mod 2*, a non-operational test vehicle.
*Mod 3*, the operational model deployed with three 500 KT re-entry vehicles. The number of SS-11s deployed at the time of the 1972 SALT agreement was 970; 66 new silos were under construction.

SS-11 sites are suitable for adaptation to cold-launch techniques in which missiles of greater diameter, stored in cylindrical containers, can be accommodated in the same silo. A missile of SS-11 proportions made its debût during the Moscow parade in November 1973 within a trailer-mounted canister (67 ft long × 9 ft diameter) towed by a fully-enclosed transport vehicle.

Although the missile itself was hidden, the end of the canister had four orifices for thrust chambers and it was assumed that the encapsulated missile could be raised vertically from its trailer for lowering into a silo.

The launch system follows the practice adopted for expelling missiles from submerged submarines. Compressed-air or gas from a generator expels the missile from its casing for ignition above ground. The new silos can be smaller and less complex because there is no longer need to have a large space between the missile and the silo wall to cater for the blast effects of hot exhaust gases, and large underground exhaust ducts can be eliminated. There is the added advantage of a modest increase in performance, acoustic damage to the silo is eliminated and there are new opportunities for hardening the site against thermo-nuclear attack.

# SS-13 Savage

First seen in Red Square in May 1965, Savage compares with the US silo-based Minuteman 1 but has not been widely deployed. It appears to have been developed in parallel with the liquid-propellant SS-11 Sego which has superior performance and warhead capacity. A total of 60 SS-13s are in service with the Strategic Rocket Forces at Plesetsk, but these are likely to be superseded by the SS-16, which embodies the latest advances in solid-propellants, silo construction, missile guidance and warhead technology.

The missile itself — like the SS-10 Scrag — is characterised by interstage trusses which separate the stages.

# SS-14 Scapegoat

This missile consists of two upper stages of the SS-13. Operationally, it is enclosed in the 'Iron Maiden' container carried on a modified JS III tank chassis. The complete system is known by the NATO code Scamp. Soviet commanders have been particularly enthusiastic for this mobile type of IRBM since it can be operated along the entire frontier of Soviet territory, from the Baltic to the Pacific. It also offers the advantage of operation from concealed positions in difficult terrain such as heavily wooded areas in the European USSR and mountain passes in areas adjoining the People's Republic of China.

For operation the missile is elevated hydraulically by the transporter to stand erect on a small launch table at the rear of the vehicle; the covers are opened and moved aside. After target coordinates have been fed into the guidance system, Scapegoat is ready to fire.

# SS-15 Scrooge

Employs a tracked transporter-erector of the type used by the SS-14 but the missile has greater performance. The 19 m (62 ft) tubular launcher is elevated for firing but does not hinge open as does the 'Iron Maiden' and it is assumed that launching is made directly from the tube.

Scrooge launchers have been identified close to the frontier with Red China near Buir Nor in Outer Mongolia. The whole of the United Kingdom and most of the Mediterranean area fall within range of Scrooge and Scamp-type launchers deployed in Eastern Europe and Western parts of the USSR. Improved weapons of this type are anticipated. (See SS-20 entry).

# SS-16

The SS-16 is part of the family of new-generation strategic ballistic weapons which embody the latest propulsion, guidance and warhead technology. Pentagon sources describe the three-stage solid-propellant missile as slightly smaller than the SS-13 Savage but with about twice the throw-weight for a given range. This implies improvements in propulsion and/or warhead 'throw yield' which may be reflected later in other weapons systems, e.g. medium-range mobile missiles.

In common with other new ICBMs tested in the first half of the 1970s, SS-16 embodies a computer-controlled post-boost vehicle capable of directing MIRV warheads sequentially along the approach path onto different targets.

SS-16 is capable of being deployed in fixed and mobile launchers.

# SS-17

A replacement for the SS-11 Sego. Giving details of three new Soviet ICBMs in 1973, Admiral Thomas H. Moorer, chairman of the Joint Chiefs of Staff, said apparent goals included the desire for better pre-launch survivability, accuracy and re-entry systems. "The Soviet Union", he said, "undoubtedly regards the achievement of a MIRV capability as an important political, as well as a military, goal."

Tests of the SS-17 were carried out during 1972, including two shots into the Pacific in November. The early trials indicated a multiple re-entry vehicle (MRV) package with three warheads. The weapon was judged to be more accurate than the SS-11 with three to four times the throw weight.

The SS-17 has since been described as suitable for use against point targets, the post-boost 'bus' dispensing MIRVs shaped for high-speed penetration of the atmosphere to ensure high accuracy.

It has also been stated that the missile employs the 'cold launch' technique being ejected from its launch silo by gas generator or compressed air before engine ignition above ground (see SS-11 entry).

# SS-18

The world's biggest military rocket and the SS-9 replacement. It employs high-energy storable propellants and is cold-launched from a new type of silo. (There have been reports that existing SS-9 silos will be modified to accept it.)

This formidable ICBM has every indication of being a first strike weapon. Pentagon sources suggest the throw-weight is 30 per cent greater than the SS-9. Flight trials have involved two versions and others (which may include satellite applications) are expected.

*Mod 1* has a single re-entry vehicle which suggests high accuracy against hard targets.

*Mod 2* carries up to eight MIRVs and (if necessary) associated decoys. A range of different warheads is anticipated to match the requirements of hard and soft targets. For example, some warheads may be mounted in pairs, one long and thin which arrives first and the other short and blunt which follows 1.5 to 2.0 minutes later with the heavier warhead.

The prime objective must be the saturation of Minuteman, Titan and other hardened or semi-hardened military bases with accurately directed high-yield thermo-nuclear bursts. Some warheads may be designed to disable silos and underground command posts by deeply-penetrating thermonuclear ground explosions causing severe seismic shocks. The post-boost computer (which triggers release of the MRV or MIRV heads) must make many thousands of calculations in the first 10 minutes of flight to compare flight errors with the pre-programmed target coordinates, and bring the manoeuvrable 'bus' onto precise course. An error of 1 ft/sec in cut-off velocity, for example, will result in a target miss of over a mile.

# SS-19

In some ways comparable with the SS-17 but less advanced technically, this two-stage ICBM is also considered an SS-11 replacement. It can be cold-launched from existing silos.

As in the case of all new-generation Soviet ICBMs employing storable liquid propellants, the missile can be held at instant readiness for long periods. Precisely what liquids are used is difficult to assess but the Russians are known to have set up a large production plant for unsymmetrical dimethyl hydrazine (UDMH) which may be used in combination with the oxidizer nitrogen tetroxide ($N_2O_4$).

Over the past 15 years, the Soviets have made large efforts to improve the performance of rocket engines employing storable liquids and some of these improvements will undoubtedly be embodied in the SS-17, SS-18 and SS-19. Academician V.P. Glushko, the veteran rocket engine designer, refers to small-size engines of exceptionally high energy characteristics achieved by the use of *high combustion pressures* (running into hundreds of atmospheres), a nearly complete combustion, the balanced and uniform discharge of combustion products, and nozzles of high expansion ratio. He also mentions improvements (embodied in the RD-253 mainstage engine of the large Proton space launcher, developed between 1961-65) in which the effort is made, in high pressure engines, to eliminate losses incurred in driving the turbopumps[*].

Glushko writes: "Further increases in the specific impulse of the engines required an increase in the initial pressure inside the chamber, and this was limited by the losses incurred in driving the turbopumps. For developed engines with thrusts in the range of 11-116 tonnes these losses in specific impulse amounted to only 0.8 to 1.7 per cent with chamber pressures of 75-90 atmospheres but increased to an unacceptable extent with higher pressures. This problem was solved by developing a new liquid propellant engine in which the generator gas, after being used in the turbine, is burned in the main combustion chamber with the rest of the fuel. As a result losses caused by the turbopump drive are practically eliminated. In such engines; propellant components entering the chamber are mixed as gas and liquid and not as in more conventional designs as liquid-liquid."

[*]V. P. Glushko, "Development of Rocketry and Space Technology in the USSR", (USSR Academy of Sciences), Novosti Press Publishing House, Moscow, 1973.

[†]V. P. Glushko, "Rocket Engines GDL-OKB", (USSR Academy of Sciences), Novosti Press Publishing House, Moscow, 1975.

**Table models of US/Soviet land-based ballistic missiles: 1. Titan II ICBM. 2. SS-7 ICBM. 3. SS-5 MRBM. 4. SS-8 ICBM. 5. SS-4 MRBM. 6. Minuteman II. 7. SS-9 ICBM. 8. SS-II ICBM. 9. SS-13 ICBM. 10. Minuteman III. 11. SS-16 ICBM. 12. SS-17 ICBM. 13. SS-19 ICBM. 14. SS-18 ICBM.**

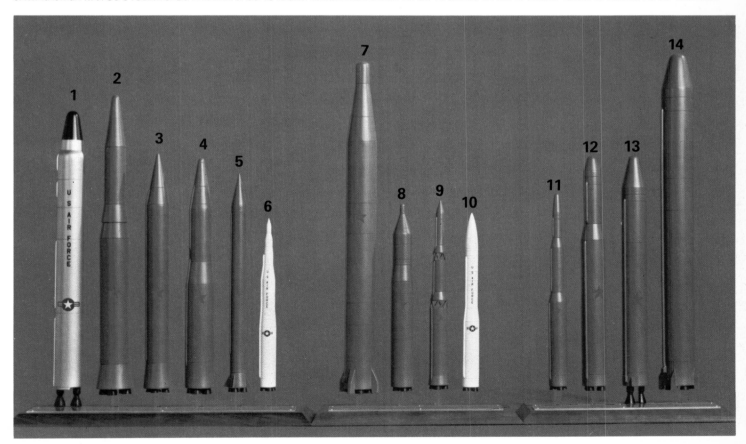

# SS-20

Examples of this land-mobile missile, which employs the first two stages of the hot-launched SS-16, were said to be deployed on the Kamchatka Peninsula in the late spring of 1976. At the same time evidence of a new lightweight nuclear warhead of possibly 50 to 75 KT yield, 136 kg (300 lb) weight, led to range estimates being revised upwards from some 2,750 km (1,710 miles)

— attainable with a 1.5 MT, 454 kg (1,000 lb) warhead — to 5,700 to 7,400 km (3,540 to 4,600 miles).

A mini-ICBM, in a land-mobile role, which the SS-20 represents, poses a powerful new challenge over an immense area of Western strategic interest from the Indian Ocean to the Pacific and including India, China, Japan, Northern parts of Australia and even parts of

the United States. It also represents a serious new threat to the entire area of NATO responsibility covering the whole of Western Europe and the Middle East from sites inside the USSR.

# CRUISE OR WINGED MISSILES

## SSC-1/SS-N-3 Shaddock

The Shaddock is a large cruise missile for coastal defence. When displayed in Red Square parades, it has been concealed in a vehicle which resembles a road tanker. In fact, the 15.7 m (51.5 ft) 'tank' contains a rail-mounted winged missile which must be at least 12 m (40 ft) long. With the container lid raised, it was possible to glimpse the nozzle of a turbojet (or ramjet) and two JATO units, one on each side of a ventral fin. The wings appear to be of the hinged 'flip out' type.

The Shaddock container elevates to an inclined launch position firing over the cab.

The **SS-N-3** variant has been deployed at sea aboard many surface ships and submarines. For example, Kresta-class cruisers have two pairs of launchers. Kynda-class cruisers have two rotatable quad launchers which elevate to 30°. Installations aboard diesel and nuclear-powered submarines have two to eight launch canisters. On E1 nuclear submarines, three pairs flush with the deck elevate for firing; the E2 class have four pairs.

When launched from surface ships, Shaddock operates in association with Scoop Pair tracking radar. Presumably, the missile is automatically gathered on the tracking radar centreline and then rides that beam to the target. However, missiles of this type can be fired far beyond the visible horizon and mid-course guidance may be applied via a cooperative aircraft or helicopter.

Shaddock can fly low or high trajectories and approaches its target in a terminal dive.

Coastal belts of the United States are vulnerable to Shaddock from nuclear submarines operating off the coast. Improved versions of this class of weapon are being introduced (see SS-NX-12 entry in table).

**Early SS-N-3 installation in Whisky Twin-Cylinder submarine, elevated to firing position**

## SS-C-2b Samlet

A cruise missile adapted from the obsolete Kennel air-to-surface missile for coastal defence, Samlet has replaced the older 130 mm coastal gun. After arriving at its appointed coastal site on a single-axle semi-trailer towed by a ZIL-157V tractor truck, it is transferred to a large rail-type launcher.

Launching is assisted by an undertail JATO unit. The cruise missile operates in association with van-mounted Sheet Bend missile control radar and long-range surveillance radars. Like Kennel, it has an active radar seeker mounted in a radome above the split-duct intake of the turbojet.

Samlet is reported to have been widely deployed by the Soviet Navy at stations ranging from the Baltic to the Pacific including the Black Sea area. It has also appeared in other Warsaw Pact countries and has been exported to Cuba and Egypt.

## SS-N-1 Scrubber

A sea-going cruise missile larger than Styx, the SS-N-1 is fired from a 'hanger'-type launcher on a 17 m (23 ft) rail. The whole assembly rotates through about 250° and elevates to the appropriate launch angle. Two such launchers were installed fore and aft on certain Krupny-class destroyers. Kildin-class destroyers have a single launcher mounted near the stern.

Launched with the help of an undertail JATO unit, the winged missile has a turbojet sustainer and operates in conjunction with ships' radar. An infra-red homing head serves for terminal guidance. Maximum range is about 240 km (149 miles).

Scrubber is being superseded by the SS-N-11.

The SS-N-1 is described in some reports as Strela but this is not the current NATO code name.

## SS-N-2a Styx

This missile is carried by Komar and Osa-class fast patrol boats. The weapon achieved notoriety on 21 October 1967 when missile boats of the Egyptian Navy sank the Israeli destroyer *Eilat* from the security of Port Said harbour. Since that time Styx has seen action in the Indo-Pakistan war of December 1971 (in the hands of the Indian Navy), and was fired by Egyptian and Syrian boats in the October War.

Styx has the appearance of a small pilotless aircraft with a slightly bulbous fuselage supporting cropped delta wings. Autopilot/command guidance control is applied through ailerons and control surfaces on each of three tail fins. The missile is capable of homing on radio

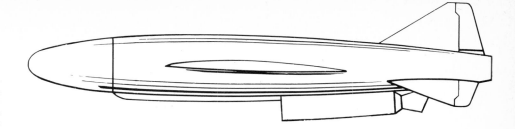

frequency energy emitted by ships' defensive radar.

Extensive use is made of Styx by Soviet bloc navies Komar and Osa-class FPBs carry two and four respectively in waterproof launch canisters mounted on

the after deck. Launching is assisted by an undertail JATO unit.

The SS-N-2b variant is reported to have additional IR homing capability.

# SUBMARINE-LAUNCHED BALLISTIC MISSILES

## SS-N-4 Sark

This huge two-stage solid-propellant missile was carried by early Golf and Hotel class submarines and was first deployed in 1961. It could be launched only when the submarine had surfaced. To accommodated the 15 m (49 ft) Sark, launch tubes projected up through the pressure hull and bridge fin. The weapon was first displayed in a Moscow military parade in November 1962. Guidance was inertial, maximum range being about 580 km (350 miles).

## SS-N-5 Serb

The Serb has been deployed in Golf III and Hotel II class submarines which have three launch tubes in an extended fin. The 10 m (33 ft) long solid-propellant missile entered service in 1964 and first appeared in a Red Square parade in November 1964. At the base were 18 electrically-operated nozzles of a gas-generator by which

Serb is expelled from the submarine's launch tube. It is assumed that the unit separates explosively shortly before

main stage ignition in mid-air. Estimated range is about 1,210 km (750 miles).

## SS-N-6 Sawfly

A much improved SLBM of greater performance, Sawfly made its debut in a Red Square parade in November 1967. It could be accommodated in vertical launch tubes within the hull of a submarine in the same way as the U.S. Navy's Polaris. In 1969 the Pentagon estimated that some 50 submarines had been built to carry ballistic missiles, half of them nuclear powered. Fifteen Y-class vessels were under construction at Severodvinsk, near Archangel, and at another smaller yard. Each was designed to carry 16 two-stage missiles of the Sawfly family.

There were three versions of SS-N-6. Mod 1 with limited range; Mod 2 having longer range with single

re-entry vehicle, and Mod 3 with longer range than either of the above with multiple re-entry vehicles.

At the same time there were reports of a new Soviet submarine of longer range and capability which had already entered the test stage. This Delta-class boat has since emerged as a formidable missile platform capable of striking at important United States targets without straying deeply from home stations. It accommodates 12 of the new-generation SS-N-8 missiles which have improved propulsion and steller-inertial

guidance conferring high accuracy (CEP = 0.4 km (0.25 mile). Two missiles of this type were launched on test over distances of some 7,890 km (4,900 miles) between the Barents Sea and the central Pacific Ocean in October 1974. Two versions of the SS-N-8 have been identified. Mod 1 with a single re-entry vehicle, and Mod 2 with three MRVs or MIRVs.

An improved Delta submarine with 16 launch tubes put to sea in 1976 and a still larger boat carrying more missiles is under construction.

# TACTICAL MISSILES
## Anti-tank

### AT-1 Snapper

First-generation wire-guided anti-tank missile no longer in production. Operator sights his target through periscopic binoculars incorporating an illuminated variable-brightness reticle and steers by line-of-sight using joy-stick control assisted by tracking flares on two of the missile's cruciform wings. Control is applied by trailing-edge vibrating spoilers. Maximum range is about 2,000 m (6,560 ft).

Remote firings are possible at distances up to about 50 m (165 ft) from the launcher. In the 1967 Arab-Israeli War, Gaz 69 vehicles had quad launchers. AT-1 was normally deployed by the Soviet Army on a triple launcher. The mounting device carried on BRDM vehicles was fully retractable, the missiles on their launchers being stored under hinged armour plates which opened when the mounting stems were raised. Missile control equipment was in the forward compartment of the vehicle.

The weapon is being replaced by the AT-3 Sagger.

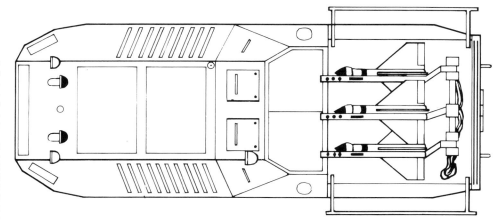

Plan front and side elevations of BRDM with triple AT-1 launcher extended. The side view shows (broken lines) the extra rough-field wheels

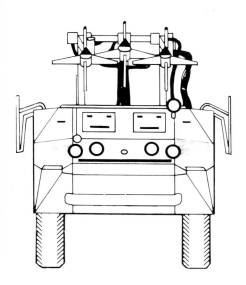

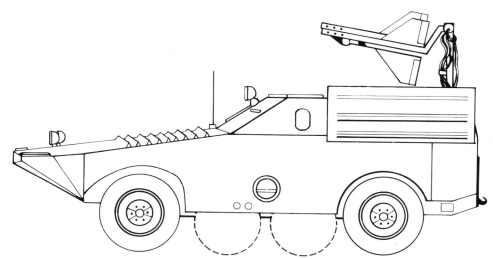

### AT-2 Swatter

Carried by BRDM vehicles on a quad launcher, this wire-guided missile, which has a range of some 2,500 m (8,200 ft), has elevons on the trailing edges of rear-mounted wings and movable foreplanes all worked together by the guidance system. Armour penetration exceeds 40 cm (15.8 in).

Examples of AT-2 are still in service in Warsaw Pact countries. On BRDMs the quad-launcher is fully retractable in the back of the vehicle, and missile control is in the forward compartment.

'B' version of Swatter has a second-generation auto guidance system.

# AT-3 Sagger

This much improved wire-guided anti-tank missile can be operated by two-or three-man infantry teams including remote firing from a portable single-rail launcher up to 100 m (328 ft) from the carrier vehicle. Hits up to 1,000 m (3,280 ft) from a target are possible with the unaided eye and 3,000 m (9,840 ft) using a telescopic sight. The missile takes 12.5 seconds to travel 1,500 m (4,920 ft).

Sagger first appeared in a Moscow military parade in May 1965. It has cruciform wings which fold for stowage and transportation and is altogether more compact than earlier Soviet anti-tank missiles, although it preserves an effective warhead; armour penetration exceeds 40 cm (15.8 in).

Carriers include the BMP-76PB, which has a single launch rail fitted above the guntube of the main armament and a total of four missiles; the BMD-1APC has one launcher, and the Polish Skot APC, two. Produced in large numbers, Sagger is in service with the Warsaw Pact countries and has seen action in Egypt and Syria. In the 1973 Arab-Israeli War, it was operated in ground-launched man-pack versions and from sextuple retractable launchers from BRDM-1 scout cars which are distinguished by a peak armoured roof which shelters the launchers even when they have been elevated into the firing position. Missiles can be fired singly or in salvoes.

Examples captured in Egypt were in "suitcase" packs for the use of infantrymen lying prone on the ground. One plastic case contained the separated warhead/booster and main propulsion and guidance system; the other the portable fire control box including joystick, firing button, power pack and optical periscopic sight. The missile launch rail was set up on hinged supports on the lid of a carrying case placed flat on the ground.

A new generation of Soviet anti-tank missiles is anticipated including those adapted for helicopter use. Stubwing launchers appear on the Mi-24 Hind-A assault helicopter.

# Short-range (battlefield support)

## Frog

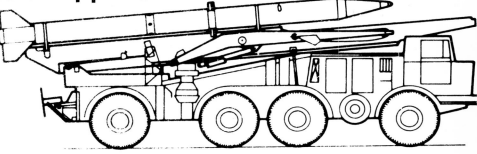

**Frog 7 on ZIL-135 erector-launcher**

The acronym of 'Free Rocket Over Ground' refers to a family of unguided, spin stabilised, artillery rocket in service with the Soviet Army on transporter-launchers. All versions employ solid-propellants with conventional main nozzles and secondary annular nozzles. Armed with nuclear, chemical or conventional HE warheads, the Frogs are intended to lay down a devastating blanket fire on battlefield and rear-area deployments of troops and armour. Frog 1, a single-stage, four-finned rocket entered service about 1957. Mounted on a tracked launch vehicle, it was cradled by a split-length casing with its heavy bulbous warhead protected by a forward framework. The estimated range was 20 km (32 miles). Frog 2, deployed the same year, was about the same length but smaller in diameter. The maximum range was about 12 km (7.5 miles).

Frogs 3 and 4, which have two tandem rocket motors, also spin stabilised and un-guided, are launched from a modified PT-76 tank chassis. Photographs of Frog 3 in action show that a forward ring of thrusters fires at the same time as the 'first stage' motor as the rocket leaves the ramp. Frogs 3 and 4 differ mainly in the shape and capacity of warheads. They have ranges of up to 45 km (28 miles) and 50 km (31 miles) respectively.

Three more variants, Frogs 5, 6 and 7, were introduced later. Frog 6 has been identified as a dummy used for training purposes. Frog 7 — a much improved weapon — employs a new erector-launch vehicle designated ZIL-135 which incorporates an onboard crane for swift re-loading. A similar vehicle is used to transport reserve rockets. (Early FROGS needed semi-trailers towed by ZIL 157V tractor trucks, and crane trucks were required to reload the transport-launch vehicles). Warheads are brought up in sealed canisters on separate trailers, the nuclear variety being under Soviet custody.

Although Frog 7 reverts to a more conventional single-stage arrangement, the four-finned rocket embodies many improvements including (it is believed) improved propellants. The warhead nosecone is streamlined with the motor casing. Estimates suggest that a 450 kg (1,000 lb) warhead could be launched over a distance of some 56 km (35 miles) with range adjustment by means of speed brakes.

Apart from countries of the Warsaw Pact, Frog 7 launchers have been supplied to Egypt and Syria. Examples were fired by the Syrian Army in the 1973 October War with Israel. Reports have mentioned a guided version.

Future developments of the Frog/Scud families could include scatter type warheads or unpowered guided projectiles which seek out active radars associated with enemy air defences including surface-to-air missile sites and/or infra-red emissions associated with tanks and other vehicles.

**Launch of Frog 3 from its tracked chassis based on the IS-III heavy tank.**

# Medium range

## SS-1B Scud A

This a battlefield support weapon is designed to strike at targets such as marshalling areas, major storage dumps and airfields behind enemy lines. Warheads can be either nuclear, chemical (persistent) or conventional high explosive

The missile, which employs storable liquid propellants, is carried on a JS-III tracked vehicle which raises it by hydraulic jacks into a vertical position for launching from a small platform. Elevating with Scud A on its erector is a ladder framework which gives the launch crew access to the full length of the missile on its platform. Missiles of the Scud family have simplified inertial guidance; an accelerometer senses that a pre-set velocity has been reached and terminates thrust. Maximum range is about 180 km (112 miles).

Crews are trained to operate from points of maximum concealment, e.g. heavily forested areas, to avoid detection. After a missile is fired the transporter is immediately driven to a new location to avoid a counter-strike and the vehicle is reloaded from a support vehicle.

## SS-1C Scud B

A larger member of the family, Scud B may have a range of 280 km (174 miles). It is carried in one of the most modern air-conditioned, heated, cross-country wheeled vehicles. The introduction of this powerful vehicle, a modified MAZ-543, gives the weapon system greater road mobility, reduces the number of support vehicles required, and offers a wide choice in selecting offroad firing positions. Scud missiles are used by all armies of the Warsaw Pact but nuclear warheads for them are in Soviet hands.

The missile itself is concealed within a ribbed split protective casing which elevates with the erector. As before, launching is made vertically from a small platform. The warhead can be either nuclear or conventional HE.

Of three Scuds fired by Egyptian forces in Sinai during the 1973 October War, all were reported to have missed their targets. A Scud is said to have been test fired by the Syrian Army over a distance of some 250 km (155 miles) in November 1975.

## SS-12 Scaleboard

A derivitive of the Scud family, the SS-12 first appeared in a Moscow military parade in November 1967. Although it employs the same MAZ 543 type transporter-erector as Scud B, the missile is larger and has much greater range — perhaps 700 to 800 km (435 to 497 miles) — which brings south-eastern England within range from forward areas of East Germany.

Scaleboard, like Scud B, has a ribbed split casing which encloses it completely and elevates with it into firing position. Good sightings of the MAZ 543 transporter show that the missile launch operator has a control console in the right hand cab (the driver being in the left hand cab). Other members of the launch crew occupy seats at the back of the cabs. The photograph shows two missiles being elevated

# SURFACE-TO-AIR MISSILES

## SA-1 Guild

First seen in a Moscow military parade in November 1960.
Not widely deployed, although large numbers were built
for test and training purposes. The missile took the form
of a canard with all-moving cruciform foreplanes and a
small aileron on each cruciform wing. There was no
separate booster and it is assumed that the motor was a
dual-thrust solid.

## SA-2 Guideline

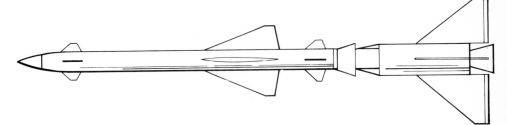

This medium-to-high-altitude anti-aircraft missile is widely
deployed in the USSR and other Warsaw Pact countries
and has been in action in South-East Asia and the Middle
East. It was first publicly displayed in 1957. An early
version is said to have brought down the U-2 aircraft
flown by Lt. Francis Gary Powers during his overflight
of the Soviet Union on May Day 1960.

The weapon system has since undergone considerable
refinement and today appears in different versions.
Examples deployed in Egypt, including power supplies
and guidance radar, were identified as the V75SM. The
missile, designated V750VK, is transported on a cross-
country semi-trailer and operates from a rotatable
launcher. The four-finned booster burns for 4-5 seconds,
two of the booster fins having gyro-controlled rudders
for initial course-setting. The SA-2 sustainer, which burns
for about 22 seconds, is fuelled by nitric acid and a
liquid hydrocarbon (probably kerosene). It has cruciform
delta wings and steerable fins. Four small canard surfaces
are mounted just aft of the nosecone.

At one time it is thought that some 4,500 SA-2s were
operational in the USSR. In Egypt and Syria they were
operated on ZIL 157 transporter/launchers in conjunction
with SA-3 and SA-6 to obtain a comprehensive all-
altitude defence system (photo, pages 54-55).

Guidance of the standard missile depends on a van-
mounted Fan Song A/B (E/F band) or D/E (G-band) radar
which acquires the target and feeds target data to a
computer. Steering commands generated by the computer
are transmitted to the missile over a UHF link vectoring it
into the radar beam to intercept the target.

A modified version of SA-2 appeared in a Moscow
military parade in 1967. Slightly longer than the original,
it had an enlarged warhead and dispensed with the usual
small canard surfaces.

The naval version of Guideline — SA-N-2 — has not
been widely deployed, probably because of difficulties
in applying the associated guidance radar to ships. A twin-
launcher replaces a gun turret on the cruiser *Dzerzhinski*,
operating in conjunction with a C-band Fan Song radar.

# SA-3 Goa

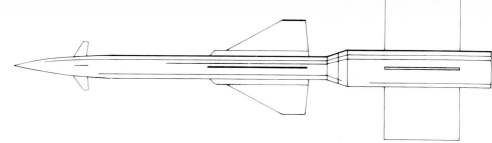

Goa is the mobile low-altitude counterpart of SA-2 and like that weapon, has been widely deployed in the USSR/ Warsaw Pact countries, South-East Asia and the Middle East. Its American equivalent is the MIM-23A Hawk. The SA-3, which has a canard configuration, has cruciform delta wings and steerable foreplanes. The boost and sustainer motors are both solid-fuelled.

Early systems were mounted on ZIL-157 tractors, others employ tracked vehicles. As in the case of SA-2, considerable information on SA-3 has been derived from captured weapons.

Guidance is by automatic radio command, targets being acquired by a truck-mounted UHF (810-850 MHz and 880-950 MHz) P-15 Flat Face radar with dual para- bolic antennae. Low Blow fire control radar operates in the I-band (9,000-9,400 MHz) on the principle of Fan Song (see SA-2). Up to six aircraft can be tracked simultaneously and one or two missiles can be fired at the same target.

The original version of Goa — the SA-N-1 — is widely deployed on ships of the Soviet Navy. It operates in association with Peel Group radar.

# SA-4 Ganef

A medium-altitude air-defence weapon, the SA-4 is pro- pelled by an integral ramjet which confers long range. It was first displayed in Moscow in 1964 on a twin-round tracked vehicle and two complete weapons systems can be air-lifted to battlefield deployments in the An-22 military freighter.

The ramjet body has a diameter of about 80 cm (31.5 in) with the centrebody projecting forward from an annular intake. Four fixed tail fins are indexed at 45° to the wings which are all-moving for control.

Ganef operates in conjunction with Long Track E-band scanning radar and Pat Hand H-band target acquisition and fire control radar. Its purpose is to provide combat troops operating in forward areas with umbrella protection against air strikes. When deployed with the Soviet Army nine SA-4 batteries comprising three twin-launchers, one loading vehicle and one Pat Hand radar, are interspersed between SA-6 batteries. The air-defence group moves up with the Army advance, the first three batteries deploying some 10 km (6.2 miles) to the rear of forward positions with the other batteries moving up in a belt some 15 km (9.3 miles) behind.

**SA-4 missiles are carried on a specially designed launcher not derived from an existing AFV (photo, page 56)**

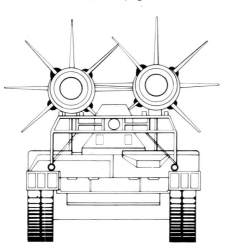

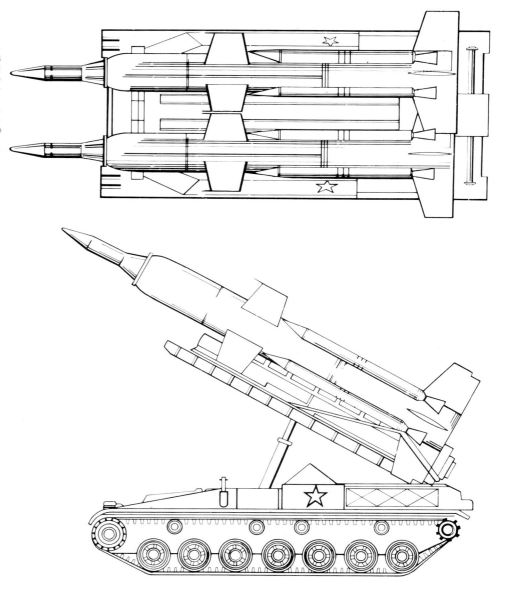

# SA-5 Gammon

This long-range, high-altitude, air defence weapon was first seen in a Moscow parade in 1963. The missile system, which has replaced many SA-2 sites within the USSR, operates in conjunction with Square Pair radar and may have limited anti-missile capability.

An improved version of the SA-5 air defence missile radar was reportedly under test at Sary Sagan in the early 1970s. The effective ceiling for intercept may now exceed 30,500 m (100,000 ft) and it is possible that some examples of SA-5 have a nuclear warhead intended to immobilise US and/or Chinese ICBM warheads by high energy neutron fluxes.

The boost and sustainer motors are both solid-fuelled. The sustainer has four cropped delta wings and steerable rear fins. Control is assisted by ailerons, and the missile responds to semi-active radar homing. An effective anti-missile capability would require a manoeuvrable warhead 'bus' which separates after second stage burn-out. Reports suggest that the up-rated system operates in association with a new mobile phased-array ABM radar.

SA-5 is described in some reports as Griffon, but this is not the NATO code name.

# SA-6 Gainful

This mobile battlefield air-defence weapon was seen to be effective against low-flying Israeli strike aircraft in the 1973 October War, often in the face of ECM. The propulsion unit is unique. After the boost phase, the combustion chamber of the solid propellant rocket motor becomes a ramjet when ram air is mixed with exhaust from a solid fuel gas generator. Components, from nosecone to tail, are (a) guidance and control unit, (b) warhead, (c) solid-propellant motor, (d) ram inlets in four external ducts between cruciform wings, (e) combined rocket/ramjet combustion chamber, (f) steerable fins and (g) exhaust nozzle.

Mounted on a triple launcher on a modified PT-76 tank chassis, a missile group consists of three triple launchers, one loading vehicle and one Straight Flush radar, also PT-76 mounted. After Long Track radars have acquired a target, fire control is taken over by Straight Flush missile site radars. Target tracking is by a 1-deg H-band (7.7-8 GHz) pencil beam and mid-course guidance commands are transmitted to the missile in I-band (8.5-9 GHz). Final intercept is by semi-active radar homing using continuous-wave (CW) radar to which in 1973 the West had no ECM answer.

Gainful has been supplied to Egypt, Syria, Libya and North Vietnam.

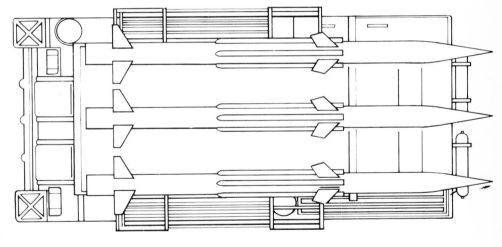

**The launch vehicle normally carries its missiles pointing to the rear (photo, page 44)**

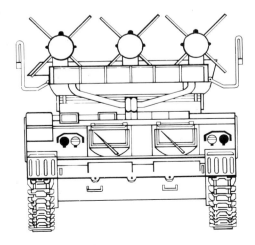

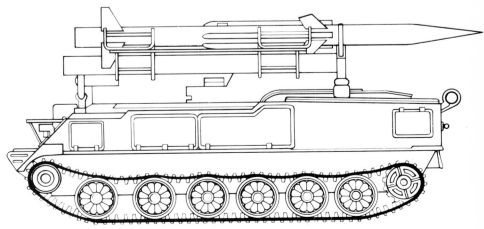

# SA-7 Grail

Grail is the Russian equivalent of the US Army's Redeye. It is tube-mounted and fired from the shoulder. The heat-seeking missile, which saw service in Vietnam and the 1973 Arab-Israeli War, was often effective against helicopters and low-flying aircraft despite counter-measures which included use of decoy flares and deflected helicopter exhaust. Some models had filters to screen out flares in the responsive part of the IR spectrum.

The Grail operator tracks the hostile aircraft through open sights. A red light appears in the optical sight when the IR seeker is energised, changing to green when the device has locked on. This is the signal for the operator to squeeze the trigger of the pistol grip. The boost motor propels the missile from the plastic tube, the sustainer igniting some 6 m (20 ft) from the operator to protect him from exhaust blast. The seeker senses the exhaust heat of the target and the guidance system, acting on cruciform canard vanes, steers the missile into the target.

Apart from shoulder-launched applications, SA-7 has been mounted on vehicles in batteries of four, six and eight and a radar-aiming system has been introduced. In the October War Egyptian forces fired salvoes at individual low-flying Israeli aircraft, although few 'kills' were reported, the main damage being to jetpipes.

The weapon is now finding its way into the hands of terrorist and guerilla organisations.

In some reports, SA-7 is referred to as Strela (Arrow) but this is not the NATO code name.

# SA-8 Gecko

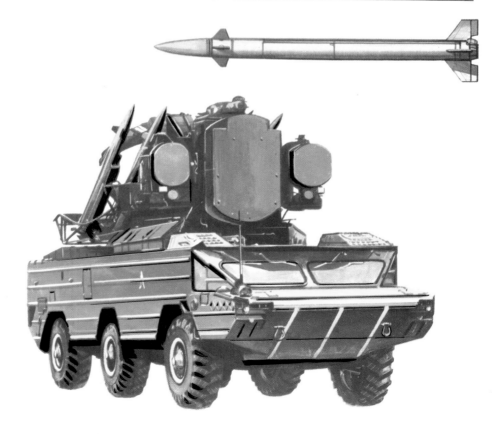

This short-range, all weather anti-aircraft weapon can be compared with the European Roland. First seen in the Moscow parade of November 1975, it is turret-mounted on a six-wheeled amphibious vehicle on which the surveillance radar antenna (folded down for transport) is flanked by quadruple missile launchers. Mounted on the same rotatable turret are acquisition and tracking radar and two guidance radars which operate in conjunction with a low-light electro-optical tracker. The two guidance radars make it possible to launch two missiles at the same target, each one responding to a different frequency to frustrate ECM.

The entire weapon system is air-transportable. The missile itself has canard steerable foreplanes and fixed tail surfaces.

# SA-9 Gaskin

Gaskin is part of a battlefield low-altitude air defence system. Installed in twin-quad box launchers on the amphibious BRDM scout car; it first appeared in the Moscow parade of November 1975. Although the missile may use the same type of IR seeker as the SA-7, it has a larger rocket motor and warhead and the canard control surfaces are non-folding. Targets appear to be optically acquired by an operator seated in the vehicle cabin, having been alerted to an approaching target by a surveillance data link. The quad launcher is fully retractable. When not in use the missile boxes rotate aft and down to rest on the rear part of the vehicle with side grilles raised for protection.

# ANTI-BALLISTIC MISSILES

## ABM-1 Galosh

An exo-atmosphere anti-missile missile, Galosh forms part of the defence system of the Soviet capital. Four complexes have 16 launchers apiece for the most part screened by birch and fir forests. The missile first appeared in a Moscow military parade in November 1964 inside a ribbed tubular container more than 18 m (60 ft) long by about 2.7 m (9 ft) diameter on a wheeled transporter. All that could be seen were the four nozzles of the missile's first stage. It is thought that the weapon is launched from the container at a high angle.

Each of the Moscow launch complexes is associated with two Try Add engagement radars made up of a large Chekhov target-tracking radar and two smaller guidance and interception radars. Dog House phased array radars in the Moscow region provide essential acquisition and tracking, and these receive early warning from large Hen House phased-array radars in peripheral areas of the USSR.

There have been reports of an improved Galosh which can loiter in the face of an ICBM attack, stopping and re-starting its manoeuvrable 'bus' warhead near the apogee of the trajectory whilst actual warheads are discriminated from decoys. A high-acceleration point defence missile, similar to the US Sprint, has been under test at Sary Sagan. Improved ABM radars (some related to a longer-range Galosh) have been extensively tested.

# AIR-TO-AIR MISSILES

## AA-1 Alkali

This first-generation solid-propellant missile armed the MiG-17, the all-weather MiG-19 and Su-9 interceptors. It has large cruciform delta wings and steerable cruciform foreplanes which operate in conjunction with wing-mounted control surfaces. Examples are still in service with Warsaw Pact countries and others.

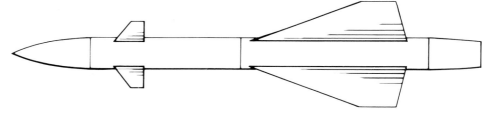

## AA-2 Atoll

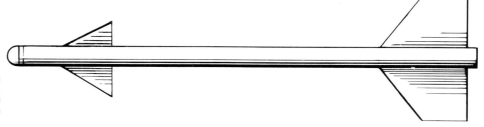

The AA-2 resembles the US Sidewinder and is carried by a wide variety of Soviet interceptors. Widely exported, it has seen action in South East Asia and during the Arab-Israeli and the 1972 Indo-Pakistan wars. India builds the weapon under licence. The Soviet designation K-13A.

The missile, which has a canard configuration, has all-moving foreplanes responsive to an infra-red seeker. A small gyro-controlled tab is inset into the tip of each fin.

Combat experience has shown weaknesses in the system, some pilots reporting that even when delivered from an optimum rearward station the seeker did not always lock on to the target. It is assumed that this deficiency has been remedied.

An AA-2-2 radar homing variant seeks to enlarge the 'kill' probability by operating in a multiple role with IR-seeking missiles. For example, the latest multi-role version of the MiG-21 Fishbed has radar homing Atolls on the outboard pylons and standard IR-Atolls inboard. The MiG-23 has been seen with a mix of Atoll and Anab.

## AA-3 Anab

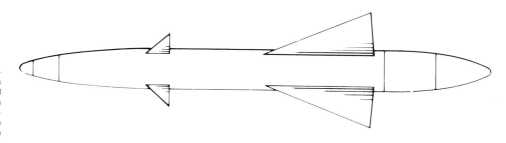

The AA-3 first appeared on the Yak-28P Firebar all-weather interceptor and later was applied to other types including the Su-11 Fishpot C, Su-15 Flagon, Mig-23 Flogger and MiG-25 Foxbat. It has highly swept cruciform delta wings and is steered by cruciform all-moving foreplanes. IR and semi-active radar homing versions have been produced and aircraft normally carry a mix of the two.

## AA-5 Ash

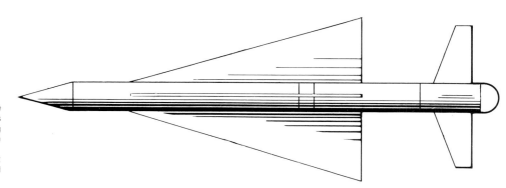

This cruciform delta winged, high-altitude air-to-air missile is steered by moveable tail fins. The Tu-28P Fiddler carries four on underwing pylons, one pair having IR homing and the other two radar homing. Examples are still in service with the Warsaw Pact countries.

The Mig-25 Foxbat A carried two AA-5s when first introduced but recent examples have four AA-6 Acrid missiles.

## AA-6 Acrid

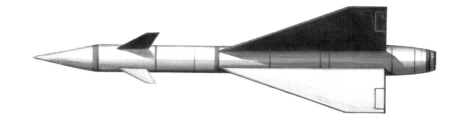

This large high-performance air-to-air missile was first identified in 1975 on the Foxbat A version of the Mig-25 high-altitude interceptor. It resembles an enlarged Anab and like that missile has been produced in infra-red and semi-active radar homing versions. The four underwing launch rails of Foxbat A accommodate two IR inboard and two SAR outboard. Wingtip fairings on the interceptor are believed to house CW target illuminating radar.

The missile itself has clearly been designed for long-range and good manoeuvrability at high and medium altitudes. It has a canard cruciform configuration with steerable foreplanes and wing-mounted control surfaces.

Performance is difficult to assess in the absence of definitive information about the rocket motor, but must be well above the Mach 3.2 attainable by the launch aircraft. The IR homing version may have an effective range of 20 km (12.4 miles), considerably more in the case of the SAR homing version which operates in conjunction with Fox Fire air intercept radar which has a 'look down' capability.

# AIR-TO-SURFACE MISSILES

## AS-1 Kennel

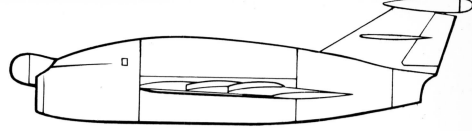

Two of these subsonic cruise missiles — the oldest of the Soviet family — were carried by Tu-16s of the Soviet Naval Air Force on underwing pylons. Turbojet-powered, they had a maximum range of about 150 km (93 miles) and were considered operational in the early 1960s, examples being supplied to Indonesia and Egypt with the parent aircraft.

The subsonic AS-1 was used extensively by naval air crew to work up techniques for guiding winged missiles against surface ships and shore targets. After being set on course by the launch aircraft, which had two large radomes beneath the nose, the missile was vectored towards its target by a radio command link; fin-mounted pods contained receiving equipment. When within striking range of the target, it responded to an active or passive radar seeker. It has since been replaced by the rocket-powered AS-5 Kelt.

A surface-to-surface variant of Kennel was developed for coastal defence (see SSC-2b Samlet entry).

## AS-2 Kipper

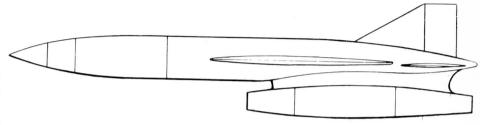

Another anti-shipping weapon, the AS-2 resembles the American Hound Dog although that missile was larger and more advanced. The Russian weapon could also be used against coastal targets.

Carried by the Tu-16, the 9.5 m (31 ft) Kipper has a swept-wing aircraft configuration and is powered by an underslung turbojet. Radar guidance equipment is carried in the nose of the launch aircraft and, according to some estimates, the stand-off range may exceed 160 km (100 miles). None of these early winged missiles would be particularly effective against the defence systems of modern warships and presumably their use would be restricted to secondary targets in peripheral areas.

## AS-3 Kangaroo

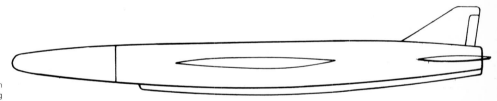

Resembling the Fitter interceptor, AS-3 is launched from the underbelly of the Tu-95 Bear. The 15 m (49 ft) long turbojet-powered missile has a stand-off range of 185 to 650 km (110 to 404 miles). Its chief targets would be ports and industrial centres. Radar guidance equipment is in the nose of the launch aircraft. The weapon must now be on the retirement list.

## AS-5 Kelt

Is a medium-long range stand-off missile resembling Styx. The hemispherical nose encloses an active radar seeker. It is carried by the Tu-16 on underwing pylons, replacing the AS-1 Kennel.

Kelt is the most widely deployed of all Soviet stand-off missiles, well over 1,000 having been produced. Some 25 examples were reported in action against Israeli targets during the 1973 Arab-Israeli War with only moderate success, many of them falling victim to air and ground defences. Hits were scored on two radar sites and a supply centre in Sinai.

## AS-6

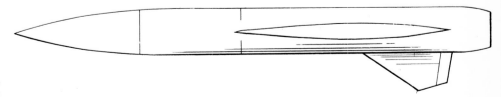

Two large supersonic AS-6 stand-off strike missiles are carried by the Tupolev Backfire B bomber on underwing pylons. The weapon clearly has nuclear capability for strikes against shore targets with particular application in the European theatre of NATO responsibility and the Mediterranean area. It could also have an important long-range anti-shipping role.

Although the Soviet authorities insist the bomber/missile combination does not have an intercontinental strategic application, US SALT 2 negotiators were apprehensive. With in-flight refuelling from Tu-95 Bear tankers, Backfire B aircraft could strike at important United States' targets and return. Estimated stand-off range is 700 to 800 km (435-497 miles). The low-altitude capability is uncertain.

The provisional drawing of AS-6 should not be taken to represent the only type of new-generation Backfire stand-off missile. Soviet designers expanding on their experience with rocket/ramjet systems are expected to develop pre-packaged, folding-wing missiles which can be accommodated within the Backfire weapons bay to preserve the aircraft's high Mach number performance.

# The Warsaw Pact

**Professor John Erickson**

Now a little more than 20 years old, the Warsaw Pact (also referred to as the Warsaw Treaty Organisation or WTO) was born of the Treaty of Friendship, Co-operation and Mutual Assistance 'done in Warsaw on 14 May 1955 in one copy each in the Russian, Polish, Czech and German languages, all texts being equally authentic'. Article 11 (1st Paragraph) stipulated that the treaty should remain in force initially for 20 years and for a further 10 years, provided that 'contracting parties' do not one year before the expiry of the treaty present 'a statement of denunciation' to the government of the Polish People's Republic. So it is that, with Albania the sole legal defector during the past decade, the Warsaw Pact can soldier on into the 1980s. (The original signatories

included the Soviet Union, Albania, Bulgaria, Czechoslovakia, East Germany [German Democratic Republic], Hungary, Poland and Rumania. Albania ceased to participate in the affairs of the pact in 1962 and officially denounced its membership of the pact in September 1968.)

At first sight and simply on an inspection of the texts of the North Atlantic Treaty (4 April 1949) and the enactment of the Warsaw Pact, it might appear that both alliance systems are basically similar and generally equivalent. Such appearances are, however, deceptive. Perhaps the major difference is that the 'Atlantic Alliance' was (and remains still) an association of independent sovereign states, a voluntary association only confirmed after many weeks of lively parliamentary debate, while the Warsaw Pact came into being at the behest,

T-62 tanks on parade during a Warsaw Pact exercise. Regular large-scale manouvres serve to ensure that the military doctrine and training of the Pact armies conform to Soviet practice

renewed to make them operative right up to the present time, these particular agreements could not of themselves promote, much less embody, a sense of unity or collective identification with Soviet interests: it was the function of the Warsaw Pact to do precisely that, ensuring at the same time Soviet predominance. (Mutual aid treaties have also been concluded and are presently maintained between the individual East European states. In addition, the Soviet Union has signed 'status-of-forces agreements' with those countries in which Soviet troops are stationed: a specific 'status-of-forces agreement' was duly concluded with Czechoslovakia on 16 October 1968 – after the invasion – covering 'the temporary presence of Soviet troops'.)

Again, there is superficial similarity in the structures of NATO and the Warsaw Pact, indeed the command, of the Soviet Union pursuing its own political and strategic pur-

poses. The immediate stimulus to the Warsaw Pact was derived from the Paris Agreements (October 1954), whereby the Federal Republic of Germany acceded first to the amended Brussels Treaty and then to NATO itself on 5 May 1955; the signature of the Austrian State Treaty on 15 May 1955, which placed a time limit of 90 days on the stationing of Soviet troops in their 'lines of communication' role in Hungary and Rumania, also injected urgency into furnishing a new set of legal justifications for the presence of Soviet forces in east-central Europe. Finally, in spite of the complex network of bilateral mutual aid treaties between the Soviet Union and separate East European states, dating back in several instances to World War II days and regularly but the reality is altogether different. In the Warsaw Pact, the Political Consultative Committee is formally required to meet twice a year under the rotating chairmanship

of each member nation (holding the chair for a year at a time); the Permanent Commission was also established to frame recommendations on foreign policy on a joint basis. Both of these agencies are physically located in Moscow, but in spite of formal stipulations the Political Consultative Committee has met only irregularly and infrequently, while the Permanent Commission seems more often than not to be bypassed in favour of bilateral consultation. (In contrast, the NATO Council of Permanent Representatives, with its numbers drawn from member nations, convenes at least once a week.) In full session, the Political Consultative Committee is made up of the First Secretaries of the individual communist parties, heads of governments, together with foreign and defence ministers: a joint secretariat under the direction of a Soviet deputy foreign minister is attached to the committee. In March 1969, in the

# The Arms Race

## US–USSR MILITARY PRODUCTION 1970–75

Approximate yearly average:

|  | USA | USSR |
|---|---|---|
| Tanks | 450 | 2500 |
| APC | 1450 | 3800 |
| Artillery | 160 | 1400 |
| Helicopters | 600 | 1000 |
| Tactical Aircraft | 600 | 1000 |
| Surface Ships | 7–8 | 40 |
| Missile Subs | less than 1 | 7 |

## TOTAL HOLDINGS OF GROUND FORCE EQUIPMENT (excluding obsolete reserves)

| | | |
|---|---|---|
| Tanks | 9000 | 42000 |
| APCs | 23000 | 41000 |
| Artillery (including mortars and multiple rocket launchers) | 9000 | 27000 |
| Helicopters | 9000 | 2300 |

## PERSONNEL

| | | |
|---|---|---|
| Active | 2.1 million | 4.8 million |
| Reserve | 1.9 million | 7.2 million |

## DEFENCE EXPENDITURE (estimated) 1975

| | | |
|---|---|---|
| Percent of GNP | 6% | 15% (estimated) |
| Comparative figures of actual expenditure | 100% | 168% (estimated) |

## STRATEGIC FORCES 1975

| | | |
|---|---|---|
| ICBM | 1054 | 1618 |
| SLBM | 656 | 784 |
| Strategic Bombers | 375 | 185 |
| Intermediate Bombers | 645 | 66 |

## FIGHTER AND ATTACK AIRCRAFT

| | | |
|---|---|---|
| Fighter Interceptor Aircraft | 374 | 2550 |
| ABM Launchers | 0 | 64 |
| Strategic SAM Launchers | 0 | 12000 |
| Tactical Attack (incl Naval) | 2300 | 5000 |

*In general Soviet totals include more obsolescent hardware*

*Above, left:* **A T-55 tank deep wading. Soviet military doctrine stresses that water obstacles must not hinder a rapid advance; consequently all Pact armies are well equipped and trained to cross rivers**

*Left:* **Developed jointly in Poland and Czechoslovakia, the OT-64 "Skot" APC replaces the BTR-60 PB in some Pact armies. It is superior both in design and construction to its Soviet counterpart**

wake of the Soviet invasion of Czechoslovakia and no doubt in response to the severe strains within the pact, hurried reorganisation set up the Committee of Defence Ministers, which includes the Soviet defence minister as well as the six East European defence ministers within this body, defined as the 'supreme military organ of the Warsaw Pact': previously these same East European ministers had been directly subordinated to the Commander-in-Chief of the Joint Armed Forces.

The military organisation of the pact consists of a Joint High Command, charged with 'the direction and co-ordination of the Joint Armed Forces': this organisation was brought into existence as early as 14 May 1955 (and thus actually preceded the ratification of the pact itself as required under Article 10). The Commander-in-Chief of the Joint Armed Forces heads the Joint High Command, which also includes the Joint Armed Forces Staff and the Military Council – in line with standard Soviet practice – which meets under the chairmanship of the Commander-in-Chief, together with the Chief-of-Staff and permanent military representatives from the East European armed forces. In 1969 the functions of the staff were enlarged to include competence in preparing training exercises, manoeuvres and war-games: simultaneously senior East European officers were appointed to this

# NATO/WARSAW PACT FORCES LOCATED IN EUROPE

In a general war situation, Warsaw Pact Forces committed against Nato might be allocated as follows:

Soviet Forces in the Leningrad Military District against Norway.

Soviet Ground and Naval and Air Forces from the Baltic Military District, plus Polish and East German airborne and amphibious forces against Denmark, the northern coast of West Germany and Holland.

Soviet Ground and Air Forces from the Group of Soviet Forces in Germany (GSFG) and the Soviet Northern Group of Forces (NGF) in Poland, and from the Moscow and Belorussian Military Districts, plus Ground Force elements of the East German and Polish armies, against North Germany (Hanover and the Ruhr); and (together with Czech army units and elements of the Soviet Central Group of Forces in Czechoslovakia (CGF) and Soviet troops from the Kiev Military District) against Central Germany (Frankfurt).

Soviet forces from GSFG, CGF and SGF (Soviet Southern Group of Forces in Hungary) plus elements of the East German, Czech and Hungarian Armies, and troops of the Kiev and Carpathian Military Districts, against Southern Germany (Stuttgart-Munich), Austria and Italy.

Against Southern Europe and Turkey Soviet troops of the Odessa and Causcasian Military Districts and elements of the Hungarian, Romanian and Bulgarian armies.

This would give a comparison of strengths as follows (Nato forces in parenthesis):
Warsaw Pact divisions 140-150(45) tanks 27,000 (10-11,000) artillery pieces 8-9,000 (6,000) men (under arms now) 1,240,000 (1,200,000).

Although the manpower under arms is approximately equal, the Warsaw Pact capacity for very rapid mobilisation would give them a 3-1 superiority in fighting troops after three weeks of mobilisation. Nato could only close the gap after a further month had elapsed.

To what extent the Soviet Union's Warsaw Pact allies can be relied upon depends, of course, on the political situation in which conflict occurs. The startling improvement in the quality and quantity of equipment with which the USSR has equipped the non-Soviet Warsaw Pact countries since 1970 would seem to indicate that these countries are increasingly being considered by the USSR as quite reliable allies. The German and Bulgarian Armies have particularly benefitted from this trend. The Poles, Czechs and Hungarian armies in addition use good quality domestically produced equipment. Only the Romanian army has failed to show a marked improvement since 1970. Presumably, due to Romania being the least controllable regime politically and having the least important position strategically, her army is accorded the lowest priority of resupply by the USSR.

It should be borne in mind that to ensure internal security in both peace and war, all Eastern European countries have very large forces under the control of their Ministries of the Interior or State Security organisations. These forces are, to all intents and purposes, military; being equipped with small warships, combat aircraft and armoured vehicles. To quote an example: A Polish conscript might find himself called up to do not two years national service in the army, but three years in the Border Troops of the Territorial Defence Force. Poland has 80,000 such troops, Romania 45,000, East Germany 80,-100,000, Hungary 20,000, Czechoslovakia 25,000 and Bulgaria 22,000. The USSR has in addition almost half a million such troops, many of whom would be used to ensure the stability of Eastern Europe in the event of war. In addition, all Eastern European countries have TA-style militia forces involving a very large percentage of their adult male populations.

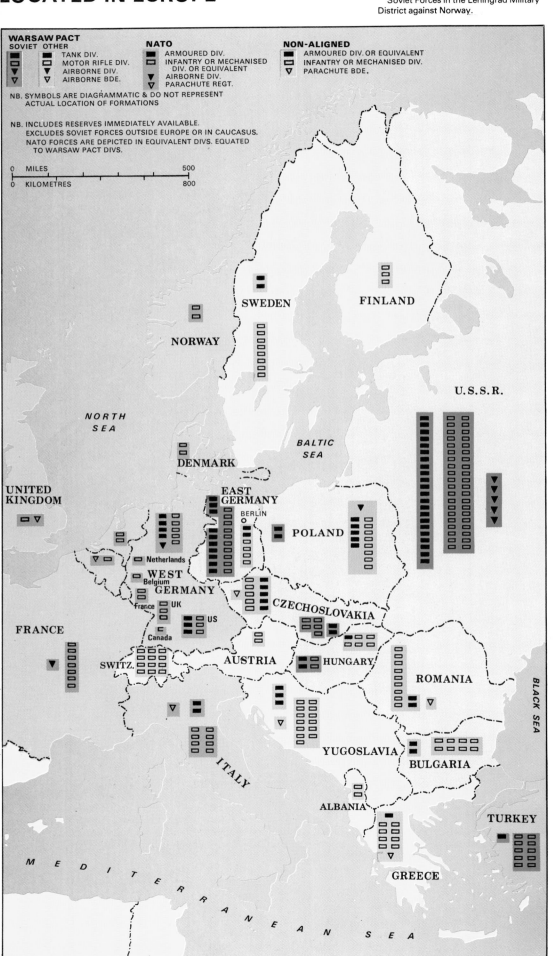

**WARSAW PACT**

SOVIET — OTHER
- TANK DIV.
- MOTOR RIFLE DIV.
- AIRBORNE DIV.
- AIRBORNE BDE.

**NATO**
- ARMOURED DIV.
- INFANTRY OR MECHANISED DIV. OR EQUIVALENT
- AIRBORNE DIV.
- PARACHUTE REGT.

**NON-ALIGNED**
- ARMOURED DIV. OR EQUIVALENT
- INFANTRY OR MECHANISED DIV.
- PARACHUTE BDE.

NB. SYMBOLS ARE DIAGRAMMATIC & DO NOT REPRESENT ACTUAL LOCATION OF FORMATIONS

NB. INCLUDES RESERVES IMMEDIATELY AVAILABLE. EXCLUDES SOVIET FORCES OUTSIDE EUROPE OR IN CAUCASUS. NATO FORCES ARE DEPICTED IN EQUIVALENT DIVS. EQUATED TO WARSAW PACT DIVS.

```
0        MILES              500
0        KILOMETRES         800
```

NORTH SEA

BALTIC SEA

SWEDEN

FINLAND

NORWAY

U.S.S.R.

DENMARK

UNITED KINGDOM

EAST GERMANY

BERLIN

POLAND

Netherlands

WEST GERMANY

Belgium

France  UK

US

Canada

CZECHOSLOVAKIA

FRANCE

SWITZ.

AUSTRIA

HUNGARY

ROMANIA

ITALY

YUGOSLAVIA

BULGARIA

BLACK SEA

ALBANIA

TURKEY

GREECE

MEDITERRANEAN SEA

*Above:* **An E. German APC is landed from an assault ship. In wartime, the amphibious elements of the Polish and E. German forces would probably be integrated with Soviet forces for operations against Denmark and the North German coast**

command group, although the key posts of Commander-in-Chief, First Deputy Commander-in-Chief and Chief of the Joint Armed Forces Staff have always been held by senior Soviet officers – presently Marshal of the Soviet Union I. I. Yakubovskii and Army General S. M. Shtemenko, respectively. Shtemenko is both First Deputy C-in-C and Chief-of-Staff; in addition, the Inspector-General of the Pact forces is a Soviet officer (Lieutenant-General Ye. Ye. Pastushenko). Even more singular is the fact that the Warsaw Pact does not have its own air defence organisation: air defence comes under the overall control of the Soviet C-in-C of the Soviet National Air Defence Command (*Protivovozdushnoi Oborony Strany* or *PVO Strany*) and a Soviet deputy commander for the Soviet *PVO Strany* acts as 'Air Defence Commander/Eastern Europe' responsible for the six air defence districts in this theatre, in addition to the 10 in the Soviet Union proper.

Two other arrangements deserve mention. The first concerns the 'military representatives of the Joint High Command', senior Soviet officers assigned to each East European capital and responsible for the Soviet military missions attached to non-Soviet Warsaw Pact ground, naval and air units. (These officers must be distinguished from

Soviet military attachés proper and also from *KGB* and other intelligence officers assigned within Eastern Europe to co-ordinate intelligence operations.) The second involves an agency never specifically identified but is seemingly a 'co-ordination body' for military equipment and arms supply, which may have some responsibility for joint procurement and may also bear on improving joint logistics facilities, including key rail-networks, the establishment of a common pool of railway wagons, the development of motor roads and the working of the oil pipeline running from the Soviet Union into East Germany, Poland, Czechoslovakia and Hungary.

Thus in origin, structure, military organisation and development, the Warsaw Pact differs substantially from NATO, nowhere more than in the political and military preponderance of a single power, in this case the Soviet Union. This nation itself contributes some 60 per cent of the first-line forces of the pact, and is the sole nuclear power within the alliance. Its hegemony within the key command positions and the political directorates remains unchallenged and unchanging, while its military grip is supplemented by multiple bilateral treaties. Finally, Soviet security in the widest sense is served since the pact also facilitates control of the internal security (and latterly the political evolution) of the Soviet Union's allies in Eastern Europe: no better example of this has been provided than the invasion of Czechoslovakia, which checked internal reform and also served, as far as the Soviet Union's allies at large were

concerned, *pour encourager les autres.*

## Warsaw Pact forces

Soviet forces deployed forward in east-central Europe have never at any time during the past 25 years fallen below the level of 25–26 divisions and at present stand at the equivalent of 31–32 divisions (five or six divisions having been added to the order of battle as a result of the invasion of Czechoslovakia in 1968). This deployment comprises four 'Groups of Forces' based in East Germany, Poland, Czechoslovakia and Hungary: Group of Soviet Forces Germany (GSFG) consists of five army HQs, 20 divisions (10 tank and 10 motor-rifle), with 370,000 men and one air army (the 16th) with 900 first-line combat aircraft; Northern Group in Poland with the equivalent of two or three divisions, 30,000 men and two air divisions; Central Group in Czechoslovakia with five or six divisions, 60–70,000 men and two air divisions; and Southern Group in Hungary with four divisions (two tank and two motor-rifle), 40–50,000 men and one or two air divisions.

This gives a total manpower figure of some 500,000 (575,000 with air and support elements), in all 16 tank and 15 motor-rifle divisions with their own tactical air support. Of these 31 divisions, 27 are deployed within the confines of the major central sector of the European front. In addition, substantial and immediate reinforcement is available from the three westerly military districts of the Soviet Union proper, the Baltic, Trans-Carpathian and Belorussian Military Districts, thus adding the equivalent of eight armies with 30–32 divisions, that is 340,000 men with a further 6,800 battle tanks.

Since 1970 these Soviet forces have undergone substantial modernisation and expansion: some 2,000 battle tanks have been added to the groups of forces (the bulk going to increase the tank strength of motor-rifle divisions), towed artillery has been increased and new self-propelled (SP) guns added, the 40-barrel multiple rocket-launcher introduced, the 'Scud' tactical missile with its 175-mile range increased in numbers by 50 per cent; tactical air power has been also increased with 25 per cent more aircraft per regiment and new ground-attack/close support aircraft introduced, such as the MiG-23 and the Su-19. Corresponding improvements in assault engineer and high-speed bridging units have been made, together with overall logistics.

To these Soviet formations must be added the non-Soviet national forces of the Warsaw Pact, generally distinguished by referring to the 'northern tier' (East Germany, Poland and Czechoslovakia) and the 'southern tier' (Hungary, Rumania and Bulgaria). Of all these states Poland maintains the largest military establishment, with a nominal order of battle of 15 divisions (five tank, eight motor-rifle, one airborne and one amphibious) with 3,800 battle tanks and 750 combat aircraft together with a significant navy, the largest non-Soviet naval force in the Warsaw Pact, with 25,000 men (2,800 officers) manning five destroyers, four submarines, 37 torpedo- and missile-firing fast patrol boats (FPBs), 41 patrol craft, two Landing Ships (Tank) and 23 Landing Craft (Tank). Poland also has a large merchant fleet and fishing fleet, plus an extensive ship-building capacity. East Germany maintains six divisions (two tank, four motor-rifle), some 300 interceptor aircraft and light naval forces (these forces are unique in the Warsaw Pact in being permanently subordinated to Soviet command in the GSFG). Czechoslovakian forces have a nominal order of battle of 10 divisions (five tank and five motor-rifle), one airborne brigade and some 500 aircraft. Taking this nominal order of battle and counting in Soviet forces, Warsaw Pact strength on the vital central sector thus amounts to some 56–58 divisions, amounting to 935,000 men with 16,000 battle tanks and 2,900 aircraft.

These gross figures, however, need some adjustment in the light of variations in the state of manning, combat-readiness and training in these 'northern tier' non-Soviet Warsaw Pact forces. From recent Soviet practice in integrating joint combat groups (East German–Polish–Soviet, or Soviet–Polish–Czechoslovak, with a multi-national variety of arms and services), it can be assumed that some, although not all, of the non-Soviet formations within 'northern tier' forces are ear-marked for first-echelon deployment alongside Soviet troops. A calculation along these lines would supply a figure of some 48 Soviet and non-Soviet divisions available without additional reinforcement for operations on the central sector, thus enabling the Soviet command to commit 200 battalion-size combat groups with 8,700 tanks and 1,750 tactical aircraft, a figure which could be rapidly expanded by reinforcement (with 50 additional divisions committed in the first 30 days of operations).

Soviet doctrine, which is uniformly applied within the Warsaw Pact, calls for high-speed day and night operations, with a rate of advance of some 30 or more miles per day under nuclear conditions and up to 20 miles in conventional operations, with Front operations (involving one or more army groups) reaching to a depth of 185–310 miles. Senior non-Soviet Warsaw Pact officers might well command one sector, although without their own national forces being assigned independent missions, operating rather with multi-national combat groups and task forces.

The relative importance of these non-Soviet forces can be gauged from the degree of modernisation they have acquired through Soviet resources: the Polish armed forces have received priority, followed by the East German and Czechoslovak forces. Similarly, non-Soviet Warsaw Pact air forces are being equipped with modern aircraft suited to an offensive role, as opposed to the previous single commitment to air defence.

Within the 'southern tier' – Hungary, Bulgaria and Rumania – the pact and scope of modernisation has lagged appreciably: the Soviet Southern Group in Hungary is supplemented by the Hungarian army, with a nominal order of battle of six divisions (90,000 men and 1,500 battle tanks) and an establishment in various stages of modernisation. Bulgaria, one of the Soviet Union's staunchest allies, has received some modern equipment, but large-scale modernisation has been impeded by economic difficulties: the nominal order of battle consists of eight motor-rifle divisions (only half of them fully

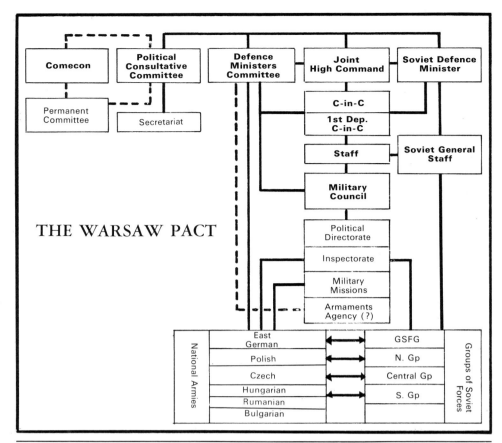

THE WARSAW PACT

# SOVIET FORCES IN EAST GERMANY

(G) = "Guards" division, a title of honour given to units/formations which distinguished themselves in the 1941-45 war

*Above:* **Impressive military parades are a prominent feature of all totalitarian societies. Nowhere is this more noticeable than in E. Germany. Here, an S-60 AA gun is seen, taking part in a May Day parade in East Berlin**

*Right:* **Coastal defence and tactical support of land operations are the main tasks of the non-Soviet Pact navies: this Polish patrol boat is typical of the type of warship with which they are equipped.**

combat-ready) and the equivalent of two tank divisions (though without full divisions being assembled). The air force has some 250 aircraft and the navy two frigates and four ex-Soviet submarines. Rumania, which has strenuously resisted Soviet efforts at 'integration' and attempts to move Soviet troops into or across Rumanian territory, has lagged appreciably in modernising its forces; the nominal order of battle consists of two tank divisions, seven motor-rifle divisions, two Alpine brigades and one airborne brigade, amounting to an effective force of one tank division, three or four motor-rifle divisions and the airborne brigade. The Rumanian navy constitutes a light coastal defence force, with six corvettes, minesweepers and FPBs.

Thus, in line with their more limited role, the non-Soviet 'southern tier' forces are appreciably weaker and less sophisticated than their counterparts on the central sector.

**Integration, standardisation, command and control**

Essentially, the Warsaw Pact constitutes a military bloc which expedites the forward deployment and the stationing of Soviet ground, air and missile forces on the territory of member states, thereby developing a major *place d'armes* within an extensive geographic zone formed by contiguous countries. This same zone also comprises a key theatre of operations, in which powerful 'shock forces', equipped with the most modern weapons, trained to a common tactical doctrine and operated under common principles of command, can be deployed, being kept at a high state of combat-readiness. To this must be added a significant, if not superior reinforcement and mobilisation capability. The facility provided by the Warsaw Pact serves three vital Soviet purposes: defence, internal security (which includes securing the continued existence of regimes acceptable to the Soviet Union) and a favourable stance for pre-emption in the event of major military operations in the European theatre.

Finally, the Warsaw Pact is not the sole mechanism or military-political arrangement whereby the Soviet Union can maintain its present military disposition in east-central and south-eastern Europe, which is heavily underpinned by bilateral treaties: it should be noted *inter alia* that the 'status-of-forces agreement' concluded in 1968 with Czechoslovakia subordinates Soviet troops in the Central Group to the Soviet high command and makes no reference to the Warsaw Pact.

In view of Soviet preponderance within the Warsaw Pact and its monopoly of senior posts, 'integration' has been and must continue to be largely on Soviet terms. Soviet hegemony in nuclear matters is absolute and likely to remain so: Rumanian and even East German dissatisfaction with the absence of any consultative procedures on the use of nuclear weapons (and targeting) led in the end to nothing. Reservations over the Soviet attempt at closer 'integration' were made both plain and public during the Czechoslovak crisis of 1968: there was (and is still) the problem of 'burden-sharing', involving the financial contributions and outlays levied for the stationing of Soviet troops abroad on members' national territory and – more serious – the expenditure required to maintain large conventional forces, together with the expense of modernisation, infrastructure and reserve forces. (Hungary is reportedly the latest member to be disquieted over support costs for Soviet troops.) The Soviet Union may emphasise its own costs in affording nuclear deterrence to cover the Warsaw Pact states, but they in turn have insisted that theirs is also a heavy burden in providing conventional forces not specifically tailored to the needs of their own national 'self-defence'.

The 'total integration' of Warsaw Pact forces has stopped short of that 'supranational' force once mooted by Moscow and resisted most strenuously by Rumania, whose armed forces were subsequently placed by special legislative enactment immutably and inalienably under Rumanian national command, although something like a special 'standing army' may be emerging in the Soviet attempt to create multinational combat groups of ear-marked contingents and detachments from member states. (In March 1975, for example, Soviet, East German and Polish units with a combined strength of several divisions exercised in East Germany, practising a rapid thrust from the Cottbus-Dresden area along a north-westerly axis). The language problem, involving as it does the use of Russian on the part of Poles and East Germans, may also hamper such 'integration'.

Nevertheless, there are important, if not decisive advantages promoting Soviet-type integration and consolidating standardisation. First, there is the matter of organisation and doctrine: there is no 'indigenous Warsaw Pact doctrine', for the national armies – with only slight allowances for national pecularities – are organised, equipped and trained along Soviet lines. Since the Soviet Union is the main source of weapons and equipment, a high degree of standardisation is axiomatic: main battle tanks (T-54/55 and T-62) are Soviet, aircraft of all types are Soviet (with the exception of some Polish and Czech trainers), artillery and mortars are Soviet, assault engineer equipment is Soviet, and Soviet APCs are standard (with the exception of some Hungarian vehicle variations). Ammunition of all calibres is completely standardised: small arms are largely Soviet, though there are some Czech variants. Soviet equipment is produced under licence in Eastern Europe. There is something approaching a common vehicle pool, although individual nations do produce military vehicles of their own: equally im-

portant is the fact that most vehicles are common to the military and civilian sectors, thus facilitating the mobilisation of 'civilian resources'. Inevitably, there are drawbacks: reliance on Soviet production can mean difficulty in enforcing deadlines, acquiring sufficient spare parts – the East German army (NVA) is reported in 1976 to be negotiating with some urgency to acquire the new Soviet self-propelled guns. The admixture of old and new equipment produces maintenance problems, but it cannot be contested that standardisation within Warsaw Pact armies is far in advance of that which prevails in NATO, with its motley of battle tank types, aircraft, missiles, ammunition and incompatibilities in logistics.

Standardised weapons and equipment, common tactical doctrine and thus standardisation in training lead inevitably to the acceptance of common principles of command and control. It is important, however, to emphasise once more that the Warsaw Pact as such is not a wartime command organisation, nor is its logistics establishment separate from that of the Soviet armed forces proper. It is essentially an administrative and training organisation, without 'command functions' in the accepted sense, for all the existence of that 'Joint High Command'. In effect, the Warsaw Pact is run and administered along the lines of yet one more Soviet military district. There have been reports of a new Warsaw Pact headquarters being sited in Lvov, but this is less a 'command organ' than a means to administer and rationalise exercises and movements along a southerly axis (possibly with an eye to instability in Yugoslavia and elsewhere). Air defence is already subordinated to the Soviet command of *PVO Strany*. For operational purposes the Soviet groups of forces in Eastern Europe would become Fronts (or army groups) directly subordinated to the Soviet high command and subject to the highly centralised control exercised through the Soviet General Staff as a main 'command organ': 'shadow' operational staffs of General Staff officers do seem to be emplaced within the various groups of forces, thus providing the true 'command staff' alongside the peacetime administrative and training structure. It is interesting to recall that the forces involved in the invasion of Czechoslovakia came under the control of the Soviet Ground Forces command, not any 'Warsaw Pact command' as such: the C-in-C of the Warsaw Pact did not command the forces committed, while logistics together with command and control (signals) did not in any way come within the competence of the Warsaw Pact. All combat-ready forces within a given Front would presumably come under centralised Soviet command, to which individual Eastern European senior officers would also be immediately responsible.

Thus, by its existence in peacetime the Warsaw Pact is designed to serve primarily Soviet military interests and certain political ends. Ironically enough, its 'disappearance' in wartime would mean that it still served those prime Soviet interests and objectives.

**T-62 Tanks attack during joint Pact exercises. Designed specifically for rapid offensive operations and deployment en masse, the T-62 relies for protection on speed and small size as well as exceptionally effective armour rivalled only by British tanks.**

# UNIFORMS OF THE SOVIET ARMED FORCES

## ФОРМА ОДЕЖДЫ И ЗНАКИ РАЗЛИЧИЯ ОФИЦЕРОВ СОВЕТСКОЙ АРМИИ

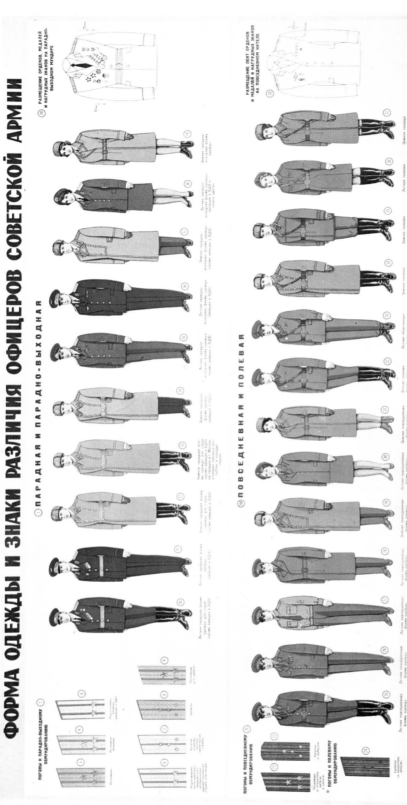

## Uniforms and Badges of Rank of Officers of the Soviet Army

1 Parade and Parade/Walking Out.
2 Shoulderboards for Parade/Walking Out uniforms:
3 Colonel.
4 Colonel-Engineer.
5 Lieutenant Colonel-Engineer (Airforce and Airborne).
6 Lieutenant Colonel (Intendant, Medical, Veterinary, Administration Services and Justice).
7 Captain-Engineer and Captain of Technical Services.
8 Captain.
9 Colonel (for greatcoat).
10 Summer parade dress when on parade (except Airforce and AB).
11 Summer parade dress (Airforce and AB).
12 Winter parade uniform when on parade (except Airforce and AB).
13 Winter parade uniform when on parade in Moscow, capitals of Republics and ''hero-cities'' (except Airforce and AB).
14 Winter parade uniform (Airforce and AB).
15 Summer parade/walking out dress (except Airforce and AB).
16 Summer parade/walking out dress (Airforce and AB).
17 Winter parade/walking out dress (except Airforce and AB).
18 Summer parade/walking out dress (Airforce and AB in blue).
19 Winter parade/walking out dress.

20 Wearing of Orders, Medals and Chest Badges on the parade/walking out uniform.
20a Everyday and Field uniforms:
21 Shoulderboards for Everyday uniforms
22 Colonel (for open-necked jackets and greatcoat).
23 Captain (on shirt).
24 Shoulderboards for field dress (for buttoned up jacket).
25 Summer everyday uniform.
26 Summer everyday uniform off duty.
27 Summer everyday uniform off duty (shirt and shoulderboards).
28 Summer everyday dress off duty (in summer coat).
29 Winter everyday dress off duty.
30 Summer everyday dress off duty.
31 Winter everyday dress off duty.
32 Summer field dress.
33 Summer light dress (in warm climates).
34 Winter field dress.
35 Winter field dress (padded jacket).
36 Summer field dress.
37 Winter field dress.
38 Wearing of ribbons of Orders, Medals and Chest Badges on everyday uniforms.
38a Cockades and Emblems.
39 Parade/walking out peaked hat.
40 Everyday hat gear of the Airforce and

AB as well as the parade/walking out beret of women officers.
41 Emblem for the crown of the parade/walking out peaked hat of officers of the Airforce and AB.
42 For everyday head gear of officers (except Airforce and AB).
43 Collar Patches:
44 For parade/walking out uniform.
45 For everyday dress and summer coat.
45a For field dress buttoned up jacket.
46 Insignia on Collar Patches and Shoulderboards:
Top Row (left to right):
Motor Rifle Troops—Artillery—Armoured Troops—Airforce—Airborne

—Engineer Troops—Signal Troops and Radiotechnical Troops—Engineer Technical Services in the Airforce—Chemical Troops—Military Technical Schools (POL Supplies Services—Fire Brigades)—''all Arms'' engineer technical personnel.
Bottom Row (left to right):
46 Pipe-laying Units—Construction and Aerodrome Engineer units—Motor Transport and Road Troops—Military Topographical Service—Railway Troops and VOSO—Intendant Services and Administrative Services—Military Bandmasters—Justice—Medical Services—Veterinary Services.

# Uniforms and Badges of Rank of Marshals and Generals of the Soviet Army

## ФОРМА ОДЕЖДЫ И ЗНАКИ РАЗЛИЧИЯ МАРШАЛОВ И ГЕНЕРАЛОВ СОВЕТСКОЙ АРМИИ

① ПАРАДНАЯ И ПАРАДНО-ВЫХОДНАЯ
② ПОВСЕДНЕВНАЯ И ПОЛЕВАЯ

1 **Shoulderboards—Parade and Parade/Walking Out and greatcoats.**
2 Marshal of the Soviet Union.
3 Chief Marshal of Armoured Troops (for greatcoats).
4 Chief Marshal of the Airforce.
5 Marshal of Artillery.
6 Marshal of Armoured Troops.
7 Marshal of Airforce.
8 Marshal of Engineer Troops.
9 **Parade and Parade/Walking Out.**
10 Summer parade uniform when on duty (except Airforce).
11 Summer parade uniform when off duty (except Airforce).
12 Winter parade uniform when on duty (except Airforce).
13 Summer parade/walking out uniform when off duty (except Airforce).
14 Winter parade uniform when on duty (except Airforce) to be worn on parades held in Moscow, capitals of Union Republics and "hero cities".
15 Summer uniform (Airforce).
16 Winter uniform (Airforce).
17 Summer Parade/walking out uniform.
18 **Shoulderboards for Parade and Walking Out uniforms.**
19 Army General.
20 Colonel General.
21 Colonel General of Justice.
22 Lieutenant General of the Airforce.
23 Lieutenant General (Engineer and Signal Troops, Technical Troops and Intendant Services).
24 Major General of Medical Services.
25 Major General of Veterinary Services.
26 **Shoulderboards for Everyday uniforms (except greatcoats).**
27 Marshal of the Soviet Union.
28 Chief Marshal of Artillery.
29 Marshal of the Airforce.
30 Colonel General of the Airforce.
31 **Shoulderboards for Field uniforms (except greatcoats).**
32 Marshal of the Soviet Union.
33 Chief Marshal of Artillery.
34 Colonel General.
35 **Everyday and Field uniforms.**
36 Summer everyday form of dress.
37 Winter everyday form of dress.
38 Summer everyday form of dress when off duty.
39 Summer everyday form of dress when off duty (with summer coat).
40 Summer everyday form of dress when off duty (in shirt and shoulderboards).
41 Winter everyday form of dress when off duty.
42 Summer field dress.
43 Winter field dress.
44 **Wearing of Orders, Medals and Chest Badges on Parade uniforms.**
45 **Wearing of ribbons of Orders, Medals and Chest Badges on the Parade/Walking Out uniforms and on the open-necked jacket.**
46 Cockade and embroidery on the parade peaked hat of a Marshal of the Soviet Union.
47 Cockade and embroidery on the parade/walking out peaked hats of Chief Marshals, Marshals of Arms of Services and Generals (except the Airforce).
48 Cockade and embroidery on the parade peaked hat of Chief Marshals, Marshals and Generals of the Airforce.
49 **Embroidery on Parade uniforms of Marshals of the Soviet Union:**
   a. peak and chin-strap
   b. collar
   c. cuffs
50 Cockade and embroidery on the parade/walking out peaked hat of a Marshal of the Soviet Union.
51 Cockade and embroidery on the parade/walking out peaked hats of Chief Marshals, Marshals of Arms of Services and Generals.
52 **Embroidery on Parade uniforms of Chief Marshals, Marshals of Arms of Services and Generals:**
   a. peak and chin-strap
   b. collar
   c. cuffs
53 **Embroidery on the collar and cuffs on the Parade/Walking Out uniform of a Marshal of the Soviet Union.**
53a Embroidery on the collar and cuffs on the Parade/Walking Out uniforms of Chief Marshals, Marshals of Arms of Services and Generals.
54 Cockade for everyday peaked hats and fur hats of Marshals and Generals (except the Airforce).
55 Emblem for the crown of the peaked hat on the parade, parade/walking out and everyday hats of Marshals and Generals of the Airforce.
56 Cockade and emblem on the everyday fur hat and peaked hat of Marshals and Generals of Airforce.
57 **Embroidery on the collar of the Everyday jacket:**
58 Of a Marshal of the Soviet Union.
59 Of Chief Marshals, Marshals of Arms of Service and Generals.
60 **Embroidery on the Field Service uniform collar:**
61 Of a Marshal of the Soviet Union.
62 Of Chief Marshals, Marshals of Arms of Service and Generals.
63 **Collar patches for greatcoats and summer coats of Marshals of the Soviet Union and "All Arms Generals":**
64 Marshals of the Soviet Union.
65 "All Arms Generals".
65a Collar patches for greatcoats and summer coats of Chief Marshals, Marshals and Generals of Arms of Service (Services):
66 Airforce.
67 Artillery and Armoured Troops.
68 Engineer and Signals Troops, Technical Troops, Intendant, Medical, Veterinary Services and Justice.

243

ФОРМА ОДЕЖДЫ И ЗНАКИ РАЗЛИЧИЯ ПРАПОРЩИКОВ СОВЕТСКОЙ АРМИИ И ЖЕНЩИН, ПРИНЯТЫХ НА ВОЕННУЮ СЛУЖБУ В СОВЕТСКУЮ АРМИЮ

① ПАРАДНАЯ И ПАРАДНО-ВЫХОДНАЯ

② ПОВСЕДНЕВНАЯ И ПОЛЕВАЯ

③ НАРУКАВНЫЕ ЗНАКИ С ЭМБЛЕМАМИ ПО РОДУ ВОЙСК ЧАСТИ

ПЕТЛИЦЫ

# Uniforms and Badges of Rank of Ensigns of the Soviet Army and for Women Accepted into Service in the Soviet Army

1 Shoulderboards for the Parade/Walking Out uniform of Ensigns and for Parade/Walking Out uniform and Everyday and Field uniforms of women accepted for military service in the Soviet Army:

2 Ensign (Motor Rifle Troops).
3 Ensign (Artillery, Tank, Engineer and Technical Troops, Signals Troops, Road, Construction, Pipelaying Units, VOSO Services).
4 Ensign (Airforce and AB).
5 Starshina.
6 Senior Sergeant.
7 Sergeant.
8 Parade and Parade/Walking Out:
9 Summer parade dress when on duty (except Airforce and AB).
10 Summer parade dress (Airforce and AB).
11 Winter parade dress (except Airforce and AB).
12 Summer parade/walking out dress (in the Airforce and AB in blue).
13 Summer parade/walking out dress (in the airforce and AB in blue).
14 Winter parade/walking out dress.
15 Wearing of Orders, Medals and Chest Badges on parade/walking out uniforms.
16 Wearing of Ribbons of Orders, Medals and Chest Badges on the everyday jacket.
17 "Those accepted as Ensigns, coming from the ranks of extended servicemen, may wear the Chest Badge for extended service on their uniforms and jackets:
18 Emblem on the crown of the parade/walking out peaked hat of Airforce and Airborne Ensigns.
19 Cockade and emblem on the parade/walking out peaked hat.
20 Star and emblem for the beret.
21 Collar patches for parade/walking out uniform.
22 Collar patches for everyday jacket.
23 Collar patches for field dress.
24 Everyday and Field Uniforms:
25 Shoulderboards for everyday and field uniforms.
26 Ensign (for everyday uniforms).

27 Ensign (for field dress).
28 Summer everyday dress.
29 Summer everyday dress off duty.
30 Winter everyday dress off duty.
31 Summer everyday dress off duty (shirt and shoulderboards).
32 Summer everyday dress off duty.
33 Summer everyday dress off duty (shirt and shoulderboards).
34 Winter everyday dress off duty.
35 Summer field dress.
36 Summer light form of dress (in hot regions).
37 Winter form of dress.
38 Summer form of dress.
39 Winter form of dress.

40 Cockade for everyday head gear of Ensigns (except Airforce and AB).
41 Cockade and emblem for everyday head gear of Ensigns of the Airforce and Airborne Troops.
42 Star for the beret (field uniform) and fur hat of women accepted for service in the Soviet Army.
43 Sleeve Patches with Insignia of Arm of Service: (from left to right): Motor Rifle Troops—Artillery—Armoured Troops—Airforce—Airborne Engineer Troops—Chemical Troops—Signal and Radiotechnical Troops—Railway Troops—Motor Transport Troops—Pipe-laying Units—Military Construction and other construction units—Medical and Veterinary Services—Military Directors of Music and Bandsmen.
44 Years of Service—Chevrons for Ensigns: (from left to right and down): 1st year—2nd year—3rd year—4th year—5th—9th year—10th year and over. Note: The chart was "signed for printing" on 27th March 1971. The new rank of Ensign (PRAPORShchlK) was only published officially at the end of 1971.

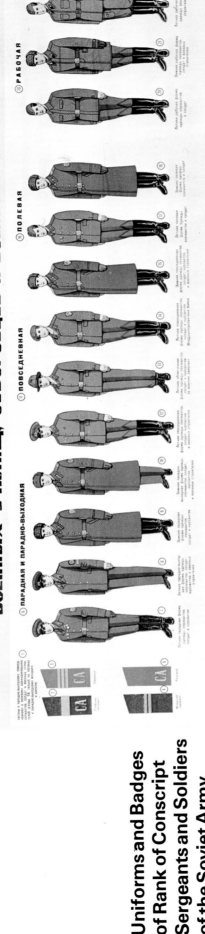

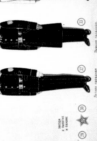

# Uniforms and Badges of Rank of Conscript Sergeants and Soldiers of the Soviet Army, Cadets of Military Schools, Suvorov Cadets and Military Construction Troops

1 Shoulderboards for Parade/Walking Out, Everyday and Field uniforms of Sergeants, Soldiers, and Military Construction Troops (the letters SA (CA) are only worn on Parade/Walking Out uniforms and greatcoats):
2 Senior Sergeant.
3 Sergeant.
4 Junior Sergeant.
5 Private Soldier.
6 Parade and parade/walking out.
7 Summer parade dress of sergeants, soldiers and cadets.
8 Parade/walking out uniform of sergeants, soldiers, cadets and military construction troops (Summer).
9 Winter parade uniform of sergeants, soldiers and cadets.
10 Winter parade/walking out uniform of sergeants, soldiers, cadets and military construction troops.

**Everyday Uniforms:**
11 Summer everyday dress of sergeants, soldiers, cadets and military construction troops.
12 Winter working dress of sergeants, soldiers and military construction troops.
13 Summer light dress for sergeants, soldiers and cadets (in hot regions).
14 Everyday summer dress of sergeants, soldiers, and cadets of the Airborne Forces.
15 Everyday winter dress of sergeants, soldiers, cadets and military construction troops.

**Field Dress:**
16 Summer dress for sergeants and soldiers.
17 Summer dress for sergeants and soldiers.
18 Winter field dress of sergeants and soldiers.

**Working Dress:**
19 Summer working dress of sergeants and soldiers.
20 Summer working dress of sergeants, soldiers and military construction troops.
21 Winter working dress of sergeants, soldiers and military construction troops.
22 Summer working dress of military construction troops.

**Shoulderboards for Working Dress of Sergeants, Soldiers and Military Construction Troops:**
23 Senior Sergeant.
24 Sergeant.
25 Sergeant.

**Shoulderboards of Officer Cadets of Military Schools (left to right):**
26 Cadet Starshina—Cadet Senior Sergeant —Cadet Sergeant—Cadet Junior Sergeant—Cadet Lance Corporal— Cadet Private.

27 **Collar Patches for Parade/Walking Out Uniforms of Sergeants, Soldiers, Cadets and Military Construction Troops.**
28 Star and emblem for peaked hat.
29 Star for fur cap with ear-flaps.
30 Star for side cap and "panama".
31 Suvorov School Cadets.
32 Summer parade and parade/walking out uniform.
33 Winter parade, parade/walking out and everyday uniform.
34 Summer everyday No 1 dress.
35 Summer everyday No 2 dress.
36 Shoulderboards, and collar patches of Suvorov cadets.
37 Collar patches for the buttoned up jacket of sergeants, soldiers, cadets and military construction troops.
38 Collar patches for greatcoats and padded jackets of sergeants, soldiers, cadets and military construction troops.
39 Wearing of orders, medals and chest decorations on the parade/walking out uniform.
40 Wearing ribbons of orders, medals and chest decorations on the buttoned up tunic.
41 **Sleeve Patches with insignia of**

**Arms of Service of the unit:** (left to right) — Motor Rifle Troops— Artillery — Armoured Troops — Airforce —Engineer Troops — Chemical Troops Signals and Radiotechnical Troops — Railway Troops —Motor Transport Troops—Pipe-laying Units — Military Construction and other construction units— Medical and Veterinary Services — Military Band Masters and Bandsmen.
42 **Sleeve Chevrons for Officer Cadets of Military Schools to denote course years: (left to right and down)** —1st Course —2nd Course 3rd Course —4th Course —5th Course 6th Course.

# Index

246

## PICTURE CREDITS

The publishers wish to thank the following organisations who have supplied photographs for this book. Photographs have been credited by page number. Some references have, for reasons of space, been abbreviated as follows:
   E and TV Films: Educational and Television Films Ltd., London.
   MOD: Ministry of Defence, London.
   Flight: *Flight International*, IPC Business Press Ltd., London.

**10, 14-19:** Novosti. **20, 22-24:** E and TV Films. **25:** bottom, E and TV Films; top, Novosti. **27, 30, 33, 36, 41:** E and TV Films. **44-45:** Novosti. **52-53, 54-55:** top, E and TV Films; bottom, Novosti. **56:** Novosti. **57-60:** E and TV Films. **61:** top, Flight; bottom, E and TV Films. **62:** E and TV Films. **63:** Novosti. **64-65:** E and TV Films. **66:** top, MOD; bottom, Novosti. **67:** E and TV Films. **68:** Novosti. **69:** top, Flight; bottom, E and TV Films. **70-71:** MOD. **72:** top, Novosti; bottom, E and TV Films. **74:** Flight. **75:** top, E and TV Films; bottom, Novosti. **76:** E and TV Films. **77:** Flight. **78:** Novosti. **79-81:** E and TV Films. **83:** bottom, MOD. **85:** Flight. **87:** E and TV Films. **88:** Novosti. **91:** MOD. **92, 95-96, 98, 102:** E and TV Films. **105-107:** MOD. **108-109:** E and TV Films. **111:** top, E and TV Films. **112-113:** E and TV Films. **114:** top, MOD; bottom, E and TV Films. **115-116:** MOD. **117:** top, E and TV Films; bottom, Novosti. **118:** E and TV Films. **119:** top, E and TV Films; bottom, Novosti. **120:** MOD. **121:** E and TV Films. **122:** top, MOD; bottom, E and TV Films. **123:** E and TV Films. **124-125:** MOD. **126:** E and TV Films. **127:** Novosti. **128:** MOD. **132, 154-157, 159:** E and TV Films. **160:** Novosti. **161-163:** E and TV Films. **165, 167-170, 173-174:** E and TV Films. **175:** bottom, Novosti. **180, 184, 187:** E and TV Films. **188:** top, E and TV Films. **193:** bottom, E and TV Films. **194:** top, Novosti; bottom, E and TV Films. **195:** Novosti. **200-201:** E and TV Films. **204:** Novosti. **205:** top, E and TV Films; bottom, Novosti. **206-207:** E and TV Films. **208:** Novosti. **209:** E and TV Films. **210:** Novosti. **211, 216:** E and TV Films. **217-218:** Novosti. **219:** Boeing. **220:** top, Novosti; bottom, E and TV Films. **221-225, 227:** Novosti. **229:** bottom, Novosti. **232-234:** E and TV Films.